NATIONALISM AND INTERNATIONALISM

European and American Perspectives

Erich Hula

With a Preface by Kenneth W. Thompson

UNIVERSITY
PRESS OF
AMERICA

LANHAM • NEW YORK • LONDON

Copyright © **1984** by

University Press of America,™ **Inc.**

4720 Boston Way
Lanham, MD 20706

3 Henrietta Street
London WC2E 8LU England

Library of Congress Cataloging in Publication Data

Hula, Erich, 1900-
  Nationalism and internationalism.

  (American values projected abroad; v. 11)
  Reprint of articles originally published in the 1940s
through 60s.
  "Co-published by arrangement with the White Burkett
Miller Center of Public Affairs, University of Virginia"—
Verso of t.p.
  Includes bibliographies and index.
  1. International relations—Addresses, essays,
lectures. 2. Self-determination, National—Addresses,
essays, lectures. 3. International organization—
Addresses, essays, lectures. 4. War (International law)—
Addresses, essays, lectures. I. Title. II. Series.
JX1417.A74 1982 vol. 11   303.4'8273 s   84-13094
[JX1391]   [341.2]
ISBN 0-8191-3704-9 (alk. paper)
ISBN 0-8191-3705-7 (pbk. : alk. paper)

AMERICAN VALUES PROJECTED ABROAD

VOLUME XI

A SERIES FUNDED BY THE EXXON EDUCATION FOUNDATION

FOUNDATIONS OF AMERICAN VALUES

Vol. I. Western Heritage and American Values: Law, Theology and History
By Alberto Coll

Vol. II Political Traditions and Contemporary Problems
Edited by Kenneth W. Thompson

Vol. III Institutions for Projecting American Values Abroad
Edited by Kenneth W. Thompson

Vol. IV Essays on Lincoln's Faith and Politics
By Hans J. Morgenthau and David Hein

Vol. V The Predicament of Human Rights: The Carter and Reagan Policies
By Nicolai N. Petro

Vol. VI Writing History and Making Policy: The Cold War, Vietnam, and Revisionism
By Richard A. Melanson

Vol. VII Traditions and Values: American Diplomacy, 1776 to 1865
Edited by Norman Graebner

Vol. VIII Traditions and Values: American Diplomacy, 1865 to 1945
Edited by Norman Graebner

Vol. IX Traditions and Values: American Diplomacy, 1945 to the Present
Edited by Kenneth W. Thompson

AMERICAN VALUES VIEWED THROUGH OTHER CULTURES

Vol. X The Elements of International Strategy: A Primer for the Nuclear Age
By Louis J. Halle

Vol. XI Nationalism and Internationalism: European and American Perspectives
By Erich Hula

Vol. XII Diplomacy and Values: The Life and Works of Stephen Kertesz in Europe and America
Edited by Kenneth W. Thompson

Vol. XIII Islamic Values and World View: Khomeyni on Man, the State and International Politics
By Farhang Rajaee

Vol. XIV African and American Values: Liberia and West Africa
By Katherine Harris

Vol. XV An Ambassador's Journey: An Exploration of People and Culture
By Charles Baldwin

Vol. XVI Selections From *The New American Commonwealth*
By Louis Heren

In
Memory
of
My Late Wife
Annemarie

TABLE OF CONTENTS

Chapters

Preface.. xi

Introduction.. xiii

I. NATIONALISM AND IMPERIALISM
National Self Determination Reconsidered 3
The Nationalities Policy of the Soviet Union: Theory and
Practice 19
The Question of Russian Objectives 45

II. PUNITIVE WAR RECONSIDERED
Punishment for War Crimes............................... 57
The Revival of the Idea of Punitive War 75

III. INTERNATIONAL ORGANIZATION

A. PAN-AMERICANISM
Pan Americanism: Its Utopian and Realistic Elements 101

B. FROM THE LEAGUE TO THE UNITED NATIONS
The Dumbarton Oaks Proposals.......................... 123
Four Years of the United Nations 139
Fundamentals of Collective Security..................... 155
The Evolution of Collective Security Under the Charter....... 181
The United Nations in Crisis 205
The United States and the United Nations 231
Fifty Years of International Government 249

C. HUMAN RIGHTS
International Law and the Protection of Human Rights........ 267

IV. POLITICAL THEORY
Practical Uses of Political Theory 297

PREFACE
by Kenneth W. Thompson

No living American scholar happily unites the values of Europe and America in proper balance better than Professor Erich Hula. His colleagues at the New School called him "Erich the Just." Walter Lippman remarked that he subscribed to the journal *Social Research* because of Hula's annual article, whether on national self-determination or the United Nations. No one has carried over the years an unchanging reputation for political wisdom to match Erich Hula.

For Hula, the present volume brings together his remarkable insights on Europe and America and the values which underlie approaches to nationalism and internationalism. Hula had assimilated the classics of European thought before coming to the United States. Their influence is evident in the essays which follow on such subjects as national self-determination and punitive war. At the same time, Hula was quick to embrace American thought enshrined in the writings on the United Nations and ethics and politics of Americans such as Reinhold Niebuhr.

The present volume treats most of the fundamental issues facing the United States and the world following World War II. What is striking and attests to the lasting value of Hula's work, is the fact that his analysis is as relevant today as when his essays were first written. Erich Hula is truly a European-American thinker for the ages.

THE AUTHOR'S INTRODUCTION

Circumstances which with some gentlemen pass for nothing, give in reality to every political principle its distinguished color and discriminating effect. The circumstances are what render every civil and political scheme beneficial or noxious to mankind.
Edmund Burke, Reflections on the French Revolution.

The essays assembled in the present volume are of more or less old vintage. Some of them were written and first published as far back as in the years of World War II or shortly after its termination, some others appeared in the fifties and sixties. Practically all of them were *Gelegenheitsschriften*, pieces that were prompted and inspired by political occurrences, issues and discussions of those earlier days. Old wine promises to be tasty stuff. But what can the reader of seemingly outdated writings of the nature described hope for? Is there any justification for republishing them?

The author of the following essays does and must leave the final judgment on this question to those who will peruse them. But he might be permitted briefly to state why he ventures to answer the question in the affirmative.

The writings, included in this volume, deal with some of the great issues of twentieth-century international politics or relating to them. Though they were composed in response to past and diverse occasions, their subject matter has in the course of years not lost its relevance. The problems of politics have a greater perseverance than we might like them to have. The discussion of those issues, is, moreover, restricted to their most fundamental aspects. Being anxious to present to the prospective reader a coherent whole rather than a medley of disparate parts, the author has confined his selection to topics that are in one way or another closely interrelated with one another. Last but not least, the recurrent attempt, made in the following essays, to disentangle the realities from mere illusions and unfounded anxieties in past and present politics and to show the futility and the perils of political action, when based on abstract principles rather than on concrete circumstances, testifies to the unity of purpose which has animated their author.

The theme, or, rather, the variations of the theme which dominates in this collection, can somewhat more concretely be described as a critical examination and evaluation of some of the political ideas and legal devices that were offered and tried out in our century in Europe and America as means for achieving lasting international peace.

The quest for permanent peace is old, but it was, at least in modern times a concern of individual thinkers rather than of acting statesmen and, least of all, political movements. This changes radically only in the twentieth century with the ascendancy of liberal, democratic and socialist ideas and of the political parties borne by them. It is no accident that Woodrow Wilson who wanted to make the world safe for democracy, also advocated and played the leading role in creating the League of Nations, the first worldwide political international organization.

Wilson's promotion of liberal democracy was motivated not by his political faith alone. It also was based on pragmatic considerations relating to the question of international peace. Only an international community, he felt, which is composed of units that are founded on the principles of liberal democracy, including in particular the right of the individual to belong to the state of his own choice, promises to be a truly peaceful community.

The belief that the application of the principle of self-determination to the political organization of mankind would further the cause of international peace, was held and professed by European liberals long before Wilson made himself its foremost apostle. When it became after World War I the ideological basis of the territorial reconstruction of Central and Eastern Europe, its nature had undergone a momentous transformation, however. The transformation of the principle, as originally conceived, into the principle of national self-determination or principle of nationalities as it also, and more appropriately, is called, resulted in the recognition of the nationality, understood as an ethnic entity, rather than of the individual as the holder of the right of self-determination.

This process and its fateful consequences form the subject matter of the essay with which the first section of this book opens. The discussion is focused on the Central and East European scene in the period between the two world wars. But the study of this particular historical case offers lessons that are applicable, and have already been proven to be applicable to other cases as well. The idea of national self-determination is, after all, one of the most potent ideas of our time. It has been stimulating the anti-colonial movement and it still is operative in the western world itself. Its most conspicuous recent manifestation is the assertion of French-Canadians of their right to separate statehood, but there are symptoms of the revival of ethnic groups pursuing similar aims also in Spain, France, and the United Kingdom.

When trying to evaluate the principle in pragmatic terms, we should remember particularly two of the lessons which its application in the aftermath of the First World War has taught us. It fails, in the first place, to eliminate national conflict wherever diverse ethnic groups are inextricably mixed with one another. The citizens of the newly established states of Central Europe were nationally no less heterogeneous than were those of the Hapsburg monarchy to which these states succeeded. Secondly, the political fragmentation, necessarily resulting from the application of the principle of nationalities, creates in the region, subjected to the operation, a vacuum of power which invites the intrusion, in some form or other, of outside states of superior strength. It was indeed the destruction of the balance of power as it existed in Europe down to World War I which made the successor states of the Hapsburg empire the victims of the expansionist policies first of Nazi Germany and later of the Soviet Union.

The assertion of the unconditional right of each nationality to its own statehood implicitly denies the legitimacy of any multinational state, the democratic state as well as the autocratic state. The slogan of national self-determination has therefore proved a potent weapon in the hands of Russia's socialist revolutionaries, including the Bolsheviks, intent on undermining the authority of the multinational empire of the Romanovs. As soon as Lenin had established his dictatorial power, he realized, however, that the slogan was a two-edged weapon. By strengthening the secessionist movements among Russia's ethnic minorities, the principle also threatened to endanger the integrity and unity of the socialist state he was trying to build, unless its application would be subordinated to the allegedly superior interests of socialism.

The theory accomplishing the adaptation of the principle of national self-determination to the interests of the victorious socialist revolution was ready at hand. In fact, it has been elaborated by Stalin already before the revolution in his famous essay on "The National Question and Socialism", published in 1913. The essay became the basis of Stalin's actual nationalities policy and has remained the basis of Soviet policy in matters related to the national question ever since, as shown in the second chapter of this volume.

Stalin did in his treatise not deny the right of the various ethnic minorities to secede from Russia, but he was indeed far from conceiving it as an absolute, unconditional right. The actual policy of the Communist party was to be determined by considerations not of the right of nations but of the interest of the proletariat, as interpreted by the Communist pary in accordance with the Marxist dctrine which puts the class above the nation. And, we may add, the only legitimate interpreter of the interests of Russia's proletariat are the central authorities of the ruling Communist Party.

The conception of the Soviet Union as a state which is based upon a supranational idea means to all practical intents and purposes the denial of the right of secession. The political and administrative structure of the Union is indeed planned in such a way as to avoid, as much as it is feasible, the institutionalization of ethnic groups and thus to check rather than foster national extremism. Such autonomy as one can speak of in the totalitarian state is an autonomy of territorial regions and not of ethnic entities. Neither the Union Republics nor their subdivisions are ethnically homogeneous.

The same tendency not to strengthen the fervor of national feelings also accounts for the liberal elements (such as one can speak of in a dictatorial regime) in Soviet nationalities policy. The Bolsheviks always believed that national oppression was likely to perpetuate nationalism while it would, under a system of tolerance, or rather indifference, rapidly wither away. Accordingly, they did not hesitate once they had conquered the state to recognize and actually pay regard to the principle of the equality of rights of Soviet citizens, irrespective of their nationality or race. The regime respects in particular the right of all citizens alike to use in public and private their native language and to receive their education in their mother tongue — in Stalin's view the one ethnic right for which the common man truly cares. It even supports, somehow, the ethnic minorities in developing their cultural institutions.

This policy is by no means inspired, however, by the ideal of genuine cultural pluralism. To try to separate culture from politics is, according to Stalin, a "ludicrous" attempt, inconsistent with Marxist tenets. The actual motive for granting linguistic autonomy is not only to deprive ethnocentrism of its psychological basis but also to facilitate the spread of the communist creed throughout the land. The Soviet Government stands ready, moreover, to use its coercive machinery for preventing a deviation, real or alleged, from the party line no less ruthlessly when it originates in an ethnic group than in any other case.

There are enough indications that the Soviet Union has not succeeded in eliminating frictions among its several nationalities. But it is by no means clear that the application of the principle of national self-determination in its unaltered sense would have resolved more satisfactorily the national question on Russia's vast territory with its ethnically mixed population. It might indeed very well have resulted in the substitution for the Tsarist empire of several smaller states, nationally no less heterogeneous and politically no more open to liberal and democratic ideas than the former, with all the upsetting consequences for the global balance of power. It might only have turned internal friction into international strife.

The third chapter of this volume is devoted to an attempt to assess the character and the objectives of Soviet foreign policy. The question of whether the Soviet Government pursues a policy of old-fashioned power politics of the classical type or of essentially unlimited imperialism aiming at the substitution of a communist world empire for the existing multi-states system, is no doubt a question of the greatest moment. The maintenance of peace between the two super-powers may indeed ultimately depend on the way in which the United States, its government and its people, feel prompted to answer it. In pondering the weight of the two assumptions on the intent of the Russian rulers, we must therefore most earnestly try to beware of unwarranted illusions as well as of unfounded fears and anxieties.

Surveying the intricate problems involved in the issue, the author poses the question whether and to what extent the communist political doctrine necessarily bears out the correctness of the assumption of unlimited objectives. Though emphasizing that a clear-cut and definitive answer to this and other questions is hardly possible, the author ventures to draw from his analysis the conclusion that current Soviet foreign policy is a continuation of the Tsarist type of power politics, adapted to present world conditions, rather than unlimited imperialism intent on attaining Russian supremacy by all feasible means, including resort to military aggression. But he also stresses that American insistence on a "position of strength" is an indispensable guarantee for keeping Russian imperialism within the limits of old-fashioned balance-of-power politics.

Ernest Renan, one of the foremost students in the nineteenth century of nationalism and its racist aberrations, was haunted by the fear the substitution of the principle of nationalities for "the sweet and paternal symbol of legitimacy" would turn the agonistic fight of Europe's princes into absolute wars of extermination. The appalling atrocities, committed by Nazi Germany in the course of World War II were the fulfillment of Renan's somber prophecy. The heinous nature and the scale of the war crimes proper and of the ordinary crimes Nazi Germany perpetrated in conducting the war and in connection with it, as well as the measures of retribution to which to resort the adversaries felt justified, are indeed likely to have by far surpassed Renan's imagination.

World War II not only brought the period of comparatively civilized warfare which had reached its very meridian in the nineteenth century to a gruesome end. It also resulted in the abandonment of legal notions relating to international war which had been uncontested throughout modern history. The appalling crimes in which Nazi Germany indulged in World War II, were only the immediate cause of the deviation from traditional conceptions. The adoption and application of the novel principles, known as Nuremberg principles, were, in fact, the culmination of tendencies which came to the surface already at the end of World War I and found manifold expression in the thinking of international lawyers and in the rhetoric of statesmen in the years thereafter.

The Nuremberg rules, defining war crimes and providing for their punishment were a matter of heated debate first in the context of World War II and later of the Korean and Vietnam war. The discussion in the second section of the present volume centers on the general aspects of the problems involved in applying those principles and examines, in particular, the assumption the Nuremberg code and the punishment of the German and Japanese war criminals, meted out under its rules, will "make war less attractive to those who have governments and the destinies of peoples in their power."

According to the conceptions prevailing down to World War I, war was a legitimate instrumentality of international politics: equal sovereigns match their limited forces for limited ends. The right of each state to decide on its own whether it was entitled to go to war, was indeed held the chief attribute of the sovereign state, the very cornerstone of modern public law. The Declaration of Independence characteristically concludes with the assertion that the United States of America "as free and independent states . . . have Full Power to levy War." It fitted these notions that the responsibility of the individual offenders of the international rules concerning the conduct of war were considered to be a responsibility of municipal law, rendering them subject, as a matter of principle, to prosecution and punishment by their own governments. The Nuremberg code not only transferred the jurisdiction over violations of the rules of warfare to an international court, established by the victorious belligerents and composed exclusively of their representatives. It deviated from traditional notions and traditional practice also by disregarding, in the formulation of the substantive rules the court was to apply, the distinction, so far generally recognized, between legal offenses subject to legal sanctions and moral offenses subject to moral sanctions alone. Last but not least the distinction was ignored by the victorious powers not only in relation to the conduct of war, but to the causing of war as well. It is the insertion in the Nuremberg code of the so-called "crimes against peace", defined as "planning, preparation, initiation or waging of a war of agression" which assures the lasting historical significance of the proceedings of Nuremberg.

But is the criminal responsibility under international law of individual persons, including the chiefs of state, for waging a war of aggression also likely, as it was suggested, to be found one of the most promising devices for preventing future aggressions?

The idea of punitive war on which the Nuremberg code and proceedings were based, is a novelty only in modern international law. Actually it is the revival of an old idea that can be traced back to the *Res publica christiana* and to the scholastic teachings of earlier times. Does the record of those olden days justify the optimistic expectations of 1945? It hardly does. It is perhaps yet more important to remember that the recognition of the right of the victor to exact punishment for the initation of unjust war not only failed to prevent it. As Vattel, the famous Swiss publicist of the eighteenth century, whom the Founding Fathers of America revered as their wisest guide in all their international dealings, has aptly remarked, it also tended in its actual operation to make war "more cruel, more disastrous in its effects, and more difficult of termination."

There is no reason to assume that Vattel's dictum would be less pertinent in the case of a punitive war, if and when waged by an international political organization.

The tendency to ascribe to the collective measures for enforcing international peace which the members of the League of Nations and of the United Nations were and are authorized to take, a punitive character, was quite conspicuous in the rhetoric both at Geneva and New York and even influenced the actual policies of the two world bodies. The impact of the punitive conception was most strongly felt in discussions in and outside of them, on the best ways of strengthening the authority and power of the two organizations. Actually, however, general political international organization, the most striking, though hardly the most significant phenomenon of twentieth-century world politics, moved in the direction of abandoning the pretensions of governmental authority and power rather than trying to augment them. It more and more resigned itself to the modest role of an essentially diplomatic body.

The third section of this book is devoted primarily to a study of general international organization from its ambitious beginning to its modest present, from the illusory hopes which gave it birth to the recognition of the realities which have shaped it and determined its course. This is not to suggest that the survey is meant to narrate and analyze the history either of the League of Nations or the United Nations. The several chapters are rather meant to take stock of some of the problems in which they became involved and to feel, as it were, the Organizations' pulse in the several stages of their development. It should also be mentioned that the discussion centers on the United Nations rather than the League of Nations. The chapter on Pan-Americanism is intended to show that the interplay of utopian and realistic elements is no less characteristic of regional than of global political organizations.

The optimistic expectation that the establishment of a general political international organization would usher in a golden age was based on the belief the maintenance of international peace was primarily a problem of providing adequate international institutions. According to this way of thinking, the deficiencies of international society which were chiefly responsible for the eternal recurrence of war were institutional deficiencies — the lack of political machinery similar to the machinery of the state which preserves peace within the national communities. The logical remedy was to set up an international government with paraphernalia of power similar to those of national governments.

This simplistic belief errs in overrating what political institutions are actually capable of achieving. Mankind has throughout history been plagued not only by the recurrence of international war but of revolution within the national communities as well. This clearly indicates that the disruptive forces shaking political society are rooted in pre-institutional factors which, common institutions notwithstanding, make for disunity and incoherence not to be overcome by legal devices alone. In fact, wherever and whenever such antagonistic forces are at work within a national body, political institutions, intended to harmonize the actions of its members in the attainment of common ends, are likely to be turned into battlegrounds of its contending factions.

The history of general political international organization has so far not contradicted the lessons of domestic politics. The moral and political prerequisites for their successful operation as organizations responsible for enforcing peace were and are badly lacking in the case both of the League and of the United Nations. Indeed the length to which the United Nations, particularly in its initial period, has gone in replacing secret diplomatic negotiation by public discussion and parliamentary procedures based on the majority principle, has often resulted in heightening rather than lessening international tensions arising from the antagonism between west and east on the one side, and north and south on the other. Ironically, the chief ideological weapon, used in the verbal warfare between the factions of the United Nations, has been the issue of human rights. (The illusions and realities of the attempt to internationalize human rights are discussed in a special chapter in the third section). Wilson's belief in the effectiveness of rational procedures in settling disputes has thus turned out to be no less faulty than other tenets of his internationalist creed, such as his conviction that an international community, organized upon the pattern of the national community, would make it possible for its members to dispense with the devices of traditional diplomacy, such as arms, alliances and balance of power for protecting their national interests.

The idea of collective security which formed the very core particularly of the United Nations system is based upon two fundamental legal principles, each of them being an abandonment of traditional notions.

The first one is a restriction of the traditional right of the sovereign state to resort to war, as provided for in the Covenant of the League, or outright prohibition of force, as stipulated in the United Nations Charter. If understood in the more radical sense, the principle implies the eradication of the distinction between just and unjust war, made both in the scholastic doctrine on the *jus ad bellum* and in the theory of modern international law. Save two exceptions, all war is aggression, even if started on account of a wrong suffered by a state. The two exceptions are war waged by an individual state in self-defense, and participation of a state in the collective enforcement action undertaken by the international community itself.

The second fundamental principle of collective security is a corollary of the first. Each and every member of the international community is, as a matter of principle, required to render assistance in some form or other, military or otherwise, to the state against which the breach of peace has been committed and to help to restore peace.

It is obvious that the members of a collective security organization can be expected to comply with the first principle, obligating them to refrain from the use of force for the protection even of their most vital interests only if they can be practically sure that overwhelmingly strong forces of the organized community will be deployed for defending them in case of aggression; for only the certainty of effective collective action is apt actually to deter potential aggressors. To assure such certain prospect, the members of the collective security organization are held to abandon the traditional right of the sovereign state to remain neutral in case of an armed conflict.

In view of the dismal record of the history of collective security, we may wonder today that it ever appealed to public opinion in the western world as strongly as it did from the twenties through the forties. It would have been somehow a political miracle if the idea had actually worked. As an Italian critic of collective security succinctly and cynically remarked, to expect the members of the entire international community to render assistance to a member which allegedly was a victim of aggression, meant to assume states can reasonably be relied upon "to make war against nature," that is for reasons they do not hold to affect their national interests. But if such expectation is unrealistic, as it indeed proved to be — the Korean case is no real exception, for the action taken against the aggressors was only formally collective — then it is not realistic, either, to expect that states will be ready to heed the prohibition of force when they feel their national interest makes its use imperative.

Neither the League of Nations nor the United Nations succeeded, frantic efforts notwithstanding, to build up a system inducing its members to dispense with the traditional right and the traditional devices of self-help. It is therefore by no means surprising that United Nations members soon began to reinterpret their obligations and their rights under the Charter. They are today prone to interpret the provision prohibiting force restrictively and to claim the distinction between just and unjust war was valid still and the decision on the justness of their use of force still a matter of their own discretion. And they tend no less clearly to interpret the Charter provision recognizing their "inherent right" to self-defense extensively. The arms race and the conclusion of military alliances for the purpose of securing the existing world balance of power are other indications that the international community of today has thus returned to notions and practices relating to war and peace that prevailed in the uninstitutionalized society of nations of former times.

Tested by the ambitious intentions of their founders the United Nations undeniably is no less in default than was its predecessor at Geneva. But the League and the United Nations have both also been assigned tasks that were performed in international society before. Moreover, not all legal principles of the Covenant and the Charter are novel principles, untried prior to the establishment of these organizations. This applies particularly to the rules governing their mediatory and conciliatory functions.

Ever since the organization of the international community under common institutions was advocated and undertaken, there has been general agreement that collective security must not be relied upon as the only means for preventing war, and that the most obvious additional requirement is to provide for pacific methods of settling international disputes and to assure their actual application, if and when the methods of bilateral diplomacy fail. Controversy has persisted over what relative weight and importance should in practice be attached, in planning and building an international peace organization, to pacific procedures on the one hand, and to procedures of collective coercion on the other. And it has been equally controversial whether and how the agencies of an international organization should combine the procedures when actually dealing with aggression.

The emphasis in planning and building the United Nations has been, in contrast to the League of Nations, on the procedures and instrumentalities of collective coercion. The same tendency prevailed in the initial period of the Organization's actual operation and it asserts itself also at later occasions. But since about the middle fifties the United Nations no longer claimed, to put it in Secretary General Hammarskjold's words, "a world authority enforcing the law upon the nations." It rather began to consider itself and act as a moderator trying to resolve international disputes and to terminate armed conflicts by initiating mediatory and conciliatory procedures, based upon and requiring the consent of the parties concerned.

There are indeed intractable issues that defy the efforts and the skill of any mediator, individual or collective. But it cannot be denied that, on the whole, the performance of the United Nations when acting, through its Secretary General, as a mediator, has been satisfactory. To be sure, in exercising such functions, the United Nations has broken no new ground. There are precedents in diplomatic history even for its armed intervention in the Suez and Congo case. But it has served well the cause of peace all the same. In fact, a general peace organization is truly indispensable for the successful operation of mediation and conciliation. To improvise in each and every case of international conflict the methods and procedures of mediation and conciliation might have met the simpler needs of international society in former times. In the complex conditions of the present world society the requirement for permanent global international institutions of mediation and conciliation has become imperative.

Modest as the achievements of general political international organizations have thus actually been, they have to all practical appearances become a permanent feature of present world politics. Traditional bilateral diplomacy has been supplemented by multilateral diplomacy operating within the framework of common international institutions. There is undoubtedly some truth in the contention that the world society of today, owing to the growing interdependence of all parts of the globe, simply cannot do without a political international organization in some form or another. The realist may add that the staying power of international organization is also due to the fact that it has become, and is apt to be used as an instrumentality in the on-going struggle between states and nations, great and small.

Illusions are entertained not by statesmen and politicians alone. Scientists are no less prone to succumb to them.

Natural scientists have promised us that by delivering things into man's power, by achieving his mastery over nature, they would promote the betterment of human life. But whatever they might have indeed accomplished in this respect, they have also brought nearer the prospect of the self-extinction of the human race. How much more terrifying is the specter of war today than it was as long as modern physics and technology had not yet conquered nature. More recently social and political scientists have ventured to claim the result of their study of political behavior, political processes and decision-making on the governmental level, in relation to both domestic and foreign policy matters, will greatly enhance the chance of securing the rationality of politics, national and international.

In the concluding chapter of the present volume the author briefly examines this claim and suggests that the empirical investigation of the facts bearing on human behavior in politics is not likely to make predictions of policy outcomes feasible. Political decisions are bound to remain based on contingent factors, varying in various combinations from one case to the other. The political scientists can help to clarify the choices open to the decision-maker as well as their possible or likely implications. But the statesman, responsible for the conduct of policy, ultimately will and must act on hunches and in compliance with the commands of his conscience.

I

NATIONALISM
AND
IMPERIALISM

NATIONAL
SELF-DETERMINATION
RECONSIDERED*

I

To all intents and purposes the present war is waged by the United Nations for the liberation of the peoples conquered by Germany and Japan. But national self-determination—in the sense in which it came to be understood during the First World War—has not been proclaimed as the guiding principle of postwar reconstruction.

To be sure, the Atlantic Charter has occasionally been interpreted as an assertion of the principle of national self-determination. Actually, however, the Charter neither contains the phrase nor suggests its meaning. Rather it proposes—if only as a basis of "a wider and permanent system of general security" to be set up in due time—the reestablishment of the European system of states as it existed before the present war. "We had in mind primarily restoration of the sovereignty, self-government and national life of the states and nations of Europe now under the Nazi yoke," said Prime Minister Churchill, commenting on the Declaration in the House of Commons on September 9,1941. This should not be taken to mean that the Charter visualizes a static world, whether in the political, economic or social sphere. It means only that the document recognizes concrete historic rights but does not proclaim abstract rational rights. It is animated by the spirit of Burke, not of the Jacobins.

This spirit is most obvious in Article 3 of the Charter, which expresses the wish of the United States and British governments "to see sovereign rights and self-government restored to those [peoples] who have been forcibly deprived of them." But it has also determined the cautious form-

*Reprinted with permission of *Social Research*, February 1943 (Vol. 10, No. 1).

ulation of the article which envisages changes of the territorial status quo ante. The two governments desire, so runs Article 2, "to see no territorial changes that do not accord with the freely expressed wishes of the peoples concerned." In other words, the Charter does not propose any territorial changes, whether on the basis of the principle of national self-determination or on that of any other abstract principle, but merely states the desire that such changes as might seem recommendable should not be effected against the wishes of the respective populations. It rejects annexations, but it does not suggest any positive principle regarding territorial reconstruction.

Insofar as the Atlantic Charter refers to the popular will it subscribes solely to the principle of self-determination. Self-determination which inspires Article 2 of the Atlantic Charter is nothing but the application—to alterations of territorial boundaries which may for one reason or another be deemed necessary—of the democratic postulate that government should be founded on consent rather than on force. The principle of national self-determination, on the other hand, or as it is more adequately called, the principle of nationalities, has come to stand for the idea that every national-ity should have the right to and should also actually form its own state. It is a regulative principle of boundary changes.[1] There is not one word in the Atlantic Charter which can be interpreted in the terms of the latter principle.[2]

It would be unjustified to conclude from this fact alone that there is a distinct trend away from the philosophy of national self-determination. In the First World War, too, the acceptance and proclamation of so revolution-ary a principle were long shunned by the leading statesmen of the western powers. President Wilson's Fourteen Points, set forth in an address to Congress on January 8, 1918, make conservative reading today in the light of later enunciations and events. The emphasis lies rather on "no annexations" than on national self-determination. The latter principle was applied to the claims of the Italians and Poles alone. The other peoples of polyglot Austria-Hungary, as well as the non-Turkish nationalities of the Ottoman empire, were not yet assured of any right to their own sovereignty. Points 10 and 12 merely demanded for them a free and absolutely unmolested opportunity for autonomous development within the political framework of the two empires. The consideration that the assurance of their complete independence, if and when the western coalition should win the war, would shatter the resisting power of Germany's allies was what finally led to the official adoption of the principle of national self-determination. This principle became a peace aim because it suited the foremost war aim: in other words, because it suited the purpose of weakening and defeating the enemy.[3]

We are on safer ground if we regard the interests at stake for the United

Nations in the present war as warranting the expectation that the history of the first world conflict will not repeat itself in the present one. After all, it is no accident that the slogan of national self-determination could be taken up by Hitler and most successfully applied against those nations which had won their political independence by appealing to the very same principle. Revolutionary ideas are easy to let loose, but hard to stop. To say it bluntly, the foremost protagonists of the principle of national self-determination in World War I find themselves in World War II in the position which was during the earlier war held and defended against them by the rulers of Austria-Hungary. The postulate that each nationality should constitute its own state is as much a threat to the resurrection, after Germany's defeat, of Czechoslovakia, Poland and Yugoslavia as it was once a deadly blow to the existence of the Danube monarchy.

There is nothing surprising in this reversion of the respective positions. The new states were national states only in theory. In fact, they were as much multi-national as the monarchy which they succeeded.

On this question we must think not only of the German minorities in those states, but also of the relationship among the peoples who were or at least figured as their founders. It is unnecessary to dwell upon the strife among Serbs, Croats and Slovenes which fills the pages of Yugoslavia's short history. Its dramatic form and the passion with which it was fought have put it into the limelight of European politics. The relations of the Czechs with the Slovaks and Ruthenes were outwardly much smoother, but disruptive forces were at work in Czechoslovakia too. The Czech attempt to rescue the Slovaks from the Magyar melting-pot, and to awaken them to the consciousness of a common Czechoslovak nationality, succeeded only in its first part; otherwise it resulted in the development of a Slovak national consciousness. The liberation of the Ruthenes worked in the same way.[4] Poland had her Ukrainian irredenta, potential or actual, not to mention her numerically lesser minorities.

The revolt of the small nations was thus followed by the revolt of the smaller ones. To be sure, it burst into flame only when Hitler found it convenient for his own sinister purposes to stir it up. But the inflammable matter was there before Hitler entered upon his career of conquest, and it will still be there after Hitler's career has been wrecked. The governments in exile of Poland, Yugoslavia and Czechoslovakia will therefore hardly care about giving new force to the idea of national self-determination, but will rather continue to base their claims to restoration on the ground of historic rights.[6]

We can scarcely assume, however, that the slogan of national self-determination has altogether spent its force. I have just referred to ethnical groups in eastern Europe which were aroused to nationalist ambitions only

5

in recent years, or whose national feeling was greatly intensified as a result of the peace settlements of 1919–20. Such examples could unfortunately be multiplied in Europe's danger zone of ethnically mixed populations. Nor can we safely be sure that we shall not witness in some not too distant future a revival of ethnical groups also in western Europe, with the disruptive consequences we know from the history of that process in central and eastern Europe. Moreover, the ideas of nationality and national independence are no longer confined to Europe. They differ in actual strength from continent to continent and race to race, but like European nationalism they have become effective all over the world, both as unifying and as disintegrating forces. The Indian question is fraught with the same complexities which beset any attempt at a reasonable solution of the national question in eastern Europe.

Thus the principle of national self-determination is still one of the most potent political ideas of our time. In these circumstances it may not be out of place to reconsider its nature and weigh its alleged merits. The following discussion of these problems is focused on the central and east European scene, the primary locus of the national problem and of national strife both before and after the First World War.

II

Political catchwords rarely convey the true nature of the principles they are supposed to express. Even less do they intimate their intricate implications. The slogan of national self-determination is no exception to this rule. It thrives on ideas that are suggested by the phrase but alien to the principle itself. The term sounds like the assertion of the free will of man, but it is essentially a determinist doctrine.[6] It promises peace and order, but actually intensifies national feeling and makes for permanent revolution. It presents itself as the crowning of democracy, but—to put it in Lord Acton's words— "sets limits to the exercise of the popular will and substitutes for it a higher principle."[7]

The difference between the principle of self-determination and the principle of nationalities, misleadingly called the principle of national self-determination, can hardly be overstressed. It will help us to grasp the true meaning of the two principles if we reflect upon them in the light of the political and legal devices that have been used or suggested for carrying them into practice.

According to the principle of self-determination boundary changes require the assent of the people who happen to live in the territory to be ceded by one state to the other. When the community of the European princes developed, under the impact of democratic ideas, into a family of nations, it

6

began to seem intolerable that the prince, or any other government, should have the right to trade territory without the assent of its inhabitants, as if they were a mere appurtenance of the soil. Thus the plebiscite came into use as a means of applying the principle of popular sovereignty to international politics. Although the law of nations refrained from making the popular referendum an indispensable requirement of every territorial change, the plebiscite was inserted into many treaties of cession concluded in the nineteenth and twentieth centuries. The few cases to which it was applied by the peace treaties after the First World War are still fresh in memory.

The plebiscite, which is a means of carrying collective self-determination into effect, was long preceded by a device of individual self-determination. As a matter of fact, inasmuch as the plebiscite gives heed, and can give heed, only to the will of the majority, individual safeguards against the consequences of boundary changes are not needless. Modern international law abounds in such individual safeguards. First of all it has seen to it that territorial rearrangements should not deprive the individual of the privileges of citizenship. The inhabitants of a territory which changes its sovereign acquire, ipso factor, the nationality of their new state. Persons who desire to emigrate rather than live under another sovereign are entitled to opt for their former nationality or any other nationality that may be open to them. The optants are entitled to retain their unmovable property in the ceded territory, and to carry with them all their movable property. No export duties are to be imposed upon them in connection with the removal of such property.[8]

Modern international law has thus tended to recognize the right of the individual to belong to the political community of his own choice, and to retain his home and property, regardless of the vicissitudes of international politics. Plebiscite and option have been the instruments of self-determination.

Neither of these devices, however, implies in itself any endorsement of the idea that every nationality should have the right to, and should also actually, form its own state. In fact, some of the plebiscites taken after the First World War resulted in the rejection of the idea of the national state. And a great many optants, in exercising the right of individual self-determination granted to them by the peace treaties of 1919–20, refuted rather than complied with the basic philosophy of the principle of nationalities.

This is not to suggest that the principle "each nationality a state" is in all circumstances in conflict with the principle of self-determination, which recognizes man's right to choose his own sovereignty. But neither should it be taken for granted that the principle of nationality is essentially in accordance with that individualist principle. The classic example of an

7

obvious clash between the principle of self-determination and the principle of nationalities is the case of the Alsatians. Although they are ethnically German they claimed in 1871 the right to remain a part of the political community of the French nation.

The holder of the right of national self-determination is significantly not the individual, but a collectivity. Again, this recognition of the distinctive personal character of the national group and of corresponding inherent group rights, does not necessarily imply the negation of any rights of the members of the group. As a matter of fact, everything depends on what is considered to be the nature of the nation, and of its relations with the individual members. If the nation is viewed, as in the subjective theory of nationality, as a phenomenon of the free human will, as an act of will, then a conflict between the national group and those who adhere to it can hardly materialize. And even in the view that the nation is constituted by objective factors, whether of a spiritual or a physical character, there is no denial to the individual of basic rights within the national order. The nationalist movement of the nineteenth and twentieth centuries, up to the rise of Hitler, was a liberal-democratic movement, its ideal being the free man in the free nation.

But the fact remains that the principle "each nationality a state," at least by implication, assigns the legitimate control over a man's actions to the government of his own nationality, and to that specific government alone, thus anticipating his free decision as to the sovereignty under which he wants to live. It takes for granted what ought to be proved—that a man's attachment to his ethnical group is by nature stronger than any other nexus of loyalties. But the Alsatians protested in 1871 against being incorporated into Germany for the very reason that their ethnical ties and their political preference did not go together. Self-determination and what is called national self-determination coincide only for the nationalist.

Moreover, modern nationalism is not so much a psychological theory of the play of loyalties in the human heart as a doctrine of man's moral obligation to put national solidarity above all other considerations and emotions. Long before Hitler tried to sap the allegiance of the Austrians and of the Sudeten Germans to their respective governments by appealing to the ties of blood which connect them with the German race, Treitschke called the claim of the Alsatians for self-determination "the plausible solution of demagogues without a fatherland," and opposed to the right of the branches of the German race to decide on their own destines "the right of the nation, which will not permit its children," as he sentimentally declared, "to remain strangers to the German Empire."[9] Nor is it Germany alone which has substituted for man's right the "divine right" of the ethnic collectivity, to put it in the words of Renan, who was haunted by the fear that the victory of

8

the ethnological conception of nation would destroy European civilization.[10]

From the middle of the nineteenth century onward the nationalist point of view was generally regarded as the only legitimate one, the only one that needed no further justification. This can be clearly seen from the way in which the principle of nationalities was carried into effect, and from the favorable reaction of public opinion to the substance and form of the nationalist policy. The establishment of national states in central, southern and eastern Europe was announced to the western world, and also accepted by it, as the realization of the principle of popular sovereignty. Actually only Cavour, the strategist of the Italian movement for national union, cared to keep up democratic appearances. But the plebiscites which Cavour cleverly made the technique of his Italian policy, informal and unilateral as they were, scarcely lived up to the standards of truly democratic referendums.[11] Bismarck's Germany was a federation of princes, forged by blood and iron. Blood and iron, sugared for western consumption by farcical plebiscites, accomplished in 1938 what was called in Hitler's terminology the establishment of Greater Germany.

It was not plebiscites that ushered in the existence or, in most cases, determined the frontiers of the so-called national states that were founded in 1918 on the ruins of the defeated Hapsburg monarchy. To be sure, the establishment of the successor states can safety be assumed to have been effected in accordance with the popular wishes of the Czechs, Poles, Serbs and Rumanians who were to occupy in their own states a dominant position. But this assumption hardly holds good for those nationalities that were to be united with them, merely on the grounds of kinship. Reared on the pattern of modern nationalist thought, the statesmen around the peace table at Paris discarded even the possibility—to refer only to one example—that the Slovaks might not mind staying with Hungary.[12] But it is even more significant and revealing for the state of mind prevailing in the Anglo-Saxon countries after Versailles that the peoples of those countries felt infinitely more worried about the cases in which their statesmen had not admitted the principle of nationalities, like those of Austria and the Sudetenland, than about the cases in which they had applied that principle, though probably against the wishes of the populations concerned. This state of mind was the psychological basis of the English policy of appeasement up to the moment when Hitler's fist reached for the first time beyond the "branches of the German race."

The determinist character of the principle of nationalities is most strikingly revealed by the device of compulsory transfer of population, specifically designed for carrying that principle into effect. To be sure, in pre-Hitler days it was applied only once. But there can be no doubt that the

9

example of the Convention of Lausanne, concluded in 1923 and providing for the compulsory exchange of Turkish and Greek nationals, has been steadily gaining ground in public opinion. It was even recommended by a member of the Permanent Court of International Justice.[13] Plebiscite and option were intended to protect the individual against being treated like an appurtenance of the soil, but compulsory transfer degrades him to an appurtenance of the race to which he is supposed to belong. Sarah Wambaugh places at the beginning of her standard work on *Plebiscites since the World War* a *Hymne à la terre,* "as the doctrine of self-determination is rooted in the passionate attachment of the peasant to his fields, the villager to the home of his fathers, and their willingness to suffer and to die rather than forsake them" (pp. xiii ff). The principle "every nationality a state," and its refined technique of compulsory transfer, are the very negation of these most elementary rights of the common man.

III

If it is true that in politics too a price has to be paid for everything, then man ought to be ready to sacrifice even his right of self-determination, provided that this sacrifice serves a still nobler cause than individual freedom. Indeed, time and again in the past and in the present century the advocates of the principle of nationalities have expressed their firm belief that its application would guarantee permanent peace. If the units of international society, so runs the typical argument, were national states whose frontiers coincided with the ethnical boundaries, war and conquest would fade out of the picture of international politics. To be sure, the organization of mankind on strictly national lines might upset the balance of power on which the system of states has thus far been supposed to rest. But that artificial structure would merely be giving way to a more natural and therefore more stable international order. In fact, so we are told, the formation of national states would be the first step toward an all-embracing confederation of states.[14]

The actual development which accompanied and followed the victory of nationalism in Europe did not, however, bear out these optimistic expectations. Rather it confirmed Renan's fear that the substitution of the principle of nationalities for "the sweet and paternal symbol of legitimacy" would turn the agonistic fight of Europe's princes into absolute wars of extermination.[15] Even if we grant that the causes and the character of modern war cannot be entirely explained in terms of modern nationalism— war is, after all, older than nationalism, and its specific character is to a large extent the result of the range and complexity of modern political, social and economic organization and also of technical development—the fact still remains that the formation of ethnically homogeneous states has tended to intensify national feeling and weakened the brotherhood of man.

The apostles of so-called national self-determination have always wanted us to believe in the irresistibility of the nationalist movement and the self-evident character of its postulate that the state in which man lives should coincide with the nationality to which he is linked by spiritual and physical ties. The truth is that the nationalist philosophy became the common belief, in so far as it ever actually did, only after man had been made to live in and undergo the influence of the national state. That this was the actual sequence of state and nation in western Europe can hardly be contested, in view of the fact that England and France had long been firmly established states when modern nationalism began to rise. But by and large it holds true also for the national states which have come into being in the last seventy years.[16]

"Italy was made; there were still to be made the Italians," said the conservative statesman d'Azeglio, reflecting upon the actual situation after the accomplishment of Italian unity.[17] Nearly forty years later the socialist Benito Mussolini could rightly remark that Italians still think in regional rather than in national terms: "Italy is not one. There are different peoples, hardly amalgamated by an administration that is fiercely unitary and centralizing."[18] And Bismarck, meditating in his *Gedanken und Erinnerungen* on the reasons for the breakdown of the democratic national movement in 1848, attributes the collapse mainly to the fact that the citizen of Prussia, Hannover, Wurttemberg, Bavaria, Hesse, felt more strongly attached to his particular dynasty than to the German nation. "Suppose," writes Bismarck, "that all the German dynasties were suddenly deposed; there would then be no likelihood that the German national sentiment would suffice to hold all Germans together from the point of view of international law amid the friction of European politics, even in the form of federated Hanse towns and imperial village communes."[19] If the events of 1918–19 belied Bismarck's fear, it is only for the reason that in the meantime the existence under one common national government had immensely strengthened the national sentiment of the German people. The history of the Weimar republic shows, however, that even half a century after the unification of Germany the German nation had not yet achieved the same degree of coherence which the western nations possess. Though the disruptive forces worked now along social rather than along state lines, without doubt the lack of national coherence as such accounts largely for Hitler's rise to power.

It is hardly an accident that national democracy failed also in many of the states that were founded in eastern and southeastern Europe after the war. But be that as it may, in their case, too, history bears out the thesis that man's alleged right to live under a government of his own nationality becomes a generally accepted axiom of a nearly religious character only after the establishment of a national government has strained man's thinking and feeling into a purely national frame of reference. The example of Czech nationalism is particularly impressive. Among the nationalities that formed the population of the Austro-Hungarian monarchy the Czechs were probably the one whose collective ethnic consciousness was most intense and most strongly politicized. Still, the common conviction of the Czech people that political independence alone would serve their national ends was rather the result than the cause of the revolution of 1918. Commenting upon how difficult it was to overcome the "pro-Austrianism" of the western statesmen, who were inspired by "the traditional view that Austria was a dam against Germany," Masaryk states that his work abroad after 1914 proved the more difficult because many of the Czechs "had long sought to persuade the world that Austria was a necessity."[20] With equal frankness Masaryk admits that his policy of liberation was regarded at home "with some degree of skepticism."[21]

The fact of the matter is that national feeling has hardly ever been equally intense, or of the same nature, among the individual members or classes of any ethnic community, not to speak of the different attitudes of the religious bodies that may coexist within an ethnic group. This is true even today, although in recent times nationalism, not least on account of its institutionalization, has undoubtedly been in the ascendant in all classes alike. The latter is about the only general statement ventured by the scholarly authors of the study on nationalism published by the Royal Institute of International Affairs in 1939.[22] Otherwise they rightly warn against dogmatizing on the attitude of the different classes of society toward the nationalist philosophy, and stress its complex character.

There is sufficient evidence, however, to support the view that the several classes of society have different predispositions toward the idea of the national state. By and large, it has appealed most strongly to and been given the most decisive impetus by the middle classes, at least in those parts of Europe with which we are here concerned. The nationalism of peasants is essentially of a passive nature. To be sure, students of the problem agree that peasants react vigorously against any policy of national discrimination unfavorable to them, and are therefore difficult to denationalize, more difficult than the inhabitants of the cities; in this sense the peasants are, indeed, the backbone of the national community. But they have not been eager to strive for national statehood. Their attitude belies, as it were, the very philosophy which has inspired the principle of nationalities, by disproving its basic assumption that the existence and integrity of a national group are dependent on its political sovereignty. Unless he is subject to a ruler who has set out to exterminate him, the peasant remains what he is through the vicissitudes of politics, like the soil that he laboriously tills. The attitude of the working class toward the idea of the national state has been less uniform. In so far as it has fallen in with the nationalist movement it has done so with a receptive rather than with a productive mind.

Thus it can hardly be denied that the establishment of the national state—corresponding as it does to the feeling of the ethnically most conscious section of the population, and setting up a mechanism of unifying the people on a level of intense ethnic sentiment—is bound to be followed by an intensification rather than by a diminution of nationalism. But the result of this process is not necessarily aggressive nationalism. As a matter of fact, the devastating effect produced by applying the principle of nationalities to the national question in central and eastern Europe lies in the resulting tendency toward an intensification of aggressive nationalism on the German side and of what might be called introverted nationalism on the part of the small nations that lie east and south of Germany.

We should be careful not to idealize small nations. The range of man's sins depends very much upon the range of opportunities offered to him. After all, the short independence which the small nations of central and eastern Europe enjoyed between the two world wars was hardly a sinless existence, though their self-restraint in exercising power was even more remarkable, human nature being what it is, than the worst abuse of power for which they may be to blame. They knew how to play the game of politics with the same moral facility, and handled the devices of the game with the same shrewdness, as the big fellows. But what nurtured their nationalist passion was essentially what the French call *l'esprit municipal,* the belief that national security lies in isolation, and the will to be let alone. The slogan of the Irish Sinn Fein, "We alone," has always, consciously or unconsciously, been the strongest motive in the policy of the so-called small nations. History compelled them to be continuously on the alert against the more powerful nations. To this fact they owe the resourcefulness of their mind and the abiding energy of their will. But it also developed in them that unfortunate defensive psychology which an Alsatian student of the national question, describing the political attitude of his own countrymen, has characterized as politics "dans le petit cadre."[23] This suspicious attitude makes the small nations difficult and stubborn partners in any political combination. It is their tragedy that the very nature of their nationalism makes them still weaker than they already are in terms of population, territory, wealth and military force.

"Circumstances," remarked Burke, "which with some gentlemen pass for nothing, give in reality to every political principle its distinguishing colour and discriminating effect. The circumstances are what render every civil and political scheme beneficial or noxious to mankind."[24] Burke's general dictum applies also to the principle of nationalities. A system of states which organizes political power units along ethnical lines is bound in the long run to give to the numerically strongest units the advantage over the weaker ones. This effect would weigh heavily enough against the principle of nationalities, even if the small state as such had not been rendered a somewhat problematic political unit by the military and economic development of recent times.[25]

Germany's relative gain in physical strength has not been the only unwelcome effect of the principle of nationalities. Germany could and did exploit the principle morally as well. The adoption of the nationalist axiom—that ethnic community and state should coincide—implicitly destroyed the legitimacy of the right of any non-German government to rule over German minorities, and even the legitimacy of a second independent German state like Austria. In fact, Germany's claim to act as the protector of the Germans living outside the Reich dates back to the days of the Weimar republic, and the discussions in the League of Nations bear witness to the vigor with which republican Germany asserted that claim.[26] Hitler had only to improve on the methods of that protection when the time seemed to be ripe to move into the vacuum of power which the peace settlement had left on Germany's southeastern flank.

No discussion of the moral implications in the principle of nationalities should fail to mention that the inextricable mixture of ethnic elements which make up the populations of central and southeastern Europe renders futile any attempt to realize the ideal of the national state. But the historical record of the postwar period, which was heralded as the fulfillment of national self-determination, makes unnecessary any further elaboration of this point. Things being what they are in Europe's zone of mixed populations, there was and can be no way of escaping the complexities of the multi-national state. To proclaim a principle which inherently denies moral validity to the multi-national state, regardless of its form of government, is therefore to destroy the only foundation upon which statesmen can build. The assertion of the unconditional right of each nationality to its own statehood is a disruptive, not a constructive principle. It plays havoc with the multi-national state, democratic as well as absolutist.

IV

Those who advocate the splitting up of the multi-national state into ethnically homogeneous separate states often take the position that democratic institutions cannot work where the population consists of different nationalities. John Stuart Mill, for example, declared that "Among a people without fellow-feeling, especially if they read and speak different languages, the united public opinion, necessary to the working of representative government, cannot exist.[27] As a statement of the fact that democratic government works best where there is common understanding among the people, the dictum is indisputable. Democracy gives free scope to the currents of public opinion. The smooth working of its governmental machinery therefore depends to a larger extent than under any other form of government upon the willingness of the people to meet one another half-way.

But ethnic differences do not necessarily exclude fellow-feeling among the citizens. And even if they did, we could hardly afford to stop at stating the fact. After all, democracy means not the mere registration of popular sentiments, but the valuation of such sentiments according to a hierarchy of ends and means. National feeling is not the only sentiment that might split and break up the democratic community. The individual's attachment to a particular religious community, political party, professional organization or social class can be as intense and emotional as his loyalty to the ethnic community to which he belongs. Still, the democratic state respects those loyalties and recognizes autonomous rights of those groups only to the extent that they are compatible with the ends which determine its own purpose and its own rights, the dignity and liberty of the human person. The same principle applies to the rights of national collectivities. They, too, are to be measured in terms of the purposes which the ethnic community serves in the human order, its service in forming and enriching the individual personality. To stretch national rights beyond the limits set by that function means to substitute for the rights of man the rights of the ethnic collectivity. Thus an unqualified principle of national self-determination is incompatible with the tenets of democracy.

The fight of the nationalities, or at least of their nationalist leaders, has often been pictured as a struggle against autocratic rulers. There was a time when there was at least some semblance of right in this interpretation, though it was not always accurate. Thus the national struggle which raged in the Austro-Hungarian monarchy was, as far as Austria proper of the constitutional era is concerned—the situation in Hungary differed essentially from that in Austria—an international struggle among the peoples rather than the fight of any of the nationalities against oppressive rulers.[28] The oversimplified interpretation was encouraged by the fact that the supranational idea, which was then the very core of the Austrian conception of the state, was clothed in the form and the formulae of dynastic paternalism, whose roots were drying up under the influence of modern currents and conditions. Dynastic loyalty failed in old Austria to be a match for the centrifugal tendencies of nationalism.

Developments during the postwar period amply demonstrated, however, that the disruptive force of the principle of nationalities, taken in an absolute sense, threatens also the existence of states founded on popular sovereignty. This threat darkened the hour of victory of Czech nationalism and brought about the final downfall of independent Czechoslovakia. In fact, if it spreads further, the doctrine which puts the ideal of ethnic self-government contrary to and above the ideal of political self-government will sooner or later destroy the national coherence of any people that is united by a political belief, and break up any country where men of different ethnical origins have so far lived peacefully together in accordance with and in obedience to the principles of democracy. Psychologically speaking, it is only a very short step from the feeling of being free to the feeling of being oppressed, if the attachment to universal ideas gives way to more primitive and narrow loyalties.

Nobody can reasonably expect that the nations and nationalities of central Europe will ever be ready to undergo a melting process like the one to which their emigrants, landing on the American shores as individuals, readily subject themselves. Nor do they need to. The example of Switzerland proves that democracy can work also where the ethnic groups are not pulverized, provided that the law does not discriminate among them but assures to all citizens alike the protection of life and liberty, without distinction of nationality or language; provided also that the citizens themselves do not indulge in ethnic particularism, but subordinate their racial loyalty as willingly as any other group loyalty to the political community which protects them all and can therefore also claim their allegiance. This and this alone is the explanation of the deservedly much acclaimed miracle that three different ethnical groups, branches of nations which, to put it mildly, have not always been on too friendly terms with one another, live harmoniously together within Switzerland. The Swiss example proves also that, given such an attitude on the part of both the authorities and the citizens, there is hardly any need for specific institutions—like the often suggested device of personal, cultural autonomy—to safeguard the legitimate rights of the members of the ethnical groups. As a matter of fact, if Switzerland had ever cared to associate her public institutions in one way or another with her component ethnic groups one might wonder whether she were still free from national strife.

Our Alsatian student of the principle of nationalities reports, somewhat bewildered, the answer to his inquiry among the inhabitants of Fiume as to whether the people of the town, altogether about 45,000 souls, preferred to stay with Italy or to join Yugoslavia: they would like, they answered, to form an independent state of their own.[29] The answer and the spirit it reveals may one day be quoted by historians in order to explain why the democratic nations of central and southeastern Europe have in our time become such an easy prey to a state employing nationalism for a policy of world conquest.

They went on thinking in terms of small political units when the objective conditions called for great designs. Nor did the forces of disintegration stop working after they had once been let loose.

There is no halt on the road to complete disintegration of the political order when institutions no longer embody ideas which unite men rather than keep them apart. And there is no hope that Europe's danger zone will finally be pacified, unless democracy reasserts the universal ideas over against the principle of nationalities, its illegitimate offspring.

FOOTNOTES

[1]See Robert Redslob, *Le principe des nationalités* (Paris 1930) p. 7.

[2]When Article 3 declares that "They [the United States and British governments] respect the right of all peoples to choose the form of government under which they will live," it simply forswears, strangely enough without any qualification, intervention in constitutional matters, according to the principle of international law that any state may settle for itself its own form of government. But it does not hold out any promise of liberation from a particular sovereignty.

[3]The several phases leading up to the acceptance of the principle of national self-determination have been surveyed by Sarah Wambaugh, *Plebiscites since the World War* (Washington 1933) vol.1, pp. 3 ff.

[4]See C. A. Macartney, *Hungary and her Successors* (1919–1937), issued under the auspices of the Royal Institute of International Affairs (London 1937) pp. 136 ff. and 487 ff.

[5]The statements of the foreign ministers of Poland, Czechoslovakia and Yugoslavia regarding the Atlantic Charter, delivered on September 24, 1941, in St. James' Palace, London, do not contain any appeal to the principle of national self-determination. See *Inter-Allied Review*, no. 9 (October 15,1941) pp. 3 ff.

[6]See C. A. Macartney, *National States and National Minorities*, issued under the auspices of the Royal Institute of International Affairs (London 1934) p. 100 and *passim*.

[7]Lord Acton, "Nationality," in *History of Freedom and Other Essays* (London 1907) p. 288.

[8]See, for example, Article 3 of the treaty between the United States, the British empire, France, Italy, Japan and Poland, signed at Versailles, June 28, 1919 (League of Nations, *Protection of Linguistic, Racial and Religious Minorities by the League of Nations*, August 1927).

[9]Heinrich von Treitschke, *Was fordern wir von Frankreich?* (1871) quoted byMacartney, *National States and National Minorities* (cited above) p.100. See the English translation of the essay in Heinrich von Treitschke, *Germany, France, Russia and Islam* (London 1915).

[10]Ernest Renan, *Qu'est-ce qu'une nation?* (Paris 1882) p. 13.

[11]Sarah Wambaugh, "Plebiscite," in *Encyclopaedia of the Social Sciences*, vol. 12 (1934) p. 165.

[12]See Macartney, *Hungary and her Successors* (cited above) p. 485.

[13]See Rafael Altamira, *Nationale Minderheiten und Bevölkerungsaustausch in Die Friedens- warte* (Zurich 1940) p. 218.

[14]See Robert Redslob, *Das Problem des Völkerrechts* (Leipzig 1917) pp. 246 ff.

[15]Ernest Renan, *Guerre entre la France et l'Allemagne* (Paris 1870), quoted by Redslob, *Le principe des nationalités* (cited above) p. 91.

[16]Common government as an integrating factor has been duly stressed in a Report by a Study Group of Members of the Royal Institute of International Affairs, *Nationalism* (London 1939) pp. 249 ff.: "The objective factors which encourage the development of common feeling may be looked upon as the result rather than as the cause of a government's existence" (p. 4).

[17]Benedetto Croce, *Storia d'Italia dal 1871 al 1915* (4th ed., rev., Bari 1929) p. 102.

[18]Gaudens Megaro, *Mussolini in the Making* (London 1938) p. 129.

[19]*Bismarck,The Man and the Statesman—Reflections and Reminiscences of Otto, Prince von Bismarck,* translated from the German under the supervision of A. J. Butler, 2 vols. (New York 1898) vol. 1. pp. 321 ff.

[20]Thomas Garrigue Masaryk, *The Making of a State* (New York 1927) p. 370:

[21]*Ibid.,*p. 374. Masaryk himself became a convert to the idea of national independence only in his later years (*ibid.,* p. 29). See also Victor Cohen, *The Life and Times of Masaryk, the President-Liberator,* with a preface by Jan Masaryk (London 1941) p. 130.

[22]*Op. cit.,*pp. 264 ff.

[23]See Redslob, *Le principe des nationalités,* p. 150. Macartney (*Hungary and her Successors,* p.365) gives a similar description and explanation of "the psychology of the weaker party."

[24]Edmund Burke, *Reflections on the French Revolution* (Everyman's Library) p. 6.

[25]See Edward Hallett Carr, *Conditions of Peace* (New York 1942) pp. 52 ff.

[26]German policy at Geneva developed along the lines which Stresemann had laid down as early as 1925 in his Memorandum to the Crown Prince. The protection of those 10 or 12 million Germans who live "under a foreign yoke in foreign lands" is stated there as one of the great tasks of German foreign policy. See *Gustav Stresemann, His Diaries, Letters and Papers,* edited and translated by Eric Sutton (New York 1935–40) vol. 2, p. 503.

[27]John Stuart Mill, *Representative Government* (Everyman's Library) p. 361.

[28]See C. A. Macartney, *Problems of the Danube Basin* (Cambridge 1942) p. 98; also Oscar Jászi, *The dissolution of the Hapsburg Monarchy* (Chicago 1929) pp. 282–97.

[29]Redslob, *Le principe des nationalités,* p. 154.

THE NATIONALITIES POLICY OF THE SOVIET UNION, THEORY AND PRACTICE*

I

The attitude of the Soviet government toward the nationalities that make up the ethnically checkered population of the Soviet Union has, from the first days of the Bolshevist revolution, attracted the attention of students of the national question. But the foreign observer can no longer indulge in a purely academic interest in this policy. The victories of Russian arms, which have assured to the USSR a leading role in European and world affairs, give this problem also a highly practical significance.

Russia's growing strength, as well as the fact that present-day politics still bristles all the world over with the unsolved problems of the nationalist age, makes a sober analysis of the nationalities policy of the Soviet Union more imperative than ever before. But these worldwide implications render infinitely more difficult the psychological detachment required for such an undertaking. A glance at the many contradictory interpretations of Stalin's nationalities policy clearly reveals the perplexities of the task. They are at least as formidable as in any other case in which we try to form a judgment on the purposes, the results and the potentialities of the Russian revolution. A Chinese sage, when asked by Guglielmo Ferrero what he thought about the French Revolution, is reported to have answered, with true Oriental wisdom, that since that event dated back only some hundred and fifty years, it was much too recent to permit of appraisal in our days. Even less are we able to appraise definitively a revolution of our own age.

We do, however, know some facts, undisputed by friend and foe of the communist revolution, on which we may base tentative judgments. Rus-

*Reprinted with permission of *Social Research*, May 1944 (Vol. 11, No. 2).

sia's nationalities policy, in particular, can be stated objectively in the terms of an indisputable record. We may even succeed, to a certain extent at least, in grasping its wider historical bearing, if we try to see and analyze it in the context of the national question in general.

I

The problems posed by modern nationalism were the subject of theoretical considerations and discussions among the Bolshevist leaders long before the party rose to power in November 1917. What was after the revolution to become an issue of state politics presented itself at the beginning of the Russian socialist movement as a problem of party politics, the problem of combining different ethnic elements into a single, indivisible political organization for the pursuit of common ends.

As czarist Russia began to catch up with the political, cultural and economic development of western countries, her many nationalities and races became more and more imbued with the nationalist spirit of western and central Europe. The disintegration of a multinational empire under the force of rampant nationalism, which was already in full swing in Austria-Hungary, seemed to be in the shaping also in Russia, with her some hundred and forty ethnic groups. As was true also in the Hapsburg monarchy, the nationalism that was gathering strength in czarist Russia was related not to the state as a whole, but to its component ethnic groups. It was not political nationalism, triumphant over ethnic and all other groups and associations standing between the individual and the state, but ethnocentrism, denying the supremacy of the state and asserting ethnic over against political values.

To be sure, only a few among the many ethnic groups that compose the Russian population displayed, around the turn of the century, nationalist sentiments of an intensity comparable to the heat of nationalist feelings in central Europe. Apart from the Great Russians, the Poles, the Finns and a few other nationalities, the national consciousness of the Russian peoples was not yet more definitely crystallized than had been the consciousness of the many ethnic groups in central and southeastern Europe before they were awakened by the French Revolution, the romantic movement and the industrial revolution. The nomadic tribes of Asiatic Russia had not reached even this stage of development. But even then it could scarcely be taken for granted in the face of the rapid growth of nationalism in the Danube basin, that those dormant nationalities of Russia would forever remain *geschichtslose Nationen*.[1]

Needless to say, the leaders of the Russian Social Democratic Labor party—which was founded in 1898 and out of which was to develop the All-Union Communist Party (Bolsheviks), the ruling group of present-day

Russia—were in no way interested in maintaining the czarist empire. Nor were they in any way inclined to support the czarist policy of legal discrimination against certain nationalities, or the attempt of the imperial government to further the Russification of the polyglot empire by coercive means. The socialist party violently and sincerely opposed the actual policies of the last Romanovs. From its first days, however, whether it confessed it openly or not, it was genuinely interested in preserving the existing political framework of Russia, in all its breadth and width, as the basis of the future socialist state. Therefore it could not fail to scent in the disruptive force of nationalism, or rather ethnocentrism, a serious threat to the socialist cause for which the party stood.

Moreover, this force was an immediate threat to the unity of the party which was to prepare and carry out the socialist revolution. In multinational Austria the unity of the socialist party had already fallen prey to the virulence of the nationalist germ. The first symptom had been, in 1897, the federalization along ethnical lines of the formerly unitary party structure. This loosening of the party ties was carried further in the following years, until, in 1911, the Austrian labor movement broke up into several political parties and trade union organizations, formed along ethnical lines and frequently cooperating not with one another but with their co-nationals on the other side of what the Marxists call the class barrier. Similar tendencies threatened the unity of the Russian Social Democratic Labor Party. The federalism of the party into ethnically delimited organizational units was an avowed demand of the Jewish Bund. Also in reflection of Austrian influence, the members of the Jewish Bund and some Caucasian socialists, supported by Mensheviks, advocated what the Austrians called "personal cultural autonomy," as a device for solving the national question in Russia.

It was these actual and potential dangers to the unity of the party and of the future socialist state which, after the turn of the century, caused Lenin and lesser Bolshevist theoreticians to give special consideration to the problems of nationalism. Among the contributions of the minor Bolsheviks Joseph Stalin's essay on "The National Question and Social Democracy," written and published in 1913,[2] holds an eminent place, not only because of the decisive role that the author was to play in determining the course of the nationalities policy of the revolution, but also because it is a clear and comprehensive statement of the basic conceptions underlying that policy. As a result of these qualities the essay is, in spite of what it lacks in theoretical finesse, a highly informative document. The following analysis will therefore concentrate on Stalin the disciple rather than on Lenin the master.

It might seem somewhat naive to refer any actions of the present ruler of Russia, the unexcelled master of communist *Realpolitik*, to theoretical conceptions stated by himself or anyone else some thirty years ago. We are cautioned, not without good reason, against overrating the significance of theoretical patterns for Stalin's actual policies.[3] But even *Realpolitik* moves in lines of thoughts, feelings and interests which may be revealed by its theoretical garment. To be sure, political realists refuse to jeopardize the achievement of their ultimate ends by a doctrinaire insistence on rigid methods. Moreover, they are ready to tread on cumbersome, winding roads when shortcuts prove to be impracticable. But unless their policy degenerates into a mere struggle for personal power, it will be oriented toward definite ends, based on definite political conceptions. In this sense Stalin's nationalities policy has always been, and still is, closely related to his political philosophy in general and his national theory in particular. Besides, the pattern of his theory fits the practical requirements of a multinational empire, regardless of whether it is used for a policy of world revolution or for old-fashioned power politics of the classical type.

Boris Souvarine hesitates to credit Stalin with the independent authorship of the essay on the national question. According to Souvarine, Lenin, "anxious to educate his co-workers, and to specialize them," provided Stalin with an outline of the study to be undertaken, and helped him to carry it out.[4] The character of the essay suggests, however, that Souvarine underrates the originality of Stalin's contribution. Lenin's own writings on the national question are essentially an array of abstract principles and statements, tied up with the Marxist theory of the state.[5] The striking feature of Stalin's pamphlet is rather the shrewdness of the concrete approach and the skilful way in which he disposes of purely ideological arguments. It reveals the Georgian politician who learned the spadework of his profession in a corner of czarist Russia where the inextricable mixture of races and nationalities, religions and customs sharpens the eye for the specific problems of the task of molding heterogeneous elements into a coherent political force.

The Georgian background and Stalin's practical sense account also for his remarkable insight into the realities of the national struggle in the Austria of 1912. According to the official party version,[6] Stalin wrote his pamphlet in Vienna, which was at that time not only the capital of an empire torn by national strife but also the center of the most serious intellectual efforts to solve the national problem. Foremost among these efforts were the profound writings of Karl Renner (Rudolf Springer) and Otto Bauer, rising talents of the socialist party, who elaborated in several books and articles specific recommendations for pacifying the quarreling nationalities of Austria. Stalin's essay is an outright condemnation of Renner's and Bauer's proposals in particular, and of the nationalities policy of the Austrian socialist party in general. Plekhanov's criticism in 1912 of the

Jewish Bund—that it "is adapting socialism to nationalism" rather than nationalism to socialism—sums up also Stalin's criticism of the Austrian socialists.[7] Both the scheme of "personal cultural autonomy," which was the very core of Bauer's and Renner's suggestions, and the disintegration of the formerly unitary party organization into several socialist parties, formed along ethnic lines, seemed to Stalin to indicate that Austria was becoming ripe for a national revolution of her several ethnic groups, but not for a socialist rovolution of the Austrian working class as a whole.

There is no sense in speculating whether multinational Austria would have been blown up by the dynamite of nationalism even without the war and defeat which overcame her a few years later. Be that as it may, the dissolution in 1911 of the socialist party into ethnic parties was a most serious symptom of Austria's political decomposition. The hope of Emperor Franz Josef, that universal and equal suffrage would push the social question into the forefront of Austrian politics and relegate the specifically national issues to a secondary place, turned out to be futile. As a matter of fact, the democratization of the suffrage system in 1907 had raised rather than lowered the tide of ethnocentrism. With the dismemberment of the "k.k. Sozialdemokratie" there was no longer any chance that a rising social class and a new international party would continue the cosmopolitan traditions of aristocracy and Catholicism, which were steadily losing ground, at least in politics proper. Rather it was to be expected that the Austrian labor movement would in the future tread in the footsteps of the bourgeois classes, among which nationalism was most virulent, and thereby lend its help to the destruction of a comprehensive and wide political structure that might one day have sheltered a socialist state. Stalin bitterly lamented in his essay the infection of the Austrian comrades with bourgeois nationalism. Seven years later he was to pride himself that the dissolution of Austria-Hungary into several national states had justified his criticism of the Austrian socialists: "Now when Springer and Bauer are standing over the spilt milk pail of their national programme, there can hardly be room for doubt that history has condemned the 'Austrian school'."[8]

With the spectre of Austria's disintegration before his eyes, Stalin formulated in his essay of 1913 a recipe for preventing the disruption of multinational states by the forces of tribalism. It has been used ever since in the Bolshevist kitchen.

Stalin did not content himself in his essay with attacking the practical propositions of the Austrian school. He opened with an assault on its basic philosophy. There is hardly any definition of nation and nationality in the numerous writings on the topic which is not at the same time a political program.[9] Renan's famous definition is the most conspicuous example, but there is no lack of political implications in other definitions. Stalin's answer to the question, "what is a nation?" is certainly no exception to this rule. In fact, it is the first precise formulation of the guiding principles which were later to determine the nationalities policy of the Soviet Union.

The nation has been described by some authors as an objective, by others as a subjective, phenomenon. Stalin definitely belongs to the objectivist school. His main exception to the Austrian doctrine was what he called its spiritualism. The characteristics which constitute a nation are, according to Stalin, community of language, community of territory, community of economic life and community of psychological make-up, the so-called national character. Time and again he emphasized that "none of the above characteristics is by itself sufficient to define a nation. On the other hand it is sufficient for a single one of these characteristics to be absent, and the nation ceases to be a nation. . . . It is only when all these characteristics are present that we have a nation" (pp. 8 ff).

This view determined the direction of Stalin's attack on Otto Bauer's definition of the nation as "the totality of people who are bound into a community of character by a community of fate."[10] Stalin showed little patience for the subtleties of Bauer, who tried very hard to keep his theory free from the spiritualist tinge of bourgeois theories.[11] But the question in which we are interested in this context is not whether Stalin's attack on Bauer was well founded, but what his attack reveals concerning his own philosophy. Stalin blamed Bauer for regarding the national character as the only constitutive element of the nation, and for assuming community of language, territory and economic life to be merely conducive to, and not altogether indispensable for, the formation of the national character and the existence of the nation. In particular, Stalin joined issue with Bauer's and Renner's view that the community of territory, under modern conditions of communication, is no longer a necessary characteristic of the national community.

The political implications of Stalin's conception are most strikingly revealed by his remarks on the problem of whether the Jews are a nation. He was greatly concerned with this question, largely as a result of the Jewish Bund's agitation for a federalization of the Russian Social Democratic Labor Party and for a constitutional and administrative reform that would recognize the Jews of Russia as a distinct national group and grant them cultural autonomy in the forms proposed by the Austrian socialists.

In view of his definition, it is hardly surprising to find that Stalin declared that the Jews do not constitute a nation, since their fate has been dispersion rather than communal life, be it in linguistic, territorial or economic terms. Stalin did not, of course, mention religion as an element contributing to the formation and preservation of national groups. Neither secular nor religious Zionism finds any place in his philosophy of the nation. In Stalin's own words (p. 12), the Jews are not a "real nation" but a "paper nation." This judgment was doubtless due primarily to his intention to discredit the ideals and tenets of the Jewish Bund, which he considered the vanguard of nationalism in Russia's proletarian ranks. But the conclusion cannot be wholly explained in tactical terms.

Stalin would hardly deny that national thoughts and sentiments may linger on in man's mind long after historical events have destroyed a people's collective existence, based on the elements that he enumerates. Nor could he reasonably deny that national ideas and feelings may strike root in individual minds and hearts long before such collective existence actually takes shape, if it ever does at all. But in either case, Stalin would definitely reject the notion that any government is under the moral or legal obligation to take cognizance of these scattered psychological facts, and to twist the individual threads into a collective texture. To do so would in his view mean to maintain or to create an artificial national consciousness.

As a matter of fact, one may wonder whether Stalin attributes genuine national consciousness even to what he himself calls a "real nation." Only the class, not the nation, is for the Marxist a true social unit. Under capitalism the nation, he maintains, is split up into antagonistic classes; under socialism the nation will wither away like the state. It is the national-ist, not the socialist, who believes in the collective consciousness of the members of an ethnic group. The Marxist is rather inclined to see in that concept a capitalist ideology, like religion an opiate for the oppressed classes. In his view the intimacy of the relationship among the members of a particular ethnic group is due only to the linguistic tie, which distinguishes that group and sets it apart from other ethnic groups with other vernaculars. According to the socialist view the integrative effect of language imparts to an ethnic group a greater political importance than is found in religious groups, and makes for special political problems, essentially problems of language policy. Stalin's arguments indicate the same trend of thought.

Stalin stressed that the nation is a historical phenomenon, which "like every other historical phenomenon is subject to the law of change, has its history, its beginning and end" (p. 8). Nations form and dissolve them-selves in a continuous process of differentiation and amalgamation which runs through all history. Stalin insisted that this process lies outside the province of government, and should be left undisturbed by governmental interference. The nationalities policy of the government of a multinational state should be guided by the laissez-faire principle. This conception explains Stalin's violent reaction against the device of "personal cultural autonomy" which the Austrian socialists advocated. It was this "subtle form of nationalism" (p. 33) against which Stalin wanted to take the field when he wrote his pamphlet in 1913.

He disregarded the differences in Renner's and Bauer's presentations of the scheme of "personal cultural autonomy," and concentrated his attack on their common purpose and common technical proposals. Their avowed end was the preservation and cultivation of the various national peculiarities. Technically this purpose was to be achieved by the establishment of legislative and administrative units, each of which would comprise all the members of its particular ethnic group, regardless of their actual domicile, and would be endowed with full self-government in all matters relating to the national-cultural interests of its members. Stalin declared that this idea of institutionalizing the ethnic group is "entirely incompatible with social democracy." The task of the socialist is not to stimulate nationalism, not to strengthen national distinctions, but to break them down and unite the population "in such a manner as to open the way for division of a different kind, division according to class." In Stalin's view the form that best serves this purpose is regional autonomy, the autonomy of territorial units with an ethnically diversified population. Common, not separate, institutions promote the spirit through which common purposes are achieved.

This rejection of the idea that ethnic groups as such have collective rights does not imply a denial of equal rights to the members of the various groups. On the contrary, the disassociation of state and nation is matched by a disassociation of the citizen's rights from his ethnic status. Laissez-faire policy, be it in the economic or in the ethnic sphere, presupposes and implies an abstract conception of the citizen and his rights. Thus Stalin defined the equality of nationalities in terms of the equal rights of their several members. It is not surprising that in doing so he stressed the equality of language rights, such as the right of all alike to use in public and private their native language, and to receive their education in their mother tongue. This, to Stalin, is the one ethnic right for which the common man actually cares. By granting and enforcing it the government of the multinational state creates an atmosphere in which inter-ethnic relations are bound to grow more and more harmonious. Linguistic autonomy, in Stalin's view, brings about the de-politicization of nationalism and thus prepares the psychological ground for the final amalgamation of the ethnic groups. Unification and amalgamation, rather than segregation and preservation of the ethnic units which compose the multinational state, were Stalin's ultimate aim.

The endeavor to make use of common institutions in order to check separatist tendencies of the nationalists is even more conspicuous in Stalin's insistence on a single proletarian party. The example of the Austrian socialist party seemed to prove that federal organization along ethnic lines, once adopted as the basis of the party structure, will inevitably develop into national separatism. "The type of organization," Stalin remarked, with keen insight into the psychological effect of institutions, "influences not only practical work. It stamps an indelible impress on the whole mental life of the workers." Therefore decentralization in the party, so far as it is necessary at all, should be based on territorial and not on ethnic units.

One might expect that a philosophy which abhors the organization of nationalities for cultural purposes would condemn in even stronger terms the most radical manifestation of the nationalist spirit, that is, the claim of ethnic groups to political independence. The right of nations to self-determination was, however, a much advertised point of the party program that the Russian socialists adopted in 1903.

It would be a mistake to attribute this point of the party program solely to agitational purposes. To be sure, the slogan of self-determination fitted very well a policy that tried to mobilize all actual and potential foes of the regime for the overthrow of the czarist government. Indeed, the stimulating effect of this slogan on the border nationalities was evident when the hour of revolution finally came. Looking back upon the turmoil of 1917, Trotsky declared that the conflict of nationalities, which the Bolsheviks had so greatly helped to intensify, "cruelly shook the February regime and created sufficiently favorable surroundings for the revolution in the center."[12]

Nevertheless, the actual and the attempted secessions of the border nationalities from the Russian state, during and after 1917, were to reveal also the risks involved in using this two-edged weapon. As a matter of fact, the wisdom of the slogan of self-determination was from the beginning a question of great controversy among the Russian socialists. It was opposed with particular vehemence by Rosa Luxemburg, the Polish socialist.[13] But she failed to convince Lenin, for whom the right of self-determination was a principle that could not be outweighed by purely tactical considerations, at least not so long as the revolution had not yet brought him face to face with the threat of secession. The stubbornness with which he clung to this principle is another interesting indication of the curious mixture in Lenin's mind of realism and utopian doctrinairism.

National self-determination was for Lenin one of the essential conditions for that "withering away" of the state which would characterize the socialist epoch of human history. This "withering away" can be expected, in his opinion, only after an amalgamation of the constituent nations, which in turn is dependent upon a complete elimination of all national friction. And this elimination can be achieved "only when complete democracy is introduced in all spheres, including the fixing of state boundaries in accordance with the sympathies of the population, and including complete freedom of secession." The transformation of capitalism into socialism through the proletarian state creates, according to Lenin, merely the possibility for the abolition of national oppression. The possibility becomes reality only if and when socialist mankind organizes its political units on the basis of consent. Therefore the right of self-determination retains its validity also for the socialist society. "This is the theory of Marxism," wrote Lenin in 1916, "from which our Polish colleagues have mistakenly departed."[14]

When Lenin came to power shortly afterward, he did not hesitate himself to depart from this theory. "The interests of socialism are indeed superior to the right of self-determination," he declared in 1918.[15] Nor was there any lack of arguments in the arsenal of Marxist theory to justify the new nationalities policy. But the fact remains that originally Lenin went very far in meeting nationalist demands. He was not afraid to ally the socialist cause with nationalism, because he was inclined to underrate the force and fervor of modern nationalism. He did not regard the latter as an equal partner, even less as a dangerous one. Nationalism, he thought, would melt away in the fire of the socialist world revolution. Socialism would knit together again what nationalism might temporarily separate.

Stalin too, in his essay of 1913, advocated, the right of self-determination as an essential element in the solution of the national problem. But that right had no organic place in the theoretical framework of Stalin's pamphlet. The Mazzinian touch in Lenin's conception of the function of the national state in the future socialist society was entirely absent in Stalin's essay. In fact, Stalin expressly refuted the idea of a "division of humanity into nationally delimited communities." He opened up no grandiose vista of an era in which nationalism and socialism would be definitely reconciled; rather he kept his eyes fixed upon the stern realities which a socialist movement faces in multinational surroundings, swept by a rising tide of national sentiments. Trotsky has blamed Stalin for his "vulgar and pedantic separation of national form from social content in the revolutionary process, as though they constituted two independent historic stages."[16]

The truth is that from the beginning Stalin saw more clearly than Lenin ever did, and weighed more realistically one against the other, the chances and the dangers for the socialist revolution which are inherent in the disruptive force of nationalism. Occasionally Stalin even used extremely harsh words against national self-determination. In 1921 he reminded the party congress that the party program of 1919 no longer spoke of "self-determination—an absolutely vague slogan—but of a better minted and more clearly defined slogan—the right of nations to political secession." But Stalin never went so far as Pyatakov, Dzerzhinsky and Bukharin, who flatly opposed the principle of self-determination and thus drew upon themselves the charge of Muscovite imperialism.[17]

In his essay Stalin purposely refrained from encouraging any of the movements for independence from Russia which were at that time gathering strength among some of the border nationalities. Certainly such independence would have to be accepted where and when it could not be prevented, if the socialist party did not want to follow the czarist policy of oppression. But the right of secession should not be the guiding principle in the solution of the national question. "The only real solution," said Stalin "is regional autonomy, autonomy for such crystallized units as Poland, Lithuania, the Ukraine, the Caucasus, etc."

Thus the *right* of the various nationalities to secede from Russia was not denied. But the actual policy of the party was to be determined by consideration not of the rights of nations but of the interests of the proletariat, as interpreted by the socialist party in accordance with the Marxist doctrine which puts the class above the nation. Or, to put it in Stalin's own words: "The obligations of Social-Democrats, who defend the interests of the proletariat, and the rights of a nation, which consists of various classes, are two different things."

The implications of Stalin's doctrine of self-determination are obvious. In customary usage that term implies both the general principle that government should be founded on consent rather than on force, and the "principle of nationalities," according to which every nationality is entitled to form its own state.[18] But neither of these principles is given any effective weight in Stalin's doctrine. In his view the legitimate interpreter of the rights that an ethnic group may and should claim is the proletariat, not the ethnic group as a whole or even its individual members, acting in accordance with their particular political convictions.

It should not be overlooked that the liberal and democratic version of the right of self-determination has also its problematic features, and that the application of the principle is not always consistent with its pretensions. Still, the democratic processes of free plebiscite and free election are a certain corrective of any theoretical shortcomings and practical abuses—a corrective that is lacking in Stalin's interpretation of the principle. To Stalin, in 1913 and afterward, the proletariat meant the rulers of the party—and not the local but the central authorities of the party.[19]

Stalin's doctrine of self-determination was clearly intended not to support the current interpretations, but to qualify them, and to transform a rigid principle into a matter of expediency. The actual policies of the soviets toward the secessionist nationalities amply illustrate the Bolshevist modifications of the doctrine of self-determination. Today the Communist party and its leader stand before the world as the restorer of a multinational empire which in 1917, and during the following years of civil war and intervention, threatened to fall apart under the assault of nationalist movements.

Empires as such are neither good nor bad. The character of their dominion over men and peoples is determined by the purposes to which their power is put, and by the ways in which the power is exercised. Therefore, in order to know the actual position of the nationalities under the Soviet Union, we have to study the concrete manifestations of its nationalities policy.

II

The Soviet Union is not, and is not intended to be, a national state in the sense in which the word has come to be understood in central and eastern Europe. It is nationally neutral; that is, none of the many ethnical groups that compose its population, not even the majority group of the Great Russians, is legally recognized as a dominant nationality, or is granted the right to use the political machinery of the Union as "the exclusive instrument of [its] own national self-expression."[20]

The time is long past in which the Soviet Union considered itself as the nucleus of a socialist world state, with its frontiers wide open to all workers of the world. The constitution of 1936 confines the suffrage to the citizens of the USSR; even more significant, the soldiers of the Red Army no longer take their oath "in the presence of the laboring classes of Russia and of the whole world," but bind themselves to defend their homeland, the USSR. The Soviet Union of today is an old-type state with definite territory and closed citizenship.

Nevertheless, the Soviet Union is still an "inter-national" community as regards the relationship among its component ethnic groups. Article 1 of the constitution of 1936 still defines the Union of Soviet Socialist Republics as "a socialist state of workers and peasants," without circumscribing their nationality, and the very name of the Union still includes no reference to its ethnic elements. Its legitimacy rests not on any title of nationality, but on its claim to be the instrument of a class. The Soviet Union regards itself as a class state, not a national state.

Actually it is not so much a class state as a party state. This distinction is necessary, for the symptoms of a new social stratification have recently been increasing, and such strata as there are exist also in the party membership itself. In any case, the legally and actually privileged group which rules the country is the All-Union Communist Party. And in view of this political reality, particular importance attaches to the fact that the purposes of the Communist party itself are related to all nationalities alike. The party wields its power over the Union not with a view to furthering the special interests of any of the many nationalities that live under its rule, but with a view to achieving social ends and to maintaining the unity of the political system. Accordingly it tries to steer a nationally neutral course and to insure, as the party program promises, "the fullest equality of all nationalities."[21]

In point of fact the Great Russians have always been predominant, as a result of their number, their geographical distribution, their economic strength and their educational level, and also because of deep-rooted historical traditions. As a result of their great weight the equality between them and the smaller, weaker and less advanced nationalities has for all practical purposes been merely a formal equality. Except for the Great Russians, who constituted up to 1939 some 52 percent of the total population of the Soviet Union, only the Ukrainians number more than 20 percent. The other minorities are hardly more than splinters, with little, if any, political weight of their own. The secession of the western provinces, after the last war, removed the nationalities that had the most intense national consciousness; even among the Ukrainians and Georgians national sentiments have lacked the fervor and the political maturity of the nationalist movements of central Europe. In so far as the Soviet population, as a result of the secessions, was more homogeneous than that of the czarist empire, and the tensions among the remaining nationalities less acute, the natural hegemony of the Great Russians was even more assured after the revolution.

The fact remains, however, that the Bolshevist regime has not attempted to maintain and strengthen by oppressive means the power proportions between the Great Russians and the other nationalities. There were even tendencies to go to extremes in leveling them down. Bukharin suggested at the Twelfth Congress of the party in 1923 that the Great Russians, as a "former great-power nation," should not hesitate in making concessions to the national tendencies of the smaller ethnic groups, and in artifically placing themselves "in an inferior position as compared with others"; only at such a price would they be able to "purchase the real confidence of the formerly oppressed nations."[22] Stalin and the other party leaders were not ready to pay this price.[23] But the opening up of new political chances, the industrialization of the most remote parts of the Union, the broadening of education, and Moscow's nationalities policy, which tried, with particular emphasis in the twenties, to promote national individualities and at the same time to integrate them into a highly centralized political system—all these developments could not fail to strike a new balance between Russian and non-Russian nationalities which at least in some cases was more favorable for the national minorities.

A precise judgment on the actual policies of the party and the government is impossible, and not only because we are dealing to some extent with intangibles. It is obvious from the discussions on the national question at several public party gatherings that the policy of neutrality toward all nationalities and races has not always been generally accepted and enforced by all party and Soviet officials. Time and again Stalin has condemned what he calls "creeping deviations" toward Great Russian chauvinism on the one side and local chauvinism on the other.[24] His scathing criticism of both types of deviators throws the most interesting light on the actualities of the national question in the Soviet Union. It deserves careful study, particularly by those who are inclined to become lyrical over an idyl which Stalin himself neither sees nor describes.[25]

These discussions destroy the illusion that the Soviet regime has succeeded in eliminating national strife from politics. Actually, no political system could have achieved so miraculous a success. In 1930 Stalin (pp. 256 ff.) even deplored "a certain accentuation of national friction," due partly to the attempt of Great Russian party officials to continue in the border regions the imperial policy of Russification, rather than inaugurating a truly inter-national or supra-national course, and partly to the attempt of local nationalism to isolate itself and shut itself up within its own shell instead of cooperating with Great Russia in the work of socialist construction. Thus in the Soviet Union, too, both extroverted and introverted nationalism seem to have been active, with all the evil consequences that we know from the history of modern nationalism elsewhere.

Stalin's speeches in the twenties abounded with illustrations of the Great Russian zeal of party and soviet officials. In 1923 (pp.180,182) he criticized the Great Russian deviators for practicing in the border regions a "policy of splitting the population from above," and for "thinking that Russian models can be transplanted to a specifically national milieu without regard for the customs of the population and for the concrete conditions"; also he objected to the activities of Marxist cadres that were unconnected with the native masses of the local regions. Great Russian nationalism appears to have continued, however, for seven years later Stalin spoke of "an endeavor to ignore national differences of language, culture and mode of life" and "to undermine the principle of national equality" (p. 256).

In the thirties Stalin began to concentrate his attacks upon the excesses of the non-Russian nationalites, but this does not mean that Great Russian nationalism had meanwhile spent its fervor. It indicates, rather, that Stalin himself had shifted his position, though without changing his principles concerning the national problem and his belief in the wisdom of disassociating party and government from ethnical considerations. Commenting in 1934 on a controversy among party members as to whether Great Russian nationalism or local chauvinism represented the more dangerous deviation from true inter-nationalism, Stalin declared that the major danger was "the deviation against which one has ceased to fight and has thus enabled to grow into a danger to the state" (p. 268). The formula still upheld neutrality, but actually it was directed primarily against Ukrainian nationalism. Hitler's rise to power was throwing its lengthening shadow also over the national problem in the Soviet Union.

The new nationalities policy was the more painful for the Ukrainians as they had hitherto enjoyed a comparatively privileged position.[26] In the twenties considerations of foreign, domestic and economic policy had combined to induce party and government to a generous attitude toward the Ukrainian cultural movement. A letter which Stalin addressed in 1926 to the Central Committee of the Communist party of the Ukraine tells an interesting and typical story (pp. 228 ff.). The party bosses at Moscow had originally decided to ride the crest of the rapidly rising Ukrainian movement, and thus to gain control of it. But difficulties soon arose. Politically reliable Ukrainian communists who were able and willing to hande the delicate job of pushing the cultural movement and at the same time applying the brake to it were not very numerous. On the other hand, the Great Russian party and Soviet officials were "imbued with a spirit of irony and scepticism towards Ukrainian culture and Ukrainian social life." In his letter Stalin tried to teach the Great Russian and the Ukrainian deviators a lesson in the true Leninist conception of ethnic culture and Soviet politics. But he seems to have failed, for some years later he turned to severe repressive measures against the Ukrainian movement. Ukrainians were to figure prominently among the victims of the purges which in the thirties shook party and country.

In spite of the oscillations of the official nationalities policy and the Great Russian deviations from inter-nationalism the Communist regime has made enormous strides toward developing in the non-Russian regions "a press, schools, theatres, clubs, and cultural and educational institutions generally functioning in the native language."[27] The regime prides itself particularly on its tolerance toward the local vernaculars, and on its initiative in scientifically promoting their further development. But even in the heyday of the policy of assisting and supporting the differentiation and development of national cultures, the inspiring ideal was not a genuine cultural pluralism. As a matter of fact, the fusion of the national cultures of the whole world into a single socialist culture, uniform both in form and in content, was the openly avowed ultimate aim of the revolution. During the transition period between capitalism and advanced communism the national cultures were expected to be distinct in form, but identical in their socialist content. The Great Russian deviators, tired of the concessions to the national minorities, even tried to utilize passages from Lenin's writings in order to justify an immediate fusion of all ethnical elements composing the Union, a fusion into a socialist-Muscovite civilization.[28]

Bolsheviks are not romantics. They do not set an absolute value on historical individualities, matured into nations. National language, folklore, customs and traditions have for them no intrinsic worth. The Bolsheviks conceive the nation not as an organic entity, mysteriously growing and decaying, but as a mechanism of aggregate elements which can be joined and taken asunder like the parts of a hydroelectric power plant. Personal attachment and loyalty to a national group have for them as strong connotations of superstition as has religion. Both, they think, will evaporate with capitalism, which has produced and utilized them for its sinister purposes. At present, however, the politician, and in particular the builder of the socialist world, has still to reckon with them. The Bolsheviks always abhorred national oppression. But they hated it not so much for the sake of national values and ideals as because they believed that it would perpetuate what under a system of tolerance, or rather indifference, would rapidly wither away. Suppression of the native language always seemed to them especially obnoxious.

The apostles of the principle of nationalities believe, or at least want to make others believe, that every man irresistibly desires the political union of all those who speak the same language. The facts of history clearly disprove this thesis of the nationalist intellectuals. And the Bolsheviks never adopted this creed. In his essay of 1913 on the national question Stalin emphatically maintained that a national minority longs not for political union with its co-nationals, but for the right to use its native language and to possess its own schools. "Give it these liberties," he declared (p. 58), "and it will cease to be discontended."

Thus the liberal language and school policy of the Soviet regime was inspired by the hope that it would deprive nationalism of its psychological basis. Moreover, what really mattered was not the language in which communist doctrine was preached and perceived, but its content. Whatever the vernacular, it could be used as "a tool of communist enlightenment of the working masses," to use the words of a resolution which the Central Committee of the Communist party passed in 1919 on its Ukrainian policy.[29] Finally, the speediest way to enable the peoples of the Union to run machines and tractors, and to master the technique of mechanized, total war, was to teach them how to read and write in their vernaculars.[30] The pluralist method was thus made to serve the uniformity of a totalitarian dictatorship and a technological civilization. The method was for that no less laudable; but it is its end with which we are here concerned.

The significance of the nationalities policy of the Soviet regime lies not in what it has done for the national collectivities, but in what it has done for their individual members. As a matter of fact, the equal rights that the revolution has proclaimed belong not to the nationalities as such, but to the individual citizens, as members of their respective national groups. National equality has a negative rather than a positive content—the prohibition of legal discrimination against anyone for reasons of nationality. Article 123 of the constitution of 1936 is an exhaustive statement of this conception. "Equality of rights of citizens of the USSR," says the constitution, "irrespective of their nationality or race, in all spheres of economic, state, cultural, social and political life, is an indefeasible law. Any direct or indirect restriction of the rights of, or, conversely, any establishment of direct or indirect privileges for, citizens on account of their race or nationality, as well as any advocacy of racial or national exclusiveness or hatred and contempt, is punishable by law."

It might be said that Article 123 should be dismissed as meaningless in view of the dictatorial character of the Soviet regime, the very essence of which is the legally and actually recognized and enforced privileged position of the Communist party and the precarious tenure of any individual rights, political or civil. Moreover, quite apart from the political character of the regime, it may be safely assumed, human nature being what it is, that the realities of Soviet life are not altogether in accordance with the high-sounding principles of the constitution. We know the discrepancy between ideal and reality from the party controversies over the deviations from the inter-nationalist party line.

The principles of Article 123 are nevertheless of practical importance. The Communist party is a privileged group, but it is at the same time an inter-national group. It started out as a political sect, and turned more and more into an administrative institution. Both as a sect and as an *Amtsadel* of a socialist society it is open to members of all races and nationalities. The political, administrative and industrial key positions in the country are held by non-Russians as well as by Russians. The Georgian origin of Stalin is generally known. But there are many other examples of non-Russian party bosses and industrial managers who share in shaping policies and wielding power for and over the Union. And this inter-nationalist climate of the country undoubtedly benefits also those who are not admitted into the ruling group. The opportunities that are open to them are, on principle, equally open to all, regardless of national origin.

Far from promoting cultural variegation, this equalitarianism of the regime, combined with and strengthened by its social equalitarianism, has prepared the psychological ground for an amalgamation of the nationalities of the Union. The dynamic forces released by the revolution itself worked the same way. Men were tossed about in the melting pot of the revolution like stones in an erupting volcano. Old ties were broken and new ties, cutting across national boundaries, were formed. The policy of equalizing the territorial distribution of industry, the mechanization of agriculture, the compulsory migrations, have shifted and blotted out cultural as well as administrative borderlines—though the natural weight of the elements that were thrown into this process was so unequally balanced that the Great Russian streak has inevitably predominated also in the new pattern.

And there is another factor that has hindered the development of national cultures. Cultural autonomy, if it is to be a real thing, presupposes that the political authorities recognize an independent, at least relatively independent, sphere of life, in which freedom reigns and conscience decides. To distinguish the religious, cultural and political spheres, and to keep them properly apart from one another, is a task that has perplexed many a political philosopher. There are involved in this problem questions of the deepest concern to mankind, not the least among them being the exclusive and at the same time complementary relationship between spirit and force as the agents that mold and destroy society and state. Total revolutions have never bothered about these subtle distinctions; at most they have taken them to be of purely opportunist character. The communist revolution was no exception to this rule.

Any cultural rights that the Soviet regime grants to the members of its various nationalities are therefore considered to be revocable, without notice, on political grounds. Needless to say, the party is sovereign arbiter on the question whether any cultural activity has turned or may turn into political activity, and should therefore be stopped by punitive measures. Praise of cultural autonomy and condemnation of the "ludicrous and non-Marxist attempt to divorce culture from politics," as Stalin once characterized the philosophy of the Ukrainian cultural movement (p. 230), can therefore be found side by side in the writings and public utterances of the representatives of the regime. Nothing more clearly reveals the purely political considerations, changing from one moment to the other, which govern Soviet cultural policy, than the orders and counter-orders regarding the latinization of the alphabet of some of the local vernaculars.

Being themselves unsurpassed masters in establishing and maintaining political cells in any kind of organization, politcal or non-political, the communists want to err on the safe side. In case of doubt as to the actual ends of allegedly cultural organizations and activities, they therefore presume politics rather than culture. Historical experience also recommends such a cautious attitude. Modern political nationalism has grown out of what were originally purely cultural movements. The nationalist age was heralded in by such seemingly innocent pastimes as "an eager delving into national history and philology; the collection of legends and folklore, the compilation of grammars and textbooks,"[31] and it culminated, if it can yet be said to have culminated, in the dismemberment and convulsion of the great multinational empires of the Ottomans, the Hapsburgs and the Romanovs. Russia was mutilated badly enough by the politicization of the nationalist movement, and the communists have not wished to expose her unnecessarily to further dangers of that kind.

The intention of preventing innate national sentiments from rising to the pitch of political nationalism has obviously guided the Soviet leaders also in shaping the organizational structure of the Union and its component parts. A certain degree of legislative, administrative and judicial decentralization is indispensable, even under a system of government with highly concentrated political power, particularly if it is of such huge territorial dimensions as the USSR. The very purpose of assuring the government the greatest possible administrative efficiency cautions against going beyond the managerial optimum of centralization. Psychological considerations point the same way. Men are likely to be more restive under an alien rule, even if it is not a nationally alien rule, than under a harsh rule by men with whom they are for one reason or another familiar. The communists have not been indifferent to such susceptibilities.

Stalin's fight against the Great Russian chauvinists in the party was inspired by these very considerations. But the attempt to help the non-Russian peoples "to develop and consolidate their own courts, administrative bodies, economic organs and government organs, functioning in the native language and recruited from among local people acquainted with the customs and psychology of the local population"[32] was undertaken against tremendous odds. The stubbornness of the Great Russian nationalists was only one of the obstacles and, at least in the most backward regions, not even the gravest obstacle to be overcome. "The acute shortage of intellectual forces of local origin in the border regions, the shortage of instructors in every branch of Soviet and party work without exception" is a constantly recurring theme in Stalin's speeches of the twenties. This shortage would have been bad enough if the regime had not at the same time embarked upon a policy of integrating all parts of the Union with the greatest possible speed into the far advanced economic system of central Russia. According to Stalin's figures there were in 1921, out of 65 million non-Russians, no less than 30 million who were still living under pre-capitalistic conditions, some 8 or 10 million even as nomadic pastoral tribes.

No wonder that the Marxist cadres that ruled over those regions were at first composed practically entirely of Great Russians. Only as the educational policy of the regime created a native intelligentsia could a system of the type known in colonial administration as indirect rule develop, making use of native personnel in executive positions. How far this system has actually been practiced by the central authorities it would be difficult to find out. The composition of the administrative personnel seems to be still a far cry from the ideal proclaimed by Stalin in 1920, that such personnel should be recruited principally from among the native peoples.[33]

The tendency to check rather than to further the blossoming of national sentiments accounts also for the fact that the territorial units of government are planned in such a way that they do not completely coincide with the ethnical stratification of the population. To be sure, the Soviet regime has gone much farther than the imperial government ever did in approximating the administrative-political set-up to the national structure of the population, at least in the southeastern and eastern parts of the country. But the fact remains that neither the Union republics nor their territorial subdivisions are ethnically homogeneous. In none of the Union republics does the autochthonous population amount to more than around 80 percent of the total. Even more striking is the ethnic mixture in the autonomous republics; some of them derive their name not from the majority, but from a minority group.

In view of the mixture of races and nationalities in the Soviet Union it would doubtless be impossible, for practical reasons, to achieve a division of governmental units that would coincide with the ethnical divisions—unless a transfer of national minorities were attempted. Moreover, administrative-political areas that might satisfy national demands would not necessarily serve best the purposes of economic administration, which are those most likely to prevail under a system of government-planned economy. But these reasons alone do not fully explain the actual administrative-political structure of the Union. The decisive reason lies in the communists' nationalities philosophy in particular, and in their philosophy of power in general.

It is not their intention to organize the nationalities of the Union; their intention is to organize the proletarian class and its political vanguard, the party, both of which cut across ethnical boundary lines. Their purpose is not to stimulate the nationalism of the various ethnic groups by strengthening ethnical partitions, but to break down such partitions by straining the thinking and feeling of Soviet citizens into a frame of reference more comprehensive than the single ethnic unit. Considerations of power politics, which loom large in the domestic policy of the Soviet leaders as well as in their foreign policy, point in the same direction. To prevent the formation of any power nuclei which might one day become able to compete with the established power, by attracting loyalties and gathering physical strength, is the main concern of any totalitarian dictatorship. If it has to operate a multinational empire it will be particularly suspicious of ethnic power groups, potential as well as real.

It is in this light that Soviet federalism, too, should be judged. Federalism as we know it in the western world means divided loyalties and divided powers. Neither is compatible with the basic concepts that prevail in the Soviet Union. To be sure, if a totalitarian regime stays in power long enough to see its revolutionary doctrines transformed into "inevitable categories of the human mind,"[34] if one generation after the other has grown, organically as it were, into the new political, administrative, cultural and economic pattern of life which the revolution has created, then, but not earlier, what was first merely a legal form without content may become a political reality. The Marxist theory of the withering away of the state is a utopia. The withering away of autocracy and its replacement by milder forms of government have occurred time and again in human history. Nobody is able to foretell whether and when this will happen also to Lenin's and Stalin's dictatorship. But we can say, on the basis of the available evidence, that it is not yet in the shaping, in spite of the constitutional reform of February 1 of this year. A real change of the power relations between Union and republics would have to be heralded not by reforms of the governmental structure but by a loosening of the party clamps that hold the Union together, not to speak of the highly centralized punitive agencies.

If we want to understand the actual working of a political system we have to look into its extra-constitutional institutions no less than into its constitutional machinery: it was Bryce's masterful description of the political parties that first revealed the realities of American democracy. And similarly, we cannot realistically appraise the federal system of any country without relating it to the party system. American federalism, both its essence and the changes it has undergone in the course of time, can be stated in terms of the history and organization of the American parties. That governmental federalism is still more than a name in this country is due, among other reasons, to the federal structure of the parties. On the other hand, the very fact that the Communist party of the Soviet Union is, in the words of the preamble to the party rules, "a unified militant organization held together by conscious, iron proletarian discipline," sets Soviet federalism far apart from what the term signifies in democratic countries. Even in purely legal terms the Communist party is a constitutionally recognized institution (Article 126).

What was said above about the native personnel in the soviets of the larger and smaller subdivisions of the Union is true also of the party leadership and party bureaucracy. Party and state are, after all, closely tied together by a kind of personal union. But the hierarchical and centralized structure of the Communist party weighs even more heavily upon the Soviet federal system. Though the official rules of the Communist party can hardly be assumed to reveal to the outsider the *arcana imperii* of the Soviet Union, they are suggestive enough of the firm grip which the party leadership holds on party and state.

Article 33 of the party rules declares it to be one of the functions of the Central Committee of the Communist party to direct the work of the central Soviet organizations through the party groups in them, thus clearly proclaiming the subordination of the state to the party. No less outspoken are the party rules on the relationship between local and central party units. The "democratic centralism" which is to be "the guiding principle of the organizational structure of the party" signifies, according to Article 18, "the absolutely binding character of the decisions of the higher organs upon the lower organs and upon the party members." The autonomy of the party organizations "in deciding local questions" is qualified to the extent that such decisions must not conflict "with any decision of the party" (Article 20). Articles 23 and 24 specify the rungs of the party hierarchy, and expressly state the subordination of the party organizations of the several Union republics to the party organization of the Union. Finally, the strict prohibition, under severe sanctions, of "factional groupings which break the unity of the party" covers also local dissensions and groupings (Articles 57, 58).[35]

As long as these party rules are maintained and enforced—and there are no indications to the contrary—the practical significance of any enlargement of the constitutional rights of the Union republics is highly problematic. But the constitutional reform of last February is not therefore altogether meaningless.

The decree of February 1, drafted by the central authorities of the Communist party and enacted by the Supreme Soviet, establishes the right of the Union republics to organize military formations, through their own agencies, and to participate, through their own agencies, in the conduct of foreign policy. But the respective commissariats of the Union republics, both the commissariats for defense and the commissariats for foreign affairs, are constituted by the decree not as republican commissariats proper, but as so-called "Union-Republican People's Commissariats," which are under the terms of the constitution strictly subordinated to the respective commissariats at Moscow. Thus in constitutional terms the reform means that in future the respective authorities at Moscow may act, both in the field of military policy and in that of foreign affairs, through corresponding agencies in the capitals of the Union republics. The sovereignty of the Union over foreign and military affairs remains undivided. The Union has merely been legally authorized to allow the Union republics to share in its exercise.

The political meaning of constitutions and constitutional amendments can never be exhaustively stated in purely legal terms. The reform of February 1, 1944, is undoubtedly another dexterous move of Stalin on the nationalities chessboard of the Soviet Union. From 1932 onward Great Russian nationalism had been in the ascendant. The February decree may indicate that the Great Russian tide has begun to recede again. The meaning of the decree in terms of foreign policy is easier to guess. In 1930 Stalin justified his benevolent policy toward the Ukrainians and White Russians by pointing out that there are a Ukraine and a White Russia not only in the USSR but also "in other states." Two years later he reversed his benevolent attitude and turned to a policy of suppression. One is entitled to assume that the attempt of today to present to the democratic world the Union republics in general, and the Ukrainian republic in particular, in the garment of independent statehood is due to similar considerations of foreign policy.

Indeed, the flexibility of the nationalities policy of the Soviet Union has always been amazing. In view of the cataclysmic events that the Union has gone through since November 1917 one may wonder, however, whether the basic consistency of that policy is not even more amazing. Its intellectual groundwork, as we have seen, was laid before the revolution, in the early Bolshevist writings. Although the Marxist phraseology has in the meantime given way to old-fashioned Russian patriotism, the nationalities policy of the Soviet Union seems to be still an application of Stalin's principles of 1913. Or to put it the other way around, Stalin's essay on the national question, published more than thirty years ago, still reads like a commentary on the present nationalities policy of the regime. The policy of the thirties, which furthered ethnic amalgamation rather than the development of national individualities, is even more in accordance with Stalin's original propositions than the policy of ethnic differentiation which was pursued up to 1932. The basic consistency of these policies, through their various oscillations and deviations, is one of methods and processes as well as of ends. They can be summed up and characterized as an attempt to assert the supremacy of the ethnically neutral class, party and state over the national group, and to achieve the solution of the national question in the Soviet Union by de-politicizing it.

This attempt suggests a striking and instructive historical parallel, encouraging and discouraging at the same time. The religious question played as much havoc with the Europe of the sixteenth century as the national question does with present-day Europe. The unity of the Catholic Church was gone, and the unity of the secular state not yet achieved. In fact, it seemed impossible ever to achieve it, as long as religion and politics remained inextricably tied up with one another. For there was no room for the Catholic believer in the Protestant state, nor for the Protestant believer in the Catholic state. The unity of the religious state could be established only by the physical extermination of the religious minority or by transferring that minority into the state of its co-religionists. It was in this situation that the *politiques* began to advocate the disassociation of religion and politics, implying, for the citizen, "the duty of loyalty to a sovereign of a different religion," and, for the sovereign, "the wisdom if not the duty of toleration,"[36] Religious peace was to be effected and maintained by turning religion into an individual quality, and by recognizing the supremacy of the unitary, religiously neutral state. Thus religious peace was bought, but at a high price, paid in religious and political values. Europe was to enter the period of cultural secularization and the absolute state.

Today nationality and politics are inextricably tied up with one another. The principle of nationalities, which has been in the ascendant during the last hundred years, inherently denies moral validity to the multinational state, although that is the only possible state in Europe's belt of mixed populations. It tends to deny, for the citizen, the duty of loyalty to a government of a different nationality, and, for the government, the wisdom and duty of national toleration. The apostles of the principle of nationalities insist that the unity of the state can be established and maintained solely in the form of the uni-national state. Accordingly they recommend either the physical extermination of the ethnic minority or its transfer into the state of its co-nationals.

The *politiques* of today who offer a solution of the national question on the pattern of the de-politicization of religion some centuries ago are the Bolsheviks. The price demanded is even higher than the one that was paid for religious pacification. Whatever the price, however, the offer is a challenge to the democracies not to be satisfied with claiming freedom, but to give it form and content.

FOOTNOTES

[1]The awakening of dormant nationalities to full national consciousness is the central topic of a brilliant study on the national question by Otto Bauer, *Die Nationalitätenfrage und die Sozialdemokratie*, Marx-Studien, vol. 2 (Vienna 1907; 2nd ed., Vienna 1924).

[2]The essay has been republished several times. Under the title "Marxism and the National Question" it opens a collection of Stalin's articles and speeches which was translated from a Russian edition published by Partizdat (Moscow 1934) and published in this country by International Publishers: Joseph Stalin, *Marxism and the National and Colonial Question*, Marxist Library, Works of Marxism-Leninism, vol. 38, ed. by A. Fineberg (New York n.d.) pp. 1–61. The following references to Stalin's article are to this edition.

[3]William Henry Chamberlin, *The Russian Enigma, An Interpretation* (New York 1944) p. 133.

[4]Boris Souvarine, *Stalin, A Critical Survey of Bolshevism* (New York 1939) p. 133.

[5]See, for example, the articles and speeches of the years 1916–17 in V. I. Lenin, *Collected Works*, vol. 19 (New York 1942) pp. 47 ff. and 267 ff.

[6]Stalin, *op. cit.*, p. 289.

[7]*Ibid.*, p. 42.

[8]The quoted passage is contained in Stalin's preface to a new publication in 1920 of his article of 1913; see Stalin, *op. cit.*, p. 289.

[9]See the survey of current definitions in René Johannet, *Le principe des nationalités* (Paris 1923) pp. 6 ff.

[10]Otto Bauer, *op. cit.*, 2nd ed., pp. 113, 135.

[11]*Ibid.*, 2nd ed., p. 121.

[12]Leon Trotsky, *The History of the Russian Revolution* (New York 1934) vol. 3, p. 49.

[13]*Ibid.*, vol. 3, pp. 38 ff., and Souvarine, *op. cit.*, pp. 135, 201 ff.

[14]Lenin, *op. cit.*, vol. 19, pp. 50 ff., 268 ff.

[15]Souvarine, *op. cit.*, p. 201.

[16]Trotsky, *op. cit.*, vol. 3, p. 59.

[17]Souvarine, *op. cit.*, p. 202; and Stalin, *op. cit.*, pp. 106, 62 ff., 168 ff., 295, 301.

[18]See Erich Hula, "National Self-Determination Reconsidered," *Social Research*, vol. 10 (February 1943) pp. 1 ff.

[19]See Stalin, *op. cit.*, pp. 64, 168 and 205, for his statements after the October revolution.

[20]C. A. Macartney, *National States and National Minorities,* published under the auspices of the Royal Institute of International Affairs (London 1934) p. 16.

[21]Point 9 of the program, under the heading "Relations of Nationalities." The text of the party program, and other pertinent source materials, can be consulted in Samuel N. Harper, "Documents on the Government of the Soviet Union," in *Source Book on European Governments* (New York 1937) Section V.

[22]Stalin, *op. cit.*, p. 301.

[23]Stalin, (pp. 168 ff) ridiculed the "repentant mood" of Bukharin, who had been "sinning for years against the nationalities, denying the right of self-determination."

[24]The term is from a report delivered at the Sixteenth Congress of the party on June 27, 1930 (Stalin, *op. cit.*, p. 256), but the theme runs through practically all public utterances of Stalin that are contained in the cited volume (down to 1934). It should be noted that in this section the bibliographical references to Stalin, although they pertain to the same volume that contains his 1913 essay, are not to that essay but to later speeches, except where otherwise indicated.

[25]See, for example, Louis Fischer, "Under the Soviet Rainbow," *Survey Graphic* (February 1944) p. 95 ff.

[26]N. Basily, *Russia under Soviet Rule* (New York 1938) pp. 155 ff.

[27]See the resolution on the national question passed by the Tenth Party Congress in 1921, reprinted in Stalin, *op. cit.*, pp. 259 ff.

[28]Stalin, *op. cit.*, pp. 198 ff., 210 ff., 230 ff., 257 ff. See also M. Chekalin, *The National Question in the Soviet Union* (New York 1941) p. 17.

[29]Walter Russell Batsell, *Soviet Rule in Russia* (New York 1929) p. 213.

[30]Edward Mead Earle, "Lenin, Trotsky, Stalin: Soviet Concepts of War," in E. M. Earle, *Makers of Modern Strategy* (Princeton 1943) p. 338.

[31]Macartney, *op. cit.*, p. 94.

[32]See the resolution on the national question passed by the Tenth Party Congress in 1921, reprinted in Stalin, *op. cit.*, p. 259.

[33]Stalin, *op. cit.*, p. 84. Wendell Willkie, *One World* (New York 1943) p. 97, offers interesting observations on the situation in the Yakutsk Autonomous Soviet Socialist Republic.

[34]See T. E. Hulme, *Speculations, Essays on Humanism and the Philosophy of Art,* ed. by Herbert Read (London 1924) pp. 50 ff.

[35]Harper, *op. cit.*, Section V, pp. 34 ff.

[36]John Neville Figgis, *Studies of Political Thought from Gerson to Grotius, 1414–1625* (Cambridge, Eng., 1931) pp. 96 ff.

THE QUESTION OF RUSSIAN
OBJECTIVES*

There is hardly an issue that arises in our relations with the Soviet Union for which our policy decision does not require our prior assessment of the "real" objectives of Russian policy. Again and again we are anxiously asking ourselves whether they are of an essentially unlimited or limited nature. Important as a precise and correct answer to the question of Russian intent is for the formulation and execution of a sound American policy, it is unfortunately one of those intriguing questions to which the clear-cut and proper answer, apt to set the mind at ease, is infinitely more difficult than we would like it to be.

In the forties and fifties we have been alternately proceeding on two extreme and contrary theories, though doubts as to their respective absolute validity were not entirely absent at any time. While during World War II we assumed that Russian policy was and would continue to be much the same as the policy of other great powers pursuing limited objectives with a view to protecting their national interests, we began shortly after the Yalta Conference to move toward and finally whole-heartedly embraced the opposite theory that the USSR was a revolutionary power with essentially unlimited objectives and an appetite practically insatiable until its ultimate aim of world domination would be accomplished. We have inferred this theory of Russian intent from Russian actions and, to an increasing extent in recent years, from communist doctrine.

I propose to examine first the question whether and to what extent this doctrine necessarily bears out the theory of unlimited objectives. Tedious as it is to follow Marxist-Leninist theory on its circuitous and sinuous roads, we may expect to be rewarded by a better knowledge of the way in which

*Reprinted with permission of the Washington Center for Foreign Policy Research from *East-West Negotiations* published by the School for Advanced Studies, 1958.

the mind of our communist adversary works. To be sure, this knowledge will not enable us to forecast communist actions. The communists themselves stress time and again that Marxist-Leninist doctrine is only a guide to action, and that "the necessary analysis of things and phenomena" must not be replaced by "merely quoting classics." The fact remains, however, that they do look at things and phenomena through the medium of their classics.

In examining the communist doctrine as far as it might be relevant for Soviet foreign policy, I shall purposely stress especially those factors that render it doubtful whether communist doctrine must indeed be interpreted as indicating and serving unlimited objectives. The particular emphasis is justified for two reasons. In the first place, we are today apt to err on the side of too pessimistic an interpretation of Marxist-Leninist doctrine rather than on the side of unwarranted optimism. Secondly, because recent political literature abounds in analyses that do not fail to bring out the most disquieting aspects of communist doctrine in full relief, there is no need to stress them once more.

The examination of the doctrine is followed by a discussion of the interrelationship between the ideological and the political objectives in communist theory and practice. The concluding paragraphs touch upon the question of the objective conditions by which Soviet policy can be assumed to be determined.

I

First, there is no Marxist-Leninist doctrine on international politics that is in elaborateness and scope equal to the communist doctrine on domestic politics. What is particularly important in our context is that there is no communist blueprint for international politics that would be comparable to the blueprint for the conquest of domestic power which Lenin has laid down in "State and Revolution." In other words, true as it is that Lenin preaches in this and other writings revolution and civil war as a means for establishing the absolute rule of communist parties within and over their respective national communities, there is no corresponding Leninist prescription to the effect that communist Russia should strive for absolute power in the world community and launch international war to attain it. Whatever else may be implied by the idea of communist world revolution and of Russia's role in this process, the Holy War as an instrument for the universalization of communism and the establishment of a Russian world empire has never been part of Leninist doctrine, though the Russian leaders, of course, have not hesitated in the past and would not hesitate in the future to exploit war, if and when it occurs, for their revolutionary and national ends.

Considering the prominent role of force in communist thought, one wonders, however, how much practical importance one can attribute to the fact that the holy-war concept forms no explicit part of the ideological armament of the Soviet Union. Adherents of a doctrine that sanctifies the use of force and coercion in domestic politics are not likely to favor their renunciation and forgo their use in international relations. In view of the communist predilection for force, the repeated assertions by Russian leaders of the ultimate triumph of their cause over ours seem to have a rather ominous sound indeed. And it is, therefore, hardly surprising that those assertive boasts are often interpreted as threats to resort some day to war for securing that triumph. But one must nevertheless ask whether the communist doctrine actually warrants such interpretation. Despite the communist emphasis on force, is the faith of the Russian leaders in the final victory of communism primarily or even exclusively due to reliance on physical force? We can answer this question only by weighing the other essential elements of their philosophy as well.

If the stress on force as a creative and even moral power is an expression of fanatic exaltation of the human will, there is strangely allied with it a strictly deterministic component, no less fanatically embraced than the first element. It is the undoubtedly sincere conviction of the Russian leaders, founded on Marxist teaching, that the laws of history are working in their favor, that the ultimate triumph of their cause is guaranteed by the operation of objective necessities. The ascendancy of the socialist system in wide parts of the globe cannot but have the effect of reassuring them of the correctness of their vision of the world to come. Once one tries to give due weight to this element of the communist doctrine, one cannot help admitting the possibility that what we are inclined to consider as threats to conquer by war are actually professions of faith, serving propagandistic purposes. Mr. John Foster Dulles' reaction to the Moscow Declaration of "the Representatives of the Communist and Workers' Parties of the Socialist Countries," issued on November 16, 1957, might have very well erred on this side. To be sure, the certainty of the Russian leaders that the angels of history are on their side does not make them any less difficult adversaries to contend with. But it might mean that we have actually less reason to fear their military assault upon us or upon other countries than we think we have. I say purposely it "might" mean this, not it "does" mean this. For there is no way of foreseeing accurately and safely which of the two elements of communist thought — the voluntaristic or the deterministic, confidence in the realization of the subjective will by means of force or confidence in the automatic operation of objective historical laws — will prevail in concrete political contingencies. One cannot possibly deny that in the history of the communist party of the Soviet Union the tendency to rely on the first rather than on the second has often proved all powerful.

In fact, there is in the deterministic faith itself an ingredient that is apt to weaken the expectation of Russian communists that "the laws of social development" will in the end secure their triumph without previous armed struggle on a global scale. While the communists are optimists as regards their long-range views on the trend of history, they entertain at the same time pessimistic notions on the laws that will govern the actions of capitalism in its period of decline. Rather than accept the irreversible judgment of history, capitalism, they are inclined to think, will try to prevent its impending doom by resorting itself to force and violence and assaulting the USSR, the citadel of world socialism. Needless to say, such belief in the inevitability of a last gigantic struggle might easily tempt the Russian rulers to forestall capitalistic aggression by launching themselves a preventive war.

It is therefore as important as it is fortunate that they have recently been moving away from the belief in the inevitability of war between capitalism and socialism. That Stalin still clung to this conviction is one of the theoretical errors of which he was accused and for which he was condemned at the XXth Party Congress. Another striking symptom of this new trend is the assertion in the Moscow Declaration of 1957 that "the forces of peace have so grown that there is a real possibility of averting wars."

Much as we may rejoice at the fact that one of the complexes that besets the Russian rulers and that might cause them to precipitate a war of aggression seems to be dissolving, there is a less pleasant side to this process as well. The qualification, not to say abandonment of the belief in the inevitable capitalist onslaught upon the bastion of world socialism reflects no doubt the realization of the growing strength of the Soviet Union on all fronts — the military, political, technological, psychological, and economic — on which it is competing with us. Now that this fear is receding, will not overconfidence in the strength of the Soviet Union instead begin to operate as an inducement to aggressive war? In trying to answer this question, we have to take into consideration the third essential element of the doctrine of communism: the stress on the imperative need to pay close attention to the realities of power when planning and executing offensive as well as defensive actions. Lenin has gone to great lengths in emphasizing this need, and has formulated in accordance with it the principles that are to govern the strategy and tactics of the communist party in whatever struggle it might become involved. In other words, ready as the rulers of Russia might be to exploit weakness, if it suits their purposes, their doctrine also enjoins on them the sober realistic appraisal of strength wherever and whenever they are faced with it. Therein lies indeed the justification of and the need for our insistence on a "position of strength," though it is difficult, as we have learned, to determine the concrete requirements for establishing and maintaining it, militarily and otherwise.

If the analysis of the most essential elements of the communist doctrine and of the interaction between them fails to yield precise and certain answers to the question of Russian objectives, it does reveal the highly complex nature of the doctrine and thus might help us not to become or remain captives of oversimplified interpretations. The result of the analysis cautions us, in the first place, against identifying the objectives proper of the Soviet rulers with the object of their faith: the coming of the one communist world. In looking for historical analogies that might throw some light on the probable impact of the latter upon the former, we need, in fact, not go very far afield. Ever since the foundation of our republic, we ourselves have staunchly and sincerely believed that American ideals will finally prevail in the world and that we have a providential role in consummating the process. Faith in the ultimate global victory of their cause has animated equally the founders and followers of all universalist religions. Historical experience also teaches, however, that such faith is no proof of aggressive intent unless it is coupled with the will to spread the religious or political gospel by means of war. Is there as surely an irrefutable presumption that this will exists in the case of communist Russia as it is obvious that there is no such will in the American case? The result of our analysis clearly speaks against such a presumption, and thus cautions us against another possible oversimplification of the communist doctrine. In fact, the idea of holy war being alien thereto, one would find it difficult to prove that the theoretical notions the Russian leaders entertain about war as an instrument of national policy are basically different from traditional notions on war as generally entertained prior to the outlawry of war. Seen in the light of communist theory, Khrushchev is not another Mohammed nor, for that matter, another Napoleon or Hitler. The Russian menace is not primarily of a military nature, though, of course, we cannot afford to rule out the possibility of Russian aggression altogether.

II

Fortunately, the examination of the evidence available in the corpus of Marxist-Leninist writings is thus apt to lessen rather than increase the fear that the Soviet rulers look upon war as an instrument for the universalization of communism and the establishment of a Russian world empire. In fact, the communist doctrine does not even bear out the suspicion that the latter is an objective of Soviet policy at all. This fact alone, however, does not yet disprove the possibility that the Kremlin is actually pursuing unlimited political objectives in the sense that it strives by means short of war to bring about a world in which no rivals are left to compete with its own power.

This possibility must be taken the more seriously since the ideological objectives pursued by the ruling party of the Soviet Union are unlimited. Admittedly, reasons of political expediency have now and then induced its leaders to tone down or even temporarily to suspend the propagation of the communist world revolution which, they believe, will assure the salvation of mankind. But we would be badly mistaken if we were to draw therefrom the conclusion that the spreading of the revolutionary gospel is solely a political means and not an ideological end in itself. It is therefore not very likely that the Russian communists will for the sake of what they call peaceful coexistence abandon their revolutionary propaganda altogether. The best we can hope for is that in the course of time their fervor will abate as throughout history the zeal of fanatical movements, religious and political, has sooner or later spent itself.

Since the proselytizing fervor of the communist party of the Soviet Union is practically boundless, is it then, one wonders, not to be taken for granted that the political objectives proper, too, of the Soviet rulers are unlimited? Is not every country won over by one means or another to the communist cause another political asset for the Soviet Union in its struggle for power? It most definitely is. But does this also prove that Soviet propaganda and even outright Soviet intervention in the affairs of other states is intended to further the gradual development of a Russian world empire? Does it prove, in other words, that Russian policy is unlimited political imperialism rather than imperialism of the traditional type which, though it wants and tries to be always more equal than others, does nonetheless at the same time sincerely accept the multi-state and legally equalitarian structure of the world community?

If proselytizing as such were conclusive evidence of schemes of world domination, we would find it somewhat difficult to disprove that we ourselves are pursuing unlimited political objectives. For we, too, hope to profit politically in the global struggle for power whenever we assist another nation in setting up or preserving a democratic government. What gives substance to the suspicions about Russia's ulterior intent is rather that, contrary to the United States, she is pursuing her proselytizing policy through an international party, an instrumentality which she also can use and has actually used for establishing and maintaining her own even though indirect rule over foreign nations. To the extent that communist parties outside the USSR are controlled by the Russian communist party, the Soviet Union, without expanding the territorial limits of its formal jurisdiction, can and has extended its political dominion. However natural those suspicions are, the complexity and flexibility of the communist theory and practice, respectively, ought not to be underrated in this case, either.

The original communist conception of world revolution has found its classical expression in the farewell letter Lenin addressed to his Swiss comrades before leaving for St. Petersburg in 1917 which is still worth quoting. "To the Russian proletariat," Lenin wrote, "has fallen the great honor of opening the series of revolutions which are the inevitable result of the imperialist war. But we do not for one moment think of the Russian proletariat as the chosen revolutionary proletariat. We know full well that the proletariat of Russia is less organized, prepared and educated than the workers of other countries. It is not any exceptional qualities, but only the exceptional historical circumstances that have made the proletariat of Russia the advance guard of the world revolutionary proletariat—may be for a very short time." The world revolution, as conceived by Lenin, has only one protagonist and subject, the international proletariat. The proletarian classes and the communist parties of the various countries, including Russia, are merely parts and detachments of one and the same world army. That the Russian detachment was to strike first in the impending world struggle, was held by Lenin, the Russian, to be due exclusively to an historical contingency but not to a providential role assigned to it. It was therefore to be entitled only to a rank of honor but not to a substantial reward redounding to Russia's political advantage. Lenin's idea of world revolution was, in other words, the expression of a genuine proletarian-communistic universalism.

One may seriously doubt whether the relations among the various national members of the communist international ever actually approximated even remotely the Leninist conception of 1917. From the position of a first among equals the Russian party rapidly moved up to a hegemonic position, and Russian national interests accordingly became, to a growing extent, a primary concern of the third international. But it was only in the Stalinist period that the universalistic conception of Lenin was reversed to all practical intents and purposes. Lenin had often been accused that he was all too ready to subordinate Russian national interests to his world revolutionary ideal. Such inclination was indeed the last thing of which Stalin could have been suspected. The amalgamation under his direction of the Russian national idea with Marxist ideas in domestic politics was reflected in foreign politics by the adoption of what Hans J. Morgenthau has called "nationalistic universalism." The communist ideology retained its universalistic flavor, but communist parties outside the USSR were actually looked upon as mere instruments of Russian national policy. They were to be subject not only to Stalin's authority in spiritual-ideological matters, as it were, but were also to be tools and servants of his temporal ambition and power. As such they were indeed used after World War II when the Soviet Union surrounded itself with satellites.

It would undoubtedly be too much to suggest that Khrushchev has abandoned the Stalinist conception of the communist international and reverted to the ideas Lenin entertained and expressed at a time when the Soviet Union did not yet exist and the exigencies of its national interests were not yet felt. But one can say that the oscillations between Leninist and Stalinist conceptions which are so obvious in Khrushchev's domestic policies, are also clearly apparent in his dealings with communist parties outside the Soviet Union, including those in the satellite states. The limits within which foreign communist parties are permitted to travel their own road to socialism have been considerably broadened under Khrushchev. Yugoslavia and Poland, both vastly inferior to the Soviet Union in size and strength but at the same time highly important for it from the point of view of its political and military security, are the most striking illustrations of the new practice. The Moscow Declaration of 1957 with its stress on "the spirit of combining internationalism with patriotism" endorses it in programmatic-theoretical terms. That these concessions have not been spontaneous but have been forced upon Khrushchev by powerful nationalist trends operating upon and within the foreign communist parties, does not deprive them of their political significance. It rather proves that the Soviet leaders realize and recognize that there are limits to the use of international communism as an instrumentality for extending and maintaining their indirect rule beyond the territorial boundaries of the USSR even within what it considers for historical, geographical, and ethnic reasons to be its legitimate sphere of influence.

III

It is not unjustified to draw therefrom the conclusion that at least their keen sense for the realities of power, if not other considerations as well, are likely to keep the political objectives of the Soviet rulers more or less within the bounds of traditional imperialism. The result of our analysis suggests, in other words, that Soviet foreign policy is rather a continuation of the Tsarist imperialist policy than a policy of the type of unlimited political imperialism. This is not to imply, however, that there are no important differences between the one and the other.

In the first place, the difference between the Tsarist regime and the Soviet regime necessarily has some bearing also on their respective foreign policies. Though it is true that imperial Russia was ruled, practically down to World War I, by an autocracy, the Romanows felt themselves bound by the moral laws of Christian statesmanship in their relations with their own subjects as well as with their fellow sovereigns. The Soviet rulers, typical revolutionaries that they are, refuse to recognize that there are any common moral bonds that unite them with their adversaries, internal or foreign. Though it also is true that old Russia was not averse to using religious affinities across national boundaries for the purposes of power politics, the communist gospel of today has by its very nature not only a geographically wider appeal but is also in the present highly secularized world a more dynamic force than Orthodox Christianity was in the eighteenth and nineteenth centuries.

But there are also differences between Tsarist and Soviet foreign policy that are in no way due to the different moral and ideological character of the two regimes, and can rather be explained by the change of the objective conditions under which the one was operating in the past and the other is operating in the present. The most important change of this nature is undoubtedly Russia's rise to the position of a super-power with world-wide interests. One wonders, however, whether we sufficiently appreciate that the role of a super-power has been thrust upon the USSR as it has been thrust upon the United States. It is the automatic consequence of victory in a war in which they were both the victims of aggression. One also wonders whether we might not be unduly inclined to attribute Soviet actions, intended to preserve the fruits of Russia's victory and protect her global interests, to unlimited objectives and warlike intentions. Instead of weighing Soviet policy in the sober light of objective factors which might account for it, we seem to have been relying increasingly on an image of Soviet imperialism suggested by an oversimplified interpretation of communist doctrine. Similarly, the Soviet rulers are inclined to judge American actions by the image which they have formed of capitalism, and they are therefore blind to the objective necessities that determine us as a super-power to pursue a policy of global defense for protecting our world-wide interests. The perils of nuclear war and the temptations of the vacuum of power created by the breakdown of the old colonial empires have further heightened the mutual fears and the mutual suspicions of the two super-powers.

Mutual fear and distrust, however, have not deterred diplomacy in the past from trying to reduce an international conflict to its rational proportions. Negotiations have served this purpose in the past, they may do so now and in the future.

II

PUNITIVE
WAR
RECONSIDERED

PUNISHMENT FOR WAR CRIMES

I

Today when we think of war crimes we all see before our eyes the horrifying pictures of the appalling criminal actions we reluctantly learned of during the recent war. In view of the character and scope of those evil deeds, outright approval of any form and kind of punishment to be meted out to their instigators and perpetrators seems more appropriate than a critical analysis of the problems actually involved in the apparently so gruesomely simple issue. In these circumstances it is an ungratifying undertaking to discuss the problematic aspects of punishment rather than merely to restate our unqualified condemnation of the abominable crimes and the persons responsible for them.

But the very fact that American public opinion, the opinion of the legal profession as well as of the laymen, is divided over the best way of coping with the Axis criminals, clearly indicates that things are in fact not so simple as they look at first sight. The division of opinion is the more significant as the alignment of pros and cons does not at all coincide with any of the usual political alignments, and coincides least of all with any differences of attitude toward the political doctrines that have inspired the criminals of the enemy nations. Nor does this division of American public opinion reflect any disagreement on the moral, or rather immoral, qualities of the truly criminal acts which have outraged mankind.[1]

The current proceedings are the result of painstaking negotiations among the governments and legal experts of the United Nations, negotiations that dragged on through practically the whole war. A common decision was essential, unless the Allies who were jointly prosecuting the war were to split wide open over prosecuting the war criminals, and to those who had to reach the decision two basically different methods presented themselves. The one method was a political, the other a judicial procedure. As regards

*Reprinted with permission of *Social Research*, March 1946 (Vol. XIII, No. 1).

the "major criminals whose offenses have no particular geographical localization," the Declaration on German Atrocities, signed by Roosevelt, Churchill and Stalin at Moscow in November 1943, definitely envisaged a political procedure, in the form of punishment "by the joint decision of the Governments of the Allies."[2] The British government seems to have preferred the political to the judicial solution up to the last stage of the negotiations among the United Nations, but the negotiations resulted finally in the triumph of the American request for a judicial procedure.

Contrary to the American position, the British thesis was founded on precedents of modern history. The example of Napoleon comes first to mind. When the so-called "Corsican monster"—an epithet which in the light of the twentieth century appears highly exaggerated—was finally struck down by the legitimate governments of Europe, the latter turned the revolutionary weapon of outlawry against the offspring of the revolution, and, without a trial, placed Napoleon, "comme Ennemi et Perturbateur du Monde," under the custody of the British government for the duration of his life.[3] Napoleon's own and his friends' hope, as one biographer puts it, to profit "from the peculiarities of English law" by gaining the rights of habeas corpus, miserably failed.[4] In a certain sense the public arraignment of Wilhelm II, decreed by Article 227 of the Treaty of Versailles, is another precedent of a political procedure aiming at the punishment of alleged international offenses, for the special tribunal which was to try the German Kaiser was not to apply substantive rules of law but was to be guided in its decision by motives of international policy and morality. The planned arraignment of the Kaiser never came off, however, as the Netherlands refused to surrender him.

The reasons that led the British government to propose a political procedure against the enemy leaders of World War II were never publicly stated. But at least one of the advantages of such a proceeding seems to be obvious: it is what it claims to be, "a matter of political expediency and of a political right of victors to punish, growing out of the fact of victory and the nature of the crimes."[5] It is one thing, however, to put a single individual under custody, without trial, as was done in the case of Napoleon, and it is quite another thing to put a great many persons to death without judicial trial. A reluctance to burden governments with such an awesome responsibility may have contributed to the final decision to institute judicial proceedings against the major as well as the minor war criminals.

Be that as it may, this decision involves no less grave responsibilities. Once made, it calls for compliance with the basic standards of justice and law, if for no other reason than that to disregard them would necessarily weaken the sense of justice within both the defeated and the victorious nations.

II

Punishment meted out by the victor for the instigation and perpetration of war crimes became a big issue for the first time in modern history after World War I. Before 1919 none of the peace instruments provided for the extradition of alleged war criminals to an ex-enemy nation and their punishment by that nation. As a rule the signatories to those earlier treaties even agreed that each of them would grant to his own subjects an amnesty for any criminal offenses related to the war.[6] As a matter of fact, the armistice concluded between the Allied and Associated Powers and Germany on November 11, 1918, still expressly stipulated in Article VI, "No person shall be prosecuted for participation in military measures prior to the signature of the armistice."[7] Once the war was over, the issue was to be definitely closed.

This practice did not mean that violations of the laws and customs of war were to remain altogether unpunished. The belligerent governments were obliged not only to observe, themselves, the rules of warfare, but also to enforce compliance with them on the part of the individual persons subject to their authority. Any infraction of the pertinent rules, including a failure of the government to prohibit and punish an infraction, constituted a violation of civil responsibility and might entitle the injured state to reprisals. But the responsibility of the individual offender was considered to be a responsibility under municipal law, rendering him subject to prosecution and punishment by his own government. It is true that the law of war also authorized belligerents to punish captured enemy combatants for offenses against its provisions committed prior to their capture. But the end of the war was supposed to revive the exclusive home jurisdiction over the offender.[8]

This lack of concern on the part of the victor about the post-war punishment for war crimes fitted perfectly the nineteenth-century conception of war as a legitimate instrumentality of international politics: equal sovereigns match their limited military forces for limited ends. Besides, in that period violations of the codes of war were far from reaching the proportions that were to dishonor the twentieth century. The long weekend of world history between 1815 and 1914 was the very meridian of comparatively civilized warfare.

The delegates who drew up and signed the amnesty clause of the armistice of 1918 were, as was aptly remarked, "professional men of arms."[9] No doubt they knew as well as anybody else about the war crimes that the Germans had committed or were accused of having committed in the course of the war just finished. But still living, as they did, in the international traditions of the nineteenth century, they were willing to terminate warfare in the spirit and in the forms of the past age. Their maxim was, so to speak,

La guerre est morte, vive la guerre!

Things were entirely different, however, as regards the Allied statesmen who were to conclude the peace. They were, or they made themselves, the spokesmen of fundamentally different sentiments and expectations. For them, the war had been a war to end all war, and to end it for good. They somehow anticipated a world in which war would be no longer a political but rather a criminal phenomenon. And they projected this view also into the past, and insisted on terminating the war as a punitive war. Nothing better illustrates the evolution of this new conception of war than a comparison of Sir Edward Grey's famous speech in the House of Commons on August 3, 1914,[10] and Lloyd George's no less famous campaign speeches of 1918.[11]

The punitive measures of the Treaty of Versailles were never carried out. The Netherlands refused to deliver the Kaiser, and Germany successfully sabotaged the trial and punishment of the other alleged war offenders. In part, the failure must be attributed to the lack of firm determination on the part of the Allied governments themselves. Their hesitation was due, however, not only to reasons of short-range political expediency but also to considerations of principle. Current writers on the subject like to ridicule the doctrinal disputes in which the legal advisers of the Allied and Associated governments permitted themselves to become entangled after World War I. Particularly the late Robert Lansing, President Wilson's Secretary of State, and James Brown Scott, the two American members of the Commission on the Responsibility of the Authors of the War and on Enforcement of Penalties, which was established by the Peace Conference at Paris in 1919, have recently become the favorite target of those writers.[12] Thus it will be useful to restate briefly the American position of that time, as laid down in Lansing's and Scott's Memorandum of Reservations to the Report of that Commission.[13]

The American Memorandum of 1919 was based throughout on a sharp distinction between moral and legal offenses and between moral and legal responsibilities. "Moral offenses," we read there, "however iniquitous and infamous and however terrible in their result, are beyond the reach of judicial procedure, and subject only to moral sanctions." This distinction between moral and legal offenses is maintained in reference to both the causing of the war and its conduct. Since a war of aggression may not be regarded as an act directly contrary to positive international law, the acts that provoked the war in 1914 should entail only moral sanctions. The principle "nullum crimen, nulla poena sine lege"—no crime, no punishment without preexisting law—should be applied also to the alleged breaches of treaties, like the deliberate violation by Germany of the internationally guaranteed neutrality of Belgium and Luxemburg. The latter acts, being illegal, incur not only moral sanctions but also the civil liability of the German state. Under international law, however, violations of treaties are by no means criminal acts, either of the state as such or of its agents.

The two American dissenters of 1919 went even further and insisted on the exclusive application of strictly positive international law in regard also to the conduct of the war. The majority of the Commission proposed that the tribunals to be charged with the prosecution of war crimes allegedly committed by Germany in the course of the hostilities should apply "the principles of the law of nations as they result from the usages established among civilized peoples, from the laws of humanity and from the dictates of public conscience." This proposal could be justified even from a purely positivist point of view, inasmuch as the Fourth Hague Convention of 1907 on the Laws and Customs of Land Warfare conceives of "the laws of humanity" and "the dictates of public conscience" as a subsidiary source of international law. The formulation nevertheless encountered determined American resistance.

"The laws and principles of humanity," the American Memorandum declared, "vary with the individual, which, if for no other reason, should exclude them from consideration in a court of justice, especially one charged with the administration of criminal law." The war crime tribunals should therefore be confined to the administration of the definitely established laws and customs of war. Moreover, the American Memorandum urged the Allied governments to use the existing legal machinery at hand, that is, national courts, rather than creating an unprecedented international criminal court for the prosecution of the offenses.

Nor is this all. President Wilson's advisers proved to be no less orthodox concerning the thorny and delicate question of the criminal responsibility, under international law, of the chiefs of state. In this, incidentally, as in certain other respects, they were supported by the Commission representatives of the Japanese government, then an Allied government but apparently endowed with the rare gift of divining future constellations of international politics.[14] Lansing and Scott recognized and affirmed that the heads of state have a moral responsibility to mankind, as well as a political and legal responsibility to their own nations. But they rejected the notion of their personal responsibility under international law. To subject a chief of state to any foreign jurisdiction, national or international, would, they held, destroy the sovereign state, the very cornerstone of modern public law.

The American position in 1919 can thus be summarized as a combination of the most orthodox interpretation of the tenets of positivist jurisprudence with the idea of sovereignty as the basic principle of international law.

III

It would be preposterous not to recognize the differences between the first and the second world wars in regard to the task of prosecuting and punishing war criminals. Both in the nature and in the scale of the offenses the two problems are hardly comparable. Also the political and legal questions involved today are in many respects unlike those of 1919. One may wonder, however, whether all these differences and changes justify a complete reversal of the American position between 1919 and 1945. This reversal finds its most significant expression in Justice Jackson's Report to the President of June 7, 1945, in which he expounds the principles to be applied in the prosecution of the major Axis war criminals. The Agreement for the Establishment of an International Military Tribunal, concluded among the United States, France, Great Britain and the Soviet Union on August 8, 1945, and the Charter of the Nuremberg Tribunal are largely based on the ideas enunciated in Justice Jackson's Report.[15]

Before attempting a critical evaluation of the instruments just mentioned it is desirable, however, to consider the extent to which the traditional precepts of international and criminal law would make it possible to exact retribution for the Nazi atrocities.

The policy of unconditional surrender, proclaimed at Casablanca in 1943 and consummated at Caserta, Rheims and Berlin in 1945, undoubtedly helps greatly to brush aside legal obstacles that would otherwise have stood in the way of giving full scope to the prosecution and punishment of the Nazi war criminals. The unconditional surrender, formally sealing the *debellatio* of Germany by the Allied military forces, has in accordance with the rules of international law established the joint sovereignty of the occupant powers over the German territory and population. This means their legislative as well as administrative and judicial supremacy over all German affairs. To state the resulting situation in purely legal terms, which are at the same time an impressive illustration of the just working of history: today the American, French, British and Russian governments jointly undertake the task of exacting retribution for German crimes, acting, legally speaking, as a German government.[16]

As already indicated, a belligerent is entitled, under international law, to punish during hostilities captured enemy combatants, whatever rank they may have, for offenses against the rules of warfare committed prior to their capture. The controversial question that disturbed the statesmen and lawyers after the end of World War I—whether, by pertinent provisions in the peace treaty, this right can be made to survive the formal termination of war by a peace treaty—does not at present arise at all, for technically we are still in the post-armistice stage, not yet in the post-war stage. This right of punishment can be assumed to apply also to German civil officials, of whatever rank, including the members of the Nazi government.[17] Hitler's suicide has spared us any scruples concerning the legitimacy of trying a criminal chief of state as a criminal pure and simple.

The wicked perversity of the late Nazi regime did not manifest itself primarily in violations of the rules of warfare by actions related to the war and the realization of its main purpose, the overpowering of the enemy, though these were indeed outrageous enough. When we think of the Nazi atrocities we think first of those that were committed in no direct connection with the military operations of the war, but exclusively for the satisfaction of beastly instincts and, in their rational function, as it were, for the establishment of German racial supremacy. What Dr. Raphael Lemkin has suggestively called genocide[18]—a deliberate attempt at the complete destruction of whole racial groups, in particular the Jews—and the actions related to it are not altogether war crimes, in a legal sense. But they are all, certainly more than any other conceivable crimes, violations of the laws of humanity and of the dictates of public conscience. And these, insofar as they are not war crimes proper, are ordinary crimes—"ordinary" in the lawyer's technical language—which are punishable under the criminal laws of the United Nations by their respective judicial authorities. The *condominium* of the Big Four allows also punishment by the United Nations for such offenses against stateless persons and German nationals, even if committed prior to the war.

This emphasis on the fact that all Nazi crimes can be punished by criminal procedures instituted by the United Nations should not be regarded as denying that it might be politically wiser to leave to German courts the punishment for the crimes that the Nazis committed against their German fellow nationals. It appears, in fact, that this is being done, at least to a certain extent, in the Russian zone of occupied Germany.[19] In any case, the essential point which is being made here is that the existing laws, both international and criminal, fully guarantee justice and retribution in regard to any atrocities committed by the Nazi chieftains and henchmen.

Thus in order to conclude one of the most disgraceful chapters of human history in the appropriate judicial way, we need not relinquish the firm basis of existing law and establish a new code of international penal offenses of doubtful legal validity and scope. As a matter of fact, if we are serious in proclaiming the opening of another and better chapter of history, we cannot be anxious enough to leave behind us all totalitarian conceptions of jurisprudence and to reestablish by the shining example of our own actions those great principles of western jurisprudence whose maintenance was one of the noblest aims of the fight against Nazi Germany. One may seriously doubt whether the Nuremberg trial and other trials still to come actually set that example of which our lawless world is in such dire need.

IV

The Charter of the International Military Tribunal is intended to be an international criminal code defining international crimes (Article 6) and authorizing the Tribunal "to impose upon a defendant, on conviction, death or such other punishment as shall be determined by it to be just" (Article 27).[20] The promulgation of such a code is a departure from the hitherto prevailing conception that so-called war crimes are crimes against, and are to be punished in accordance with, the municipal law of the respective belligerent states.

In characterizing war crimes proper, that is, violations of the laws or customs of war, as technically international crimes, the Nuremberg code is objectionable from a formal point of view. On this score, however, it is open only to formal criticism, because it does not in itself imply any substantive change in the rules of warfare under which the defendants are held to be accountable.

Things are different in regard to the so-called "crimes against humanity." It need not be repeated that this legal charge, too, would not be objectionable in principle if it could be understood as a general reference to what are in the terminology of the criminal lawyer ordinary criminal offenses, clearly defined as such and subject to definite punishment according to the existing criminal laws. Nor could the formulation be justly attacked if it were intended to be a reference to humanity as a subsidiary source of law. But unfortunately it cannot be interpreted in either way. It means, to all practical intents and purposes, the vesting of a criminal court with a blank authority to determine crimes and punishments in accordance with subjective rather than objective criteria of criminality.

The complete eradication of any distinction between moral and legal offenses, and moral and legal responsibilities, is even more obvious and important as regards the first offense established by the Nuremberg code, the so-called "crimes against peace." Article 6a of the Charter of the International Military Tribunal defines crimes against peace as "planning, preparation, initiation or waging of a war of aggression, or a war in violation of international treaties, agreements or assurances, or participation in a common plan or conspiracy for the accomplishment of any of the foregoing." Before entering into a discussion of the problems involved in the concept of crimes against peace, this writer would like to state emphatically, in order to avoid any possible misunderstanding, that he is as strongly convinced of the moral war guilt of Nazi Germany as anybody can be. In his view, the Third Reich is morally guilty not only of aggressive but also of unjust war—and, contrary to a generally held opinion, the two are not necessarily the same. The problem to be discussed in the following para-

64

graphs is not the question of Nazi Germany's moral guilt, but the question of the sanctions that are legally permissible.

In his Report to the President, Justice Jackson oscillates between suggesting that the Tribunal's jurisdiction over crimes against peace arises from existing rules of international law, and interpreting the pertinent provisions of the Charter as the statement of a new rule of international law, based on the prerogative power of the victors. Let us first examine the arguments dressed in the garments of conservative jurisprudence.

In their center stands, of course, the Kellogg Pact of 1928, with its condemnation of recourse to war for the solution of international controversies, and the renunciation by its signatories of war as an instrument of national policy in their relations with one another.[21] To be sure, Germany was a signatory to the Pact, and thus committed a breach of contract by deliberately and ignominiously disregarding its solemn obligations. There is no doubt, either, that by doing so Germany incurred the civil liabilities which traditional international law provides for breach of contract; the Potsdam Agreement on Germany's reparations is the staggering bill due for those liabilities. But Mr. Jackson's interpretation, supported as well as contested by reputable international lawyers,[22] goes much further and deduces from the two short articles which form the essence of the Kellogg Pact the criminal responsibility of the individual persons who act as the agents of the aggressor state.

This interpretation is such a radical departure from long-established principles of international law that it could never be deduced from merely ambiguous terms of the agreement supposedly incorporating it. The interpretation is even less tenable if the terms, as is actually the case in the Kellogg Pact, point in the opposite direction. The Pact establishes neither the criminal responsibility of the law-breaking state nor that of any of the latter's agents. Nor does it contain any provision intimating the use of collective or individual punishment as a sanction.

This is not to deny that between the two world wars international lawyers were busy in devising codes of international penal offenses. It is further true that some of them were considering inserting aggressive war in those codes, as one of the international crimes—either by affirming the criminal responsibility of the state or its individual agents, or by affirming a combined collective and individual criminal responsibility.[23] But it is no less true that the governments never even thought of taking up such far-reaching proposals. All that can be said is that between the two world wars the idea was somewhat in the air, and that it is a highly interesting idea, indicating entirely new trends in international thought which, if ever adopted, would revive, in new forms and on a much more comprehensive plane, medieval conceptions regarding the structure of the *Res publica Christiana*. In the present context there are only two points that count: first, in 1939 war, including aggressive war, was not an international crime according to the legal rules that prevailed at that time and were subscribed to by all governments; second, international law was then still regarded in the traditional way as a law which in principle governs the relations between states, and therefore violations of the Kellogg Pact's prohibition of war could not be and actually were not interpreted in terms of the individual responsibility of the agents of an aggressor state.

Nor should it be overlooked that the United Nations Charter of San Francisco and the Statute of the new International Court of Justice tacitly reject the very notions on which the Nuremberg prosecutions of crimes against peace are founded. Neither of these most recent international instruments characterizes aggressive war as an international crime, and neither of them affirms any individual criminal or civil responsibility under international law of any sort. One may wonder how it can be honestly maintained that basic precepts of international public law were no longer valid in 1939 which were solemnly reaffirmed by the victors themselves in 1945.

Therefore it is not surprising that Justice Jackson deems it advisable to hold another iron in the fire, by regarding the prerogative power of the Big Four as further basis for the claim that the Allies have jurisdiction over the so-called crimes against peace. But here he runs into another difficulty, no less formidable than those mentioned. Anglo-Saxon jurisprudence, and not Anglo-Saxon jurisprudence alone, rejects retroactive criminal laws, "making a certain deed criminal which was not so when it was performed, or increasing the penalty attached to crimes already committed."[24] When Nazi Germany abandoned the principle, "No crime, no punishment without preexisting law," this was generally taken to mean that she deliberately spurned a basic legal maxim of modern Western society. That action assuredly does not now, morally speaking, entitle the dethroned rulers of Nazi Germany to the benefit of the principle which they withdrew from their subjects. But neither can it be a reason for undermining its validity in the countries that have upheld it.

To be sure, the doctrine in question, like any other absolute principle, requires certain qualifications in its practical application.[25] Such qualifications have been repeatedly suggested by the jurists who have been plagued by the intricacies involved in the task of assuring the just punishment of the war criminals without violating the very essence of the principle of non-retroactivity. Professor Glueck, for example, to mention only one of them, maintains that the principle is meant to apply only to the "protection of substantial rights" of the accused.[26] But the same writer, who in this as well as in most other respects has developed very radical views on the punishment of Axis war and ordinary crimes, does not even contemplate the idea that violations of treaty obligations and the waging of aggressive war should be included in the list of punishable crimes.[27]

The main objection to be raised against Justice Jackson arises, however, from the fact that his retroactive law shares only in the inherent deficiencies of an ex post facto law, and not in its positive quality. A retroactive law is one of dubious validity, but it is meant to be a law all the same. It is meant to be applied, from the moment of its enactment, as a general rule relevant to all cases similar to the one that caused its existence, to past cases as well as to future ones. But the Nuremberg rule is not, according to the Charter of San Francisco, intended to be applied to future aggressive wars that may be launched, contrary to the obligations contained in the Charter, by any of the victorious powers, and certainly least of all to such a war launched by any of the Big Five. Nor does there seem to be any intention of applying it to the past cases of Russian aggression against Finland, Poland and the Baltic states, in part executed jointly with the accused German criminals, or to Russia's attack against tottering Japan last August, unprovoked by the latter, though instigated by the other prosecutor states.

Thus the Nuremberg rule on crimes against peace, if somewhat more closely analyzed, is not so much what any law is meant to be, that is, a general rule to be generally applied, but rather what was called in Jacobin France *une loi de circonstance.*[28] In other words, the Nuremberg rule on crimes against peace aims exclusively at a definite group of purposely selected men.

That the arbitrary constitution of so-called crimes against peace was not necessary in order that the arm of justice might reach the instigators of the war crimes and the other Nazi atrocities, can be seen from the fact that, among all the individual and collective defendants at Nuremberg, Hjalmar Schacht is the only one whose indictment charges him only with crimes against peace. All the other defendants are accused also of war crimes and of crimes against humanity.[29] The justification for proclaiming and applying a new principle of law, without regard to the existing rules, rests solely on the expectation that this revolutionary action will, to put it in Justice Jackson's own words, "make war less attractive to those who have governments and the destinies of peoples in their power."[30] Whether this expectation is well founded would be a debatable question, however, even if the new rule were not exclusively directed against the leaders of the defeated enemy nations.

At present it is not clear where the responsibility lies for putting the Nuremberg trial on what is, legally, such a slippery basis. It would seem that Russian conceptions of revolutionary justice have been combined with new ideas of international law in general and new trends of western jurisprudence in particular. Be that as it may, the mixture of genuinely judicial functions with functions of a primarily political nature cannot fail to have baneful effects on an otherwise irreproachable cause.

V

At Nuremberg the accused are being tried in procedural forms which maintain more "peculiarities of English law" than any of the defendants were morally entitled to expect. This respect for the judicial forms is, indeed, what distinguishes the trial at Nuremberg from the proceedings of the revolutionary tribunals of Jacobin France and Bolshevist Russia. "It is unbearable," Robespierre once exclaimed in the Jacobin club, "that a tribunal instituted to make the revolution march forward should make her march backward by its criminally slow pace. The tribunal," Robespierre continued, "must be as active as the crime, and it must always be on the plane of the crimes."[31] There is no Robespierre behind the judges of Nuremberg, urging them to degrade the trial "au niveau des délits." As a matter of fact, one might even wish that somebody would speed up the pedantic proceedings, obviously but mistakenly inspired by a desire to project the quality and quantity of the charged crimes into the dimension of time. But these more or less laudable features of the Nuremberg trial do not erase the unpleasant fact that it does not altogether apply laws.

It seems to me that this fact also outweighs the objection that the Nuremberg court is an agency of the victors pure and simple. There is no doubt, however, that one should not minimize the psychological effect, particularly on the defeated nation, of the onesided composition of the court. This will not fail to be felt especially in regard to the Tribunal's assumption of jurisdiction over the waging of aggressive war. To be sure, as long as the right to take up arms is not subject to the judicial decision of a supra-national authority, the victor cannot reasonably be expected to submit the judgment on the rightness of his cause to anyone above himself, after he has sacrificed blood and treasure for it. But neither can it be reasonably anticipated that the vanquished will accept the verdict of his victorious foes as the verdict of impartial judges. To expect anything else would mean to indulge in childish illusions. There was therefore much wisdom, and also justice, in the former practice of refraining, in a world of sovereign states, from a legal disqualification of even the most obviously morally guilty state and its agents.

The lack of a truly international character—"international" in the comprehensive sense of the former Permanent Court of International Justice—is a rather serious disability of the Nuremberg Tribunal also in regard to its jurisdiction over violations of the laws and customs of war. Distinguished

American lawyers insisted, even in the heat of the past war, on the establishment of a genuinely international criminal court, either composed of nationals of the United Nations and of neutral states, possibly including nationals of the Axis countries as well, or consisting of representatives of neutral states alone. Some were even willing on principle[32] to grant that court the authority to try anyone accused of violations of the laws and customs of war, regardless of which of the belligerents he was identified with. The International Military Tribunal of Nuremberg meets neither of these requirements of truly impartial justice.

Violations of the war rules on both sides are the regular concomitant of any war. Moreover, modern technological inventions have introduced into warfare weapons of a character which eradicates any distinction between combatants and non-combatants, or between military and private objectives, distinctions that formed the very core of the nineteenth-century rules of warfare. The end of the war has brought home to the defeated nations the import, in its most literal sense, of the Biblical warning, "For they have sown the wind, and they shall reap the whirlwind." But unless we are willing to assert self-righteously that we stand as the angels of the avenging Lord, under no law, we have at least to admit that the deliberate omission, in the Nuremberg indictment, of the bombardment of Warsaw, Rotterdam and London is not sufficient to settle the question of the moral and legal responsibility for the destruction of Dresden, Hiroshima and Nagasaki.[33]

Nor should we overlook another aspect of the war trials. What counts in international politics is not only moral and legal but also political responsibilities. No doubt the Allied statesmen are to be acquitted of any moral or legal responsibility for having launched the second world war. But could they also answer satisfactorily the charge that they did not live up to their political responsibilities? This is a question in the clarification of which the victors should be even more interested than the vanquished, if they intend to learn how to avoid another holocaust. It is an ugly fact that the different phases, episodes and manifestations of the policy of appeasement have to be hushed up in the trial of the Germans, in order not to implicate Allied statesmen themselves in what, in the Nuremberg terminology, might easily be called conspiracy.

And even more serious is the fact that the trial, by diverting public attention from the illusions and blunders of the twenties and thirties, fails to teach the adequate political lesson. Justice Jackson seriously states in his Report to the President that "we relied upon the Briand-Kellogg Pact and made it the cornerstone of our national policy."[34] This amazing statement, and other symptoms as well, suggest that a lesson of warning against belief in the magic power of diplomatic words may still be needed. One might even suspect that the Nuremberg trial, and the Tokyo trial still to come, with their hoped-for deterrent effects upon potential future aggressors, are another substitute for a political foreign policy.

VI

In one of the many discussions that the International Law Association devoted between the two world wars to the establishment of an international criminal court with jurisdiction over war crimes, among other offenses, an eminent delegate concluded his objections to the proposal with the words, "A bas la guerre des procés, vive la paix de l'oubli et de l'espérance."[35] Probably nothing signifies more clearly Hitler's degradation of politics to pure criminality of the most appalling kind that the fact that after World War II any plea for a peace of forgetfulness would be an outrage against the most elementary sense of justice. Accordingly this article has not been directed against punishment for the Nazi crimes. It is solely meant to criticize, in the concrete solution that is being applied, the specific features which turn the victors' allegedly judicial liquidation of those crimes into a continuation of war beyond the actual end of military warfare.

Because of the involved and complex character of the issues discussed, it may not be out of place to summarize the theses and arguments of the present essay.

The nature and the scale of the crimes committed demand stern punishment, based primarily and essentially on considerations of retributive justice. Modern criminological theories stress the corrective and deterrent purposes of punishment. But the insufficiency, not to say the immorality, of the prospective approach to the question of punishment is more glaringly illustrated by the Nazi crimes than by any other possible criminal offenses.[36]

The imperative need for inflicting just punishment upon any guilty criminals, accomplices and accessories as well as instigators, could easily have been met within the framework of the existing rules of international and criminal law. This is true not only in regard to the war crimes proper, but also in regard to the other Nazi atrocities which were merely ordinary crimes, in a legal-technical sense, though they were extraordinary in their purpose and scope, their heinous character and the devilish refinement of the techniques by which they were accomplished. Therefore it was not necessary to base the crimes against humanity on subjective tests of criminality and thus go beyond definite legal limits.

Even more to be regretted is the insertion in the Nuremberg code of the so-called crimes against peace. In so far as this category is presented to us as the application of existing rules of law, the attempt fails to convince the positivist lawyer. In so far as it is recommended to us as the symbol of new legal conceptions, it fails to satisfy even those who would be willing to forego any positivist objection to the dubious origin of a new legal principle, provided it could be reasonably assumed to herald a reconciliation of morality and law in international politics. The fact that the application of this revolutionary maxim is most carefully restricted to the leaders of the defeated nations is liable to shatter any such lofty hopes.

A limitation of the charges against the Nazi ringleaders to ordinary crimes and to the most obvious violations of the rules of warfare would have made possible a more expeditious judicial proceeding than the pompous and ambitious Nuremberg trial. To be sure, the Nuremberg court is by name a military tribunal. But at the same time it is assigned a task which precludes the performance of its duties in the simplified forms of a truly military judicial body. It may very well be found that a more expeditious proceeding would have been morally more impressive and effective.

Justice Jackson frankly confessed, in his opening address to the Nuremberg tribunal, that prosecution and judgment are carried out "by victor nations over vanquished foes."[37] In view of the character and the particular termination of the second world war, there are, indeed, compelling reasons for burdening the victors with this tremendous responsibility. One may affirm this necessity, and still quarrel over the concrete execution of the task which has fallen to the victors. But the very fact that the current proceedings fail by implication to meet the indispensable requirements of truly impartial justice should warn us strongly against any easy anticipation that they will have wholesome effects, either on the defeated or on the victorious nations.

The latter consideration leads to the problems of punishment for war crimes apart from the context of the past war. But the intricate questions involved in punitive war in general fall outside the scope of the present discussion.

FOOTNOTES

[1]The diversity of attitudes and views is conspicuous throughout the pertinent literature published before and after the institution of the present proceedings against the alleged Axis war criminals. In regard to the one group see in particular: George A. Finch, "Retribution for War Crimes," in *American Journal of International Law*, vol. 37, no. 1 (January 1943) pp. 81 ff.; American Society of International Law, Thirty-Seventh Annual Meeting, *Proceedings* (Washington 1943) pp. 39 ff.; George Manner, "The Legal Nature and Punishment of Criminal Acts of Violence Contrary to the Laws of War," in *American Journal of International Law*, vol. 37, no. 3 (July 1943) pp. 407 ff.;

Clyde Eagleton, "Punishment of War Criminals by the United Nations," *ibid.*, pp. 495 ff.; Albert G. D. Levy, "The Law and Procedure of War Crime Trials," in *American Political Science Review*, vol. 37, no. 6 (December 1943) pp. 1052 ff.; C. Arnold Anderson, "The Utility of the Proposed Trial and Punishment of Enemy Leaders," *ibid.*, pp. 1081 ff.; Sheldon Glueck, *War Criminals. Their Prosecution and Punishment* (New York 1944); Hans Kelsen, *Peace Through Law* (Chapel Hill 1944) pp. 71 ff.; Quincy Wright, "War Criminals," in *American Journal of International Law*, vol. 39, no. 2 (April 1945) pp. 257 ff.; Pan-American Union, *Report on the International Juridicial Status of Individuals as "War Criminals,"* prepared by the Inter-American Juridical Committee in Accordance with Resolution VI of the Inter-American Conference on Problems of War and Peace, held at Mexico, D.F., February 21 to March 8, 1945 (Washington, August 1945).

In regard to the present Nuremberg trial see especially: U. S. Department of State, Publication 2420, *Trial of War Criminals* [Documents: 1. Report of Robert H. Jackson to the President; 2. Agreement Establishing an International Military Tribunal; 3. Indictment] (Washington 1945); "The Nuremberg Novelty," in *Fortune*, vol. 32, no. 6 (December 1945), pp. 140 ff.; Rustem Vambery, "Law and Legalism", in the *Nation, vol. 161, no. 22* (December 1, 1945) pp. 573 ff.; Milton R. Konvitz, "Will Nuremberg Serve Justice?," in *Commentary. A Jewish Review*, vol. 1, no. 3 (January 1946) pp. 9 ff.; Erno Wittmann, *The Inalienable Rights of Aliens*, with an introduction by Roger N. Baldwin (Washington 1946); Ernest O. Hauser, "The Backstage Battle of Nuremberg," in *Saturday Evening Post*, vol. 218, no. 29 (January 19, 1946) pp. 18 ff.

[2]"Declaration on German Atrocities," released November 1, 1943, in U. S. Department of State, Publication 2423, *The Axis in Defeat. A Collection of Documents on American Policy Toward Germany and Japan* (Washington 1945) pp. 3 ff.

[3]*British and Foreign Papers* (1814–15) pp. 665 ff.; *ibid.* (1815–16) pp. 200 ff.; Albert Sorel, *L'Europe et la revolution francaise*, vol. 8 (Paris 1904) pp. 419 ff.

[4]J. H. Rose, *The Life of Napoleon I* (New York 1924) vol. 2, pp. 484 ff.

[5]Charles Warren, "Precedent for Punishment," in Letter to the Editor, New York *Times*, February 7, 1945.

[6]See Colemen Phillipson, *Termination of War and Treaties of Peace* (London 1916) pp. 243 ff.; also Alfred Verdross, "Die Amnestieklausel in den Friedensverträgen," in *Wörterbuch des Völkerrechts und der Diplomatic*, ed. by Karl Strupp, vol. 1 (Berlin and Leipzig 1924) pp. 38 ff.

[7]See *American Journal of International Law*, vol. 13 (1919), Supplement, p. 98; also *Der Waffenstillstand 1918–1919*, herausgegeben im Auftrage der Deutschen Waffenstillstandskommission mit Genehmigung des Auswärtigen Amtes, vol. 1 (Berlin 1928) pp. 23 ff.

[8]See the analysis of George Manner, *op. cit.* (n. 1), particularly pp. 407 ff. and 419 ff. The Peace of Vereeniging of May 31, 1902, formally terminating the Boer War, was "not a peace treaty proper, . . .but was an arrangement following the subjugation and annexation of the vanquished States" (Phillipson, *op. cit.* [n. 6] p. 246), and therefore the denial by the British of reciprocal amnesty for penal offenses against the rules of warfare cannot rightly be considered an exception to the view and practice stated above.

[9]George A. Finch, *op. cit.* (n. 1) p. 84.

[10]Sir Edward Grey, in *Speeches on Foreign Affairs, 1904–1914*, ed. by Paul Knaplund (London 1931) pp. 297 ff.

[11]On the development after the armistice see David Lloyd George, *Memoirs of the Peace Conference*, vol. 1 (London 1939) pp. 52 ff., 109 ff.

[12]See, for example, Sheldon Glueck, *op. cit.* (n. 1) passim.

[13]Carnegie Endowment for International Peace, Division of International Law, Pamphlet No. 32, *Violations of the Laws and Customs of War*, Reports of Majority and Dissenting Reports of American and Japanese Members of the Commission of Responsibilities, Conference of Paris 1919 (Oxford 1919) pp. 58 ff.

[14]See *ibid.*, pp. 79 ff.

[15]*Trial of War Criminals,* cited above (n. 1).

[16]See Hans Kelsen, "The Legal Status of Germany according to the Declaration of Berlin," in *American Journal of International Law,* vol. 39, no. 3 (July 1945) pp. 518 ff.

[17]This view is supported also by Lansing's and Scott's above-mentioned Memorandum; see *Violations of the Laws and Customs of War,* cited above (n. 13) pp. 23, 70. In regard to the "act of state" defense see the literature mentioned in note 1, and Alfred Verdross, *Die völkerrechtswidrige Kriegshandlung und der Strafanspruch der Staaten* (Berlin 1920) pp. 59 ff.

[18]Raphael Lemkin, *Axis Rule in Occupied Europe* [Laws of Occupation. Analysis of Government. Proposals for Redress], Carnegie Endowment for International Peace (Washington 1944) pp. 79 ff.

[19]New York *Times,* January 3, 1946.

[20]*Trial of War Criminals,* cited above (n. 1) pp. 15 ff.

[21]See David Hunter Miller, *The Peace Pact of Paris. A Study of the Briand-Kellogg Treaty* (New York and London 1928) pp. 246 ff.

[22]See note 1. For a legal evaluation of the Kellogg Pact see also the discussions that followed its adoption, particularly: Edwin M. Borchard, "The Multilateral Treaty for the Renunciation of War," in *American Journal of International Law,* vol. 23, no. 1 (January 1929) pp. 116 ff.; American Society of International Law, Twenty-Third Annual Meeting, *Proceedings* (Washington 1929) pp. 88 ff.; and Twenty-Fourth Annual Meeting, *Proceedings* (Washington 1930) pp. 79 ff.; Quincy Wright, "The Meaning of the Pact of Paris," in *American Journal of International Law,* vol. 27, no. 1 (January 1933) pp. 39 ff. Neither the public documents relating to the Pact of Paris (see D. H. Miller, *op. cit.* [n.21] pp. 154 ff.) nor any of the contributions to the scholarly discussions just referred to envisaged the possibility of interpreting the Kellogg Pact as an instrument of international criminal law which implied the criminal responsibility of either the states or the individual persons that contravened its stipulations. On the contrary, some participants in the discussions, basing their arguments on the British and French reservations to the Pact and on the recognition of those reservations by the American government, went so far as to maintain that the Pact reserved to the signatories such a wide discretion regarding the meaning of aggression and self-defense as to render it legally inoperative. See especially Edwin S. Borchard, *op.cit.* (n. 22) and Roland S. Morris's analysis in the *Proceedings* (1929) of the American Society of International Law, cited above (n. 22) pp. 88 ff.

[23]See the references to this movement in George Manner, *op cit.* (n. 1) pp. 410 ff., 428 ff.; Albert G. D. Levy, *op. cit.* (n. 1) pp. 1069 ff.; Hans Kelsen, *Peace Through Law,* cited above (n. 1) pp. 110 ff.

[24]Walter Denton Smith, *A Manual of Elementary Law* (St. Paul 1896) p. 31.

[25]On the problems involved see the well balanced analysis by Jerome Hall, "Nulla poena sine lege," in *Yale Law Journal,* vol. 47, no. 2 (December 1937) pp. 165 ff.

[26]Sheldon Glueck, *op. cit.* (n. 1) p. 106.

[27]*Ibid,* pp. 37 ff.

[28]See Carl Schmitt, *Die Diktatur* (2nd ed., Munich and Leipzig 1928) p. 150.

[29]*Trial of War Criminals,* cited above (n. 1) pp. 65 ff.

[30]*Ibid.,* p. ll.

[31]Albert Mathiez, *La revolution francaise,* vol. 3 (Paris 1928) p. 82.

[32]See, for example, Charles Cheney Hyde, in American Society of International Law, Thirty-Seventh Annual Meeting, *Proceedings* (Washington 1943) p. 43; Clyde Eagleton, *op. cit.* (n. 1) p. 498; Sheldon Glueck, *op. cit.* (n. 1) p. 115; Quincy Wright, "War Criminals," cited above (n. 1) p. 279.

[33]The wanton destruction of "cities like Rotterdam," carried out "for no military purpose," figures in Justice Jackson's Report to the President as one of the most flagrant violations of the rules of warfare; see *Trial of War Criminals,* cited above (n. 1) p. 6. But the reference to Rotterdam is

missing in Count Three of the Nuremberg indictment (*ibid.*, pp. 56 ff.). On the legal aspects of aerial bombardment see L. Oppenheim, *International Law, A Treatise,* edited by H. Lauterpacht, vol. 2 (6th ed., London-New York-Toronto 1940) pp. 406 ff., and Charles Cheney Hyde, *International Law, Chiefly as Interpreted and Applied by the United States,* vol. 3 (2nd rev. ed., Boston 1945) pp. 1822 ff.

[34]*Trial of War Criminals,* cited above (n. 1) p. 10.

[35]International Law Association, Thirty-Third Conference, held in 1924, *Report* (London 1925) p. 95.

[36]See the pertinent discussion on penological doctrines with regard to war crimes in Catholic Association for International Peace, *Transition from War to Peace, A Report of the Post-War World Committee* (Washington 1943) pp. 28 ff. Punishment for war crimes is analyzed and rejected, from the point of view of utility, by C. Arnold Anderson, *op. cit.* (n. 1) pp. 1081 ff.

[37]New York *Times,* November 22, 1945.

THE REVIVAL OF THE IDEA OF PUNITIVE WAR*

I

The course of human affairs often fails to bear out the historical importance which contemporaries are inclined to attach to events they have been witnessing. This experience should caution us against premature assertions on the epoch-making significance of the trials which have followed World War II as a judicial epilogue. However, we may venture to presume that the proceedings of Nuremberg and Tokyo against the leaders of defeated Germany and Japan will for a long time to come figure among the *causes célèbres* of international law. For they have raised problems and questions that go to the roots of the system of states under which Western society has been living during the last few centuries.

The far-reaching moral, political and legal implications are today impressively suggested by the division of American public opinion, the opinion of the legal profession as well as of laymen, on the merits of those trials, or rather of some of their aspects. For the point of the debate has been, generally speaking, neither the lawfulness of the authority of the two International Military Tribunals nor their right to try and punish the Axis leaders for the abominable violations of the rules of warfare, war crimes proper in the traditional sense of the term, which those men have instigated. Spirited discussions have been occasioned mainly by the insertion in the indictments of the so-called "crimes against peace," consisting in the planning and initiation of a war of aggression. It seemed to many critics, though they were no less strongly convinced of the moral guilt of the Axis leaders than the proponents and advocates of that charge, that the latter failed to have a valid basis in existing international law.[1]

The criminal responsibility under international law of individual persons for waging a war of aggression, which forms the very essence of the "crimes

Reprinted with permission of *Thought*, Fordham University Quarterly, Vol. XXI, No. 82, Sept., 1946.

against peace," is, however, presented to us not only as the imperative response to a unique situation, but as a general proposition to be applied in all future cases of aggressive war. As a matter of fact, it is occasionally held to be the most promising device for preventing future aggressions. The idea therefore deserves to be discussed apart from the context of the Hitlerian war which has given rise to it. The present moment—when the circumstances which fashioned that context have begun to recede into the past— might seem to be particularly propitious for this undertaking.

II

That the charge of "crimes against peace," as contained in the indictments of Nuremberg and Tokyo, lacked the foundation of a crystallized rule of international law, does not necessarily mean that its insertion in an international criminal code might not have conformed to actual trends in the doctrine and practice of international law. In point of fact, it is only apt to enhance the historical significance of the recent war trials that they actually were the culmination of a development that can be traced back to the first world war.

If we are to appreciate the changes of the concept of war which form the basis of that development, we have first to understand the principles that prevailed prior to 1914.

The international law of the nineteenth century did not admit an unqualified right of the sovereign states to wage war. But it did recognize their practically absolute right to use and rely on their own judgment as to the justness of their cause as well as the moment they might be entitled to resort to war in order to take justice into their own hands. At best, the principle of a just war could be said only to be lingering on, and it is hardly a matter of surprise that its character as a rule of positive international law finally became a controversial issue among the publicists themselves.

Moreover, war as such was considered an inevitable phenomenon of social life, deeply rooted in human nature, and in this sense was taken to be a legitimate instrumentality of international politics. Thus, to try to outlaw war did not seem to make sense. But it did appear feasible and actually proved to be within the reach of civilized men to regulate and limit its conduct. In fact, the very idea of prohibiting war altogether or subjecting it to legally defined conditions—substantive or procedural—was considered to be as much an unwarranted interference with the basic rights of the states as it was an illusion. Being unable to count on a community that has the will and the power to protect the interests of its members, the latter must be free to resort to self-help for redressing wrongs and vindicating rights.

The lack of any effective protection by the international community suggested still another right of the sovereign state. Dependent as it was on

76

self-help, it had to be allowed to render the latter as effective as it could possibly do, both by strengthening its own forces, military as well as others, and by joining them with the forces of other states. The full power to contract alliances figures therefore in the Declaration of Independence side by side with the full power to levy war, and "other acts and things which independent states may of right do." In seeking alliances, a state might go as far as it could in making friends, provided only its policy aimed at the maintenance of the existing balance of power and not at its destruction.

The balance of power was, however, more than a mere means for securing the effectiveness of the self-help of the individual states in a world lacking a supranational authority. The function assigned to the scheme up to the first world war was not so much to act as a makeshift good enough as long as the concentration of power in an authority superior to that of the single states would be unattainable, as to be the permanent mechanics of a pluralistic system of states that was definitely set against the very idea of a politically unified world.[2] Modern international society was to be in the true sense of the word a society of nations and not a world state. It was to be governed by a law *inter gentes* and not by a world law.

Only the states should be able to create by their mutual consent legally binding rules of international law, they alone should administer them, and they alone should be the judges of the rights and duties stipulated by their common agreements. It is true that this view did not imply the rejection of common moral standards to which all states and governments alike should be subject. But the lack of any supranational legal institutions, related to the society of nations as a whole, could not but help to impair the sense of legal responsibility toward the international community itself. For responsibility is apt to be felt more strongly when and where there are institutions to keep it alive.

The primitive legal character of the community of nations explains not only the bilateral nexus of responsibilities under modern international law, rendering the law-breaking state liable only to the aggrieved state itself, that is, to the state's peer and not to a superior authority. It determined also the very nature of international liabilities, or, more specifically, the absence of criminal responsibility. Not every wrongful act is, by the terminology of municipal law, a punishable crime. What is generally held to constitute it as such is its atrocious character and its harmfulness to the respective community as a whole, requiring retribution by the public authorities. Acts that are supposed to affect private persons only and therefore subject to modes of private redress alone, are considered to lack the constitutive elements of a crime.[3] It was thus logical that the international community, being a society of equals not recognizing any superior authorities, a society, in other words, in which interests affecting it as a whole were hardly recognized, should also be without criminal laws and criminal procedures.

This view rules out the very idea of punitive war. "No war among independent states," says Kant, "can be a punitive war (*bellum punitivum*)." The victor is therefore not allowed to base his conditions of peace upon an alleged right of exacting punishment. Even if he merely implied a punishment for the war waged against him, he would be insulting the vanquished.[4]

The conception of the international community as a society of equal nations *superiorem non recognoscentes*[5] determined also the position of individual persons under modern international law. International law was to govern the relations among states alone as well as it was to be created and administered only by states. Where there is no world community represented and held together by supranational institutions, there is, juristically speaking, no world citizen either. Man's rights and duties are based on municipal, not on international law.

The international practice, prior to 1914, with regard to the punishment of individual malefactors for violations of the rules of warfare was the consequence of this conception. The law of war was supposed to bind only the states as such. The belligerent governments were obliged not only to observe, themselves, the rules of warfare, but also to enforce compliance with them on the part of the individual persons subject to their authority. Any infraction of the pertinent rules, including a failure of the government to prohibit and punish an infraction, constituted a violation of civil responsibility and might entitle the injured state to reprisals. But responsibility of the individual offender was considered to be a responsibility under municipal law, rendering him subject to prosecution and punishment by his own government alone. Violations of the rules of warfare were thus punishable not as international crimes, but as crimes under the local law of the individual offender.

It has of late become fashionable to picture the system of international law just outlined in the darkest colors, and to brand it as international anarchy pure and simple. Indeed, it would be of no avail to disregard and deny its very grave defects. The catastrophe of the first world war into which nineteenth-century Europe was finally plunged would all too obviously refute any nostalgic eulogy. But neither is it permissible to judge that system in purely organizational terms, and to see exclusively its failure to express the moral precepts of a peaceful and just world order in legal institutions as well. Important as the forms of society are, they are not the only nor, still less, the decisive criteria to be applied to the evaluation of the different ways and means by which men may order their private and public relations with one another. It is true, the concentration of power in the members of the international community left the governments of the sovereign states legally uncontrolled masters of their moral rights and duties. But it is only fair to add that the exercise of their powers compares not unfavorably with the record of other periods of history.

III

No doubt, the consistency of the principles prevailing in the society of nations prior to 1914 was not nearly as complete as the preceding lines would seem to suggest. Examples of theories and practices contrary to them could be easily produced. Moreover, the Hague Peace Conferences of 1899 and 1907 already foreshadowed the ideas and devices that were to grow into maturity after World War I. But the sway of the concept of sovereignty was and remained strong enough to orient doctrine and action in all basic questions the same way. It was only after the end of the first world war that we actually entered a period of transition to forms of international life, not yet foreseeable, with the bewildering variety of fundamental moral and legal tenets that is so characteristic of the great crises of history.

The ambition of the twenties and the early thirties—Hitler's rise to power in Germany practically broke the elan of the peace movement—reached out much farther than the ambition of the nineteenth century ever did. The first world war started as an old-style war in terms of its moral, legal, political, military and economic as well as of its psychological features. But it turned during its long course of four years into a war to end all war, and to end it for good. That was at least the way the nations that were to be the victors became inclined to interpret its ultimate meaning. Once the war against war was won, the task ahead therefore seemed to be to make permanent peace come definitely true. Comparatively less attention was paid to attempts to keep up, or rather restore and lift the standards of civilized warfare to be complied with by the belligerents in case armed conflicts should recur all the same. For technological developments appeared to nullify any serious chance of limiting and controlling the progressive destructiveness of modern warfare.

Though men despaired of being able to retain the comparatively modest goal of regulating war, they entertained, strangely enough, the more excessive hope of being able to eliminate war altogether. The very character of present-day warfare, its tendency to involve the whole population of the belligerents, the so-called noncombatants of the law of war of former times no less than the combatants, the gigantic material losses and sacrifices which it inflicted upon all belligerents alike, the economic disorder in which it left even the victor nations, its destructive impact upon the very foundations of civil order—horrifying as all those features and effects of modern war were, or rather because they were of such a horrifying nature, they were looked upon as deterrent factors promising to uproot the last vestiges of the view that war could from anybody's point of view be a desirable thing. There was, therefore, in line with other *illusions du progrès*, less readiness than ever before to accept war as an inevitable phenomenon of politics, springing from the belligerency of an unchangeable human nature.[6] That the rejection of the philosophy of pessimism was based on the belief in the certain blessings of the irresistible forces of science, which was at the same time multiplying the technical possibilities of human self-destruction, hardly justified expectations of the peaceful future of mankind, but they were gaining ground all the same.

This change of objective and subjective circumstances combined to discredit the idea of war as it was held prior to the catastrophe of 1914. No doubt, the foundation upon which the new conception was based was in some parts not impressively strong. But this fact does not detract from the merit of the advocates of permanent peace in having given to the old fight against the curse of war a fresh impulse at a moment when there was an imperative need for renewed efforts.

The new conception found its expression not only in the increased stress which was laid upon the moral issue involved in war. As a matter of fact, its historical significance lies rather in the attempt to transform the code of the moral precepts regarding war into a code of positive rules of international law and to assure their effectiveness by adequate structural reforms of the society of nations.

The attempt to limit the lawful resort to war was not undertaken at one stroke. The Covenant of the League of Nations imposed upon its members only specific obligations not to resort to war, but did not contain a general prohibition of war. The emphasis was on procedural restrictions of the members of the League, obligating them to try the pacific settlement of their disputes and restraining them by time limits before war could be lawfully resorted to. The implications of the League system for the place and role of war in international law were, however, not exhausted by circumscribing the conditions of lawful war.

The protection of the state against aggression or any threat of war was under the Covenant no longer the individual concern of the state alone that was immediately affected by the hostile actions of another state, but was declared to be "a matter of concern to the whole League" which was obliged to take any measures "that may be deemed wise and effectual to safeguard the peace of nations." This assumption of responsibility by the international community was bound to make for notable changes in the international atmosphere. It was apt to invalidate the hitherto recognized principle, already undermined by the Hague Conferences, that a nation's armaments were purely a matter of its own concern. It was bound to affect also the right of each state to form alliances, both the unqualified right to arm and to contract alliances being the concomitants of the formerly isolated positions of the single states, having no alternative but self-help. As a matter of fact, the guarantee of the state's security was no longer to be the maintenance of the balance of power, but the institutionalized international cooperation of all states.

The rights to be ceded by the nations were rights due them as long as they had to live, as it were, in a state of nature, but they were no longer to be recognized once the states entered into an organized society which would relieve them of the *privilegium onerosum* of self-help. Membership in the new society implied, however, the acceptance of obligations not only in the form of negative prohibitions, but of positive obligations as well. The establishment of a machinery for coordinating the peace-securing efforts of the member nations thus coincided with the creation of responsibilities on the part of the nations toward the international community as a whole and their common agencies. To the bilateral nexus of responsibilities under international law were henceforth added responsibilities to the institutionalized community of nations.

It is therefore no accident that the terminology of criminal law makes its reappearance on the international scene at the very moment when the attempt is being made to reawaken in the nations and their rulers the sense of responsibility toward the world community as a whole by creating worldwide institutions. It is true, this terminology was carefully kept out of official instruments that defined in legally binding form the states' rights and duties. None of the existing governments was yet ready to accept the risks involved in recognizing an international criminal law, and least of all was any of them inclined to recognize international "crimes against peace" in a juristic sense. The new terminology indicated only trends in international law, to which the legal rules themselves, actually agreed upon by the governments, did not yet conform. However, the great historical significance of those trends has clearly been borne out by the recent war trials.

IV

The so-called sanctions of Article 16 of the League of Nations Covenant and the so-called outlawry of war by the Kellogg Pact very well illustrate the point just made.

Article 16 of the Covenant provided for the case of a state having resorted to war in disregard of the obligations to which it had subscribed as a member of the League. The unlawful act of war against another member was, under the provisions of the article, considered to be an act of war against all members of the League and, accordingly, an act to call forth their collective economic and military measures against the covenant-breaking state. Nothing in the text of the article suggested either the criminal character of the unlawful act of war, or the punitive nature of the collective measures. Still, in the oratory of Geneva the latter were from the beginning called "sanctions"—a word that has a definite penological connotation[7]—and the former "crime." No doubt, the terms were originally merely the expression of moral views and sentiments, but soon they were frequently understood to have a juristic significance as well.[8] The so-called "war of sanctions" of Article 16 can thus be said to have played in the present revival of the idea of punitive war at least as important a role as the Kellogg Pact was to do.

The League of Nations Covenant left the member states under certain conditions free to take such action, including war, "as they shall consider necessary for the maintenance of right and justice." It restricted the range of lawful wars, but it did not abolish war as an institution. War was still recognized as a legal remedy of self-help in case there was no other alternative open for obtaining satisfaction. In the words of Mr. Kellogg himself, the Kellogg Pact was meant to be a declaration against war as an institution.[9] The High Contracting Parties accordingly agreed "that the settlement or solution of all disputes or conflicts of whatever nature or whatever origin they may be, which may arise among them, shall never be sought except by pacific means" (Article II). Whereas under the League Covenant even a war that might in a technical sense constitute aggression might be a lawful war, the material cause of war was to lose by the Briand-Kellogg Pact its legal relevancy. Though this came very near to an absolute prohibition of war, it came, however, no more than close to it. For in the negotiations preceding the conclusion of the Peace Pact the governments agreed on reservations that expressly exempted an act of self-defense from the prohibition of war.[10]

As a matter of fact, the governments carefully refrained from pronouncing the "outlawry of war" in the text of the treaty. They merely declared with solemnity "that they condemn recourse to war for the solution of international controversies, and renounce it as an instrument of national policy in their relations with one another" (Article I).

This did not, however, hinder the repetition of what we already observed in the history of Article 16 of the League Covenant. The tone was set by no less a person than M. Briand, the coauthor of the Peace Pact. In his address of welcome to the representatives of the governments that were gathering around him in Paris in order to attach their signatures to the agreement, M. Briand praised the pact as an instrument that "by mutual accord truly and regularly outlawed" war "so that a culprit would incur the unconditional condemnation and probably the enmity of all its co-signatories."[11] What was in legal terms a diplomatic document, with implictions not fundamentally different from any other international treaty, was given at its baptism the name "international criminal law." It may be worth while mentioning that Mr. Kellogg, the co-father of the Pact, used in referring to his child the old-fashioned names of nineteenth-century diplomacy.[12]

The ground for interpreting the Briand-Kellogg Pact as a charter of international criminal law was prepared not only by oratorical exercises within the League of Nations. When the penal provisions of the Treaty of Versailles failed of execution, there sprang up a movement that tried systematically to develop the ideas somewhat haphazardly expressed in the improvised clauses of the peace treaty, and to have them permanently incorporated by all governments into the body of twentieth-century international law.[13]

The short-range goals of the individuals, mostly international lawyers, and of the organizations that joined in the movement differed widely according to theoretical conceptions of public law and political considerations of a more practical nature. Membership in the movement ran the whole scale from moderate to the most radical reformers. Some urged the necessity of first establishing a substantive code of international crimes, differing again among one another over the scope of such a code. The others wanted to see preference given to the setting up of an international criminal court. The most important division of opinion occurred on the question whether states or individuals, the collective entities or their personal agents from the governments down to the lower rungs of the state administrations, or states as well as individuals should be held criminally accountable and punishable under future international law.

But whatever their differences were as to those more or less relevant details, all reformers agreed that the international community had outgrown its primitive character of which the merely civil and bilateral liability of its members was the most conspicuous expression. In their view, the form as well as the nature of this responsibility had become outdated by the establishment of international institutions, such as the League of Nations and the Permanent Court of International Justice, which made of the international community all but a kind of superstate. In fact, if those institutions were to be effective, they had to be implemented by agencies administering criminal laws and procedures.

The demand for the recognition of individual criminal liability got support from still another side. The emergency of an organized world community rendered the traditional view that man has a legal standing only under municipal law more and more problematic, or, to put it the other way around, the states remained no longer the undisputed monopolistic subjects of international law. To be sure, in this case, too, one can speak only of a trend, the governments being very reluctant to give to the new ideas an expression that would be legally binding. But there were at least some symptoms of a crystallization in positive juristic rules, apt to encourage the advocates of a world law which, they hoped, would first supplement the law *inter gentes* and finally replace it altogether.

The central question which the movement for an international criminal jurisdiction had to solve was, of course, the scope of the contraventions of international law that should be classed as punishable international crimes. The starting point of the movement being the abortive penal provisions of the Treaty of Versailles, it was taken for granted that the international criminal code should cover the violations of the rules of warfare, transforming them thus from offenses under municipal law into offenses under international law as well. The main historical significance of the movement lies, however in the fact that it also propagated the inclusion in an international criminal code of what the Charter of Nuremberg of 1945 was to call "crimes against peace."

V

There were thus in the twenties several parallel, or rather confluent, developments afoot which produced the weapons that were later to be directed against the conservative interpretation of the Kellogg Pact. The attack was opened in 1928, lost some of its vigor in the middle of the thirties, gained momentum again during World War II, and finally scored the triumph of winning over the governments of the victorious United Nations. The great war trials of 1946 were the first application of the principles stored up in that continuously expanding arsenal of novel ideas and devices. They were, furthermore, the application of the most radical views that had been propounded by any of the several wings of the antitraditionalist school.

The radicalism of these views is due to their inconsistency with what, after all, has continued to be the basic character of the society within which they are to be applied. For the new views derive their validity from principles applicable to a world state under a world law, and not to a society of nations under international law. The international community of today, in spite of legal trends to the contrary, is still such a society; and it seems likely to remain so. In fact, those who would apply the new principles to it have for their alleged purpose to transform our society of sovereign nations into a sovereign world community. They are proposing to punish the rulers of states for a breach of the peace as though this were an act of sedition within a world state. They are doing this at a moment when—in spite of the recent reassertions of the principle of just war—states and their policy makers are still recognized by international law as their own and sole judges of their right to resort under certain conditions to war.

It is true that the period between the two world wars made great strides—backward rather than forward, however—toward establishing legal criteria for distinguishing just and unjust wars similar to those that were, in times preceding the growth of the modern society of nations, generally recognized as binding upon the princes. As a matter of fact, the prohibitions of the Kellogg Pact were broader than were those of the Scholastic doctrine on war which always admitted war as a legal remedy of self-help—even though it might be, in a technical sense, an offensive war. But even the Kellogg Pact was not understood by any government to withdraw from its signatories "the right to have recourse to war in self-defense and to judge for themselves whether a situation has arisen calling for such action."[14]

Considering the bewildering variety of views in the theory and practice of international law on "what constitutes the right of self-defense and the necessity and extent of the same,"[15] the practical effect of the legal prohibition of war, as laid down in the Pact, was bound to be dubious. It could hardly be different from the effect of the principle which prevailed throughout the history of modern international law that the sovereignty of the state did not imply its absolute right to wage war but only the state's free judgment on the exercise of its basically limited right. Moreover, the signatories of the Kellogg Pact refused, implicitly at least, to submit even the ultimate determination of a dispute that might have arisen on the actual exercise of the supposedly inherent right of self-defense to a superior political or judicial authority.

Nor is it surprising that the states should have been reluctant to accept absolute prohibitions of self-help as long as they could not rely on safer guarantees of protection by the community as a whole than those which the League of Nations actually afforded them. To be sure, under the terms of the Covenant, the League had definite responsibilities toward its members who had accepted on their part no less definite positive and negative obligations toward the League as well as its single members. But here again the states were left their own judges on the questions whether they were in a concrete case legally bound to take action, and what action they should take in order to implement those responsibilities and obligations. That the members of the League were inclined to interpret their duties under the Covenant more strictly than they would interpret their rights could be very well foreseen in the early twenties, and was clearly confirmed by the failure of the League in the Sino-Japanese and the Italo-Ethiopian conflicts.

The League of Nations was, in strictly legal terms, a machinery which should and which actually did facilitate agreement among its members on common actions and the coordination of the common actions to which they might have consented. But it was not a body politic with discretionary powers over the member states. Its agencies were not governmental agencies, but basically still had the character of diplomatic organs intended to assure the closest possible cooperation among sovereign states.

The fateful problem of giving practical effect to the legal prohibition of unjust war was therefore just as little solved by the confederate society of sovereign nations as it had been solved by international law in its pre-institutional stage. Armaments, alliances and balance of power which continued, even after 1918, to be the paraphernalia of international politics were much more the consequences of that failure than, as is often suggested, its causes.

The actual structure of the international community thus remained essentially unchanged by the many peace instruments that were enacted after the first world war. Its new common councils being only international and cooperative, but not supranational agencies holding discretionary powers, the world community continued to be fundamentally a society of nations *superiorem non recognoscentes*. However, the absolute sway of a consistent doctrine was gone, because of the impact of the war and its aftermath, and new ideas and devices began to be harbored in the old structure. Ironically enough, they were to have the profoundest effect not on peace, but on war. For the melancholy truth is that the great efforts to abolish war succeeded merely in changing its concept and nature.

But it might, at least, have been hoped that the transition to punitive war which we are witnessing should be a change for the better.

VI

The concept of punitive war which became the very basis of the war trials of Nuremberg and Tokyo is new in relation to the views that prevailed in what used to be called the period of modern international law. In truth, however, it is rather the revival of an old idea with a longer history than the history of the modern juristic conceptions of war. If we want rightly to appreciate the principles applied in those trials as a precedent to be generally followed in future cases of violations of the laws of peace and war; if we want, in particular, to weigh the merits of the claim that the criminal responsibility under international law of the individual statesmen will prove to be an effective instrument for preventing future aggressions, we might do well to ask what lessons the past can offer us.

The Scholastic doctrine of just war can be traced back to St. Augustine. It is, however, the doctrine of the late Scholastics of the sixteenth century—and its fate—that is apt to shed most light on our present-day problems. For it was only then that the Scholastic teachings on war were meant to be applied within an international framework not too different from the one within which we live today. The Spanish Dominican Francisco de Vitoria

(c. 1483–1546) and the Spanish Jesuit Francisco Suarez (1548–1617) who were the most eminent representatives of those teachings wrote in and for the incipient society of sovereign states which at present still exists, though we are trying very hard to overcome its grave deficiencies. As a matter of fact, we try to overcome them by returning to the ideas of those founders of modern international law.

This makes for striking similarities in the problems posed to the publicists and statesmen of the sixteenth and to us in the twentieth century. However, the Schoolmen of the sixteenth century endeavored to work their way in a direction opposite to the way that men are groping today. We are striving to square the circle by creating a world authority without a diminution of the national authorities. The sixteenth-century Schoolmen attempted to fortify the state authorities without also cutting through the universal spiritual ties which survived after the universal political institutions of the Middle Ages had practically ceased to operate.

The oppositeness of directions accounts for important differences in the respective attitudes toward the problem of war. The emphasis of the present discussions is on the unlawfulness of war, though exceptions are readily admitted in the case of self-defense and of a police action to be undertaken by the organized international community against single law-breaking states. To be sure, the writings of the Scholastics are far from being panegyrics upon the virtues and blessings of war. Apostles of war as such can find no comfort in them, but only the strongest possible condemnation of their perverted notions. In fact, the very purpose of those writings is to draw sharp lines between lawful and unlawful wars. Still, the emphasis is rather on the recognition, though it is a very strongly and carefully qualified recognition, of war as a legal institution of self-help in a world of sovereign states that are coordinated to one another, but not subordinated to any superior political authority. The emphasis may even be said to be on the assertion of the right to wage a lawful war as an essential attribute of the sovereign prince.

The insistence on the *jus ad bellum* of the sovereign prince which seems somehow strange to the present-day reader can be easily understood in the tragic historical context of the disintegration of the *Res publica Christiana,* as originally conceived. The dictum on the right of the prince to wage war, provided it be, by reason of its substantial causes, a just war, was to settle a centuries-old controversy. The Christian Commonwealth of the Middle Ages was a strictly hierarchical order, supreme power residing exclusively in its highest spiritual and temporal authorities. Its members were therefore as little entitled to wage war against one another as are the citizens of the modern state. Only the Pope and the Emperor were held to have the legal authority to wage war. This conception became untenable when the per-

87

sonal nexus between the members of the Christian society was disrupted by the emergency of territorial political units whose rulers proved to be strong enough to assert their own supreme power against the claims of any superior political authority. *Rex in regno suo est Imperator regni sui.*[16]

Although the replacement of the hierarchical medieval order by a society of coordinated states *superiorem non recognoscentes* was in the sixteenth century very far advanced, it was still in need of the strongest possible affirmation. This explains the emphasis by Vitoria as well as Suarez on the rights of the sovereign princes, and especially on their right to wage war. This situation accounts also for Suarez' attitude toward the settlement of interstate disputes by secular arbitration. Though insisting on the duty of the sovereigns to employ their best efforts in order to avoid war with all the appalling calamities consequent on it, he maintains that they are not bound by the natural law to accept the decision of arbitrators who are not instituted by their common accord.[17]

The very essence of sovereignty is thus considered to be the absence of a superior authority which would be entitled to decree ordinary legal remedies against the wrongful actions of a state. War is therefore recognized by the Scholastic jurists as an extraordinary legal instrument of self-help by which one state may redress the wrongs inflicted upon itself by another state, provided the wrong is grave and proportionate to the evils engendered by war.[18] This view excludes the justification of war by considerations of political expediency. Both Vitoria and Suarez emphatically denounce the extension of empire, personal glory of the prince and other supposed advantages to him or to the state itself as just causes of war.[19] But their view is equally far from implying the rejection of offensive or aggressive war, if the latter is intended to redress a wrong suffered. Aggressive war is also allowed to the injured state for avenging itself and its subjects. For the state "cannot adequately protect the public weal and the position of the state if it cannot avenge a wrong and take measures against its enemies, for wrongdoers would become readier and bolder for wrongdoing, if they could do wrong with impunity."[20]

Aggressive war thus figures side by side with the war of self-defense as a just war, provided the war has been commenced for redressing or avenging a wrong or is aiming both at civil redress by and criminal punishment of the persons responsible for the wrong inflicted. The Schoolmen are therefore far from giving unconditional preference to peace, if it seems to be incompatible with the maintenance of justice.

The redress of an injury suffered was held to justify an offensive war throughout the following centuries until the general prohibition of war by the Kellogg Pact made this kind of war illegal. However, the notion of a just aggressive war waged for inflicting criminal punishment upon offenders against the law of nations faded away later on, to be revived only in the twentieth century.[21]

It is true that Vitoria and Suarez, like other publicists of their age, rejected the views that ascribed to the Pope or the Emperor the political lordship over the world, and made themselves the advocates of the sovereign rights of the emerging nation states. However, they continued to think of the world as a spiritual whole of which the single states should be only parts. Their society of nations was based on an objective moral order, and the individual states were supposed to find and not to make the law. Though they paved the way for modern international law by insisting on a clear distinction between the *jus naturae* and the positive *jus gentium,* the idea of later times that international law was a body of legal rules which derived their binding force exclusively from the wills of the respective states would have horrified them. The subjects of the *jus gentium* were to be the states as the politically organized members of mankind. However, men retained their individual status under natural law with regard to their rights as well as their duties.[22]

Thus, international rights and duties continued to be related to the world community itself rather than conceived as merely bilateral relationships among its constituent parts. It is this conception which accounts also for the Scholastic doctrine on the punitive power under natural and international law.

Society at large, in order to be held together, requires that there be "somewhere a power and authority to deter wrongdoers and prevent them from injuring the good and innocent. Now, everything needed for the government and preservation of society exists by natural law, and in no other way can we show that a state has by natural law authority to inflict pains and penalties on its citizens who are dangerous to it. But if a state can do this to its own citizens, society at large no doubt can do it to all wicked and dangerous folk. . ."[23] The dissolution of the hierarchical *Res publica Christiana* under supreme authorities into a pluralistic society of nations without a lord over them is thus not held to have made the vindicative right of the all-comprehensive community itself obsolete. It still exists by natural law.

But in view of the lack of a central superior authority this right must now be considered to reside in the members of the community. In exercising it, however, the latter act only as the instrumentalities of the community. Still, Vitoria goes so far as to maintain that the right of punishing is due the injured state by natural law.[24] Suarez more consistently relates it, at least in *De legibus ac Deo Legislatore,* to the province of positive international law. "For owing to natural reason," Suarez says, "it is not indispensable that this power should be held by the injured state. Men could have established another mode of punishment, for instance, by assigning this power to a third authority, and instituting it as an arbiter with coercive power. However, the present mode having been adopted by custom as more convenient and conformed to nature, it is just to the point that one may not resist it."[25]

Whatever were their differences concerning the character of this right, Vitoria and Suarez agreed on its content. "Princes have authority not only over their own subjects, but also over foreigners, so far as to prevent them from committing wrongs."[26] On the basis of this authority they may commence against the wrongdoing state an aggressive war in order to inflict punishment upon it. On its basis, too, they may, if implicated in a defensive war, punish the aggressor once victory is won. The wrongdoing state is subject to their criminal jurisdiction *ratione delicti.*[27]

The fact that this jurisdiction makes one and the same state accuser and judge at the same time imposes upon the victor the duty to try by all means to deliver the judgment as judge rather than accuser.[28] But it does not entitle the vanquished to reject it for this reason. For in view of the lack of an authority superior to both of them, the injured state as well as the offender, the jurisdiction of the victor over the vanquished is the only means of effecting the criminal responsibilities of the offending state and its agents, the prince himself as well as his counsellors. "Indeed, it is undeniable," says Suarez, "that under this circumstance the same person has in a certain way the role of plaintiff and judge, as we see it to be true of God to whom the public power presents a certain analogy. The reason is that this act of vindicative justice is indispensable to mankind, and that neither in nature nor in the ways of human affairs has one been able to find a better procedure."[29]

As long as the human race, being still conceived as "a certain moral and quasi-political unity,"[30] and not the various peoples and kingdoms, was considered to be the basis of international rights and duties, the principle of individual rather than collective responsibility for international offenses could not fail to be taken for granted. The problem discussed at great length by the Schoolmen was therefore not whether individual responsibility of the agents of the state was to be assumed at all, but to what categories of persons criminal responsibility should be imputed. Considerations for the security of the state being in the ascendant, there was a distinct tendency to restrict the range of persons who were held to be bound and entitled to follow their own conscience rather than the command of their prince in deciding the question whether a war waged by their prince was just or unjust. Accordingly, the number of persons who could be assumed to be responsible for international wrongs also tended to be continuously narrowed.[31] Vitoria thus summarized his own views by the dictum that "in general among Christians all the fault is to be laid at the door of their princes."[32]

VII

The princes were thus burdened by the Schoolmen with the main responsibility for offenses against the law of nations. How far the practice actually corresponded to that teaching is, to be sure, another question. Alberico Gentili, an Italian publicist of the sixteenth century, in discussing historical examples of punishment inflicted upon captive leaders of the enemy, feels induced to comment ironically that the ancient practices were quite opposed to the habits of modern warfare. "For now it is the common soldiers who are slain. The leaders, the rich, are saved, that they may ransom themselves."[33] Be that as it may, even greater than the responsibilities with which the Scholastic doctrine charged the princes, might be considered the rights that it conferred upon them. For it recognized them, in strictly legal terms, as their own judges on the broad powers that were granted to them with regard to the substantive and procedural distinctions between just and unjust war.

This is not to say, however, that they were not held subject to any institutional control. For the princes, in deciding doubts on the lawfulness of a war, or any other action, are in the forum of conscience not allowed to rely on their own or on their lawyers' judgment, but have "to seek the advice of those whom the Church has appointed for that purpose, such as prelates, preachers, and confessors, who are people skilled in divine and human law." Unlawful war is sin. And "in those matters which belong to his salvation a man is bound to yield credence to the teachers appointed by the Church, and in a doubtful matter their ruling is law."[34]

The doctrine of the indirect power of the Pope *in temporalibus* is the application of those teachings to the relationship between the Christian princes and the head of the Church. In accordance with that doctrine, the Pope has the right to assume in a concrete case jurisdiction over the cause of a war, and to pronounce a judgment to which the parties to the dispute are bound to conform. It is true that the Pope can choose not to interpose his authority in order to avoid a greater evil. In this case the sovereigns are not obliged to ask for papal authorization before going to war, but may pursue their rights according to their own decision. However, they have to take care not to be themselves the reason why the Pope does not dare to intervene.[35]

This subjection of the temporal rulers to the control of religious authorities formed an essential part of the Scholastic teachings on war. In fact, it was its very foundation. The ever-widening split within Christendom and the process of secularization of public and private life that followed it destroyed its spiritual and institutional basis.

However, not all the changes which the Scholastic doctrine on the *bellum*

91

justum underwent in the course of time are due to the breakdown of its religious-institutional foundation. The idea of the just cause of war itself suffered modifications that paved the way for the views which were to be propounded by the statesmen and publicists of the following centuries. Nor can those modifications be ascribed to the influence of the Protestant writers on international law alone. For they clearly appeared in the very writings of the Schoolmen of the sixteenth century, as compared with the Thomistic doctrine proper.[36]

One side of this process has been aptly described as "the obliteration of the difference between the objective criterion of justness and the subjective criterion of good faith."[37] It manifests itself in Vitoria's admission, hardly consistent with his own basic teachings and contrary to other express statements of his own, that a war can be just on both sides. "Assuming a demonstrable ignorance either of fact or of law, it may be that on the side where true justice is the war is just of itself, while on the other side the war is just in the sense of being excused from sin by reason of good faith, because invincible ignorance is a complete excuse."[38] A similar trend reveals itself in Suarez' probabilism. The prince has to follow the more probable opinion, Suarez maintains, if he arrives after a careful examination of the legal merits of the controversy at the conclusion that there is a probability on either side.[39] Though both views were set forth in a cautiously elaborated form, they easily lent themselves to an extensive interpretation of the *jus ad bellum*. The temptation to consider the opinion that is more favorable to one's own interests as the more probable one is no doubt particularly great.

The successive introduction of subjective elements into the just causes of war was bound to spell sooner or later the doom of the idea of punitive war. Punishment must not be founded on probabilities, but on certainties. It is therefore no accident that Suarez tends to remove war out of the sphere of vindicative into that of distributive justice, and to substitute for criminal responsibilities civil liabilities.[40]

This tendency was later on furthered by the weakening of the idea that the human race is a moral and quasi-political unity. Accordingly, international rights and duties came to be conceived as purely mutual relationships among the constituent members of the society of nations. Thus there was not any longer a community to which punitive power could be attributed. Even less did it seem permissible to subject any one state to the vicarious criminal jurisdiction of any other state. The several states being held to be the sole basis of international rights and obligations, there was no room left for the individual responsibility of the states' agents.

However, all these conceptual changes do not yet exhaust the reasons for the disappearance of punitive war from the theory and practice of international law. Strange as it may seem, humanitarian considerations also contributed to it.

VIII

The so-called law of war formed an essential part of the Scholastic teachings on war. Vitoria and Suarez devoted considerable space to the discussion on "what kind and degree of stress is lawful in a just war."[41] In point of fact, it is to their lasting credit that they were among the first modern publicists who tried to limit warfare by subjecting its conduct to legally defined restraints. Christianity had not been able to wipe out war in this sinful world; it should at least prove to be capable of mitigating its horrors.

One of the main concerns of our Schoolmen was to give practical effect to the legal distinction between guilty and innocent. They encountered, however, difficulties in this undertaking which were directly due to their doctrine of just war. The shocking logic of war permits actions that are otherwise generally considered crimes pure and simple. It even stamps on them a heroic value. If the concept of just war is to be legally meaningful and effective, we can exempt only the killing by those who wage a lawful war from the precepts that prevail in society apart from war. The leaders and soldiers on the side of the unlawful belligerent are murderers. However, this status hardly recommends them to the kind regard of the other belligerent. The discussion of the Schoolmen on the law of war is an instructive comment on the perplexities involved in the efforts to reconcile humanitarian considerations with a strict application of the principles of just war.[42]

To the extent that the just causes of war lost in the course of time their precise character, the untoward effects of this doctrine upon the legal status of the unlawful belligerent became problematic even from the point of view of justice. The latter as well as purely humanitarian considerations combined and led to the proclamation of the principle that states at war with one another have the same legal status and can therefore claim the same rights, both for themselves and for their subjects, regardless of whether they wage a lawful or an unlawful war.[43]

The heralds of the new principle took great pains to stress that it was not meant to abolish the moral distinction between just and unjust war. Nor did they want it to be understood as rejecting the idea of religious and moral sanctions against those responsible for an unjust war. "The persons," to quote Grotius, "who knowingly perform such acts, or cooperate in them, are to be considered of the number of those who cannot reach the Kingdom of Heaven without repentance."[44] It is supposed, in other words, to abolish the distinction between just and unjust war only "externally and in the sight of men"[45] But the fact remains that the principle of just war was henceforth to be, in strictly juristic terms, a *lex imperfecta*.

It testifies to the complexities of human affairs that the emasculation of the legal distinction between just and unjust war should contribute to the humanization of warfare. However, it would be hard to deny that the milder practices of warfare that were to characterize the eighteenth and nineteenth centuries were at least partly due to the concept of war as a duel between equals which is the very opposite of the idea of war as the prosecution and punishment of a criminal.

Nobody has seen more clearly the effect of the punitive concept of war on the way in which war is being conducted and terminated, nor has anyone expressed it more eloquently than Vattel, the famous Swiss publicist of the eighteenth century who was followed by the Founding Fathers of America "as the most competent, the wisest, and the safest guide"[46] in all their international dealings. "Since each Nation claims," Vattel remarks, "to have justice on its side, it will arrogate to itself all the rights of war and claim that its enemy has none, that his hostilities are but deeds of robbery, acts in violation of the Law of Nations, and deserving of punishment by all Nations. The decision of the rights at issue will not be advanced thereby, and the contest will become more cruel, more disastrous in its effects, and more difficult of termination."[47]

On the basis of the historical record, the return to the idea of punitive war is thus unfortunately rather the symptom of grim prospects for the future conduct of wars than a guarantee of the elimination of war as such. Under these circumstances it is no doubt a matter of comfort that we are anxious, as is borne out by the negotiations on the outlawry of the atomic bomb, to reopen also the discussion of the Schoolmen on "what kind and degree of stress is lawful in a just war."

FOOTNOTES

[1]The present writer has sided with those critics in his article "Punishment for War Crimes," in *Social Research*, XIII. No. 1 (March 1946) p. 1 ff.

[2]See Alfred Vagts, "The United States and the Balance of Power," in *The Journal of Politics*, III, No. 4 (November 1941) p. 434.

[3]Walter Denton Smith, *A Manual of Elementary Law* (St. Paul, 1896) pp. 132 ff.

[4]Rechtslehre, 2. Teil, 2. Abschnitt, §§ 57, 58, in Immanuel Kant's *Werke*, Herausgegeben von Ernst Cassirer, VII (Berlin, 1916), p. 154 ff.

[5]On the historical origin of this formulation see Angelo Piero Sereni, *The Italian Conception of International Law* (New York, 1943), p. 59.

[6]See Alvin Johnson, "War," in *Encyclopaedia of the Social Sciences*, XV (1935), p. 340 ff.

[7]See Quincy Wright, *A Study of War* (Chicago, 1942), II, p. 939 ff. See also L. Oppenheim, *International Law. A Treatise*, edited by H. Lauterpacht, II, (6th ed.; London-New York-Toronto, 1940), pp. 133 ff.

[8]See Paul Barandon, *Das Kriegsverhütungsrecht des Völkerbundes* (Berlin, 1933), pp. 259 ff, 279 ff.

[9]See David Hunter Miller, *The Peace Pact of Paris*. A Study of the Briand-Kellogg Treaty (New York-London, 1928) p. 283.

[10]See the British Note of May 19, 1928 and the American Note of June 23, 1928 in David Hunter Miller, *op cit.*, pp. 196 ff, 213 ff.

[11]Address of M. Briand, August 27, 1928, in David Hunter Miller, *op. cit.*, p. 257.

[12]Addresses of the Honorable Frank B. Kellogg, Secretary of State, in D. H. Miller, *op. cit.*, pp. 269 ff.

[13]See the references to this movement in George Manner, "The Legal Nature and Punishment of Criminal Acts of Violence Contrary to the Laws of War," in *American Journal of International Law*, XXXVIII, No. 3 (July 1943), p. 410 ff.; Albert G. D. Levy, "The Law and Procedure of War Crime Trials," in *American Political Science Review*, XXXVII No. 6 (December 1943), p. 1069 ff.; Manley O. Hudson, *International Tribunals, Past and Future* (Washington, 1944), pp. 180 ff.; Hans Kelsen, *Peace Through Law* (Chapel Hill, 1944), pp. 110 ff.

[14]L. Oppenheim, *op. cit.*, p. 154. See Also David Hunter Miller, *op. cit.*, pp. 39 ff., 46 ff., 83 ff., 195 ff., 213 ff.

[15]Roland S. Morris in the *Proceedings of the American Society of International Law*, Twenty-Third Annual Meeting (Washington, 1929), p. 90. See also Edwin M. Borchard, "The Multilateral Treaty for the Renunciation of War," in *American Journal of International Law*, XXIII, No. 1 (January 1929), p. 117 ff.

[16]See Angelo Piero Sereni, *op. cit.*, pp. 57 ff. and 86 ff., and Arthur Nussbaum, "Just War—A Legal Concept?" in *Michigan Law Review*, XLII (1934), p. 455 ff.

[17]Francisco Suarez, *De Bello*, translated in Alfred Vanderpol, *La doctrine scolastique du droit de guerre* (Paris, 1919), p. 391, §§ 355 f.

[18]Suarez, *op. cit.*, p. 378, § 334.

[19]Franciscus de Vitoria, *De Indis et De Jure Belli Relectiones*, translated in *Classics of International Law* (Washington, 1917), p. 170, §§ 10–12, and Suarez, *op. cit.*, pp. 377 f. § 333.

[20]Victoria, *op. cit.*, p. 168, § 5 and p. 182, § 44. See also Suarez, *op. cit.*, p. 366, § 315 and p. 368, § 318.

[21]In speaking of punitive war, we shall do well to distinguish two concepts which are closely related to each other, but not identical. Punitive war proper is offensive war waged for punitive purposes. Its present revival has been effected by the punitive interpretation of Article 16 of the League of Nations Covenant. Somewhat different is the defensive war in which the defender employs his victory for inflicting punishment upon the aggressor. The latter concept underlies Justice Jackson's proposition based upon the Kellogg Pact.

The Schoolmen of the sixteenth century maintained the right to wage aggressive war for punitive purposes as well as the incidental right of the belligerent who originally fought a purely defensive war to inflict punishment upon the aggressor once victory is won. In the first case, the war begins as a punitive war; in the second case, it only ends as one.

[22]See Heinrich Rommen, *Die Staatslehre des Franz Suarez, S.J.* (M. Gladbach, 1926), pp. 270 ff.

[23]Vitoria, *op. cit.*, p. 172, § 19.

[24]Vitoria, *ibid.*

[25]Suarez, *De legibus ac Deo legislatore*, II, c. xix, translated in Alfred Vanderpol, *op. cit.*, p. 505, § 520. In *De bello* Suarez sides with Vitoria on the question regarding the character of the right of the punishing state. See *op. cit.*, p. 368, § 318; p. 380, § 337, and especially p. 381, § 339.

[26]Vitoria, *op. cit.*, p. 172, § 19.

[27]Suarez, *De bello, op. cit.*, p. 380, § 337.

[28]Vitoria, *op. cit.*, p. 187, § 60.

[29]Suarez, *op. cit.*, p. 381, § 339.

[30]Suarez, *De legibus ac Deo legislatore,* II, c. xix, *op. cit.*, p. 506, § 521.

[31]See Heinrich Rommen, *op. cit.*, p. 303.

[32]Vitoria, *op. cit.*, p. 187, § 60. The highly interesting and important qualification "among Christians" is due to considerations that fall outside the scope of our present discussion.

[33]Alberico Gentili, *De Jure Belli Tres Libri,* translated in *Classics of International Law* (Oxford-London, 1933), III, chap. viii, p. 325.

[34]Vitoria, *op. cit.*, pp. 116 ff., §§ 1–3.

[35]Suarez, *De bello, op. cit.*, p. 371, § 323. See also Heinrich Rommen, *op. cit.*, pp. 235 ff.

[36]See Alfred Vanderpol, *op. cit.*, pp. 250 ff.

[37]Arthur Nussbaum, *op. cit.*, p. 460.

[38]Vitoria, *op. cit.*, p. 177, § 32.

[39]Suarez, *op. cit.*, p. 389, § 352.

[40]See especially Suarez, *op. cit.*, p. 389, § 352. Cf. also Heinrich Rommen, *op. cit.*, p. 301.

[41]Vitoria, *op. cit.*, p. 171, § 15 and pp. 178 ff., §§ 34 ff.; Suarez, *op. cit.*, pp. 397 ff., §§ 363 ff.

[42]See especially Vitoria, *op. cit.*, p. 183, § 48.

[43]See Hugo Grotius, *De Jure Belli ac Pacis Libri Tres,* translated in *Classics of International Law* (Oxford-London, 1925),III,chap. iv, § 3, p. 643 ff.; E. de Vattel, *Le Droit des Gens, ou Principes de la Loi Naturelle, appliqués à la Conduite et aux Affaires des Nations et Souverains,* translated in *Classics of International Law* (Washington, 1916), III, chap. xii, §§ 188 ff., p. 304 ff.

[44]Grotius, III, chap. x, § 3, *op. cit.*, p. 719.

[45]Vattel, III, chap. xii, § 190, *op. cit.*, p. 305.

[46]Albert de Lapradelle in his *Introduction to Vattel, op. cit.*, p. xxxv.

[47]Vattel, III, chap. xii, § 188, *op. cit.*, p. 304.

III

INTERNATIONAL ORGANIZATION

III(A)

PAN-AMERICANISM

PAN AMERICANISM: ITS UTOPIAN AND REALISTIC ELEMENTS*

Pan-American solidarity has been more often and more solemnly affirmed in recent years than ever before in the history of Pan-American rhetoric. The impact of recent catastrophic events has indeed caused a crescendo of manifestations strong enough to make the continental brotherhood express itself also by some deeds. For the first time in their history, the twenty-one American republics intervened in world affairs as a collective unit, though not exactly with striking success. Is Pan-Americanism finally going to become a reality in world politics? What chances are there that the Western Hemisphere will emerge out of the present chaos as a distinct political entity within the international order of tomorrow? How far, if at all, is continental regionalism a political objective worth striving for?

The memory of the ignominious breakdown of the League of Nations being still fresh in our minds, we are hardly inclined to indulge in illusions about the chances for success of any other attempt at establishing a workable collective system. We have rather to beware of unjustly withholding from such an endeavor the credit it might deserve. Undue pessimism would be, however, as little justified and as harmful as unfounded optimism. Besides, the chances of Pan-Americanism have to be weighed on the basis of its specific merits and faults.

First, however, we had better examine the recent achievements of the policy of Pan-American solidarity in the light of the legal record. Legal documents, stripped of the diplomatic arabesque, speak a sober language. And soberness we need, living as we do in an age of catchwords which all too often lull us into complacency.

*Reprinted from *Problems of Post-War Reconstruction*, Edited by Henry P. Jordan, American Council on Public Affairs, Washington, D.C., 1942.

When the Sixth International Conference of American States, held in Havana in 1928, undertook to put the Pan-American Union on a treaty basis, it inserted into the convention the express provision that "both the Governing Board and the Pan-American Union shall discharge the duties assigned by this convention subject to the condition that they shall not exercise functions of a political character." Since the convention has so far not become effective, the legal basis of the Pan-American Union is still somewhat problematic. But what matters more is that such great pains should have been taken to emphasize the non-political character of an inherently political agency.

If this strange quibbling fails to reveal what the delegates to that Pan-American gathering did have in mind, it does at least show that they did not want Pan-America to be understood as a separate political entity, acting through corporate agencies of its own. In other words, the refusal to grant the exercise of political functions to the Pan-American Union meant the rejection of a truly regionalistic conception of Pan-Americanism.

In fact, the Pan-American agencies do not fundamentally differ from the old-style agencies of international intercourse. The elaboration of institutions and procedures of what has been called international government which culminated in the establishment of the League of Nations, the International Labor Organization, and the Permanent Court of International Justice was greatly furthered by the initiative and support of American states. Yet no such institutions of inter-American government were set up in the Western world.

To be sure, arbitration and conciliation, as means of amicably settling international conflicts, were suggested and adopted in the Western Hemisphere, too. As a matter of fact, arbitration figured on the agenda of the First International Conference of American States, convening at Washington in 1889, ten years before the First Hague Conference. It is no accident, however, that arbitration was then and afterwards recommended most strongly by Argentina, the very same state which was, then and afterwards, most emphatically opposed to any collective system on the American continent. The Argentine delegation left no doubt that the arbitration scheme, submitted to the Washington conference, did not aim at establishing an amphictyonic council or American confederation. Far from proclaiming the indivisibility of peace in the Western world, Argentina rather wanted to emphasize the bilateral character of inter-American relations.

Nor does the actual inter-American peace machinery for the settlement of international disputes show any trait of a collective system. The several treaties and conventions concluded in the twenties of the present century—such as the Gonda Treaty of 1923, the General Convention of Inter-American Conciliation of 1929, and the General Treaty of Inter-American

Arbitration of the same year—do not provide for corporate agencies, representing the American community of nations as a whole; they stick to the principle of party representation on the various boards of adjudication. Only the legal basis of the American peace machinery is *Pan*-American, but the system as such is of a predominantly bilateral nature.

Even more indicative of the basically individualistic conception prevailing in the Pan-American movement is the character of the Pan-American institutions proper. They are diplomatic agencies of essentially the same type as the normal diplomatic agencies of the family of nations. The Pan-American organization has been called an American League of Nations minus the political functions of the League. The difference of scope would be considerable enough, indeed, but this is not all. For, even within the fields which both organizations are equally competent to cover, the status of their respective organs and the mode of their collective action are far from being identical.

This is more obvious in the case of the Governing Board of the Pan-American Union and the League of Nations Council than in that of the International Conference of American States and the League of Nations Assembly. The jurisdiction of the League of Nations Council is to a certain extent concurrent with that of the Assembly, whereas the Pan-American Union and its Governing Board are merely the executive agencies of the Pan-American Conference. However, the truly revolutionary feature of the Geneva Council was its hegemonic structure, for the permanent seats on the Council were assigned only to the great powers. But equality is the very corner-stone of the Pan-American edifice. Each American republic accordingly enjoys, as of right, equal representation both at the Conferences and on the Governing Board of the Pan-American Union. That the Governing Board is practically identical with the diplomatic corps representing the American republics at Washington fits into this picture. As late as in 1923, a proposal suggesting the establishment of the Governing Board of the Pan-American Union as a separate organization composed of representatives other than the regularly accredited diplomatic agents of the American states in Washington failed to win the unanimous approval of the Fifth Pan-American Conference. Since 1928, however, it has been left to the discretion of the several member states whether they should be represented on the Governing Board of the Pan-American Union in the traditional way, or by special delegates appointed *ad hoc*.

One may wonder whether the League of Nations should be referred to at all as an example of international government. As the League was essentially a legal device for coordinating, by means of some permanent agencies, those actions upon which the member states had *voluntarily* agreed in a concrete case, it might be more exact to characterize the League as a specific form of international cooperation. How much, or how little, this has actually meant, we know from bitter experience. At any rate, the American nations did not go even that far in adjusting their instruments for joint continental action, although this action was supposed to be restricted to nonpolitical matters.

The comparison of these two systems, the Pan-American and the League of Nations, is all the more illuminating as the majority of the American republics were at the same time members of both organizations. Though the League Covenant hardly touched the sovereign status of the member states, the American republics refused to concede to the Western Hemisphere organization the few rights which they had recognized as belonging to the League. As far as they consented to a collective system at all, they were champions of universality rather than of regionalism.

The disappearance of the League of Nations from the scene of world politics could not fail to bring into full relief such faint collective traits as may be distinguished in the Pan-American setup. Where there are no mountains, hills dominate the landscape. But, despite the perspective, they remain hills. Nevertheless, Pan-American organization has, in the last fateful years, grown in breadth and depth on its own account. The very same events which brought about the disintegration of a League aiming at universality have strengthened the forces making for a closer integration of the Western World. Pan-Americanism enters into a new phase of its history.

When the Inter-American Conference for the Maintenance of Peace met at Buenos Aires in December, 1936, the trend towards a regional orientation of Pan-American policy was not yet strong enough to carry the day. Argentina had made it clear from the outset that she would be unconditionally opposed to any regional distinctions or separation of continents. A Brazilian project, aiming at establishing a united front of the American republics against the interposition of a non-American power in any American country, was therefore watered down to the colorless "Convention for the Maintenance, Preservation, and Reestablishment of Peace," which timidly refrained from specifying geographically the very menace to the peace of the American states it was intended to check. However, the fact that the discussion at the Buenos Aires conference centered on the respective merits and faults of the principle of regionalism as against the principle of universality revealed the fresh impetus given to the Pan-American idea by the latest international developments. Under their impact, the conference also adopted the principle of consultation, to be applied by the several American republics in case of threatening or actual war, though it neglected to provide for procedural rules. Even so, the decision was an important step in the direction of a regional organization, since it meant the first departure from the bilateral pattern of the inter-American peace machinery, hitherto strictly adhered to. The conference thus practically subscribed to the indivisibility of peace in the Western Hemisphere.

The controversy over universalism or regionalism was soon to be settled, by further international events, in favor of the regional conception. For the Eighth International Conference of American States, held at Lima in December, 1938, the necessity of regional distinctions was a foregone conclusion. To be sure, the separation of the Western Hemisphere from the other continents has never been understood by any of the American republics in an absolute sense. "It cannot be fairly said," remarked Secretary Hull at the Lima Conference, "that we are trying to shut ourselves off in a hemisphere of our own; any such effort would be futile." And as late as July, 1940, the American nations, through the mouths of their foreign secretaries assembled at Havana, solemnly declared that, faithful to their ideals, they would coordinate their own interests with the duties of universal cooperation. Thus Western Hemisphere regionalism as it has evolved in late years is an open, not a closed regionalism.

The Declaration of Lima definitely establishes the indivisibility of peace in the New World by proclaiming that any threat—by acts of any nature—directed at the peace, security, or territorial integrity of any American republic is to be the common concern of the American nations. It also specifically refers to foreign intervention or activity that may threaten the principles upon which continental solidarity is based and pledges the American nations to defend those principles, thus recognizing the twenty-one American republics as a distinct political unit. The Monroe Doctrine has finally become continentalized. "The unilateral assertion by the United States of the necessity of protecting the Western Hemisphere against aggression from abroad is now the declaration of the Hemisphere itself."[1]

To make continental solidarity effective, the Lima Conference undertook to institutionalize consultation, though in a rather tentative way. Rejecting the farther-reaching suggestion of the delegation of Chile to create a permanent organ of consultation, the conference decided that the Ministers for Foreign Affairs of the American Republics should meet, at the initiative of any one of them, in their several capitals in rotation, and without protocolary character, whenever consultation among them was deemed desirable. At the same time the conference extended the procedure of consultation from purely political matters to any economic, cultural, or other question in the examination or solution of which the American states have a common interest.

The outbreak of what was then called "the European war" necessitated the calling of the first consultative meeting of the foreign ministers. Both the meeting at Panama, held in the fall of 1939, and the second consultative meeting of the foreign ministers, which convened at Havana in July, 1940, shortly after the collapse of France, specified the tasks of continental cooperation and improved the machinery for carrying them out.

The "Declaration of Panama," establishing a safety-belt around the American continent to be kept free of belligerent activities, has not met with conspicuous success. Its significance lies rather in that it supplied the legal basis, somewhat ambiguous though it is, for the first collective action of the twenty-one American republics, bearing upon rights and interests of third powers outside the Western Hemisphere. In accordance with one of the provisions of the declaration, the signatory states made joint representations to the European powers that had been involved in the *Graf Spee* incident off the harbor of Montevideo. Similarly, the Declaration of Neutrality, likewise agreed upon at Panama, must be considered not so much an event-shaping act of policy as an expression of regional solidarity.

Moreover, the Panama conference made great and partly successful efforts to adapt the Pan-American machinery to the growing needs of hemisphere policy. Both the Inter-American Financial and Economic Advisory Committee and the Inter-American Neutrality Committee owe their existence to the meeting of 1939. The latter committee, though less important in a practical sense than the former, is a new type of continental agency in that it consists of only seven members, who represent not their respective states, but the whole body of the American republics. However, the sole function of the committee is to study and formulate recommendations concerning the problems of neutrality.

The Foreign Ministers, assembled at Havana in July, 1940, reiterated the pledge of the American nations to reciprocal assistance and coooperation for the defense of their territory, sovereignty, and political independence, and resolved to expand the scope of the financial and economic cooperation which had been agreed upon the year before at Panama. However, the regional trend culminated in the Act of Havana, which continentalizes the principle of non-recognition of the transfer of territory from one to another non-American power, a tenet until then supported rather precariously by the Monroe Doctrine alone. The Act provides for the establishment of an Emergency Committee, charging it with the provisional adminstration of any island or region, located in the Americas, which is in danger of becoming the subject of a territorial barter or change of sovereignty among non-American states. The committee is composed of one representative of each of the American republics, but is to be deemed constituted and entitled to act on behalf of all of them as soon as two-thirds of its members shall have been appointed by the respective governments. If action by the committee cannot be taken promptly enough, any of the American republics, singly or jointly with others, is given the right to act in the manner which its own defense or that of the continent requires. The other states, on their side, are bound to acquiesce in these measures, provided they consider the need for emergency action to be sufficiently urgent. The convention, supplementing the Act of Havana, also formally vests "the American Republics, as an international community which acts strongly and integrally," with the "international juridical capacity" to take any such island or region under their provisional administration and to deliberate as to its destiny.

In short, the Western Hemisphere has at last received legal recognition as a separate political entity, acting through corporate agencies of its own.

The study of the legal record of Pan-Americanism, as it has developed during late years, clearly confirms the slowly but continuously growing force of a truly regionalistic conception, the absence of which was so conspicuous in the earlier history of the Pan-American movement. But one cannot yet speak of more than a trend towards regionalism, and must accordingly beware of overrating the effectiveness of the present system To be sure, the peace and security of the American continent and of any of the American republics have been repeatedly proclaimed to be the common concern of all and each of them; nevertheless, it has always been understood "that the governments of the American republics will act independently in their individual capacity, recognizing fully their juridical equality as sovereign states," to use the phrase with which the Declaration of Lima qualifies the coordination of the "sovereign" wills of the American republics by means of the procedure of consultation. In other words, the final decision as to whether the *casus foederis* has arisen under the concrete circumstances, and the measures to be taken if peace and security are considered threatened, is left to the discretion of the several American republics.

The regionalistic trend was strong enough to make the American states subscribe to the principles of a continental system. But so far it has not been strong enough to cause them to accept an *effective* continental system. To render such a system effective, the individual states would have to be ready in certain cases to renounce the *exercise* of rights inherently theirs as sovereign subjects of international law; moreover, they must be prepared to acknowledge that this surrender is made in order to preserve their *status* as sovereign nations, realizing that those rights would become imaginary if the international order guaranteeing them should collapse. Instead, the Declaration of Lima and other instruments of Pan-American solidarity proclaim the equal sovereignty of the signatory states not only as the goal of their continental policy, but also as the means of attaining it.

The language of those instruments whose stipulations in part clearly neutralize one another proves that they are the product of conflicting tendencies, painfully covered up by subtle formulas of diplomatic compromise. This accounts also for the fact that the regionalistic principles are laid down in "resolutions" and "declarations," to say nothing of the many reservations qualifying the agremeents concluded. Only the provisional administration of European colonies and possessions in the Americas was made the subject of a "convention" which is intended to supplement the Act of Havana. This convention, however, has been ratified by no more than three of the twenty-one signatory states: Costa Rica, the United States of America, and the Dominican Republic.

Thus, the legal record shows that while the strictly regionalistic conception of Pan-Americanism is in the ascendant, it is still counteracted by antagonistic tendencies powerful enough to emasculate the covenants entered into. However, if we want to appraise correctly the strength of forces and counter-forces, we cannot rest content with an analysis of legal documents. The mere fact that the American republics have so far subscribed in principle to reciprocal assistance and cooperation, but have refused to renounce in advance the right of interpreting for themselves the extent of their obligation, does not necessarily mean that they would not join in undertaking concerted action if the need arose. It is altogether possible that political and moral bonds might prove closer and more effective than the legal ties alone would indicate, as the example of the British Commonwealth of Nations suggests.

Collective policy means sharing responsibilities in order to further common interests. It was a long time before the American republics, including the United States, were ready to recognize, even in theory, the mutual responsibilities involved in continental policy.

So much has been said and written about the abuse of the Monroe Doctrine, and comparatively so little about how much the Latin American nations have benefited by it that misconceptions have arisen. Thus the agreements of Montevideo (1933) and Buenos Aires (1936), pledging the contracting parties, including the United States, not to intervene, directly or indirectly, and for whatever reason, in the internal or external affairs of any other of the parties, were hailed as the end of the Monroe Doctrine. Indeed, the Latin American republics had come in the course of time to see only the negative and to overlook the positive aspect of that Doctrine. In reality, however, the good neighbor policy is not so much the abandonment on the part of the United States of the principles of the Monroe Doctrine as a recognition of them, on a reciprocal basis, by the Latin American nations.

The Roosevelt corollaries of 1904–1905 made the Monroe Doctrine an instrument for the exercise by the United States of international police power in Latin America. This happened at a time when the doctrine seemed to have definitely lost its original function of shielding the Americas against any European inerference which might threaten the political *status quo* on this continent. When Argentina was asked in 1862 to join a confederation of South American states, then under discussion among some of them, her foreign minister politely answered that he could not see any reason for such a union. Though he conceded that a serious threat to the independence of the South American republics could come from a European League directed against the Americas, he was sure that such a League could hardly crystallize. Plausibly enough, this feeling of security was not shared by the less powerful sister republics, at a moment when Spanish, French, and English troops stood on Mexican soil. Shortly afterwards, Peru also found herself involved in a war with Spain. But before the nineteenth century came to its peaceful end, practically all Latin American republics had formed the conviction that their political existence was no longer seriously menaced by European powers. Instead the shadow of real, disquieting danger seemed to be cast by the "Colossus of the North."

Yet, when President Monroe delivered his famous message of December 2, 1823, he was glorified by an Argentine as a crusader who had pulled out his sword, stood in the middle of the bridge, called the Holy Alliance to a halt, and set free the Latin American nations.[2] Even less rhetorically and more critically minded citizens of the newly established republics were ready to admit that the policy of the United States of America, embodied in the Monroe Docrine, had aided them greatly—first to gain and then to preserve their political independence. The only fault they found was the fact that the United States did not consider the Monroe Doctrine a pledge.

As early as 1824 the Colombian Minister to Washington inquired of President Monroe what help could be expected from the United States if France should make war upon his country. A few months later the Brazilian Chargé d'Affaires proposed on behalf of his government that the United States should enter into an alliance with Brazil to maintain its independence in case Portugal should be assisted by any foreign power to reestablish her former rule. In 1826 Mexico called upon the United States to fulfill the "memorable pledge" of President Monroe and assist her in fending off the threat of French interference. Two years later it was the Argentine government which anxiously sounded out the scope of the doctrine. Then and later when similar inquiries came from the Southern republics, the United States made it emphatically and consistently clear that, while the declaration was an act of the chief executive of the United States and there was every reason to believe it was in accord with public and congressional opinion, it "must be regarded as having been voluntarily made, and not conveying any pledge or obligation, the performance of which foreign nations have a right to demand."[3]

Nor was the United States any more ready to accept the responsibility read into the Monroe Doctrine by the Latin American sister republics after she had begun to arrogate to herself under its terms the right of policing the continent. "The Monroe Doctrine," said President Wilson in 1916, at the very moment when he enlarged its scope further by his doctrine of Constitutionalism, "was proclaimed by the United States on her own authority. It always has been maintained, and always will be maintained, upon her own responsibility."[4] Similarly the United States delegation to the Fifth International Conference of American States (1923) emphasized, when rejecting a proposal of Uruguay to establish an American League of Nations, that the Monroe Doctrine was a unilateral declaration, implying no obligation whatsoever on the part of the United States.

The persistency with which the United States refused to pledge herself to undertakings to which the Monroe Doctrine was intended to supply the title would have been less confusing and embarrassing for the Latin Americans if such an attitude could have been interpreted as a simple aversion to the legalization of an otherwise fixed policy. That would not have been hard to understand. However, the refusal to enter into any engagements with the Latin American states had to be looked upon in the light of the other maxim of American foreign policy, "to steer clear of permanent alliances," a maxim which, in the long run, can but frustrate a consistently regional policy. To be sure, Washington referred in his Farewell Address exclusively to alliances "with any portion of the *foreign* world," by which he clearly meant Europe. But in terms of public opinion, Washington's continentally qualified isolationism soon became total isolationism.

If the comparatively weak Latin American countries, under the lulling influence of long-continued peace, eventually arrived at the belief that they had achieved security, it is not surprising that the United States, potentially so much more powerful than her sister republics, should be prone to forget what the founding fathers had fully realized, namely, that liberty and safety have to be paid for by the constant readiness to fight for them. Jefferson and Madison, when consulted by Monroe before he delivered the message which he knew would shape the future of America, spurred him to action, though they were fully aware that such a challenge to the continental powers of Europe might lead to war. But Congress, in whose hands rest the measures necessary to enforce the Doctrine, proved reluctant to sustain it from the very beginning. Thus it refused to act upon a resolution affirming its principles, introduced at the same session in which Monroe delivered his message. Nor was time to change the attitude of the legislative body toward the Monroe Doctrine.[5] As late as 1935, when Congress passed the first Neutrality Resolution, it ordered the embargo on arms, munitions, and loans to be applied in all wars alike, regardless of whether they were waged solely among non-American powers or among non-American and American powers. Total isolationism triumphed once more over continental solidarity, though only for a short while.

The foreign policies of the Latin American states are likewise characterized by tendencies that conflict frequently, sometimes to the point of irreconcilability. But whereas a consistently regional policy of the United States is thwarted by her fundamentally isolationist leanings, the regionalism of the Latin American republics is tempered by their basically universalistic outlook. The two elements of Latin American policy do not exist in the same ratio in all countries or at all times, but they do continuously act upon and counteract each other. Certainly it was no accident that the United States, after having initiated the League of Nations, finally refused to join in, nor that the Latin American nations did become members of that supposedly universal organization—not failing, however, to display their regional solidarity at Geneva. The Latin American universalism is conditioned by many factors, not the least important of which is the determination of the Latin American republics to counterpoise the "Colossus of the North" by holding the door to Europe wide open. Cultural traditions and economic considerations no doubt play a role, but so do occasional blunders committed by the United States in her dealings with her neighbors. However, far more than these factors combined, it is the political structure of the Americas which makes the Latin American nations so reluctant to follow a strictly regional line. Rather than admit the existing inequality among the members, they prefer not to organize the American family of nations at all.

But it is not the preponderance of the United States alone which blocks the road to the establishment of a closer continental organization, based on the principle of cooperation. For the political weight of the several Latin American nations themselves runs the whole gamut—from the great powers through the middle states and down to the small nations. In the light of European experience, the results of this political structure should cause no surprise. Lord Bryce appropriately compared the relationship among the South American states to the former European balance-of-power system, in which there were several great powers playing the "great game" with and against one another, and with and against the smaller powers.[6] It is in accordance with the rules of this game that Argentina is the champion of bilateral relations among American states, and Uruguay the advocate of comprehensive continental schemes.

The structural factor likewise explains why the idea of a Latin American confederation, sometimes coupled with an all-comprehensive Pan-American system, but sometimes opposed to it, has failed to materialize. Although conceived at the beginning of the free political existence of the Latin American nations and supported by the moral authority of Simon Bolivar, the idea never took tangible form. As a matter of fact, the Congress of Panama, which Bolivar called in 1826—an event so often described in lyrical tones—foreshadowed the later rivalries among the Latin American nations rather than a policy of brotherly solidarity.

Thus the historical as well as the legal record would serve as a warning that, even if we take due account of the achievements of the recent years, the willingness of the members of the American community of nations to share the responsibilities of a collective policy should not be over-rated.

The difficulty of coordinating the actions of the several American republics and of molding these nations into a political unit will be recognized as perfectly natural if we reflect upon the diversity of conditions and interests which shape the course of policy in the different countries and which have to be considered and reconciled with each other in pursuing a continental policy. Pan-Americanism, as we know it from the past and as it is understood today, stands for the democratic organization of the Western Hemisphere; it stands for cooperation. In other words, the emphasis is upon consent rather than upon force. But the consent of the members, be it of a national or international community, can be obtained only if the body politic has some coherence. National as well as international democracy, to be a working system, requires common ideas and interests.

It has been the fundamental fallacy of organizational pacifism not to realize this prerequisite of a working international government, based on democratic principles. Thinking in terms of an ill-founded analogy between international and municipal law, the pacifists came to the conclusion that the establishment of institutions as such, if they were only shaped upon the pattern of the democratic state institutions, would secure perpetual peace. As an excuse for this fatal delusion the argument may be advanced that this kind of Utopian thinking is in no way restricted to the international field. Modern man is no longer willing to see that basically it is not so much the institutions as the complexity of things which accounts for the faultiness of the political and social order. However that may be, it is obvious that modern international society is much less of an integrated whole than the modern state, and that the forces of disintegration in the international community cannot be sufficiently checked or balanced by the setting up of democratic international machinery.[7]

The few Pan-American institutions which did actually come into being grew in a more organic way. The Pan-American movement should therefore be given credit for making no pretensions to a unity not yet really achieved.

Nothing bears out the dubious character of Western Hemisphere unity more clearly than the fact that not even the geography from which the political conception borrowed its name confirms the basic assumptions of Pan-American philosophy. It is no accident that America is the only continent to which scientific and colloquial language refers in the dual and plural rather than in the singular. The saying has become familiar that both North and South America look toward Europe, and away from each other. On no continent except America are the physical barriers which separate the different regions of such a nature as to render any plan for overland communication virtually impossible or, if ever attained, quite useless. To be sure, the airplane has reduced the size of the continent, but it has reduced the size of the globe at the same time. Geographical proximity has thus kept its relative meaning, and is still not concerned with imaginary continental frontiers. In drawing conclusions from these geographical factors for the specific defense problems of a Western Hemisphere "unit," Professor Staley is therefore right when he declares that what is called continental solidarity is essentially maritime solidarity.[8]

Among the geographical conditions which influence the nature of human society, climate plays the most important part. One need not subscribe to the climatic explanation of history to realize that the diversity of climatic conditions has not furthered political uniformity among the American republics, but has, on the contrary, contributed to political discord on the continent. But even where climatic conditions are more or less equal, as in the temperate zones of North and South America, they have been an element of disintegration. For under the same climate the same agrarian products are usually grown, a factor which hampers the economic integration of the continent.

While the political aspect of the strictly regionalistic conception of Pan-Americanism has found at least some organizational expression, in the field of economics the formation of a Pan-American customs union is still as remote as it was in 1889 when the first International Conference of American States discussed and rejected the idea. The principles of universalism and bilateralism still sway the commercial policy of the American republics, both in their relations with non-American states and among themselves. Whatever tendency there may be toward more closely knit economic arrangements, so far it has been restricted in scope to the sub-regions of the American continent, as demonstrated by the deliberations and decisions of the La Plata Conference in February, 1941.

Though it is true that the balance of economic forces can be considerably modified by human action, there are definite limits to the effectiveness of economic voluntarism. This is not the place to discuss the technical merits and faults of the several devices which were recently suggested for increasing hemispheric self-sufficiency by integrating the national economies of the several American republics into a harmonious whole.[6] But, in this

113

connection, a warning should be given against the fallacious view that the coordination of widely divergent economic structures is a purely economic task to be solved by purely economic means. The Havana Conference of 1940 proposed to the American nations "immediate measures and arrangements of mutual benefit tending to increase trade among them without injury to the interests of their respective producers." But it is obvious that the practical impossibility of integrating the economic system of a vast continent without injuring interests which are particular but none the less powerful, makes such a task an eminently political one, to be solved only by the actions of a closely integrated political body. No attempt to establish close economic units has ever succeeded where and when the political stimulus was lacking. That record of failure clearly bears out the fact that the *direct* integration of divergent national economies is a futile hope.

Given the problematic character of America's geographical unity and the lack of economic coherence, neither the rhetoric nor the actual force of the Pan-American movement would be understandable if it were not for the common history of the American republics. National character has been called "frozen history." In the same way the Pan-American spirit could be called frozen history, the history of the political emancipation of this continent from Europe.

It is this common historical experience that works as a unifying factor rather than the legendary spiritual unity often conjured up on solemn occasions. The spiritual partnership of which Wilson once spoke is, after all, not really closer than the spiritual partnership of the ever-quarreling European nations. For that matter, the Central and South American nations can no more disclaim their spiritual link with the Spanish and Catholic world than the United States can disown her Anglo-Saxon and Protestant tradition. These two streams of European origin have left the marks of their different cultural conceptions wherever they touched. Moreover, these differences did not disappear under the influence of colonial life, and also managed to hold their own against the later influx of the ideas of the Enlightenment and the French Revolution. Even where the fruits of the process of secularization have grown ripe, they still have the flavor of the old sap.

It would be surprising, indeed, if these cultural conceptions had not also shaped the political ideas and political institutions. True, there have been special factors operative in the several American states which have given them their peculiar political form, but the dividing line between the two types of political systems existing on this continent runs along the cultural watershed.

Whatever the cause, the dualism of form as such is an indisputable fact. The Latin American countries are the *locus classicus* of dictatorship rather than of democracy as it is understood in the United States and as it once was understood also in Europe. To be sure, Latin American dictatorships do not altogether correspond to the totalitarian pattern which characterizes the European dictatorships of today. The regime of a Francia is the exception, not the rule. The normal Latin American dictatorship is—or at least has been so far—a technique of government, but not a social system which merges private and public sphere. Even so, the co-existence of two different governmental systems is bound to render inter-American cooperation more difficult. It is up to the citizens of the North American democracy to exercise great care and avoid giving offense either by expressing complacency over their own political regime or disdain for the political system of other countries. After all, democratic machinery cannot be expected to work equally well under all conditions and, even where it does run smoothly, some price has to be paid for it. Besides, what counts ultimately is the values for which a political system is being operated. That is more important than the way of operating it—although this does not, of course, suggest that every means is justified. The many asseverations of adherence to the ideals of democracy which recur time and again in Pan-American declarations are, therefore, not necessarily mere lip-homage to principles disowned in political workaday life.

But it must be borne in mind that the duality of the governmental systems coexisting in the Western Hemisphere has become strongly felt only very recently. When Monroe, in his historic message, rejected any attempt by the European powers to extend their political system to any portion of this hemisphere, he could point to the Old and the New Worlds as the antagonistic exemplars of his time: republic and monarchy. The republican form then blanketed whatever political variations there may have been among the newly established states. Seventy-two years later, Secretary of State Olney, in his famous discussion of the Monroe Doctrine, was still able to refer to the monarchical and republican principles as the basic and "irreconcilably diverse" characteristics of the European and the American systems.[10] The Latin American nations have likewise always seen their emancipation from the old continent as the victory of the republican symbols. The common history of the Americas has been a republican history.

Since that era, however, the struggle between republic and monarchy has spent its fervor, and the world has become divided into democracies and dictatorships, the two systems into which the American continent itself seems to be split up. Does this mean that the common history of the Americas has also come to its end?

If it were only the republican idea that linked the American nations together, their historical partnership might be doomed indeed. But the community of ideas and interests which has been the foundation of this

115

partnershp reaches deeper and farther than that, though the American nations were not—and could not be—conscious of it to the same degree in all periods of their common history. In the last analysis, what unites the American nations is their mutual stake in the maintenance of the European balance of power. To that source, they owe their national independence as well as the non-military character of their political institutions. To sum up a paradoxical situation in paradoxical terms: the American nations have their common stake in that continent, detachment from which they consider to be the very essence of their national and their hemispheric history. And so colonial nations, anxious though they are to look only towards the future, have to pay their tribute to the past, with which men and women alike are indissolubly bound.

Canning's dictum—that he called into existence a New World in the West in order to redress the balance of power in Europe—reveals why England believed it to be to her advantage to act as the godmother of the Latin American republics and of the Monroe Doctrine alike. But it also throws light upon the conditions under which the Southern republics could dare to proclaim their independence and the North to assume their guardianship. "If we can effect a division in the body of the European powers, and draw over to our side its most powerful member, surely we should do it," Jefferson advised President Monroe in the correspondence already mentioned. It could not be stated more clearly that, whatever reasons England might have to lend her support to the New World, the United States was no less interested in restoring and maintaining a balance of power in Europe which would assure the existence of that nation with which "we should most sedulously cherish a cordial friendship." For, said Jefferson, "Great Britain is the nation which can do us the most harm of any one, or all on earth; and with her on our side we need not fear the whole world."[11] Such an expression of the vital interest of the United States in the traditional structure of the European system of states had already been contained in Washington's Farewell Address, where it was perhaps least to be expected, with its emphasis upon the thesis of the remoteness and separateness of European and American concerns. But statesmen, unlike ideologists, cannot indulge in a refusal to qualify the principles they proclaim. Pointing to Europe, Washington warned Americans not to implicate themselves "by artificial ties in the *ordinary* vicissitudes of her politics or the *ordinary* combinations and collisions of her friendships or enmities."[12]

As an American statesman observed thirty years later, Canning had somewhat overrated the extent of the dislocation of the Old World, and his

American contemporaries had made the same error. The real or imaginary dangers threatening the New World, however, gave the first impetus to the idea of continental solidarity and led to Monroe's declaration as well as to several attempts at establishing a Latin American confederation. But with the disintegration of the Holy Alliance, which had set out to unify Europe and her colonial possessions on the basis of monarchical principles, American statesmen were freed from the nightmare of a European League interfering in the life of the new continent. At the same time, the endeavors to unite all or some of the American states came to a standstill, to be revived again only briefly when the shadow of Napoleon III fell upon the American scene. The Western Hemisphere began to feel itself, in the words of Secretary Olney, "practically invulnerable as against any or all other powers." That a closely integrated Europe should interfere with American affairs did not seem any more conceivable. And as this happy situation continued, there was a steady dwindling of the consciousness that the maintenance of such a condition depended upon the existence of a European constellation of powers which did not jeopardize the naval supremacy of Great Britain, the guardian of the Atlantic sea-lanes connecting the European and the American shores.

Both in national and international politics the foundations upon which society rests are remembered only in times of crisis. Such a crisis, threatening to shake the foundations of the political structure of the Western Hemisphere, approached when the First World War broke out. If the threat did not materialize, it was solely because of the intervention of the United States, which prevented the establishment on the European continent of a hegemonic system which would at least have matched, if not surpassed, the power of England. Wilson acted as Washington and Jefferson would have acted. One may speculate on what the Latin American nations would have finally done if the German menace had grown more serious than it actually did at that time. Aside from Brazil, which associated herself with the Allied Powers as a belligerent, only the Central American republics, swayed by the influence of the United States, went to war. Some other Latin American republics adopted a policy of benevolent neutrality or non-belligerency, both in favor of the Allies. But such powerful and important members of the American family of nations as Mexico, Argentina, and Chile stuck to the classical concept of absolute neutrality. Pan-American solidarity expressed itself in words rather than in deeds.

Not Wilhelm II but Hitler was to make the whole continent realize the German menace and thus give to the Pan-American idea a new stimulus. Though it is true that the regionalistic policy of recent years was initiated and has been most strongly pushed by the United States, the Latin American republics gladly fell in with a course from which they could derive nothing but gain; for they could no longer remain blind to the dangerous implications of European events. Whether they like it or not, the American nations find themselves thrown back to the common origin of their political existence. Frozen history has been reliquefied into political actuality, the only difference being that the present menace is more real and potent than the menace of the days when the ghost of the Holy Alliance seemed to loom on the Eastern horizon.

Even though historians are still debating the question of how seriously the Holy Alliance ever considered engaging in an American adventure, the outcome of such an attempt can hardly be open to speculation. Its chances of success would have become almost nil after England had thrown the weight of her navy on the side of the New World. Hitler might turn toward the West if, as, and when he defeats Great Britain. But can he be assured to have such a sinister aim as the conquest of the Americas?

To speak the political language of the nations which are to be the victims of his policy is part and parcel of Hitler's technique of conquest. Goebbels accordingly implores the Latin American nations to remain forever faithful to the ties connecting them with the old continent, simultaneously beseeching the English Americans to forget all about that rotten world. He talks universalism in the South, and isolationism in the North. The Monroe Doctrine, he tells us, will no longer be a purely American policy, but a globe-wide program, the very basis of the new, brave world, organized along strictly continental lines. Actually, of course, Hitler is not striving for the balance of autonomous continents, but for *Weltherrschaft*. Even if we did not have the testimony of Rauschning and other equally reliable corroborations of Hitler's true intentions towards the Western Hemisphere, we could be sure that the great technician of power in Berchtesgaden knows about the interrelationship of continents in the small world of today. In the arsenal of Hitler's conquest of the world, "continentalism" is what bilateralism was in his conquest of Europe: the diplomatic and propagandistic preparation for the military pincer movement.

There is a saying that a political system can be best maintained by the same means through which it was established. If the American nations want to weather the storm which is rapidly gathering about them, they will have to grasp anew the truth in this maxim and return to the principles they announced and applied when they challenged the Old World and set themselves free. What are the chances that they will pursue such a course?

If we could be only sure that men and nations act in accordance with their long-range interests, we should not have to worry about the freedom of the

Americas. But since human nature is what we have seen it to be, the prospects are not too reassuring. Nor can we rely too much upon the assumption that common danger will unite by suppressing other passions. The dismal fate of European nations, all members of the League of Nations, but each taking its single turn to fall prey to Hitler's conquest, scarcely furnishes encouraging evidence. When neither future events nor the human reactions to them are to be foreseen, prophecies are out of order. The only thing we can do is try to strike a balance between the forces which make for harmony and the elements which make for discord among the members of the American community of nations.

The crux of inter-American relations is the political structure of the continent. The size of her population and the wealth of her economic resources assure to the United States a natural hegemony. If she abuses her privileged position, Pan-American unity is threatened from within. If she does not turn it to account, Pan-American unity may be destroyed from without. To steer a course between abuse and non-use of the political possibilities which are open to the United States because of her hegemonic position is one of the most difficult tasks American statesmanship has to face. Therefore, occasional departures from this course should not arouse surprise. But, in view of the present grave circumstances, is it possible to commit such errors without doing irreparable harm?

Since the good neighbor policy of forswearing any intervention in the internal or external affairs of any other of the American nations was inaugurated, the chance of a deviation toward a continental *laissez-faire* policy is somewhat more likely than overzeal in policing the hemisphere.[13] Given such a possibility, the Latin American republics would be ill-advised if they were to demand too circumspect a policy on the part of the United States at a moment when the world order upon which their sovereign existence depends is threatened by greater dangers than ever before in their history. An emergency situation can be mastered only by emergency measures. If that truism is acknowledged—and who will deny it?—let us not make the mistake of failing to realize with equal clarity that leadership, to be accepted and followed, has to be firm and unconditional.

So far it has been the lot of Pan-Americanism to thrive only in times of crisis—so much so that one may wonder what would happen to it if the world should return to the state of affairs prevailing in the nineteenth century and up to recent years. For, if the freedom of the European continent and the British Isles should be maintained, the American nations might be inclined again to believe that there is no necessity for organizing themselves into a more closely knit political unit. But there is some substantial ground for the hope that they will in the future remain more conscious than in the past of the interplay of forces on this and the other side of the Atlantic.

In any case, continental regionalism, and particularly Pan-American continentalism, is definitely doomed if Germany defeats England. Hitler does not seek a mere partition of the world among equal powers—neither along continental nor any other lines. Total and universal domination is Hitler's goal.

FOOTNOTES

[1]Charles G. Fenwick, "The Monroe Doctrine and the Declaration of Lima," *American Journal of International Law* (April 1939), p. 266.

[2]See Gaston Nerval, *Autopsy of the Monroe Doctrine* (1934), p. 46.

[3]Instruction sent by Secretary of State Clay to the American Chargé d'Affaires at Buenos Aires in 1828. See J. R. Clark, *Memorandum on the Monroe Doctrine* (1930), pp. 107 ff., 182 ff.

[4]*Ibid.*, p. 178.

[5]Clark, *op. cit.*, pp. 132 ff., 182 ff.

[6]James Bryce, *South America, Observations and Impressions* (1914), p. 503.

[7]The case against organizational pactificism has been most admirably stated in an otherwise somewhat disputable book by E. H. Carr, *The Twenty Years' Crisis, 1919–1939: An Introduction to the Study of International Relations* (1940), pp. 219 ff.

[8]Eugene Staley, "The Myth of the Continents," *Foreign Affairs* (April 1941), p. 487.

[9]For this problem compare Henry P. Jordan, "Hemisphere Policy as Implemented by Economics," in *Problems of Post-War Reconstruction.*

[10]Clark, *op. cit.*, p. 158.

[11]Clark, *op. cit.*, p. 97 ff.

[12]*Ibid.*, p. 15.

[13]For the legal implications of that policy see Fenwick, *loc. cit.*

III(B)

FROM THE
LEAGUE OF NATIONS
TO THE
UNITED NATIONS

THE DUMBARTON OAKS
PROPOSALS*

The Dumbarton Oaks proposals for the establishment of a general international organization are not yet the definite charter of the future world organization. In strictly legal terms they are a tentative agreement between the United States, Great Britain, Russia and China which lays the foundations of the future organization. Preparation of its final charter is the task of the conference at San Francisco, convened for April 25th, of representatives of all the United Nations, small and large alike. It can be taken for granted that the structure that will ultimately emerge from the general conference will not in all details resemble the structure agreed upon by the four great powers at Dumbarton Oaks. The criticism of the scheme by the governments of the middle and small states will have to be met by somehow blunting its hegemonic edges.

It is less likely, however, that any such changes will affect the substance of the scheme so far agreed upon, and therefore the following analysis is based on the Dumbarton Oaks proposals in their original form. In this discussion I shall disregard the economic and social functions which those proposals assign to the future world organization, and shall confine myself to an analysis of political purposes and agencies.

I

Throughout human history periods of devastating wars have been productive of great designs, intended to redeem mankind once and for all from the curse of bloody, ruinous strife by devising a more just and more stable international order. We have seen a recurrence of this pathetic effort during the present worldwide struggle. Particularly in this country, an ever-

Reprinted with permission of *Social Research*, May 1945 (vol. 12, no.2).

widening stream of well-meaning projects for permanent peace began to pour forth shortly after the outbreak of the war. As was to be expected, most of them were too perfect to fit the stubborn realities of the world in which we live. If we hope to do justice to the Dumbarton Oaks proposals, we should therefore avoid measuring them by the standards of maximum schemes which testify to the laudable intentions of their authors rather than to their political awareness. The framers of the Dumbarton Oaks proposals had to face the imperious necessities of international politics, and deal with them on the level of actual circumstances.

We are fully justified, however, in comparing the Dumbarton Oaks plan with what are to all practical intents and purposes minimum schemes of international organization. Therefore in the following pages I shall repeatedly refer to two instruments of this kind, the Covenant of the League of Nations, and what can be called the American Design for a charter of the general international organization. As regards the latter, some words of explanation seem desirable. The American Design is not an official draft, in the sense that it would ever have been presented as such to the American public. It grew out of the deliberations of a private group of American and Canadian experts on international affairs which was constituted early in 1942 and arrived at a community of views late in 1943. The content of this agreement was revised in 1944 by a smaller group, consisting exclusively of Americans. Though the history of Dumbarton Oaks has not yet been written, we are on safe ground in assuming that this revised draft, published in August 1944, formed the basis of the suggestions which the American delegates submitted at Dumbarton Oaks to the British, Russian and Chinese colleagues. In wording as well as in structure the Dumbarton Oaks proposals closely resemble that American Design, though there are certain striking and very interesting differences between the two documents.

The Dumbarton Oaks organization is to be a comprehensive and permanent association of the nations of the world. Membership will be open to "all peaceloving states." Actually the original members will be the states represented at the San Francisco conference, but other states may be admitted later on. The Big Three have made it clear that at San Francisco only those states will qualify for original membership which were by March 1, 1945, at least formally participating in the present war on the side of the United Nations. This explains the recent rush into the ranks of the United Nations by states that had hitherto failed to declare war on the Axis powers. In fact, "The United Nations" is to be the very title of the organization set up at the San Francisco conference. Later admittance will have to be granted by the General Assembly upon recommendation of the Security Council.

It can be safely assumed that the present enemy countries will be admitted, if at all, only after a period of probation. The situation is somewhat more complex as regards the states that remain neutral throughout the present war. Russia's abstention from the International Air Conference at Chicago last December, and the official reasons given for it, forbode a reluctant attitude on the part of at least the Security Council to admit the neutral states without insisting on further conditions than proof of their peaceful intentions. Nor is it certain that the neutrals themselves will all be ready to join the organization, even if they are put under the pressure which the Dumbarton Oaks proposals envisage for such an eventuality. It may thus be some time before the organization develops into a truly universal association.

But from its first day it is to be a permanent organization, in the sense that voluntary withdrawal from it will not be legally permissible. Once a member of the organization, a state is bound to remain a member for good. The proposals empower the General Assembly, upon recommendation of the Security Council, to suspend a member from the exercise of any rights or privileges of membership, and even to expel it, but unlike the Covenant of the League of Nations they do not authorize any member to leave the organization at its own volition. This permanency of membership in the United Nations is a radical deviation from practically all precedents in the history of modern international organization. It is the more noteworthy as only the big powers are assured the right of absolute veto against constitutional amendments.

Also precedent-breaking are the broad powers assigned to the general international organization, or more precisely, to its Security Council. In regard to both the settlement of disputes and the prevention and repression of war, the powers of the Security Council far surpass the powers of the League of Nations organs, at least in relation to the minor members of the organization.

The wide range of powers is particularly conspicuous in the provisions on the pacific settlement of disputes. Unlike the League Covenant, the Dumbarton Oaks proposals stipulate an absolute prohibition of war. The charter is to bind all members to refrain in their international relations from the threat or use of force in any manner inconsistent with the purposes of the organization. Legally the threat or use of force is to be the monopoly of the organization. This absolute prohibition of individual wars means that all members are obliged to settle their disputes by peaceful means, in such a manner that international peace and security are not endangered. Member states are free only as to the methods by which they try to achieve the peaceful settlement.

If the parties to a dispute fail to settle it by "negotiation, mediation, conciliation, arbitration, or judicial settlement, or other peaceful means of their own choice," they are bound to refer it to the Security Council. If the

Council is of the opinion that "the continuance of the particular dispute is in fact likely to endanger the maintenance of international peace and security," it is empowered to settle the matter by its own decision. And the Security Council need not wait until a dispute is referred to it, for it is empowered to assume jurisdiction on its own initiative at any stage of a dispute. Under the League of Nations Covenant the parties to a dispute were not bound to accept the terms of settlement even if the latter were unanimously agreed upon by all members of the Council other than the disputants themselves. Under the Dumbarton Oaks plan the disputants are obliged to accept and carry out even a majority decision of the Security Council, though in relation to a great power the terms of settlement are not enforceable.

The political implications of these provisions will become fully clear only when we discuss the voting procedure. But even in the present context we should consider briefly what the Dumbarton Oaks proposals have to say about the rules and principles by which the Security Council is legally bound in establishing the substantial terms of settlement.

The proposals stipulate that in discharging this function the Security Council should act in accordance with the purposes and principles of the organization. The purposes of the organization are the maintenance of peace and the maintenance of security. What are its principles? The Dumbarton Oaks recommendations do enumerate the principles in accordance with which the organization and its members should pursue its purposes. But the fact of the matter is that all these principles, with the possible exception of one, merely circumscribe and underline the obligations of the member states to comply with the decisions of the Security Council. They do not lay down rules or standards to be complied with by the Council. The preamble of the League of Nations Covenant referred to the "firm establishment of the understandings of international law," the "maintenance of justice" and a "scrupulous respect for all treaty obligations" as means of promoting international peace and security. No less emphatically does the American Design insist on the supremacy of international law. But in the Dumbarton Oaks proposals we seek in vain for any reference to international law and justice. It is certainly true that solemn reference to the prescriptions of law and justice does not in itself assure their actual observance. But what we are concerned about in this context is that the Dumbarton Oaks plan purposely refrains from declaring the maintenance of legal and moral standards to be one of the conditions of maintaining peace.

That in stressing this omission I am not overemphasizing legal niceties is proved by the omission of still another and much more important clause of the League Covenant. In fact, we are here face to face with the basic philosophy of Dumbarton Oaks.

Article X of the League Covenant obligated the members of the League to respect *and preserve* from external aggression the territorial integrity and political independence of all members. This collective guarantee of the members' territory and independence against external aggression was highly problematic from a practical point of view. Both the decision whether a case for guarantee had actually arisen and the decision on the measures to be undertaken against such aggression were left to the discretion of the individual members. Under Article X the Council was empowered only to advise upon the means by which these obligations should be fulfilled. Still, the article contributed greatly to the defeat of the Covenant in the United States Senate, the principal argument of its opponents being that it implied a guarantee by the United States of the status quo all over the world. To be sure, the no less famous Article xix of the League Covenant tried to introduce a dynamic element into international relations by authorizing the Assembly to recommend from time to time a revision of treaties and other procedures of peaceful change. But the fact remains that the Covenant leaned toward a static conception of international law. In view of the role played by Article X of the League Covenant in the discussions of the Senate some twenty-five years ago, it can be taken for granted that the American delegates to Dumbarton Oaks were as little eager as the other delegates to insert into the proposals a guarantee clause of worldwide scope. On the contrary, they agreed that the door should be left open for peaceful change of existing territorial and political conditions, if and when the maintenance of those conditions should prove to endanger the preservation of international peace.

The Dumbarton Oaks proposals make provisions for the establishment of an International Court of Justice to replace the present Permanent Court of International Justice at The Hague. At the same time, however, they clearly indicate a distinct preference for the political rather than the judicial settlement even of disputes that by their very nature lend themselves to decision by a court. International conflicts concerning the territorial integrity and political independence of a state are generally considered to be of a nonjusticiable character. Thus it is only consistent that in the Dumbarton Oaks plan their settlement falls under the jurisdiction of the Security Council. Being a political body, the Council will be inclined to decide such issues in conformity with considerations of political expediency rather than of international law. It will be particularly inclined in that direction when a disregard of international law is the sole price at which international peace can be maintained. In other words, the Dumbarton Oaks proposals mean the legalization of settlements in contradiction to the law whenever the ratio of the disputants' physical strength suggests and warrants such a solution as the only possible means of avoiding an armed conflict among the great powers of this world.

This is borne out by the proposals' intentional failure to limit the arbitral authority of the Security Council by a code of substantive principles, including a guarantee of the territorial integrity and political independence of the members of the so-called security organization. The proposals concerning the settlement of international disputes are a set of rules of procedure but they do not recognize inalienable rights of the member states which the Security Council would be bound to respect in settling a dispute. Thus the Dumbarton Oaks plan, in contrast to the League of Nations Covenant, leans toward a dynamic conception of international relations. The full degree to which this fact lessens the actual security value of the organization for the small states will become evident only when we discuss the voting procedure of the Security Council.

In brief, the Dumbarton Oaks proposals lay the main emphasis on the enforcement of peace rather than on the enforcement of law. The more important, therefore, is the question to what extent they assure the effectiveness of the organization in dealing with an actual or potential aggressor state, and thus enable it to accomplish its principal purpose. This brings us to a discussion of the powers entrusted to the Security Council for the prevention and repression of war.

As indicated above, these powers, too, are in a sense much broader than those that were assigned to the League of Nations Council. They are also more flexible, and the greater flexibility of action makes for greater stress on the prevention than on the repression of war. It is true that the League Covenant did not altogether neglect preventive intervention by the League agencies. But the terms of the Covenant lend themselves to controversial interpretations, which made it difficult to strike a reasonable balance between the preventive and the repressive conceptions. Moreover, according to Article XVl of the Covenant, coercive measures, whether in the form of economic sanctions or of military sanctions, could be applied only against a member actually resorting to war in disregard of the provisions contained in the Covenant.

Under the Dumbarton Oaks plan no uncertainty can ever arise as to the *right* of the Security Council to interfere at any time with the external affairs of member states whose actions are in the considered opinion of the Council a "threat to the peace, breach of the peace or act of aggression." In deciding whether it should interest itself in the matter, the Security Council is not bound by any defintion of actions that constitute a threat to the peace, breach of the peace, or aggression. Also, it is completely free to enjoin on such member states the taking of certain specified measures in order to eliminate the dangers to the maintenance of peace. And finally, it is empowered to apply coercive measures, including military measures, whenever it considers such sanctions indispensable as a thwart to aggressive intentions. Not alone an actual resort to force, but even a threat to use force warrants the taking of coercive measures by the Council.

These rules mean not only that would-be aggressors are subject to further restrictions than those imposed upon them by the League Covenant but also that the members of the organization which is to enforce the peace are given greater responsibilities. But these responsibilities are far from unlimited. In this case the conferees of Dumbarton Oaks have taken great pains to define and circumscribe clearly the authority of the Security Council.

The role of the Security Council in relation to coercive collective measures is, unlike the role of the League Council, of a directing and not of a merely coordinating character. As regards diplomatic, economic, financial and commercial sanctions against the potential or actual aggressor state, the members are obligated to comply with any decision that the Security Council finds appropriate to the particular situation. Constitutional processes in the several states are not allowed to stand in the way of enforcing at short notice the diplomatic and economic measures determined by the Council. The latter is free to exempt states from participating in these sanctions, but no state is entitled to such an exemption.

The Dumbarton Oaks plan tries also to assure adequate and prompt action by military measures, if peace can be maintained or restored only by such extreme means. In precommitting the members of the organization to the use of military force it goes much less far, however, than it does in precommitting them to follow the Council's decisions on other sanctions. As a matter of fact, the charter as such is not to contain any specifically military stipulations. The Dumbarton Oaks plan merely directs the member states to conclude among themselves special agreements, to be approved by the Security Council, whereby the Council will be supplied with strictly limited forces. These agreements will provide for two types of armed forces. The first type is national air force contingents for combined international enforcement action, to be kept immediately available by the parties to the agreements. The second type is armed forces and other military facilities which the parties will undertake to make available to the Security Council whenever the latter calls upon them to assist it in maintaining or restoring peace. Thus the plan does not provide for the establishment of an international police force, but contents itself with the provision of contingents to be supplied by the national armies in accordance with these special agreements. The latter are to be ratified by the signatory states "in accordance with their constitutional processes."

In invoking military action the Security Council may insist upon the cooperation of all members of the organization, but it is free to call upon only some of them. It will be assisted and advised in such action by the Military Staff Committee, which is responsible under the Security Council for the unified strategic direction of any armed forces placed at the Council's disposal. The Military Staff Committee will consist of the Chiefs of Staff of the great powers and, if need be, of other associated members representing the minor powers. Only the Chiefs of Staff representing the great powers will have the right to vote.

This does not mean that the Security Council will not be entitled to ask for military support by the members of the organization beyond the limits set by the special agreements, if it should prove that the forces at the disposal of the Council are not fully effective for maintaining or restoring international peace. It means only that the military precommitments of the members are definitely limited. The conferees of Dumbarton Oaks wanted to make it absolutely clear that collective military measures involving the use of additional forces would be dependent upon the free discretion of the member states. The special agreements are to obligate the members of the organization to participate in police actions of a limited range. It is up to them to decide whether they will cooperate with the Security Council in military actions of a warlike character.

It is a safe guess that this provision, too, is primarily due to the insistence of the American delegates at Dumbarton Oaks. It clearly meets in the most satisfactory way the issues arising in this connection under the American constitution, which reserves to Congress the right to declare war, and authorizes the President only to the lesser uses of force in international relations.

From a strictly technical point of view, it may be said, in short, that the Dumbarton Oaks proposals satisfy the conditions of effectiveness in peace machinery to a higher degree than did the League of Nations Covenant. This does not imply, of course, that they satisfy those conditions to a sufficient degree. Nevertheless, there is no doubt that they go far toward assuring promptness and unity of action against an aggression of minor scope; they do put teeth into the Covenant.

II

But the greater effectiveness of the present apparatus of peace enforcement does not in itself mean a greater certainty that there will actually be a decision to use it when there is need for it. In fact, the flexible character of the Dumbarton Oaks provisions is a twosided matter. It means that the Security Council is only *empowered* to take collective measures. Its powers are permissive, not mandatory. It is hardly a mere accident that the Dumbarton Oaks proposals speak of the right of the Security Council to take military actions, whereas the League Covenant speaks of the duty of the Council to recommend military sanctions to the members concerned.

The probability that the Security Council will act to settle international disputes and to prevent and repress war depends ultimately upon the rights and duties which the Dumbarton Oaks plan assigns to the individual members of the organization. Therefore it is necessary now to consider those provisions of the plan which define the legal status of the several members.

This question's significance for the fate that awaits the San Francisco treaty in the United States Senate can hardly be overrated. In 1920 the League of Nations was wrecked in the Senate by the charge that it was a superstate, although none of the provisions of the Covenant warranted such a charge. Because of its comparatively broad powers the Security Council of the Dumbarton Oaks organization will come closer to a world government than any other international body in recent history. How then may it be possible this time to meet the charge of superstate?

The question turns on the problem in what sense, if any, and to what extent the Dumbarton Oaks proposals are actually intended to establish an organization that would hold superior powers over the governments of its member states; for we would be entitled to speak of a world government or a superstate only if any of the agencies of the United Nations organization were empowered to take actions independently of the governments of the respective members, and without their previous approval in each case.

A close analysis of the Dumbarton Oaks proposals shows that the general international organization is to hold such independent powers only as regards the medium and small member states. The great member states, including the United States of America, retain their discretion concerning any collective actions to be taken by the organization. In other words, the Security Council through which the Dumbarton Oaks organization will exercise its arbitral and its security functions will have a dual character: within its sphere of jurisdiction it will be a governmental body in relation to the lesser members, and a merely coordinating agency in relation to the great powers.

There is no denying that the Dumbarton Oaks proposals group the member states into two classes of different legal status, although Chapter II of the plan proclaims the principle of "sovereign equality" as the very basis of the organization. To be sure, the equality of states, understood as their equal capacity for rights, has become generally recognized only in comparatively recent times. Moreover, the League Covenant, too, by legalizing the actual inequality of great and small states, through its provisions on the composition of the Council, contravened to a certain extent the idea of the legal equality of states. But though the small states did not have equal representation on the League Council, the vote of those that were members of the Council carried legally as much weight as the vote of the big fellows.

Decisions of the Council required, generally speaking, a unanimous vote of the members. Besides, under the Covenant the Assembly, in which every member of the League was equally represented, held by and large concurrent powers with the Council. In these respects the Dumbarton Oaks organization will differ fundamentally from the League of Nations. It is therefore no exaggeration to say that the proposals mean a reversal of the direction into which the family of nations seemed to move until recently.

The only agency in whose deliberations and decisions all the members of the organization will participate on a footing of complete equality is the General Assembly. That body will elect the non-permanent members of the Security Council, the members of the Economic and Social Council, and, upon recommendation of the Security Council, the Secretary-General of the organization. The General Assembly will approve the budgets of the organization, and decide on the proportion to be borne by each member. Generally speaking, the Assembly is to control the organization's activities. Important decisions of the General Assembly, including its electoral functions, will be made by a two-thirds majority, all other decisions by a simple majority vote.

The functions of control assigned to the General Assembly do not, however, include actions on peace and war. All that it is authorized to do for the maintenance of international peace and security is to make recommendations. In fact, it is not even allowed to make on its own initiative any recommendations concerning a matter that is pending before the Security Council. Under the Covenant of the League of Nations the Assembly and Council held concurrent powers, but the Security Council has an absolute monopoly in all matters relating to the maintenance of international peace and security. It is this monopolistic position of the Council which magnifies the importance of the provisions concerning its composition and procedure.

The Security Council is to consist of five permanent and six non-permanent members. The permanent seats are assigned to the United States, Great Britain, the Soviet Union, France and China. The non-permanent members are to be elected by the General Assembly for a term of two years, and they are not to be immediately eligible for reelection. Thus the composition of the Security Council is clearly based on the idea that power should go with responsibility. At least the principal responsibility for maintaining peace will rest with the militarily, economically and financially strongest states. Their permanent representation in the organization's executive council, which is to hold the key to war and peace, is therefore, in practice, indispensable. In this respect the Dumbarton Oaks proposals merely follow the precedent set by the League of Nations Covenant, which otherwise scrupulously adhered to the principle of equality among its members.

As a matter of fact, neither the expediency nor the justice of the distinction between permanent and non-permanent members of the Security Council is seriously contested. What is being criticized is rather the concrete application of this distinction. It is more than doubtful whether all the five states that are assigned permanent seats are actually, not merely potentially, great powers. Moreover, if power and responsibility are to be proportionate, it seems plausible that the middle states, too, should be granted a special position, perhaps in the form of semi-permanent membership in the Security Council; the Netherlands, Canada, Brazil and certain other countries can rightly claim a military, financial and economic strength far superior to that of such states as Costa Rica, Nicaragua or Albania. And is not the total of six non-permanent members too small to provide for a fairly adequate representation of middle and small states alike? Finally, one may wonder whether the provisions on the composition of the Security Council should not be made more flexible. As they stand today, any change regarding either the status or the number of its members would require a constitutional amendment, which in order to become effective would have to be ratified by each of the five privileged members of the Council.

The privileged position of the great powers is due not only to the permanency of their tenure and the hegemonic structure of the Security Council. Equally if not even more important are the voting privileges granted them under the procedural rules of the Dumbarton Oaks plan. The vote of a great power is not only actually but also legally to carry more weight than the vote of a middle or a small state represented on the Council. We touch here upon the much discussed veto power of the permanent members of the Security Council.

Under the Covenant of Geneva, decisions of the Assembly or Council required the agreement of all the members of the League of Nations represented at the meeting. This unanimity rule of the League was in conformity with the then prevailing idea of the equality of all states, as well as with the usual procedural practice of the main organs of other international organizations. But it could not fail to weaken considerably the efficiency of the League machinery, particularly in security matters. The authors of the Dumbarton Oaks plan therefore agreed that the future security organization should be strengthened by application of the majority principle to the decisions of all its agencies. Departure from the unanimity rule was facilitated by the fact that in many fields a distinct trend away from it has been evident in international development between the two world wars, and especially during the present war.

Acceptance of the majority principle for the decisions of the Security Council brought the delegates of Dumbarton Oaks face to face, however, with the same crucial question which many times before in history has challenged the wit of the builders of confederate or federative organizations. For an example we need only remember the discussions of the Constitutional Convention at Philadelphia in 1787, concerning proportional or equal voting in Congress. Because of the entirely different nature of the United Nations organization and its specific purpose, it is hardly surprising that some kind of proportional voting was at Dumbarton Oaks a foregone conclusion. Small as the total number of the lesser states represented on the Security Council may be, they nevertheless hold a majority of six to five. It would be preposterous to allow the Security Council to form a decision involving coercive actions without making sure that at least some of the great powers that are strong enough to enforce those measures are ready to back up such a decision.

Contrary to a widely held belief, the American delegation was not altogether opposed to granting voting privileges to the Council's permanent members. As a matter of fact, the American Design went so far as to recommend that in *all* agencies of the general international organization the majority should in some cases be required to include the votes of the states continuously represented in what the Dumbarton Oaks proposals were to call the Security Council. The obstructive controversy of Dumbarton Oaks turned exclusively on the question whether a great power which is itself charged with aggression should forfeit its right to vote. The Russians insisted on the absolute great-power veto, the Americans and British wished to see it qualified.

The Yalta compromise establishes three different categories of decisions of the Security Council, to which different voting rules are to be applied.

To the first category belong all decisions on purely procedural matters. These are carried if they are made by an affirmative vote of seven out of the eleven members of the Council. This means that a great power—indeed, several of them at once—may be outvoted on procedural matters.

The second category comprises decisions of the Council taken in the exercise of its arbitral functions in the settlement of international disputes. In these cases parties to the dispute have to abstain from voting, even if they hold a permanent seat in the Council. Decisions on such matters are carried if they are made by an affirmative vote of at least seven members, provided the seven or more votes include the concurring votes of the permanent members other than the parties to the dispute.

The third category comprises all other possible decisions, in particular the determination by the Council of the existence of a threat to peace or a breach of the peace and decisions on coercive measures of any kind. All decisions of this type are carried only if made by at least seven members, including the concurrent votes of *all* the five permanent members. In other words, the fact that a great power is itself charged with aggression does not disqualify it from voting on and vetoing any decision of this third type: a great power can veto any enforcement action directed against itself.

The Yalta compromise thus incorporates what is not quite correctly called the absolute veto of the great powers. But it incorporates it in a somewhat mitigated form. To be sure, a great power can prevent the Security Council from invoking physical force, or even from ordering diplomatic or economic sanctions. But no great power that is a party to a dispute can prevent the Council from investigating the dispute and proposing a settlement. If charged with aggression, a great power would at least have to state its case at the bar of public opinion.

The lack of universal coercive power in the supposedly universal peace organization is a shock to the believers in an integral collective security system. But it is legitimate to ask whether a right of the Security Council to take coercive measures against one of the great powers would not be a merely fictitious right. Coercive measures against Great Britain, or Russia, or the United States would mean, in effect, total, worldwide war. No state, large or small, can reasonably be expected to take such measures unless it considers its vital interests to be at stake. Neither can it be presumed that the United States would risk a war against Russia to prevent the latter, let us say, from annexing Rumania, nor that Russia would go to war against Great Britain or the United States to prevent aggressive actions on their part in matters not touching upon Russia's vital interests.

The voting procedure in the Security Council is no doubt open to many more or less well founded objections. But the plan should definitely refute any unqualified charge that the world organization constitutes a super-government which would deprive the United States of her freedom of decision on war and peace. The voting privilege of the great powers legally precludes coercive actions by the Security Council against any of the great powers, including the United States. It is to the honor of this country, and speaks for its peaceful intentions, that in spite of this advantage it was opposed to the absolute veto. But the fact remains that the absolute veto, once adopted, enlarges the discretion of the American government. More important, in actual practice, is the fact that under the voting rules the United States cannot be compelled to participate against her will in collective coercive actions against another state. Any such measure would require the assent of the American representative in the Security Council, who will act under the instructions of the President. Measures of a warlike scope would have to be previously endorsed by a formal declaration of war by Congress.

Thus by joining the Dumbarton Oaks organization the United States would not forfeit her sovereign right to decide for herself on war and peace. All she would obligate herself to do would be to cooperate with the other members of the organization in maintaining or restoring international peace, a task from which she could not shrink anyway, unless she would again gravely neglect her own interests. As regards the great powers, including the United States, the Dumbarton Oaks organization is nothing but institutionalized international cooperation—machinery for the coordination of collective measures voluntarily agreed upon by the five powers.

Things are different in regard to the middle and small states. For them the security value of the organization is likely to be diminished by the very provision that assures freedom of action to the great powers: because of the latter's voting privilege, the smaller states cannot be certain of obtaining the organization's support against even an attack by another medium or small state, not to speak of an attack launched against them by a big fellow. And at the same time a medium or small state is bound to participate in collective coercive measures invoked by a body in which it may not even be repre- sented. Canada and the other Dominions would thus find themselves in the strange position of being subordinated to the Council of the general in- ternational organization, while at the same time enjoying a status of com- plete independence and equality within the supposedly closer framework of the British Commonwealth of Nations.

But it is only fair to add that no great power, either, can count on receiving coercive action from the organization against another great pow- er. Nor can a permanent member rely, in any matter, on absolutely certain action by the Security Council. Finally, the Dumbarton Oaks proposals are clearly intended to assign to the privileged members of the organization not only greater rights but also greater responsibilities. We should therefore suspend judgment on the relative positions of the great, middle and small states until we know, from the special agreements still to be concluded among the members of the organization, to what extent their rights and duties are truly proportionate.

III

The small states are greatly interested in still another question. Is the Security Council, under the terms of Dumbarton Oaks, authorized to interfere also in the internal affairs of the member states? The proposals contain only one direct reference to this question, and this reference would seem to indicate that any such intervention is precluded. According to this provision the arbitral powers of the Security Council will not apply to situations or disputes arising out of matters which by international law are solely within the domestic jurisdiction of the states concerned. In any concrete case it is the Security Council itself, however, which will have to decide whether a matter pertains to municipal or to international law. Moreover, the Council's right to "determine the existence of any threat to the peace," and to take appropriate countermeasures against any such threat, would easily lend itself as a legal basis for any kind of interference by the Council, even with the internal affairs of the member states. As a matter of fact, Joseph C. Grew, Under-Secretary of State, is reported to have stated on March 3 that the Dumbarton Oaks plan contemplates "suppression of revolutions that might bring international war." By the same reasoning it would have to be added that the plan might also operate to encourage revolutions.

Be that as it may, intervention by the Security Council with the internal affairs of member states would demand the concurrrent affirmative vote of all the great powers plus two votes of non-permanent members of the Council. In view of the conflicting political philosophies of the states concerned, it is not very likely that such a majority vote could easily be reached.

This contrast in the basic political beliefs of the five powers may prove to be the greatest liability of the organization. It has already led to the inability of the Dumbarton Oaks conferees to agree on common principles that would direct the relations between governments and their respective citizens. The membership of the organization will range from states which cherish the traditions of government by law, down to states in which the relation between government and opposition is determined by conceptions approximating the rules of absolute, unlimited warfare. A common interventionist policy by the Security Council would therefore be no simple thing to achieve.

This still leaves untouched, however, the problem of interference by one great power with the internal affairs of its smaller neighbors, serving not the interests of the organization as a whole but the particular interest of the one particular state. It leaves untouched the problem of a surreptitious interventionist policy by one great power against the will of the other powers, great and small alike. The chances that such a policy will be pursued depend greatly on the answer to another question of tremendous political importance, which is not yet definitely settled by the Dumbarton Oaks proposals.

As the plan stands now, primary responsibility for the settlement of disputes and for the prevention and repression of war is assigned to the Security Council, as the central authority of the organization. The present discussion is based, in fact, on the assumption of this alignment of responsibility. But the plan does not altogether exclude a far-reaching delegation of authority by the Security Council to regional agencies. Indeed, the Conference of Mexico City, and in particular the Act of Chapultepec, point in the direction of a final solution that would go rather far in stressing the regional as against the universal conception. Needless to say, a decision in favor of a highly decentralized security organization would approximate the system of spheres of influence. This could not fail to have, among other important effects, a bearing on the question to what extent the great powers will be able to turn their small neighbors into satellites.

One short word about another possibility that seems to be in the shaping. The Dumbarton Oaks proposals strongly suggest that the enforcement of the peace terms to be imposed on defeated Germany and Japan should not be entrusted to the Security Council of the world organization, but should be the concern of the great powers alone. Senator Vandenberg's plan points in the same direction. This solution would relieve the incipient organization of a tremendous responsibility.

It would corroborate, on the other hand, the interpretation that the future international organization will be founded on the hegemonic conception of a worldwide Concert of Powers. But unlike the European Concert of Powers in the nineteenth century, it will be closely tied up with a more or less representative organization of the minor states. It will be a combination of a World Concert of Powers and a League of Nations.

The builders of a world organization face the problem which is the very central problem of politics. To put it in the words of Abraham Lincoln, how can we establish a government which is not too strong for the liberties of the people, but strong enough to maintain itself? Only the future can prove whether and to what extent the conferees of Dumbarton Oaks have succeeded in laying the foundations of a structure which will be able to avoid arbitrariness as well as weakness—the two dangers inherent in any political system. It would be useless to deny that both dangers loom on the horizon. Certain features of the structure can be said to invite an abuse of power. But no less real is the danger of weakness. The Dumbarton Oaks plan stands or falls, politically as well as legally, with the unanimity of the five great powers. If this nucleus falls apart, the whole edifice will crumble to the ground.

FOUR YEARS OF THE
UNITED NATIONS*

The attempt to review and appraise the work of the United Nations on the basis of its four-year record is admittedly a bold and problematic undertaking. Such short experience does not seem to warrant even merely tentative conclusions. And yet, the attempt may actually be less presumptuous than it appears at first sight.

The United Nations is, after all, by no means an entirely novel experiment in building an international political organization of projected universal scope. To be sure, it was part of the propaganda employed in selling, or rather overselling, the new organization to the American public, to present the United Nations as a hitherto untested remedy for the evil of war. Inasmuch as references to the defunct League of Nations could not altogether be avoided, they were made only in order to illustrate the constitutional superiority of the new over the old organization.[1] Actually, the United Nations does differ from its predecessor in some, not wholly irrelevant, respects. These differences, moreover, are not confined to the institutional and functional features of the two organizations, but extend to their moral, ideological, and political settings as well. Nevertheless, the United Nations and the League of Nations are, fundamentally, variants of one and the same organizational type—the confederate system. Both were conceived by their founders as international bodies composed of sovereign member states, yet charged with the task of upholding the authority of the community of nations as a whole. The basic identity of structure and purpose has made for a continuity of issues and problems that is already very striking and is bound to become ever more so. Their fundamental unity of structure, purpose, and problems makes it possible—indeed, even imperative—to analyze and weigh the short record of Lake Success and

Reprinted with permission of *Social Research*, vol. 16, no. 4 (December 1949).

Flushing Meadow in the light of the somewhat longer record of Geneva.

The limits of experience do not present the greatest stumbling block in the way of assessing the accomplishments and failures of the United Nations. A record short in terms of years is not necessarily deficient in terms of work actually undertaken. The Charter assigned to the United Nations and its specialized agencies tasks of a variety and scope unprecedented in the history of international organization. And even the severest critic of the United Nations could not possibly maintain that it has not been eager to make the fullest use of its powers. The formidable number of items on the agenda of each year's General Assembly and the length of its annual sessions clearly testify to a work load that very definitely puts the activities of the League of Nations in the shade. This quantitative difference is no less impressively indicated by the respective staff figures for the League of Nations Secretariat and that of the United Nations. Whereas the maximum number of staff members employed in the former was approximately 800, there are today some 3,000 staff members employed in the latter, not counting the civil service of the specialized agencies.[2] Thus, instead of being frustrated by lack of material, the student of the United Nations finds himself overwhelmed by its abundance.

It would be impossible to evaluate in any one paper all the activities of the United Nations with anything close to accuracy. This holds true especially for the functions assigned to such organs as the Economic and Social Council and the Trusteeship Council. To appraise their actual accomplishments would require not only a careful scrutiny of the whole host of resolutions passed by those bodies and the General Assembly. We would also have to find out to what extent the member governments have taken practical steps to implement the several decisions.[3]

It is not only necessary, but justifiable as well, to limit the following stocktaking to the record of the United Nations as an agency for maintaining international peace and security. Maintenance of international peace and security is the purpose that stands highest in the hierarchy of aims which the United Nations is designed to fulfill. Its success is therefore primarily determined by its actions and failures to act in the political field proper. In fact, all the other activities of the United Nations being of an essentially auxiliary character, they too must be measured in terms of their respective contribution to peace and security.

I

By far the greatest expectations aroused in us by the establishment of the United Nations were based on its alleged merits as a security organization. Chapter VII of the Charter was considered to be its very core. The technical features of the collective security system, incorporated in the Chapter, were supposed to assure the effectiveness of the new peace machinery to a much higher degree than the League of Nations Covenant had done. The powerful protection which the system was presumed to offer the smaller members of the organization was to reconcile them to its hierarchical structure and its authoritarian spirit. Actually, however, not even the legal features of the Charter's security system justified such fervent hopes, quite apart from the doubtful validity of its political assumptions.

According to the concept of collective security, the national security of the individual state is a matter of concern to the community of nations as a whole. A threat to the security of one is a threat to the security of all. The other nations are not only entitled, but obligated, to come to the help of the state threatened. In exchange for receiving protection from the international community, the individual state is expected to give up, or rather accept limitations of, such important attributes of its sovereignty as the right to arm, to form alliances, and to wage war. Collective enforcement of peace and security is to replace individual self-help.

The close interdependence between the obligation of the community and the undertakings of its members is obvious. In fact, it operates as a vicious circle in which any system of collective security is bound to be caught. No nation, including the most peaceable one, can afford or be willing to renounce, without reservation, the paraphernalia of power and the right to employ them, unless it can be virtually certain of effective collective protection. But the confederate structure of the system of collective security precludes the only true guarantee of such efficacy, a supranational authority superior to any and all of the national governments in terms of political, moral, military, and economic strength. The advocates of world government, therefore, are no doubt right in maintaining that the problem of collective security is insoluble within the framework of a confederate system. They are wrong merely in assuming that a world government proper would be attainable or workable.

The short history of the United Nations security system is a melancholy illustration of this vicious circle. It is the more discouraging as it is, *mutatis mutandis,* a repetition of the League of Nations experience, the main difference being the greater rapidity with which the disintegration of the San Francisco system has been consummated. As a matter of fact, it would be more appropriate to say that it has not come into existence.

What are the legal features and political assumptions of that system, and what are the causes and symptoms of its disintegration?

Universal membership is the ultimate goal of the United Nations. But this was never meant to imply that its coercive powers were to be universally applicable. On the contrary, as a security organization proper, the United

Nations to all intents and purposes has had from the very beginning an extremely narrow scope. In view of the right of the permanent members of the Security Council to veto any enforcement measure—a right upon which we insist, even today, as strongly as the Russians do—the organization could not, even in purely legal terms, be expected ever to be in a position to institute enforcement proceedings against any of the great powers. Neither can we count on its support against the Russians, nor can the Russians count on it against us. What is worse yet, none of the smaller powers is entitled to regard collective protection as certain or even likely, if and when its security should be threatened by a great power.

At best it could be hoped that the legal security mechanism of the United Nations might operate in cases of conflict between minor powers. But the veto applies in these cases as well, though its subjective aspect is somewhat different. By exercising it, a permanent member of the Security Council would not stave off collective action against itself, but would refuse to participate in such action against another United Nations Member, thus blocking enforcement procedures against the latter. And it is quite likely to do so if its supposed national interests suggest this course.

To emphasize the restrictive character of the veto is not to imply that the political problems involved in collective security could and should be solved by abolishing the veto in its application to enforcement measures. The veto is a symptom, not the root, of the difficulties that are inherent in the political realities. To remove the legal obstacle which precludes enforcement action against a permanent member of the Security Council would mean to endow the organization with a merely fictitious right, unless it is ready to launch what would be essentially a global war, the very catastrophe which the organization is intended to prevent. Nor would it be any more useful to abolish the veto as a means of blocking collective action against a medium-sized or small Member of the organization. If one of the great powers, and especially if one of the superpowers should consider it, rightly or wrongly, necessary for political reasons to identify itself with the nation against which preventive or repressive collective action is to be taken, such action would again ultimately mean global war. The veto is nothing but the legal form in which a permanent member of the Security Council states what it holds to be the zone of its vital interests on which it is not ready to compromise. Without the veto, it could be legally outvoted, but not actually brought into line.

Given the limited scope of the United Nations security system and the uncertainties of its operation within this scope, the fact that the technique of the enforcement measures provided for in the Charter is an improvement over that of the Covenant has meant very little in a practical way. Moreover, the most important of those improvements has not materialized. As it has been so aptly put, the Security Council "has had its teething troubles, but it has not yet acquired its teeth."[4] According to Article 43 of the Charter, there was to be placed at the disposal of the Security Council a military establishment composed of national contingents. However, owing to the inability of the Big Five to come to an agreement on the character and size of those armed forces, diplomatic and economic measures are still the only coercive powers of the Security Council. The formal authorization to use them, even for merely preventive purposes, is all that is left of the much-praised advance of Chapter VII of the Charter beyond Article 16 of the Covenant.

That the enforcement machinery has not yet been completed weighs in the total balance less heavily than the fact that the political assumptions upon which the security system of the United Nations has been based have failed to come true. The former is rather a mere indication of the latter. The security structure has remained unfinished, because its foundation has fallen apart.

The very word "veto" has today a derogatory connotation. But the actual and potential abuse of the veto privilege should not make us forget that the veto is the reverse of a positive idea of long standing, adapted to the parliamentary procedures of current international politics. The idea that the maintenance of international peace and security depends, primarily and ultimately, upon the existence of what, in the predemocratic age, was called the concert of the leading powers, has not become any less valid because the stubborn facts of world politics displease our tender liberal hearts. Whether we like it or not, far from being a substitute for the concert of powers, the system of collective security has a reasonable chance to work only within a hegemonic framework. The fathers of the United Nations were therefore wise in recognizing the uanimity of the foremost powers as a basic prerequisite for the new security system.

The chances for successful operation of collective security are slim enough when the interests of great powers that otherwise entertain the most cordial relations with one another do not run parallel with regard to enforcement measures called for by the alleged disturbance of peace by a third minor state. The Indonesian case with its alignment in the Security Council of colonial versus anticolonial powers, instead of the usual alignment of east versus west, was a typical illustration of such a situation. That what the French veto defeated was not an enforcement measure proper only corroborates the problematic value of the collective security system even under comparatively auspicious conditions.[5]

But practically speaking, the system is unworkable if the great powers are divided by a deep and permanent rift. To be sure, even within the context of a cold war there might arise situations in which its protagonists are, for one reason or another, willing and able to pursue common enforcement policies. In the Palestinian case, the Security Council went so far as to base its final cease-fire order explicitly upon Chapter VII of the Charter, and to declare that failure to comply with the order would require its immediate consideration with a view to further action. It is an open question, however, whether the Security Council could have ever agreed on actual enforcement proceedings, if subsequent developments in Palestine had called for them. As the record stands, the case testifies to the value of the United Nations as a conciliatory agency rather than as an international policeman. Be that as it may, the case typical of the problem of enforcing peace and security by the collective action of an organization torn by a cold war among its leading members was and still is the Greek case.

The breakdown of the security system of Geneva was dramatically signalized by the failure of the League of Nations in the Sino-Japanese and Italo-Ethiopian conflicts to impose any sanctions in the former case and effective sanctions in the latter. The disintegration of the security system of Lake Success has not followed from any spectacular enforcement experiment, not even one tried on a small nation. But, even so, the symptoms are no less definite and clear. They can be summarized as a return, on almost all sides, to the idea and devices of self-help.

The tempo of the return to international normalcy, as it were, was in each case determined by the length of time for which the belief in collective protection as a working substitute for individual self-help endured. As a matter of fact, the Russians never lost themselves in the pleasant maze of hopes and illusions that nurtured organizational pacifism in the liberal democracies of the west. Being extremely distrustful of the security value, for a socialist state, of international institutions in a world dominated, according to them, by monopoly capitalism, they saw in the establishment of the United Nations no valid reason for discontinuing the game of power politics pure and simple.

This is not to imply that Russian policy can be explained in terms of supposedly realistic security considerations alone. The very dynamism of the communist idea would refute such a simple interpretation of Russia's aggressive actions. It is only to suggest that the obsession about security, deeply rooted in her history, is one of the factors that account for her actual policies.[6] Its force may be the more considerable since Marxist-Leninist doctrine holds that war, international as well as domestic is the world's inescapable fate, so long as capitalism is working disruption. Unfortunately, wherever there prevails the fatalistic belief in the unavoidable clash of arms, be it founded on religious or scientific conceptions, defensive and offensive motives and actions merge all too easily, as has been amply borne out by history.

Security has become also an American obsession, ever since we fully realized that the political and technological developments of recent years have deprived us of the benefits of an isolated position. Contrary to the Russians, however, in our quest for safety in a shrunken world, we turned to the idea and the contrivances of collective security. True, we hoped to gain our new security at a cheap price, and some of the most important provisions of the Charter, as well as certain omissions in it, all of them tending to emphasize the powers of the Member states over against the authority of the United Nations Organization as a whole, are due to American initiative taken for the sake of American sovereignty.[7] But we were inclined to attribute to the world confederacy a very high security value, because our long liberal tradition had made us prone to believe in the triad of Wilsonian internationalism: the fundamental harmony of divergent opinions and interests, the potency and justness of public opinion, and the effectiveness of rational procedures in settling disputes.

Admittedly, our basically optimistic philosophy has never induced us to neglect completely our actual and potential instruments of national power. The atomic bomb is, after all, hardly a typical expression of the Wilsonian faith. But the pace of our rearmament began to quicken only with the growing realization of the deficiencies of the United Nations security system. The degree which our disillusionment has reached today is indicated by the fact that our military planning has caught up with Russian policy in completely disregarding the United Nations as a security factor. In this atmosphere of absolute lack of international confidence, proposals for the regulation of conventional and atomic weapons are, on the part of all powers, likely to be propagandistic gestures rather than serious efforts to arrive at agreements.

Another phase and symptom of the disintegration of the world security system has been the formation of political and military alliances. This trend revealed itself first in the east by a vast network of bilateral treaties between Russia and her satellites as well as between the satellites themselves. The western world soon followed suit with multilateral security agreements. The pattern was set by the Inter-American Treaty of Mutual Assistance, signed at Rio de Janeiro in 1947. Its counterpart in western Europe is the Treaty of Brussels concluded in 1948. The development finally culminated this year in the North Atlantic Treaty and its military implementation.

By far the most momentous of those particular political and military understandings is the Atlantic Pact. It also demonstrates more clearly than any other how far, in spite of ourselves, we have moved away in the brief span of four years from the ideas of Dumbarton Oaks and San Francisco. To be sure, the Pact is based upon and formulated in strict accordance with Article 51 of the Charter, which recognizes the right of individual and collective self-defense. To that extent it can no doubt correctly be called an implementation of a Charter position. But this does not alter the fact that the Pact is based upon political and legal conceptions that are fundamentally different from those underlying the Charter.

Wilson conceived of the League of Nations as the very negation of the European system of alliances and balance of power, in his opinion one of the main causes of the ever-recurring wars on the Continent. Nor did his heirs who were to build the United Nations hold these devices in any higher esteem. The structure they planned for it and the stress they laid on the paramountcy of the world organization to any regional arrangements were a clear rejection of the allegedly immoral and outdated notions and techniques. It is all the more indicative, therefore, that American statesmen became the main architects of the Atlantic Pact which is, whatever we choose to call it, an alliance based on the balance of power idea.[8]

It signifies that the nation which believed in the efficacy of collective security with almost religious fervor has reluctantly come to the conclusion that the very objective of the system, to check in advance any potential aggression by assembling at least equal or possibly superior forces against it, will be better achieved by the diplomatic methods of olden times. Indeed, it is not entirely unjustifiable to presume that the very concreteness of the system of alliances may well render it a more effective means of assuring peace than the abstract system of collective security with its "twilight zone," where, to quote Mr. Hamilton Fish Armstrong, "one side assumes that collective security exists and the other counts on taking advantage of the fact that it does not."[9] Therein lies our hope that the disintegration of the United security system does not necessarily mean that the cause of peace is lost as well.

No less a discrepancy exists between the legal conceptions that underlie the Charter, on the one hand, and the Atlantic Pact, on the other. In trying to prove to ourselves and others the rightness of our novel policy of alliances, we have recently tended to assign to Article 51, on which the Atlantic Pact is based, a central position in the system of the Charter. Nothing could be more ominous than this attempt to interpret Article 51 as expressing the very essence of the United Nations constitution. The actual position and function of Article 51 in the Charter render it very close to the emergency provisions in a national constitution which authorize, under certain conditions and within more or less clearly defined limits, the suspension of the constitution. In this sense, Article 51 of the Charter might be compared, for example, with the ill-famed Article 48 of the ill-fated Constitution of Weimar.

In accordance with the idea of collective security, the Charter stipulates a general prohibition of war as a means of individual self-help. Any lawful use of force is, under the principal terms of the Charter, the monopoly of the

United Nations Organization acting through its central agency, the Security Council. Article 51 establishes the exception, the right of the individual Member states to wage defensive war. True, it also defines the only conditions and limits under and within which the exception may lawfully be considered to apply. But by leaving the previous determination whether a state may in a concrete case resort to self-defense to the discretion of the individual state in question, Article 51, to all practical intents and purposes, restores the right to war to the position it held in modern international law prior to the establishment of an organized international society.

In view of the likelihood of a deadlock in the Security Council in case of an international crisis, which would block collective protection by the organization of the victim of an armed attack, Article 51 is undoubtedly a reservation that no Member of the United Nations can reasonably be expected to renounce. But to shift the emphasis in interpreting and applying the Charter from the provisions that constitute the very core of the system of collective security to the provision which envisages its suspension, and to speak at the same time of implementation of the Charter, is a not very profitable attempt to deceive ourselves and others about the bankruptcy of the political and legal system whose establishment was the primary purpose of the Charter.[10]

II

What are the lessons to be drawn from this disheartening record? The question poses the same basic problems that faced the Members of the League of Nations in 1936 when the failure of its first, and last, sanctions experiment caused them to explore the conclusions to be inferred from that failure. Nor are the types of answers given to the question then and now very different. They recommend either the strengthening of the respective organizations, or adaptation of their methods and procedures to the political realities.[11]

There is no need to comment on the organizational approach to the problem after our lengthy analysis of the United Nations security system. A revised Charter could devise on paper new and broadened legal competencies, but it could not create a political entity willing and able to exercise and enforce them. Moreover, what would have been very sensible from a political point of view between 1936 and 1938 would make no sense and serve no purpose in 1949. The Members of the League were shortly afterward to be the victims of aggression by states outside the League. To strengthen the League would have meant virtually to form, by a free act of will, an alliance that was a few years later imposed on them by their common enemies. It is to Russia's lasting credit that, foreseeing this

147

contingency, she proposed reforms of the League which, if adopted, would in the form of a strengthened Covenant have realized a defensive alliance.[12] The United Nations of today has no common foes, but is split within itself into potentially hostile camps of another world war.

There remains, therefore, only the other alternative, namely, to adapt the methods and procedures of the United Nations to the political realities. This is by no means intended to suggest a policy of passive acquiescence in those explosive realities, and even less a policy based on the belief in the inevitability of an American-Russian war. The proposition suggests resignation only to the unalterable fact that the problems and issues of international politics are not amenable to any novel devices, so long as the structure of international society remains what it is today. But apart from that, it is founded upon the positive and perhaps all too optimistic assumption that the time-honored diplomatic methods of persuasion and negotiation can still be made to contribute to the pacification of the world. If this assumption is correct, at least within those rather narrow limits within which it can reasonably be expected to apply, the chances of the United Nations as a *pacificator orbis terrarum* will be the better, the more it follows diplomatic rather than governmental patterns.[13]

The annual report on the work of the United Nations Organization which Mr. Trygve Lie submitted to the General Assembly this fall points very clearly in the direction of our proposition.[14] After stating that "in the past a somewhat misleading emphasis has sometimes been placed on the enforcement functions of the Security Council," the Secretary-General exhorts the members to concentrate their future efforts on practicing and developing the instruments of Chapter VI of the Charter under which the Security Council has powers of recommendation only. Mr. Lie finally proceeds, in diplomatic language, to enlighten the great powers on the value of diplomacy as a means of making the United Nations a going concern.

In his desire to open up new vistas of hope, Mr. Lie somewhat overstates the successes of the United Nations as a mediatory and conciliatory body. To gauge the actual contribution of the pacific efforts of the United Nations to the positive results achieved in such cases as those of Syria-Lebanon, Iran, Egypt, Palestine, Indonesia, and Kashmir would require a detailed study of each of them in political as well as legal terms. But this qualification is not intended to detract from the credit due the United Nations in this field. The record compares not altogether unfavorably with that of the League of Nations, especially in view of the fact that throughout the twenties the organization of Geneva was an exclusive club of liberal democracies. And it is very definitely better than our overemphasis on the frustrating effect of the Russian veto would lead us to expect. In point of fact, as far as political disputes proper are concerned, the Russian veto has had a decisive negative effect only in the Greek question.

The good record of the United Nations is the more remarkable because the legal provisions of Chapter VI of the Charter would have easily lent themselves to efforts at paralyzing the Security Council for good. What has actually happened is that the Security Council, in dealing with the political disputes, has developed a body of rules, of customary law, procedural and substantive, that tends to strengthen considerably its legal authority as a pacific agency. To be sure, this authority will be of no practical avail whenever a dispute is engineered with the connivance of, if not directly instigated by, one of the great powers, as is illustrated by the Greek case. But the significance of this development in regard to disputes on the periphery, as it were, of international politics is therefore no less great.

It would hardly be justifiable to ascribe to any of the great powers, or even to the minor ones, a consistent policy in this process of constitutional growth by usage of either Jeffersonian strict or Hamiltonian loose construction. National interests prevail in international politics over considerations of consistency as surely as party interests do in national politics. The one and the same state, or even representative of state, may in one case urge the members of the Security Council to stick to the text of the Charter, and in the other, to apply logic and common sense. All that can safely be said and presumed to hold valid for the future as well is the following: Russia, forming with her satellites a permanent minority bloc, has shown and will continue to show a much greater reluctance to agree to procedures and decisions that seem to touch upon the basic structure of the United Nations than is displayed by the members of the permanent majority bloc. Four of Russia's forty-one vetoes were directed at preventing the strengthening of the General Assembly over against the Security Council, the citadel of Soviet voting power in the United Nations.

III

It is hardly surprising that the good record of the United Nations as a mediatory and conciliatory body includes no achievements in the cold war between the United States and Soviet Russia. To think and speak of the United Nations as if it were a political entity is a fallacy, though the United Nations does have a legal personality. The name signifies a political relationship, not a substance, and the character of the relationship depends primarily upon the attitude of its leading Members toward one another. It would therefore not be reasonable to assume that the organization could have prevented or halted the cold war. It can, on the other hand, point to some resolutions and actions, especially in relation to the Berlin issue, that were due to the initiative of the minor powers, and may even have exerted some mitigating influence.

But one may wonder why, in the total balance of the cold war, the United Nations has heightened rather than lessened the international tension. This poses the question whether and to what extent the specific procedures practiced by the United Nations might have been conducive to that deplorable effect. Since the United States has played the decisive role in determining, shaping, and employing those methods, it poses also the question of our own responsibility for that unfortunate result.

The United Nations has gone to extremes in trying to replace secret diplomatic negotiation by public discussion and parliamentary procedures based upon the majority principle. It is the most radical attempt made thus far to apply to international politics the methods of domestic democratic politics. Measured in terms of this experiment, the League of Nations looks like the incarnation of old-time diplomacy. The unanimity principle prevailing in both Assembly and Council, the League Members felt compelled to come to an agreement before they proceeded to vote. Secret negotiation preceded and shaped the public discussion, at least in the Council. To put it in Paul-Henri Spaak's revealing words: ". . . the atmosphere of Geneva was very different from that now at Lake Success. It was more prearranged. There were some public debates from time to time, but I do not think I am betraying any secrets or saying anything unpleasant when I say that the public debate, in which the opposing theses were presented, were quite carefully prepared in the corridors, and that in reality everyone there was playing a role which he had learned in advance. When anyone deviated from the role which had been written by the authors, he was immediately considered to be a very bad character."[15] Public expression and voting thus served only to underline and express a diplomatic agreement.

Since the unanimity principle of long standing still prevails among the permanent members of the Security Council, one should have expected that voting in the Security Council would more or less regularly be prearranged by negotiations among them. Actually, no previous consultation approaching a serious effort to reach agreement seems ever to have taken place. Certainly there are no indications that the speeches of Mr. Austin and Mr. Gromyko or Mr. Malik have been the product of cooperative efforts in the corridors.[16]

It would be naive to suggest that the methods of Geneva might in all cases have positive results at Lake Success as well. The point I am driving at is, rather, that in international politics, and especially in dealings among great powers, parliamentary proceedings cannot replace diplomacy proper, but depend for their part upon the successful operation of diplomacy. If diplomatic agreement proves to be impossible, outvoting the recalcitrant state, whose cooperation is probably necessary for carrying out a recommendation of the Security Council or General Assembly, serves no practical purpose with regard to the matter at hand. Its only effect is to deepen the rift between the powers concerned, the avoidance of which—if it can be avoided at not too high a price—is the main function of the art of diplomacy.

Instead of dealing with the individual cases as they arise in the councils of the United Nations exclusively with a view to our long-range interests, we, as a power certain of majority support, have often succumbed to the temptation to score parliamentary triumphs, expressed in what are, in terms of international power, imaginary figures. Public discussion and voting are, on all sides, no longer regarded as procedures serving primarily the integration of divergent opinions and interests; they are, on the contrary, in danger of degenerating into weapons of the ideological and political cold war.

The adoption by the Charter of the majority principle, side by side with the principle of concurrent majority applying to the permanent members of the Security Council, has charged the United Nations atmosphere with an explosive constitutional issue that is apt to intensify the cold war. "The Nature of the Union" could very well serve as the title of quite a few chapters in the history of the United Nations.

The constitutional controversy over the nature of the union centers on the veto issue, though that is not the only one to fall under this heading. Speaking precisely, it is a dispute over the scope and exercise of the veto rather than over its existence and legitimacy.[17] For we are as little ready today to subject our foreign or domestic policy to majority decision of the United Nations, as we were at the time of Dumbarton Oaks, Yalta, and San Francisco. Commenting upon the veto in the Senate discussion on the Charter in 1945, Mr. Vandenberg said: "It is our defense against what I venture to believe would be bitterly condemned in many quarters as our 'involuntary servitude' if our veto power did not exist. It is the complete answer to any rational fears that we may be subordinating our destiny to alien commands. . . . It guarantees our perpetuated independence of international dictation."[18] In the meantime we have, of course, learned from Russia's two vetoes in the Czechoslovakian case that the veto can also be abused to facilitate the imposition upon a free nation of "involuntary servitude." But we still neither have any reason, nor have we declared any intention, to forego the veto as a protection of what we rightly consider to be our vital interests. Nor do we want any other of the great powers to renounce the privilege altogether. If the limitations upon the veto which we have proposed were to be adopted, the flag, to paraphrase Mr. Vandenberg, would still fly from the dome of the Capitol as well as from the Kremlin.

We should not, however, be surprised that the Soviet Union, as a minority power, is not ready to accept even minor limitations upon what is

151

essentially a minority privilege. In fact, never in history has the majority principle appealed to permanent minorities that could not expect ever to profit from a free swing of the political pendulum. The Soviet Union is, therefore, inclined to see even in innocent and well-meant attempts to smooth the operation of the Security Council by limiting the scope and exercise of the veto the first axe-stroke against what she considers to be the democratic foundation of the United Nations.

Her suspicion, in this case, is the easier to understand since we have not—I regret to say—been fair to the Russians with regard to her veto policy. If the Russians have abused the veto, we have not failed to abuse their abuse. To be sure, in six cases the exercise of the veto was clearly intended to protect the Soviet satellites, and it blocked United Nations action that would have been justified or required under the Charter. In the great majority of the forty-one vetoes, however, Russia's motive was to maintain her relative power position in the United Nations rather than to obstruct its activities. It is only natural that this is a concern as dear to the Russians as it is to us, though as a majority power we need not for its sake employ the veto. No less than twenty-two vetoes were directed against the admission of new members in order to prevent an increase in the size of the majority in the General Assembly. And at least four vetoes, as has already been mentioned, can be interpreted as "the prevention of any formal action which, directly or by implication, would increase the competence of the General Assembly."[19]

The constitutional controversies in the United Nations thus make one thing abundantly clear. Any move on our part in the direction of extending the application of the majority principle, be it directly by limiting the veto or indirectly by strengthening the General Assemly, will confirm the Soviet Union in her belief—a belief that is, unfortunately, based on a *Weltanschauung*—that we intend to transform the United Nations, originally planned as an organization within which the great powers would deal with one another on an equal footing, into an instrument of domination over Russia. Nor can we actually deny that this policy does fit our national interests better than those of Soviet Russia, at least as understood by her present rulers. They feel confident that they see through to the purely ideological roots of this policy. What they cannot see, what their very *Weltanschauung* prevents them from realizing, is that this policy, rather than being primarily inspired by utilitarian motives, is deeply rooted in our national history, and in our idealistic desire to see the governmental procedures of domestic democracy extended and applied to international politics, not for our sake alone, but for mankind's sake as well.

Dreaming of the Parliament of Man, we, for our part, find it no less hard to realize that anything coming close to an attempt to make the dream come true is bound to nurture Russia's suspicion of encirclement. But we cannot any longer afford to ignore the evidence, if we want our United Nations policy to fulfill what is the main purpose and function of diplomacy: to remove unfounded suspicions and thus to decrease international tension. Reliance on ideas and techniques of diplomacy proper will better serve this end than any move toward world government.

FOOTNOTES

[1]See Leland M. Goodrich, "From League of Nations to United Nations," in *International Organization*, vol. 1 (February 1947) pp. 3–4

[2]See A. Pelt, *The League of Nations Compared with the United Nations*, lecture delivered at Lake Success, April 4, 1949 (mimeographed 49–10351) p. 7

[3]Recent discussions in the Economic and Social Council seem to indicate that the record of implementation is poor. See *United Nations Bulletin*, vol. 7 (August 15, 1949) pp. 174 ff.

[4]B. A. Wortley, "The Veto and the Security Provisions of the Charter," in *British Year Book of International Law*, 1946, p. 107.

[5]See Raymond Dennett, "Politics in the Security Council," in *International Organization*, vol. 3 (August 1949) pp. 430 ff.

[6]See John N. Hazard, "The Soviet Union and the United Nations," in *Yale Law Journal*, vol. 55 (August 1946) p. 1018.

[7]See Clyde Eagleton, "The United Nations: Aims and Structure," in *Yale Law Journal*, vol. 55 (August 1946) pp. 974 ff., and Leo Gross, "The Charter of the United Nations and the Lodge Reservations," in *American Journal of International Law*, vol. 41 (July 1947) pp. 531 ff.

[8]The question whether the North Atlantic Pact is a military alliance proper played some role in the Senate discussions on the Pact. See *North Atlantic Treaty*, Hearings before the Committee on Foreign Relations, U. S. Senate, 81st Congress, 1st Session (Washington 1949) Part I, pp. 143 ff.

[9]Armstrong, "Coalition for Peace," in *Foreign Affairs*, vol. 27 (October 1948) p. 13.

[10]Hans Kelsen, "Collective Security and Collective Self-Defense under the Charter of the United Nations," in *American Journal of International Law*, vol. 42 (October 1948), pp. 795–96. See also Kelsen, "The Atlantic Pact and the United Nations Charter," in *New Leader*, June 4, 1949, p. 9.

[11]See "Documents relating to the Question of the Application of the Principles of the Covenant," in League of Nations, *Official Journal*, Special Supplement, No. 154 (Geneva 1936).

[12]*Ibid.*, pp. 10–11.

[13]Hans J. Morgenthau, "Diplomacy," in *Yale Law Journal*, vol. 55 (August 1946) pp. 1067 ff., and *Politics Among Nations: The Struggle for Power and Peace* (New York 1948), especially pp. 419 ff. The latter is a brilliant defense of the ideas and techniques of old diplomacy.

[14]United Nations, *Annual Report of the Secretary-General on the Work of the Organization, July 1, 1948–June 30, 1949*, General Assembly Official Records, Fourth Session, Supplement No. 1(A/930) (Lake Success 1949) pp. ix ff.

[15]Spaak, "The Role of the General Assembly," in *International Conciliation* (November 1948), p. 612.

[16]Only a short time ago the Big Five decided to set up machinery for consultation prior to voting, probably in compliance with a suggestion from the Secretary-General in the annual report mentioned above. See New York *Times,* November 1, 1949.

[17]George De T. Glazebrook, "The Middle Powers in the United Nations," in *International Organization,* vol. 1 (June 1947) p. 314.

[18]U. S. Senate Document 59, 79th Congress, 1st Session, p. 10, quoted in Norman J. Padelford, "The Use of the Veto," in *International Organization,* vol. 2 (June 1948) p. 230[6].

[19]Dennett, *op.. cit.,* pp. 429 ff. This article and the one by Norman J. Padelford (cited above) contain judicial analyses of the veto question.

FUNDAMENTALS OF COLLECTIVE SECURITY*

The question of the way in which an organization for collective security ought to deal with aggression, if and when it occurs, has been a matter of heated discussion ever since the founding of the League of Nations. To recall some of the ideas that were set forth theoretically in those endless controversies on the fundamentals of collective security may help us to appreciate and understand the problems which we have confronted in the recent practice of the United Nations and which no doubt will plague us in the future as well.

I

The system of collective security is intended to assure the peaceful existence of all members of the international community by establishing and implementing two basic legal principles.[1]

The first fundamental principle of collective security is the prohibition of force. Every war, and even every threat or use of force short of war, by one state against another is legally prohibited and thus unlawful. Since the prohibition of force is meant to be absolute, it applies to what the classic theory of international law has called just wars as well as unjust wars. According to the philosophy of collective security, "there is no distinction between *just* and *unjust* wars. Save two exceptions, all war is aggression, even if started on account of a wrong suffered by a State."[2] The two exceptions are war waged by an individual state in self-defense, and participation of a state in collective enforcement action undertaken by the international community itself.

The second fundamental principle of collective security is a corollary of the first. Every violation of the rule prohibiting the threat or use of force is

*Reprinted with permission of *Social Research*, Spring 1957 (Vol. 24, No. 1).

legally a matter of concern to the whole community of nations, and not only to that state which is immediately affected and directly injured by the breach of that rule. This principle is as radical a departure from nineteenth-century notions as the absolute prohibition of force. War waged by one state against another was, according to traditional international law, a strictly bilateral affair. No general rule of the law of nations prevented other states from adopting and pursuing, in case of war, a policy of neutrality involving the same rights and duties on their part toward both belligerents. According to the philosophy of collective security, each and every member of the international community is, as a matter of principle, required to render assistance, in some form or other, to the state against which the breach of the peace has been committed, and to help in some way or other to restore the peace.

This collective guarantee[3] is, it is true, designed to assure to all members of the family of nations the enjoyment of peace and security just as much as is the prohibition of force itself. The obligation of mutual assistance has no other purpose but to render the prohibition of force effective. Hence the notion that the planning and preparing of a practically fool-proof mechanism of collective measures for repressing aggression and war is the best way of preventing them. The certain prospect that overwhelmingly strong forces of the organized community will automatically be deployed against an aggressor is assumed to have a deterrent effect on the use of individual force. It is further true that the international community, if and when it is actually compelled to take collective action, does so, strictly speaking, to ensure respect for its own authority and interest. The action, including military measures of all kinds, is therefore, by intent, both politically and legally different from war as an instrument of national policy waged by individual states.

However, being virtually a contest of arms between the law-upholding community and the law-breaking aggressor state, the execution of what is meant to be a guarantee of peace is still war, in terms of human misery, political and social dislocation, and economic losses. In Woodrow Wilson's words, it turns what "is intended as a constitution of peace" into a "League of War."[4] But it is not the only and not even the most striking paradox of the system of collective security that the very agency whose *raison d'etre* is to save mankind from the scourge of war should serve as the machinery for waging war. By obligating, in principle, all members to participate in the taking of collective measures, including military measures, against an aggressor state, it is apt to transform any particular war into a general war, and thus tends by widening war to increase its evil effect.[5]

The system of collective security is the legal expression of a change in our moral evaluation of war. From the moral approval of just wars and an attitude of moral apathy toward unjust wars, we have in recent times been moving in the direction of unqualified moral condemnation of all individual wars except those waged in self-defense. The system is also a recognition of the change in the character and the consequences of modern war. It expresses the realization that its increasing destructiveness and its tendency, due to the growing interdependence of the contemporary world, to implicate other states are likely to make war—any war—a threat to civilization as such. Unfortunately, however, it can hardly be maintained that the system of collective security offers a truly novel answer to the age-old question of how we might prevent war. For it is fundamentally nothing but an adaptation to current international politics of the time-honored but somewhat dubious maxim: *Si vis pacem para bellum.* In fact, the war by which the system of collective security proposes to fight war is a "contingency to be dreaded"[6] more than the war envisaged previously in that maxim.

Thus, ever since the organization of the international community under common institutions was advocated and undertaken, there has been general agreement that collective security must not be relied upon as the only means for preventing war. Even the system of collective security itself has often been defined in much broader terms than those comprising merely the prohibition of recourse to force and the guarantee of its observance by a mechanism of collective coercive measures.[7] But regardless of whether or not one restricts the concept of collective security to these two basic legal principles, there can be no doubt that they need to be supplemented by other principles, devices, and procedures, if the elimination of war from international politics is to become possible and the dire contingency of sanctions be avoided.

The most obvious additional requirement for preventing war is to provide for pacific methods of settling international disputes and to ensure their actual application, if and when the methods of traditional diplomacy fail. But it is not sufficient that mediatory and conciliatory procedures begin to operate "when the spectre of war appears."[8] To render a system for the organization of peace effective, its agencies must possess authority to intervene before a situation has actually led to serious international friction or given rise to a more or less clearly defined dispute. In fact, they require some general authority to promote and preserve an international order in which the rational causes of international conflict will no longer be operative. To put it in General Jan Smuts' words, an organization of peace, if it is to be effective and to last, "must become part and parcel of the common international life of states, it must be an ever visible, living, working organ of the polity of civilization. It must function so strongly in the ordinary peaceful intercourse of states that it becomes irresistible in their disputes; its peace activity must be the foundation and guarantee of its war power."[9]

There is thus, in theory, general agreement that for preventing war effectively the collective-security powers of an international peace organization need to be supplemented by other devices and policies. There is also agreement that, on the other hand, the effectiveness of the mediatory and conciliatory powers of such an organization is likely to be increased by the prospect of coercive measures, if its members fail to fulfill the obligations they have undertaken for peaceful settlement of international disputes.[10] But it has always been controversial what relative weight and importance should in practice be attached, in planning and building an international peace organization, to pacific procedures on the one hand, and to procedures of collective coercion on the other. And it has been equally controversial whether and how the agencies of an international organization should combine those procedures when actually dealing with aggression.

The two main trends of thought to which this controversy on the fundamentals of collective security has given rise have been most clearly elaborated in the discussion on the definition of aggression that started in the early 1920s and has ever since been carried on inside and outside first the League of Nations and then the United Nations.[11] It is therefore appropriate to reconsider those basic issues in the context and terms of that discussion.

II

The movement for a legal definition of international aggression was initiated and sustained by statesmen and scholars who were inclined to rely primarily on the coercive measures provided for by the system of collective security as an effective means of preventing war. The definition of aggression was conceived of by them as one of the essential requirements for assuring the practically automatic operation of the system and thus guaranteeing its intended effect of deterring aggression. This function of the proposed definition is clearly indicated by the historical context in which the movement originated. The first attempts at definition coincided with and were a part of frantic efforts made in the early 1920s to strengthen the collective-security provisions of the League of Nations Covenant. In fact, in those attempts probably lies the chief historical significance of both the abortive Draft Treaty of Mutual Assistance of 1923 and the equally abortive Geneva Protocol of 1924.

The Draft Treaty of Mutual Assistance gives us yet another clue to the philosophy that inspired the endeavors toward a legal definition of international aggression. The authors of the Covenant of the League conceived of unlawful resort to war as an act morally so atrocious and socially so harmful to the entire international community as to call for counteractions on the part of all of its members, rather than for mere redress by the party immediately affected by the breach of the law. Municipal law qualifies morally opprobrious and socially harmful unlawful acts as crimes subject to public punishment. Thus the fathers of the Covenant, following the terminology of municipal legal systems, might very well have qualified unlawful resort to war as crime, and repressive measures against it as punishment. Actually, however, they refrained from extending these domestic notions to the international field, preferring to keep within the traditional terminology of international law, which "resembles tort law rather than criminal law in the national legal system."[12] It was only in the Draft Treaty of Mutual Assistance of 1923 that the prospective parties were to "solemnly declare that aggressive war is an international crime,"[13] thus making explicit what Article 16 of the Covenant only implied. To be sure, the Draft Treaty never became positive international law. But the idea remained alive that, for all practical purposes, aggressive war ought to be considered a crime, and that the task of an international agency called upon to deal with aggression was accordingly a function pertaining somehow to international criminal justice rather than to diplomacy. The definition of international aggression was to be the legal instrument for giving expression and effect to what one may call the penal conception of collective security.

The definition of aggression is formally an implementation of the first fundamental principle of collective security—the prohibition of force—in so far as it circumscribes the acts that fall under this prohibition. Its practical purpose, however, is to secure the prompt and effective operation of the mechanism of collective repressive measures by which that principle, or rather its observance, is guaranteed.

Aggression has always been one of the vaguest and most controversial concepts in the political and legal vocabulary. According to the proponents of definition, it is this general uncertainty regarding the facts constituting acts of aggression which accounts to a large extent for the practical weakness of the system of collective security. The lack of agreement on the meaning of aggression, they maintain, enables the aggressor to present with some semblance of justification offensive acts as legitimate measures of self-defense. What is even more unfortunate, the vagueness of the notion of aggression is apt to tempt the international agency itself, charged to deal with aggression, to evade taking collective action. Finally, and not least important, it is an inducement for the members of the security organization to shirk the obligations that are incumbent upon them pursuant to the principle of mutal assistance.

The remedy for the uncertainty concerning the nature of aggression and its untoward effect of weakening the deterrent power of the system of collective security is, we are told, a precise and legally binding definition of aggression. Once any doubt as to what facts constitute aggression has been removed by a clear definition of aggression, there will no longer be any room for disagreement on whether or not a particular act charged against a particular state qualifies as aggression. At the same time, the definition of aggression would allegedly dispose of the thorny question of what constitutes legitimate self-defense by implicitly restricting the latter to the use of force in response to acts falling under that definition. All the international agency called upon to deal with aggression would have to do in a concrete case of armed conflict is determine which state actually committed the act defined as aggression. When this determination had been made, there would automatically be against the author of that act an irrefutable presumption of aggression,[14] binding upon both the organ and the several members of the security organization. The definition of aggression would thus make it impossible for them to disregard the obligations imposed by the system of collective security. Moreover, the definition would supposedly alleviate the responsibility they assume in executing repressive measures against the aggressor state. Being deprived of free discretion in deciding whether the alleged act constitutes aggression, they cannot be held liable by the aggressor or any other state for considering and treating the act as what it is legally defined to be.[15] In other words, the definition of aggression would not only secure the automatic operation of the system of collective security, but also lend it the impersonal character that marks the enforcement of objective rules of law in the national legal system.

But if the adherents of this school of thought agree on the desirability of defining aggression, they differ among themselves on the type of definition they want to see adopted. The discussion has turned chiefly on the alleged respective merits and demerits of the general and the so-called enumerative definition. Those who advocate the former content themselves with defining aggression as employment of force for any purpose other than self-defense. This definition is quite obviously a naive and futile attempt to define the vague and controversial concept of aggression by the no less vague and controversial notion of self-defense, and is virtually nothing more than a useless repetition of the rule prohibiting the resort to force (*Question,* pars. 242–44, 478). It is therefore hardly surprising that the discussion has from an early date centered on the enumerative type of definition which, being more elaborate and precise, can more reasonably be expected to serve the ends for which definition of aggression is recommended.

The most famous example of the enumerative type is the so-called Politis definition in Article 1 of the stillborn "Act relating to the Definition of the Aggressor," drafted by a committee under Nicolas Politis' chairmanship at the Disarmament Conference of Geneva in 1933. The Politis definition was, in turn, based on a proposal the Soviet Union had submitted to the Conference. Both of these proposed definitions have decisively and lastingly influenced subsequent discussions on the definition of aggression prior to and even since World War II.

According to the Politis definition, "the aggressor in an international conflict shall . . .be considered to be that State which is the first to commit any of the following actions: (1) Declaration of war upon another State; (2) Invasion by its armed forces, with or without a declaration of war, of the territory of another State; (3) Attack by its land, naval or air forces, with or without a declaration of war, on the territory, vessels or aircraft of another State; (4) Naval blockade of the coasts or ports of another State; (5) Provision of support to armed bands formed in the territory which have invaded the territory of another State, or refusal, notwithstanding the request of the invaded State, to take in its own territory all the measures in its power to deprive those bands of all assistance or protection."[16]

Granting the validity of the assumptions and considerations on which the demand for a definition of aggression is based, there can be no doubt that the Politis formula, or any other formula of the same pattern, is more suitable than a general definition for dispelling the nebulous vagueness in which the notion of aggression has so far been shrouded. Being an exhaustive enumeration of the facts that constitute acts of aggression, the Politis formula can be and has been criticized for forestalling the legal possibility of qualifying and treating other unforeseen and unforeseeable breaches of the peace as acts of aggression, a possibility that is claimed to be the very merit of a general definition. But the apostles of the Politis formula, even if they should concede that this limitation, inherent in any enumerative definition of aggression, is indeed the vice of its virtue, are convinced that the practical significance of this vice is as small as the practical significance of the virtue of enumeration is great. The historical record of the system of collective security being what it is, its operation, they believe, is more likely to be hamstrung by deliberate evasion of vaguely stipulated obligations than by lack of legal authority to take and execute collective action.

The proponents of the Politis formula not only claim for it the merit of excluding for the future any doubt as to whether or not a concrete act alleged to be aggression actually constitutes aggression in the legal sense. They also praise the proposed definition as a means of simplifying the ascertainment of the responsibility for an armed conflict. All that is required in determining the aggressor is to establish which of the parties to the conflict has first committed one of the acts specified in the definition.[17] Once such a definition as is suggested by Politis and his followers is adopted, "it is no longer necessary to inquire into the psychological motives behind the resort to force, the righteous or unrighteous intention of the State committing the forbidden act" (*Collective Security*, p. 304). Nor is it necessary for the international agency dealing with aggression to consider any of the events prior to the act of aggression, since the definition of aggression covers provoked acts of aggression no less than unprovoked acts (*ibid.*, pp. 23, 297).

As a matter of fact, the definition, being an implementation of the absolute prohibition of force, is deliberately intended to rule out even the consideration by the security organization of any but the objective facts of aggression. In the words of Article 2 of the "Act relating to the Definition of the Aggressor," drafted by the Politis committee in 1933, "no political, military, economic or other consideration may serve as an excuse or justification for the aggression" (*Question*, par. 78). Like the absolute prohibition of force, the definition of aggression is meant to give legal effect to the idea that "it is of paramount importance that peace be maintained, whatever may be the wrongs endured by the State which has attacked" *(Collective Security,* p. 298). Nothing is more revealing for the philosophy underlying the Politis definition than the contention of at least some of its adherents that the invasion of the territory of a state qualifies as aggression even when the attacked state possesses no legal title to exercise authority over the invaded territory, but holds it only de facto (*ibid.*, p. 316). The unqualified protection of the peace and the status quo is the fundamental purpose of the definition of aggression, as it is also of the absolute prohibition of force.

To be sure, the separation of the responsibility for aggression proper from the responsibility for the dispute or the situation that has led to the breach of the peace is in no way intended to bar a state whose rights and interests have been violated from taking all appropriate measures for safeguarding them. It is meant exclusively to limit the aggrieved state to recourse to methods of peaceful settlement and adjustment of its claims and grievances. "Domestic law does not allow the individual to take the law into his own hands by violent means. The same principle should be followed in the international field" (*ibid.*, p. 298). As aggressive self-help by means of force has always been a crime under domestic criminal law, it is henceforth also to be a crime under international criminal law.

III

One cannot but admire the logical consistency with which the Politis school tries to apply principles that govern social relations within the national community to the broader community of nations. But it is precisely on account of the extreme length to which this school is driven by its abstract reasoning that the fallacy of the analogy between relations among individuals and relations among collective political entities is in this case even more obvious and dangerous than it is in other twentieth-century legal schemes for organizing international society on the basis of this analogy.

Realization of the fallacy underlying the penal conception of collective security is what distinguishes the school that denies the desirability of defining aggression from the school that upholds it. To be sure, aggressive war is a matter of deep moral concern for the opponents of definition, no less than for its proponents. Nevertheless they refuse to accept the conclusion that ideas, principles, and procedures of criminal justice offer the best means of fighting the evil of war. They oppose to the penal conception of collective security what one may call the diplomatic conception.

Criticism of the Politis school is based on several grounds. It is, first of all, directed against the validity of the assumption that definition would ensure the deterrent effect which the system of collective security is intended to exert upon potential aggressors. This expectation, according to the adherents of the diplomatic conception, is too unrealistic to be warranted. What actually renders it doubtful whether aggression against a particular state is going to provoke the reaction and resistance of the entire international community is that states cannot reasonably be relied upon "to make war against nature," that is, for reasons they do not hold to affect their national interests (Francesco Coppola in *Collective Security,* pp. 7, 144 ff.). It is true that the definition of aggression might deprive the security organization and its members of the argument that an act of aggression actually committed did not legally qualify as such; and in this case they might find it more difficult, if they refused in a concrete case of aggression to take collective action, to justify their policy in terms of the legal obligations they have subscribed to. But it is somewhat naive, the diplomatic school maintains, to assume that they will not try, and will not be able, to overcome this difficulty, if considerations of interest seem to advise against accepting the risks and burdens involved in collective action. Moreover, while the definition of aggression is apt to preclude for the future any honest disagreement among governments on whether or not a specific act constitutes aggression in the legal sense of the term, it does not and cannot provide for the automatic ascertainment of the responsibility for having committed it. There still remains the possibility of honest, and even more commonly of dishonest, disagreement on the matter of which of the parties to the conflict first committed one of the acts of aggression specified in the definition (see *Question,* par. 33).

But lack of realistic appreciation of the political factors that render doubtful any attempt to devise a fool-proof mechanism of collective security has not been the only objection against the proposal of definition. The representatives of the diplomatic school have for moral, no less than political, reasons questioned also the validity and the wisdom of the philosophy itself on which the proposal is based. More specifically, they have questioned the moral validity and the political wisdom of the ideal of automatic sanctions in the first place, and of the punitive ideal in the second.

IV

The great merit of definition, according to the penal school, is that it would make it simpler, when hostilities break out, to determine aggression and aggressor. But even if this effect is assumed to be as striking as alleged, one may very well doubt whether the attempt to resolve the complexity of international war into the elements of an ordinary criminal case is justified. As things actually are, the method of applying to war the principles and means of criminal justice cannot but assure "a purely artificial simplicity" (*Question,* par. 229).

As a matter of fact, the Politis definition is intended to reduce the crime of aggression to a degree of simplicity at which, as a rule, even municipal criminal codes do not aim in defining ordinary offenses. According to a time-honored maxim of criminal law, *Mens Rea* usually forms a constituent part of crime. An individual therefore is commonly not guilty of an offense against the criminal law unless he has a guilty mind.[18] No guilty mind is required for committing the crime of aggression, as far as the Politis definition is concerned. Intention, motive, and purpose of the act of aggression need not—indeed, must not—be inquired into by the international agency when faced with aggression (*Collective Security,* pp. 337 ff.). Any resort to force, provided only that it falls under the enumeration of objective facts that constitute aggression, calls for the immediate taking of collective action against the state committing aggression in the defined sense, even if the aggressive act was in no way intended to initiate an aggressive war, and even if the parties to the armed conflict resulting from that act merely stumbled, as it were, into what Sir Austen Chamberlain and others have described as "accidental war." Thus, the diplomatic school charges, the definition of aggression might very well have the effect of precipitating a collective action where there is a reasonable chance to stop aggressive acts and restore peace and the status quo ante without resort to the most extreme and calamitous measures (see *Question,* pars. 40 ff., 51, 116, 260).

Admittedly, accidental wars, as opposed to deliberate wars, may have occurred in history less frequently than a naive philosophy of international politics has been inclined to assume. But there have in the past been wars that fit Sir Austen's description of accidental wars, and there still is and always will be the possibility of "wars arising without premeditation, without the desire for war on the part of anyone, out of some question which suddenly brings passions to the boiling point, which affects, or is thought to affect, the national honor, or out of some imbroglio into which nations have been led, not knowing what they did, and from which they see no possibility of extracting themselves without a loss of honor and repute" (*Collective Security*, p. 35). No doubt, such a war as Sir Austen has so described offers to a security organization an ideal opportunity for proving itself true to its task of composing conflicts and restoring peace. But there is even less doubt that by premature application of coercive punitive measures against one of the parties to the conflict the organization would deprive itself of any chance of exploiting that opportunity successfully. The criminal prosecutor would from the very beginning crowd out the *amiable compositeur,* and a particular war, capable of being ended easily by pacific procedures, would unnecessarily and unjustifiedly be transformed into a general war infinitely more difficult of termination.

The diplomatic school's criticism that the vaunted simplicity of the proposed definition fails to take into account the "tangled political situation" (*ibid.,* p. 308) and the no less tangled moral situation in which wars usually originate applies not only to accidental wars. Also in deliberate, premeditated war the responsibility for committing aggression, in the' military-technical sense of the definition, is likely to be only one element, though undoubtedly a very important one, in a composite pattern of moral and political responsibilities for the conflict which has exploded into war. To put it in the blunt words of a Swedish statesman, Mr. Osten Unden: "It has been contended that the relationship between the attacking country and the defending country is similar to the relationship between a murderer or bandit on the one hand and his victim on the other. Such a concept, however, has nothing in common with the type of situation that most frequently arises. In reality there are numerous degrees of responsibility in the case of aggression" (see *Question,* par. 232).

The usual complexity of the pattern of responsibilities in deliberate, premeditated wars of aggression is impressively suggested by the way in which both history and jurisprudence have commonly approached the question of war guilt. As far back as Thucydides, historians concerned with the interconnection of events and their explanation have tended to regard the "immediate cause" plunging states into war as a subordinate question compared with the "real cause," which, according to the great Athenian, is also the one that is "formally most kept out of sight." Concentrating their attention on the latter, the historians, again following Thucydides, are inclined to consider and describe as "inevitable" the war whose origin they thus try to explain.[19] Seeing the parties involved in war as instruments of fate or of irrepressible casual forces, rather than as free agents, they even tend to exculpate them from moral and legal guilt.

In the traditional doctrine of international law, as it prevailed prior to the first world war, there was a similar tendency to look upon war as a natural phenomenon, as it were, outside the reach of moral and legal norms, or, what is practically the reverse of this naturalistic conception, to admit, explicitly or implicitly, an absolute right to war. But in so far as that doctrine did retain the normative character of the *bellum justum* theory of the schoolmen and recognized only a qualified right to war, it displayed—in weighing and balancing against one another the "numerous degrees of responsibility in the case of aggression"—a distinct tendency to emphasize the responsibility for the remote causes of war rather than for the opening of armed hostilities, the proximate cause. According to the *bellum justum* doctrine, it was not aggression per se, but the lack of valid cause in launching war that constituted war guilt.[20]

To eliminate any legal justification for starting war is the very purpose of the absolute prohibition of force achieved by twentieth-century international law. Indeed, the fact that under traditional international law each state could claim the right to decide for itself the validity of the cause for which it resorted to war invited an attempt to prevent any further abuse in the exercise of the *jus ad bellum* by abolishing the right as such. But however weighty the arguments for the outlawry of war may be, it cannot reasonably be expected that the situations in which aggressions occur will henceforth be any less complex, morally or politically, than they were prior to the legal prohibition of force. Nor can it reasonably be taken for granted that a collective-security organization should not be entitled carefully to balance the rights and wrongs on both sides when dealing with acts of aggression. It is for these reasons that the advocates of the diplomatic conception of collective security oppose a definition of aggression that ignores the usual complexity of the context in which wars, including deliberate aggressive wars, originate, and prevents the international authorities, charged with the task of halting them, from taking that complexity adequately into account.

The case of provoked aggression is undoubtedly the strongest argument on which the diplomatic school can base its warnings against artificial simplicity and its plea for the recognition of divided responsibility for armed conflict. Moreover, use of the idea of provocation as a qualifying element in the determination of war guilt is sanctioned by long-established practice in international law. Time and again, treaties of defensive alliance have limited the obligation of their respective parties to assist one another to cases in which they are the innocent victim of "an unprovoked attack," "an unprovoked war," or "an unprovoked aggression" (see *Question*, pars. 202 ff.).

The members of the diplomatic school do not feel that their plea for the recognition of divided responsibility in cases of provoked aggression is any less well justified because it has proved to be as difficult to define provocation in precise legal terms as it is to define aggression or self-defense. They want to see international authorities, when called upon to deal with breaches of the peace, as little shackled by a definition of provocation as by a definition of aggression. All they insist upon is that "the previous conduct of the attacked party"[21] be one of the factors those authorities should be free to take into consideration when deciding on and carrying out collective action against aggression. From this point of view, three categories of acts that might constitute provocation, depending upon the individual case, have been mentioned in the course of the discussion on the definition of aggression: first, preparations for aggression at some time in the near or distant future; second, some breach of international law, involving another state or its nationals; and third, an unfriendly attitude of governments or public opinion, even if not a breach of international law (see *Question,* par. 338).

According to the representatives of the diplomatic school, there are still other factors to be taken into account in measuring the responsibilities for a war. The Politis formula is practically "a territorial definition of aggression" (*Collective Security,* p. 316). As such it covers the territory which a state holds only de facto no less than the territory it holds de jure. In terms of this definition it therefore makes no difference whether territory of the one or the other kind is invaded. Moreover, the definition applies to any case of aggression, regardless of whether the territorial sovereignties of the aggressor state and the attacked state are clearly marked off by a boundary line that is definitely established in law as well as in fact (*ibid,* pp. 300, 334 ff.). To be sure, the prohibition of force is meant to be absolute. Thus the aggressor state has no legal right to claim justifying causes of one type or another in the sense of making its acts lawful. But it may very well be maintained that the aggressor's moral and political responsibility does not weigh so heavily when the aggression is committed in an unsettled state of affairs as it does when occurring within a politically and legally stable order.

V

By emphasizing the moral and political complexity of the situation in which wars usually originate, and stressing the usually "numerous degrees of responsibility in the case of aggression," the diplomatic school exposes itself to the suspicion that it is trying to restore by indirect means the right to war to the extent that it was generally recognized prior to the absolute prohibition of force. But to infer this intention from the position of the diplomatic school is in no way justified. It would be equally unwarranted to interpret its rejection of the ideal of automatic sanctions, and the stubbornness with which it insists on reserving to the security organization liberty of action in dealing with aggression, as inspired by the motive of preserving for the organization unbounded legal freedom to evade the task of taking collective action whenever it pleases to do so.[22] After all, the members of the diplomatic school object to the definition of aggression not only insofar as it would imply a legal obligation to resort to enforcement measures even in cases where for political or other reasons the latter could and should be avoided. They oppose definition no less sincerely on the ground that it might legally forestall collective action in cases where it ought to be taken. All the same, it would be useless to deny that free discretion of the security organization in dealing with aggression is apt to operate in practice as a legal temptation to escape the commitments of collective security.

But whatever the consequences of liberty of action on the part of the security organization might be, they do not diminish the weight of the moral objections to which the idea of automatic sanctions is open. To establish or imply an obligation on the part of the security organization and its members to take the most extreme measures in case of aggression, including measures of military force, irrespective of the attacked state's own previous conduct or of other factors relevant to the question of war guilt, would mean subscribing unquestioningly to an absolute general guarantee of protection. Even if guilty of the most serious infringements of international law against the aggressor, the attacked state would be disposed to count on, even to feel justified in expecting, international support against suffering the not altogether undeserved consequences of its own unlawful deeds. In fact, the encouragement of such an expectation might easily operate as an inducement to lawless conduct, inasmuch as by indulging therein nations would run only a greatly reduced risk of war.[23]

The moral implications of a system of automatic sanctions are no less objectionable and absurd from the point of view of the security organization and its members. Opposition to the idea of collective security has often been stated in terms that make it appear to be the expression of a philosophy of power politics pure and simple, unconcerned with considerations of morality and justice. Indeed, when Francesco Coppola (*Collective Security,* pp. 7, 144 ff.) ridicules the prohibition of force in international politics as an attempt to prevent the states from making war according to nature, that is, for their own national interests, he not only seems to suggest the probable futility of what he considers a dubious legalistic effort. His dictum also recalls the notion, recurring time and again in the history of political thought ever since the days of the sophists, that might ought to be the standard of right.[24] Similarly, when he refers ironically to the obligation which a security organization imposes upon its members to assist the victim of aggression as an obligation to make war against nature, inasmuch as such obligation does not accord with their national interests, he again seems to voice doubts not only about the effectiveness of this legal prescription but about the very validity of the moral principle of mutual aid underlying it. Admittedly, the diplomatic school shares with Coppola and other opponents of the system of collective security a doubt in the unfailing efficacy of its devices. Even so, its rejection of the proposal to bind an international organization by a legal definition of aggression that would not permit it to consider duly all pertinent responsibilities, when dealing with a breach of the peace, is in no wise caused by a lack of concern for the moral duties of international fellowship.

Far from conceiving of the obligation of assistance as a human convention of contestable validity, because it contradicts nature's law that each state should seek exclusively its own advantage and comfort, the diplomatic school merely insists, for moral reasons, on the conditional character of the duty of mutual assistance. If an attacked state is not morally entitled to expect the support of the international community, irrespective of its own previous conduct, neither can the security organization and its members be justly held bound by an obligation to risk the dire contingency of collective action for the purpose of assisting the object of aggression, regardless of the actual balance of rights and wrongs among the warring states. Indeed, it appears that even Mr. Politis was not completely blind to the morally preposterous implications of his own proposition. At any rate, he was anxious to disprove that an absolute obligation to take sanctions could be legitimately deduced from it.[25]

In sum, the ideal of automatic sanctions which inspired the proposal to define aggression is, in the first place, a phantom, unrealistic by virtue of the assumption that a legal formula will ensure to the system of collective security a deterrent effect upon potential aggressors which it can for political reasons never be expected to have. In the second place, the ideal is open to the most serious objections on moral grounds. Since the simplicity to which the proponents of definition try to reduce the problem of war is "purely artificial," it is not surprising that the proposed solution, based on such artificiality, is contestable in ethical terms as well. Oversimplification of complex moral problems cannot but lead to morally objectionable solutions.

The advocacy of a definition of aggression is nevertheless not wholly lacking in merit. Inasmuch as the discussion it has provoked has brought out in full relief the morally doubtful nature of the ideal of automatic sanctions, it has contributed to the elucidation of a central problem of collective security. Ever since the system was proposed and applied, its advocates have been obsessed with the quest for the certainty of sanctions. Definition of aggression is only one among various devices that have in the course of the last forty years been recommended for assuring that certainty. If it is the merit of such political realists as Coppola and Morgenthau[26] to have proved the political fallacy of this frantic quest for certainty, it is the merit of the proponents of definition—in view of their real intentions, an entirely involuntary merit, to be sure—to have carried its advocacy to a point where also the moral fallacy of the quest becomes obvious. The ideal of *automatic* collective sanctions against aggression is a false ideal, politically and morally.

VI

The representatives of the diplomatic school have not only questioned the moral validity and the political wisdom of the ideal of automatic sanctions. Their criticism of the philosophy underlying the proposal to define aggression has been directed also against the punitive ideal, which forms no less an essential part of that philosophy than the notion of automatic sanctions.

The qualification of aggression as an international criminal offense is intended to serve the same purpose as is the automatic operation of sanctions. The prospective condemnation of an aggressor as an international criminal by the competent international authority is meant to exert, and even expected to intensify, the deterrent effect upon potential aggressors which the certain prospect of collective action in case of aggression is designed and assumed to have. As an alleged means of preventing war, the conception of aggression as a criminal act, subject to criminal punishment by the organized international community, is therefore open to the same criticism of lack of realistic assumptions as the idea of automatic sanctions itself, and has been subjected to this criticism by those who adhere to the conceptions of the diplomatic school.

Doubting the efficacy of the punitive notion as a means of preventing war, the adherents of the diplomatic school hold it the more important and urgent to concern themselves with the question what effect the penal conception is likely to have upon collective action taken for repressing war, once open hostilities have broken out. How, they ask, is the substitution of the idea of collective retribution for the idea of mutual assistance going to influence collective security *in action?* The objections to the penal conception raised by the diplomatic school from this point of view retain their full interest and value in spite of the fact that no definition of aggression and no express designation of the latter as a criminal offense has ever been incorporated either into general international law or into the law of the League of Nations or of the United Nations. Collective action in case of aggression is, for political reasons, as apt to be turned to punitive objectives, even without any rules of positive law to legitimize them, as punitive

170

war has tended in the twentieth century to be revived without such sanction.

It would seem, in the first place, that the cognizance of aggression, conceived of as an international crime, ought to be given to an international judicial tribunal of one kind or another. The most elementary principles of criminal justice practiced by civilized nations require that independent courts alone conduct criminal proceedings, that they discharge their penal functions without paying attention to political considerations, and that they comply most strictly with evidential and other rules safeguarding objective procedures. These principles are essential requirements of international no less than of municipal criminal justice. To advocate, as some proponents of the penal conception of collective security have been doing, that the power of passing judgment on the guilt of the crime of aggression be assigned not to a political but to a judicial authority is therefore only consistent and fair. It is hardly surprising, however, that most of the members of the penal school have rejected the idea of having the responsibility for aggression determined by judicial agencies and procedures. "In theory," to quote Professor René Cassin (in *Collective Security,* p. 331), "this is a magnificent plan. But we feel that it does not correspond to reality." One may wonder indeed that the learned author does not go a step further and draw from his realization of the inapplicability of criminal procedures proper to the reality of international war the conclusion that the penal notion is altogether out of place. Yet one cannot but agree with his view that only a political organ is capable of dealing adequately with the problems to which aggression gives rise.

In cases of aggression, what precludes resort to a judicial authority is, first of all, the momentous and far-reaching consequences of a decision to take collective action for halting hostilities and restoring peace. Whatever punishment a municipal court inflicts upon a murderer or bandit, the execution of that punishment will most likely not directly affect the national community as such. To punish an aggressor state by taking collective military action against it may very well shake the entire international community to its foundation. The implications and possible consequences of the judgment to be passed in the case of aggression thus rule out the possibility of ever basing the decision on purely legal considerations without examining and weighing the political aspects and factors involved in the case. Only a political organ, therefore, can be expected to be equal to the task.

Nor does the nature of the case make it permissible to bind the international authority dealing with aggression by rules of evidence and other rules guaranteeing objective procedures, such as the most fundamental principles of criminal justice would require, if punishment of the aggressor rather than halting aggression and restoring the status quo ante is the very purpose of collective action. The success of the latter could easily depend upon an instantaneous response to the aggression committed, and this not only for reasons of the character of the twentieth-century warfare (*Collective Security*, p. 315). Even in less urgent cases, circumstances might call for taking collective action at a moment when the available evidence for establishing which of the parties to the armed conflict first perpetrated the act of aggression is at best presumptive, and by no means conclusive. Thus compliance with procedural principles that are indispensable for rendering objective criminal justice would very likely delay the operation of sanctions, and accordingly defeat the purpose that the penal conception of collective security is intended to serve.

Its advocates, faced with this awkward dilemma, are, for the most part, not ready to pay so high a price, but insist rather on the pursuit of punitive objectives by purely political agencies and procedures. It is true, an attempt to fight aggression by collective action decided upon in judicial proceedings would no doubt be doomed to failure, the reality being what it is. Nevertheless it would indeed be a magnificent and noble attempt, inasmuch as it is inspired by the aim of extending the rule of law. But to fight aggression by collective punitive action decided upon in political proceedings cannot but result in extending the rule of force rather than that of law, for collective action in pursuit of punitive purposes is bound to make more difficult both the termination of the action and the settlement of the issues that have caused the armed conflict. Thus the eventuality of collective action against aggression becomes still more dreadful than it already unavoidably is. This effect of the penal conception upon collective security in action is the point on which the diplomatic school has concentrated its criticism of the punitive philosophy.

It would be naive, not to say preposterous, to suggest that an international agency called upon to deal with aggression should, in all circumstances, subordinate its enforcement policy to conciliatory efforts, with a view to ending the armed conflict at any price and thus also shortening the collective action. Rather, one would be entitled to insist that it concentrate wholly on repression and suspend any attempts at conciliation if, and as long as, the military superiority of the aggressor state over the attacked state is so overwhelming as to assure the former an easy and quick victory, enabling it to impose its political will upon the defeated party. For an unimpeded military triumph of the aggressor over his victim might very well make any conciliatory efforts purely "academic."[27] But although the spirit of collective security could, under certain conditions and for their duration, require the subordination and even the outright suspension of conciliatory exertions, that spirit would be definitely violated if the peace organization, in pursuing repressive measures, were to neglect any reasonable chance of terminating the contest of arms by pacific procedures. The latter are no less, if indeed they are no more, than the former a legitimate means for attaining what is the object of collective security, if and when aggressive war has been launched: the restoration of peace.

It would be equally naive and preposterous to deny that the difficulty of pursuing at one and the same time a policy of repression and a policy aimed at conciliation and pacific settlement is indeed formidable, for political and also for military reasons. The task might easily prove too difficult for the skill of even the most consummate statesman. Undoubtedly it becomes still more formidable if the international agency, in exercising its security function, assumes or is legally held to assume the role of a criminal or quasi-criminal prosecutor, judge, and executor, directing its efforts to the punishment of the aggressor.

As was mentioned above, the advocates of the penal conception have never gone so far as to pretend that the responsibility for committing aggression is necessarily identical with the responsibility for the dispute or the situation that finally exploded in armed hostilities and war. They reject, it is true, the recognition of causes that in the eyes of the law might justify an act of aggression, and therefore insist that, in dealing with aggression, the pertinent authority refuse to take allegedly justifying causes into consideration. But they do not rule out the possibility that the aggressor state could have well founded grievances against the attacked state "which might later be invoked" (*Collective Security*, pp. 332, 298). In other words, the attempt to simplify the determination of aggression and aggressor, in case of an outbreak of hostilities, is not meant to imply that the issues that have given rise to the armed conflict should be disregarded when it comes to its final settlement. One is entitled to wonder, however, whether any agency, once it has become engaged in punitive procedures against the aggressor state alone, will ever find its way back to a full and objective appreciation of the complex political and legal context of which the aggression forms only one element. And one may wonder still more whether the aggressor state will ever be ready to accept its prosecutor as an authority morally, legally and phychologically fit to determine objectively what is its due.

The deliberate exclusive concentration on the crime of aggression, the "immediate cause" of the armed conflict, cannot but result, in the first place, in the obliteration of the political factors that have been its "real causes." This obliteration is a classic example of what Morgenthau has called the "fragmentation" of international issues. "The facts of life to be dealt with," he says,[28] "are artificially separated from the facts that precede, accompany, and follow them, and are transformed into a legal 'case.'" The extent to which this transformation of an intricate and involved political question or set of questions into an apparently simple criminal case is bound to complicate and delay the settlement of the former can hardly be over-rated.

This effect will necessarily be the more powerful as the exclusive concentration on the legal case of aggression results, in the second place, in the obliteration of its wider legal and moral aspects as well. The attacked state may itself be guilty of violations of law and morality so serious as to qualify as international crimes. But the proceedings directed against the criminal aggressor to the exclusion of any other malefactor give the victim of aggression the chance to emerge as a shining example of innocence and probity. Right and justice will be proclaimed to be all on its side, and none on the side of the aggressor. No sooner has a collective action aimed at the punishment of the aggressor been initiated than it automatically becomes a collective war for righteousness, with all the consequences we know from the history of individual wars for righteousness.[29] Passions are inflamed; the temptation to resort to the sternest methods of warfare is increased; and complete victory over one culprit, rather than the halting of aggression and restoration of peace between two guilty parties, becomes the objective of the collective action.[30] Moreover, with the shifting and widening of the goal of such action, and the consequential lengthening of its duration, new political complications are bound to arise that will add to the original hazards of the collective action and may even endanger its ultimate success.

VII

In the course of discussion on the fundamentals of collective security, probably the most consistent and most radical proposal that has been made with a view to avoiding the pitfalls of the punitive approach is the scheme promoted in the 1930s by Dr. Georg Cohn, a Danish scholar and statesman.[31]

Reciprocal undertakings of military assistance form an essential part of the system of collective security, as well as of the system of defensive alliance. The two devices differ from one another, however, in that the alliance is intended to guarantee the security of a limited number of states against the supposedly aggressive policy of one or more particular states, while the collective organization of security is designed to protect the security of all against each and every other state. The system of alliance "is necessarily directed against someone, even if it is completely free from all thought of aggression," but the collective organization of security is directed against war as such (*Collective Security*, pp. 161 ff.). It is the abstract character of the system of collective security, as opposed to the concrete nature of the system of alliance, that renders the effectiveness of the former so much more doubtful than that of the latter in the eyes of Coppola and others.

Cohn sees in the abstract character of collective security not a vice but a virtue, and tries to preserve that character for it even throughout the collective action which the security organization resorts to when hostilities have broken out. According to Cohn, the collective action must be taken not against aggression, and even less against the aggressor, but "against war as such, as fact"—defensive as well as offensive war. For "to direct the reaction . . . against the guilty party and in the interest of the victim" would mean that the organized international society "becomes active against someone and no longer merely against war itself."

This principle that the enforcement measures are to be taken not against the aggressor, but against both or all belligerent states, is not the only indication of Cohn's effort to prevent the collective action from turning into a war proper that will, as such, be no more easily limited and terminated just because it is being waged by collective society. Though the members of the security organization are, under Cohn's scheme, legally held to participate in the enforcement measures according to directives of its central agency, their status is conceived by him in terms of neutrality, rather than of belligerency. To be sure, unlike the neutrals of former times, they are bound by the rule of participation, rather than that of abstention. But the principles of traditional neutrality would apply to them, inasmuch as they are expected, while engaged in enforcement measures, to maintain absolute impartiality toward the belligerents and to keep the balance between them rather than assist in the defeat of the one by the other. The elimination of the question of legal and moral responsibility for the immediate as well as for the real causes of the armed conflict does not, according to Cohn, in any way weaken the system of collective security, but on the contrary is likely to render it "more and more effective and universal."

If Cohn's scheme is the most systematic elaboration of the anti-punitive notion of collective security, it is by no means the only expression of the opposition of the diplomatic school to the penal philosophy. Others of its members subscribe to fundamentally the same idea as that underlying Cohn's proposal, when they insist that the ideal attitude for an international authority to take in dealing with aggression is "that of a policeman in a street fight, who is completely unconcerned with the rights and wrongs of the quarrel, but determined to separate the combatants" (*Collective Security*, p. 139)

That the execution of sanctions or enforcement measures by the collective society is essentially a police action, rather than war in the traditional sense of the word, is today common parlance, accepted and used by members of the penal, as well as of the diplomatic, school of collective security. In fact, during the last decades international and constitutional lawyers have been considering and discussing to what extent the rules concerning war proper are also applicable to collective police action. Important as it is, however, this question is not the only and not the chief concern of those who advocate what we have called the diplomatic conception of collective security. What they are primarily interested in is the question of the political principles and objectives that should guide an international organization and its members in taking and executing collective action, if and when the prohibition of force has been disregarded. And their answer is less that the collective action ought not to be legally conceived as war than that it must not be politically waged as war.

Their question and answer are both determined by their realization of what a dreadful contingency a collective action conceived and conducted as a war of sanctions would be. To put it in the words of the student of collective security whose plea for the ideal of police action has just been quoted: "The true function of a collective system is rather that of a scarecrow than a gun; the principal benefits are forfeited when it breaks down as a deterrent and has to proceed to action, since this may involve a more disastrous collision than that which it is designed to prevent" (*Collective Security*, p. 139). It is with a view to mitigating the effects of such a collision, in case it cannot be avoided altogether, that the diplomatic school rejects not only the idea of collective retribution but, explicitly or implicitly, even that of collective assistance to be rendered to the victim of aggression, inasmuch as the latter would practically result in and justify a war of alliance against a particular state. Not only must the security organization not wage a punitive war; it must not wage any war in the proper sense of the word. Its only legitimate object in taking collective action is to separate the belligerents, and it must not in the process become itself a belligerent in a political or legal sense. Only under these conditions will it remain acceptable and fit to act as a diplomatic conciliatory body as well as a peace-enforcing authority.

The diplomatic school doubts that the prospect of condemnation and punishment for aggression would prove an effective deterrent, and therefore reproaches the advocates of the penal conception of collective security with lack of realism. But one may wonder to what extent the idea of police action proper is itself a realistic proposition, considering the practical requirements of collective action and the psychological climate that is likely to prevail at the moment the action is called for. The analogy with simple social relations within the national community is as deceiving in this case as it is in other cases. If it is naive to assume that the international community can, as a rule, afford to deal with an aggressor state as if it were a murderer or bandit pure and simple, it is hardly less naive to expect that an armed conflict between two states is likely to be as easily manageable as a simple street brawl.

In the first place, whatever name be given to the collective action, to the extent that it is military action it is from the very beginning subject to military requirements of strategy and tactics, and becomes ever more so the longer it lasts. Its very termination is as much dependent upon military as upon political considerations. Moreover, unless the combatants display an equal degree of willingness or resistance about being separated, the international organization and its executive agency will sooner or later find themselves aligned, and thus practically allied, with one of the belligerents against the other. Assuming, as one is entitled to assume, that the aggressor state is less likely than its victim to comply with a cease-fire order issued by the community organ, the latter will be actually forced into the position it has conscientiously tried not to occupy by refraining from any judgment on the responsibility for aggression.

In the second place, an abandonment of the role of the policeman, "completely unconcerned with the rights and wrongs of the quarrel," could be the very price to be paid for the possibility of initiating the collective action at all. The champions of the policeman ideal are themselves compelled to recognize that "at present such sublime detachment from the merits of a dispute is hard to find" (*Collective Security*, p. 139). Admittedly, this obstacle might be somewhat less formidable if there were an international police force in existence, and if therefore the members of the international organization would not have to become directly involved with their own military establishments in the collective action to be taken. But be that as it may, so long as no international police force exists, the policeman will actually be a composite military machinery to be set and sustained in motion exclusively by the national wills of its component parts. This being the case, is it then likely that the pallid abstract ideal of a mere police action against "war itself," rather than against any concrete enemy guilty of crime, will prove powerful enough to make nations agree to the sacrifice of their blood and treasure?

The question touches upon what is indeed the most paradoxical and tragic complexity in the system of collective security. One, and probably the most important, of the reasons that make the prevention of war in our age urgent and imperative is the character of modern warfare. To ascribe its wantonness and cruelty to the destructiveness of contemporary weapons would merely explain what makes the horrors technically possible, and would not state their real cause. The latter must be sought in those ideological and political factors which ended the brief period in Western history when wars came close to being fought like duels, and which gave new impetus to the idea and practice of war for righteousness. It would be surprising if actions of the collective society taken to repress armed conflict did not tend to be colored by the kind of war that unfortunately dominates in our time. But it is much more ominous that the peculiar conditions of collective action are fatally conducive to such action being initiated and conducted as punitive war, with all the calamitous consequences it entails. Regardless of whether or not one subscribes to the dictum that the members of a security organization are called upon "to make war against nature," it can hardly be denied that, human nature being what it is, the motive power for their assuming the risks and burdens of participating in collective action is likely to stand in need of being reinforced by an appeal to such vindictive instincts as can be aroused only against a particular concrete *hostis,* allegedly guilty of an atrocious crime.

The members of the diplomatic school can perhaps be reproached with having underrated the extent to which their ideal of the policeman is at odds with the realities in which their scheme of collective action would necessarily operate. But this can in no way detract from their historical merit in having pointed out the direction in which our thinking on collective security should, for the sake of peace, be moving. Their merit is the greater in that they attacked the position of the penal school long before "that best oracle of wisdom, experience" taught us a lesson on the problems involved in collective security *in action.* The experience of both the League of Nations, including the sanctions experiment of 1935–36, and the United Nations up to June 25, 1950, tended to focus the attention of statesmen and scholars on the ways and means of increasing the chance of preventing war, rather than on the problems involved in repressing war by collective action. It was the United Nations action in Korea that first brought home to us the full significance of the latter question.

Professor Herbert Butterfield is inclined to see in the Korean war a notable exception to the current twentieth-century type of punitive war for righteousness and a return to "that warfare-for-limited-purposes which has been so despised since 1914."[32] It is true, the Korean war did not end as a punitive war. But it would be hard to maintain that it did not begin as such, and that there were not strong forces at work also to terminate it as such. It is for this reason that the Korean war must be recorded in history as a dramatic contest between the advocates of the penal and those of the diplomatic conception of collective security. Indeed, the discussion inside and outside the United Nations from 1950 to 1953, and even afterward, on the methods by which and the objectives for which the collective action in Korea should have been conducted, were a repetition of the theoretical arguments and counterarguments exchanged in the discussions on the definition of aggression carried on in the twenties, thirties, and forties. It was, however, only in the course of this first experiment in military collective action that the proper objective of enforcement measures emerged as one of the paramount practical issues of collective security.

FOOTNOTES

[1] League of Nations, *Preparatory Commission for the Disarmament Conference, Committee on Arbitration and Security. Memorandum on Security Questions, submitted by M. Politis, Rapporteur,* League of Nations Document C.A.S.10 (1928.IX.3) p. 14, par. 53.

[2] *Question of Defining Aggression,* Report by the Secretary-General, U. N. Assembly, Seventh Session, A. General, A/2211 (October 3, 1952) par. 349, quoting a statement made by Mr. Ricardo J. Alfaro in the International Law Commission. Text references to *Question* are to this Report.

[3] The term "guarantee" is used by Politis in League of Nations, *op. cit.*

[4] David Hunter Miller, *The Drafting of the Covenant* (New York 1928) vol. 2, p. 562. Some forty years later, Sir Benegal N. Rau was to remark in relation to the United Nations action in Korea, "Circumstances have forced the Security Council into an unprecedented role; in fact, we are functioning at the present moment almost like a war council": U. N. Security Council, *Official Records,* 478th Meeting, July 28, 1950, p. 6.

[5] League of Nations, International Studies Conference, *Collective Security,* ed. by Maurice Bourquin (Paris 1936) pp. 7, 146. Text references to *Collective Security* are to this volume.

[6] League of Nations, *Reports and Resolutions on the Subject of Article 16 of the Covenant. Report by M. de Brouckère,* League of Nations Document A.14.1927.V (1927.V.14) p. 70. The French text of this document speaks of *une eventualité redoutable.*

[7] In League of Nations, *Collective Security* (cited above, note 5), the term "collective security" covers practically all functions of a peace organization. Somewhat less broad is the scope Paul Barandon gives it in *Das Kriegsverhütungsrecht des Völkerbundes (Berlin 1933) pp. 1 ff., 279 ff.*

[8] Miller (cited above, note 4) vol. 2, p. 25.

[9] *Ibid.*

[10] *Charter of the United Nations. Report to the President on the Results of the San Francisco Conference* by the Chairman of the United States Delegation, The Secretary of State, Dept. of State Publication 2349. Conference Series 71 (Washington 1945) p. 87.

[11] A bibliography of important writings on the question of defining aggression is contained in Louis B. Sohn, *Cases and Other Materials on World Law* (Brooklyn 1950) pp. 801 ff.

[12] Philip C. Jessup, *A Modern Law of Nations* (New York 1948) p. 10. See also Erich Hula, "The Revival of the Idea of Punitive War," in *Thought,* vol. 21, no. 82 (September 1946) pp. 408 ff.

[13] League of Nations, *Records of the Fourth Assembly, Minutes of the Third Committee (Official Journal),* Special Supplement No. 16, p. 203.

[14] See League of Nations, *Collective Security* (cited above, note 5) p. 297. The present discussion on the definition of aggression leans heavily on the analysis in this volume.

[15] League of Nations, *Report of the Committee on Security Questions. Rapporteur: M. N. Politis,* Geneva, May 24, 1933. Conf. D./C.G. 108, in *Conference for the Reduction and Limitation of Armaments. Conference Documents,* vol. 2, League of Nations Document 1935, IX.4, pp. 679 ff. (par. 8). See also C. A. Pompe, *Aggressive War an International Crime* (The Hague 1953) pp. 88 ff.

[16] League of Nations, *Report . . . on Security Questions* (cited above, note 15) p. 683.

[17] Ibid., p. 679.

[18] For a recent discussion of the concept see J. LL. J. Edwards, *Mens Rea in Statutory Offences* (London 1955).

[19] Thucydides, *The Peloponnesian War,* Modern Library ed. (New York 1951) p. 15. See the interesting discussion on guilt and culpability in politics in the work of a contemporary historian, Herbert Butterfield, *Christianity, Diplomacy and War* (London 1953) pp. 41 ff. and passim. The same author, in *History and Human Relations* (New York 1952), devotes a special chapter to the problem of "moral judgments in history" (pp. 101 ff.).

[20] The best survey and analysis of the doctrine of war prior to World War I can be found in Leo Strisower, *Der Krieg und die Völkerrechtsordnung* (Vienna 1919).

[21]Pompe (cited above, note 15) p. 49.

[22]An example of such interpretation can be found in Jean Ray, *Commentaire du Pacte de la Société des Nations selon la politique et la jurisprudence des organes de la Société (Paris 1930) pp. 534 ff.*

[23]The Protocol that was to be annexed to the "Act relating to the Definition of the Aggressor," drafted under Mr. Politis' chairmanship by the Committee on Security Questions of the Disarmament Conference held in 1933, implicitly recognized the danger involved in ruling out the consideration of justifying causes. The list exemplifying such causes was followed by the provision: "The High Contracting Parties further agree to recognize that the present Protocol can never legitimate any violation of international law that may be implied in the circumstances comprised in the above list": League of Nations, *Report . . . on Security Questions* (cited above, note 15) p. 684. See the similar provision in the concluding paragraph of the Annex to the USSR Convention for the Definition of Aggression, signed at London on July 3, 1933, in League of Nations, *Treaty Series,* vol. CXLVII (1934) p. 75.

[24]The sophist Antiphon mentioned among the human conventions enjoining us to do things that are unnatural the laws bidding us never to be aggressors against our neighbors, but at the most to defend ourselves against their aggressions: see Ernest Barker, *Greek Political Theory. Plato and his Predecessors,* 3rd ed. (London 1947) pp. 66 ff.

[25]"It should . . . be noted," said Politis in his report of 1933, "that the question of the definition of the aggressor and that of sanctions to be taken against the aggressor while, of course, closely connected, are nevertheless separate questions. The strictness of the definition of the aggressor does not necessarily lead to the automatic application of sanctions": League of Nations, *Report . . . on Security Questions* (cited above, note 15) p. 679. More consistent with the basic philosophy of definition of aggression is the statement by another of its representatives, to the effect that "the automatic application of collective sanctions in cases of aggression was essential": *Question of Defining Aggression* (cited above, note 2) par. 267. On this question see also *Collective Security* (cited above, note 5) p. 315, note 2.

[26]Coppola's position has already been cited: *Collective Security,* pp. 7, 144 ff. Hans J. Morgenthau, *Politics Among Nations* (New York 1954), discusses collective security on pp. 274 ff. and 388 ff.

[27]This argument played a decisive role in the Korean case. See U. N. Security Council, *Official Records,* 474th Meeting, June 27, 1950, p. 2.

[28]Morgenthau (cited above, note 26) pp. 523 ff.

[29]See Butterfield, *Christianity, Diplomacy and War* (cited above, note 19) p. 17 and passim.

[30]Vattel's classic statement on the characteristics and effects of a war for righteousness is applicable also to punitive collective action. See E. de Vattel, *Le droit des gens, ou principes de la loi naturelle, appliqués à la conduite et aux affaires des nations et souverains,* transl. in *Classics of International Law* (Washington 1916) bk. III, ch. XII, p. 304, par. 188.

[31]The following references in the text to Georg Cohn's scheme are based on League of Nations, *Collective Security* (cited above, note 5) pp. 22 ff., 402 ff. See also Georg Cohn, *Neo-Neutrality,* transl. by Arthur S. Keller and Einar Jensen (New York 1939), especially pp. 294 ff.

[32]Butterfield, *Christianity, Diplomacy and War* (cited above, note 19) pp. 16, 22.

THE EVOLUTION OF COLLECTIVE SECURITY UNDER THE UNITED NATIONS CHARTER*

It would be difficult to gauge the extent to which disappointment in the United Nations contributes to the malaise that manifests itself so clearly in current American discussions on foreign policy. There is no question, however, but that this disappointment has some share in creating and fostering the general discomfort. True, there has recently been no marked increase in the perennial discontent caused by the failure of the United Nations to live up to the expectations that we originally placed on it as a collective security organization. We seem to have resigned ourselves to the modest role it is actually capable of playing. At any rate, we have ceased to look upon it as an instrument that could conduce to our military security. Realizing that the ideal of an international community of power, organized upon the pattern of the national community, is beyond reach, we have turned to the device, employed in traditional diplomacy, of balancing power against power. We try, accordingly, to ensure the global equilibrium between our forces and those of potential enemies by means of national armaments and defensive alliances, and, in general, by lending our individual support, military or otherwise, to the potential victims of aggression. Though we have thus been thrown back, very much to our own dislike, upon the conventional methods of protecting the national interest, the maintenance of international peace and security, the end for which the United Nations was established, remains the lodestar of our actions. It is for this reason that we are sincerely convinced that our policies serve ultimately not only our own interests but also the interests of the international commu-

*Reprinted with permission of the Johns Hopkins Press from Arnold Wolfers (ed.), *Alliance Policy in the Cold War*, 1959.

nity as a whole. For this reason also we felt certain that our obligations under the Charter could not possibly prove burdensome for us in pursuing our peaceful objectives. But there is no denying that recent experience has somewhat shaken us in that certainty. Nor can there be any doubt that the growing realization of the difficulty of bringing into harmony the rules of the game of power politics, which we are unfortunately compelled to play, with the principles of a system that was intended to end this game, is producing feelings of uneasiness about the United Nations that differ in kind from the usual sentiments of distress due to its limited effectiveness as an instrument of peace.

We became keenly aware of that difficulty for the first time in the Suez Canal crisis of 1956–1957. Neither the North Atlantic Treaty nor any of the other collective defense arrangements to which we are party obligates us, admittedly, to lend our allies military or any other assistance in case they themselves resort to the use of force prohibited by the Charter. In fact, those agreements, being all subject to the higher law of the Charter, do not even obligate us to remain neutral in such a case. The British-French military action against Egypt did not present us, therefore, with a legal dilemma, properly speaking. But the political dilemma for that reason was not any less perplexing for us. The landing of armed forces on Egyptian soil, preceded by bombardment from the air, was undoubtedly prima facie a violation of the Charter. The political objective of the British and French, however, was none other than to protect vital interests of their own as well as the *status quo* in the Middle East, in the maintenance of which we were hardly less interested than the United Kingdom and France themselves, considering that these two countries are the main pillars of our alliances. Thus, in terms of balance of power politics, the attitude for us to take would have been to lend the two Western governments our diplomatic support, though not necessarily without exercising a restraining influence upon them. To be sure, it is questionable whether the British-French action, leaving aside the moral issues involved, was good power politics or whether it would have been good power politics for us to back them. It is indeed arguable that concern for our relations with the rising Arab nations, and for the Russian competition with us in currying their favor, were equally relevant elements in a realistic evaluation of the situation and the ways in which we might meet it. But the fact of the matter is that the ideology on which the collective security system of the United Nations presumably rests left us no choice but to take sides against the two Western powers and thus to imperil the very alliance that is meant to give us the security the United Nations system does not provide.

Hence we found ourselves voting in the United Nations, together with the Soviet Union, for the immediate withdrawal of the French-British forces from Egyptian territory. Nor might it have remained a matter of merely voting against our principal allies had they not actually desisted from pursuing their precipitate course, thus sparing us the prospect of confronting the dilemma in its most cruel form. Since our participation in sanctions against the United Kingdom and France almost certainly would have had disastrous effects upon our whole defense posture, one wonders whether we could have afforded to run so formidable a risk rather than to shrink from the commitments of the Charter. In fact, from the very moment we submitted the case to the United Nations we purposely refrained from proposing an explicit moral censure of the alleged aggressors, and thus tried to soften the diplomatic defeat we helped to inflict upon them. This moderation must undoubtedly be credited, among other factors, with the quick healing of the wounds the Western alliance had suffered from that unfortunate incident. The ease with which friendship was restored among the three Atlantic powers could not, however, dim again our awareness of the problems that are liable to arise whenever the universal abstract commitments of collective security happen to cut across rather than coincide with our particular concrete alignments.

Another recent experience to suggest that the obligations of the Charter might after all be more burdensome than we had assumed was the Middle Eastern crisis of 1958, which focused on Lebanon and Jordan. It was of a less serious nature than the Suez crisis, but the lesson it taught was hardly less significant. In the first place, it was an American action this time, the landing of our Marines on the shores of Lebanon, that aroused strong opposition in the United Nations. This reaction was far from surprising in so far as it was based upon political objections. True, we were sincerely convinced that we had to comply with the request of the lawful Lebanese government, friendly to us though not formally allied with us, to assist it against domestic subversive forces aided from abroad, not only because we had ourselves a stake in maintaining the Middle Eastern *status quo* but also because we felt our action was required in order to assure respect for the purposes and principles of the Charter. But it was nonetheless not unlikely that our own appraisal of the situation and our choice of the means of meeting it would be challenged, and not merely by members of the Soviet bloc. In fact, the political necessity and wisdom of the action were also seriously questioned by large sections of American public opinion itself.

What we hardly expected, however, was that the legality of our action in terms of the Charter was to be questioned, and again not only by members of the Communist bloc. The Charter implicitly forbids intervention, in the sense of coercive interference, by one state in the domestic affairs of another. Such intervention is obviously inconsistent both with the principle of sovereign equality and with the prohibition of the use of force. But the

Charter does not preclude the assistance of one government to another at the latter's request. The right to request and render assistance against domestic subversion, recognized in general international law, is today, in fact, even more indispensable than it has been at other periods, since indirect aggression plays an exceptionally large role in the current international struggle for power. In a revolutionary age like ours, domestic subversive forces are more often than not supported, if not instigated, by foreign governments bent upon extending their dominion or at least their influence. Nor is it reasonable to argue that governments that are threatened by domestic subversion and possibly indirect aggression should rely exclusively upon collective protection by the United Nations instead of resorting to the traditional method of seeking the assistance of a friendly power. For the United Nations is hardly less problematical as an instrument for dealing effectively with indirect aggression than with direct aggression. We have proved, at considerable risk, by our policy in the Suez crisis that we do not propose to revert to the doctrine, applied and upheld by statesmen and international lawyers of former times, that intervention in the affairs of another state against its will is lawful if it is intended to preserve the balance of power. But we have made it equally clear in the Lebanon case that we are not ready to accept the view according to which our commitments under the United Nations Charter forbid us to lend military support to those potential victims of indirect aggression that request such aid.

The experience of the Suez and Lebanon cases may easily repeat itself. Indeed, it is likely that the difficulty of harmonizing our own policies with those of the world body will increase rather than diminish, owing to the steadily growing membership of the United Nations and its changing political complexion. Moreover, the weakening of our diplomatic position in world politics must unavoidably lessen our influence inside the organization. The disappointment about this trend will be the keener because initially we swayed the councils of the United Nations as no single power ever was a able to sway those of the League of Nations. The development might even give new impetus to those who want to get along without the United Nations, hoping vainly to escape from the ugly realities of current international politics by turning away from the mirror reflecting them. Such counsel should not be heeded and in fact is not likely to be. But we certainly have good reasons for re-examining our actual commitments under the Charter and the degree of freedom of action they leave us for securing our national existence by alliance policy and other devices of traditional diplomacy. Since the same obligations are incumbent upon us as upon other members of the United Nations, the question can also be asked in general terms: What is the actual law of collective security?

To speak of the actual law of collective security is to imply that it is not necessarily identical with the written law of the Charter. The application, or for that matter the nonapplication, of legal rules is apt to modify their original meaning or even to affect their validity. The Charter has been subject to the law of change no less than any other constitutional document, international or municipal. But we must nonetheless go back to the original legal conceptions underlying the Charter if we want to appraise the subsequent development correctly. There is another reason for analyzing once more the philosophy of Dumbarton Oaks and San Francisco. We are often tempted, by idealistic or by practical motives, to take or declare as law what in truth is only the ideology, or rather a specific ideology, of collective security, superimposed upon the legal content of the Charter. In fact, the discrepancies between a political idea and the norms by which it is translated into a legal system could hardly ever be greater than they are in this case.

The political idea and the technical term of collective security imply that all members participating in the system enjoy equal protection against aggression launched from any quarter whatsoever. One may wonder therefore whether the legal system conceived at Dumbarton Oaks and presented to the conferees of San Francisco as a genuine collective security system actually deserves this designation. The Dumbarton Oaks Proposals and the law of the Charter based upon them were in many respects more reminiscent of the philosophy of the European Concert of Powers than of that of the League of Nations, the historical prototype of a collective security system. The Charter system of San Francisco was not meant to be universally applicable. The monopoly of the Security Council in all matters relating to the enforcement of international peace and security and the requirement of unanimity of its five permanent members made collective action against any of the great powers practically impossible. The lesser powers were thus left unprotected against the gravest danger threatening them, aggression by a superior power. It could be little consolation to them that the great powers themselves could not expect the assistance of the organization against one of their peers. Like the European Concert, but unlike the League of Nations, the collective security system of San Francisco was designed to enforce peace among the smaller nations only. The proponents of the Charter felt—and rightly so—that the organization would hardly be capable of deterring a great nation from aggression. They also were inclined to think—though mistakenly—that the chief threat to the new international order was likely to be the renewal of aggressive policies by the Axis powers, defeated in World War II.

The collective security system of the Charter was and still is deficient in yet another important respect. The scope of the substantive protection it offers to members of the United Nations, within the limits of the protection it offers, is legally narrower than the protection afforded by the Covenant of the League. The members both of the League and of the United Nations were and are bound to respect the territorial integrity and political independence of other nations. But only the Covenant imposed upon its parties the additional obligation of preserving one another against external aggression. No positive guarantee of territorial integrity and political independence, be it as an obligation of the several members or of the organization itself, was incorporated into the Charter of the United Nations, although suggestions to that effect were made at San Francisco. It is hardly surprising, therefore, that the minor powers wondered how much worth they could attach to the collective protection they were promised against aggression, considering that at the same time they were denied a guarantee of their existence and possessions. In view of the deliberate omission of a positive guarantee, it is all the more significant that the Charter does not even stipulate the nonrecognition of territorial acquisitions or of other advantages obtained in defiance of the prohibition of force. Proposals submitted to the San Francisco Conference that the Charter should subscribe to the principle *ex injuria jus non oritur* failed of acceptance.

The fact that the Charter, as a spokesman of the smaller states bitterly remarked at San Francisco, was to contain "no clear declaration that the security of individual members is the objective" was not the only reason the minor powers felt disturbed. They noticed other symptoms as well that seemed to point to a system of collective security in which the territorial integrity and political independence of its members, not to mention their lesser rights, might be considered expendable. In fact, they were inclined to see in the future Security Council under the domination of its permanent members an instrumentality for effecting settlements on the Ethiopian or Munich model.

Politically speaking, their fear of a concert of the great powers that would actually be capable of taking common action was as unrealistic as was the hope of those who tried to revive what Lord Salisbury once called "the federated action of Europe," now on a global scale and in such democratically modified form as the spirit of the twentieth century required. But one can understand nevertheless, even today, why the legal concepts underlying the collective security system of the Charter should have disturbed the smaller nations. The primacy of peace was stressed so strongly that one could very well wonder whether the organization would not feel tempted, if not entitled, to neglect considerations of law and justice for the sake of peace. One can appreciate this anxiety all the better because the Charter also seemed to be leaning in the direction of a highly dynamic conception of peace that favors the peaceful change of the *status quo* where it is needed in the interest of peace. It can hardly be denied, moreover, that the Security

Council was intended to possess sufficiently broad powers, legal and physical, to effect policies based upon such a philosophy.

The tendency to overemphasize the value of peace was particularly striking in the Dumbarton Oaks Proposals in which references to international law and justice, as standards to be observed by the organization in its several activities, were almost completely lacking. This tendency is still visible in the Charter itself, though to a lesser extent. For the minor powers were not entirely unsuccessful at San Francisco in their efforts to inspire into the Dumbarton Oaks Proposals, as one of their representatives put it, "something like a soul power." The Charter provides that the organization should strive for the settlement of international disputes "in conformity with the principles of justice and international law." But it is significant that an Egyptian amendment according to which the United Nations should be bound by the same requirement when discharging its enforcement function under Chapter VII of the Charter was rejected at San Francisco.

The dynamic conception of peace, too, is less conspicuous in the Charter than in the Dumbarton Oaks Proposals. In Chapter VI of the Charter, the Security Council is given only recommendatory powers when engaged in the adjustment or settlement of international disputes or situations. But it was felt all the same, and not merely by the smaller states that the Security Council might also make use of the compulsory power it was to possess in the case of enforcement measures to impose its own terms of settlement upon the parties to a conflict. Instead of simply applying existing law, the Security Council might change it and create new law, thus exercising legislative power for all practical intents and purposes. In other words, like the members of the European Concert before them, the permanent members of the Security Council might consider themselves entitled to assert, through the instrumentality of the Council, the legal power to regulate important matters concerning other states, including territorial and even domestic constitutional questions, without being subject themselves to a higher authority. That the Charter lent itself to such an interpretation of the powers of the Security Council and at the same time did not stipulate a positive guarantee of the integrity and independence of the member countries, seemed to indicate that the organization was intended to assure the peaceful evolution of the international political order through collective procedures rather than the strict maintenance of the *status quo*.

Any device to secure the peaceful revision of treaties and of other conditions causing grave international friction is highly commendable. There can be no permanent peace even in a national community if its members insist on absolute rights and deny to the government the authority and power to control and limit them. All that the members of a national community can legitimately claim is that they participate in some form or other in the operation of the government and that the exercise of governmental authority and power be subject to the law. As the United Nations was originally conceived, the small nations' share in controlling activities and decisions of the organization was far from equal to that of the great nations. Moreover, the Charter can hardly be said to contain the constitutional safeguards required for a government of law. Its authors purposely refrained from inserting in the Charter what might be called an international bill of the rights of states. Out of the seven principles, enumerated in Article 2, which shall determine the conduct of the organization and its members, only two are formulated in terms of rights of states, namely, the principles of sovereign equality and of the exclusion of domestic matters from United Nations jurisdiction. The five other principles set forth the duties they must observe in their relations with one another and with the organization. Last but not least, the statement of principles concerning the rights and obligations of members is sufficiently broad to permit a flexible interpretation. This flexibility could be expected to work in favor of the several members rather than of the organization in case the latter should fail to acquire the authority and power with which the fathers of the Charter tried by legal means to endow it. But it is hardly surprising that the smaller nations asked themselves, nonetheless, what the weakness of constitutional safeguards for assuring a government of law would mean for them, particularly if the Security Council should develop into a supranational government.

We have so far discussed the general legal notions underlying the collective security system envisaged in the Charter and have come to the conclusion that they differ greatly from those upon which the League of Nations was based. They resemble, instead, *mutatis mutandis* the ideas underlying the nineteenth century European Concert of Powers. To what extent can the same be said of the enforcement machinery and the character of the enforcement measures for which the Charter has made provision?

Such successes as the European Concert had in maintaining international peace were undoubtedly due to the potential military power that it could mobilize to enforce its decisions. The actual display and use of collective force were left to improvisation, however. The same held true for the sanctions of the League. The United Nations was to be far more advanced than any collective peace system preceding it, in that the availability to the Security Council of armed forces would be assured by previous military agreements concluded between the Council and the members of the organization. Nor was the participation of smaller nations in the proceedings and measures of Chapter VII to be permitted to cause undue complications and delays. Contrary to the League system, which left the decision on the *casus*

188

foederis and on sanctions in the hands of the several states, the enforcement system of the United Nations was to be highly centralized. The determination whether enforcement measures should be taken, and if so what kind, was to be the exclusive prerogative of the Security Council in which the great powers were to be dominant. The Council was also to determine whether all or only some of the members of the United Nations should participate in a particular collective action. The latter provision subsequently became the basis of the legal contention that, contrary to the League, the status of neutrality was not necessarily incompatible with the obligations of United Nations membership; the same conclusion might also be drawn from the legal character of the enforcement measures in general.

A sober analysis of the peculiar character of enforcement measures under the Charter is more suggestive than anything else of the wide discrepancies between the legal content of the Charter, as it was conceived by its authors, and the ideological layer superimposed thereupon.

The Concert of Europe, and in fact also the League, operated at a time when, according to a widely held view, the sovereignty of the state implied its practically unlimited right to go to war. True, the Covenant established some restrictions on that alleged right, but essentially they were merely procedural limitations. Only the Kellogg Pact and, following it, the Charter, took a further step toward prohibiting war and any use of force regardless of the substantive reason for resorting thereto. Once the use of force is considered a contravention of law, except in self-defense, it is only natural—in view of the moral opprobrium attaching to it and of its disastrous consequences in human terms—to look upon the breach of the prohibition of force as a crime and to interpret collective action against such a breach as a criminal procedure serving a punitive purpose. One might hope, moreover, that the deterrent effect of a prohibition of war and force upon a potential aggressor would be still greater if he could expect not only to be repelled by the united counterforce of the international community but to be publicly condemned as a criminal. The founders of the United Nations could have been tempted to adopt the punitive conception for still another reason. Thinking of the Security Council, acting under Chapter VII, as a kind of supranational government, they would have been only consistent had they construed the enforcement power of the Council in analogy to the punitive power of a municipal government. They were less anxious, however, to be consistent than they were to devise a legal procedure that would suit the structure of international society and best serve the interests of international peace, the paramount purpose of the United Nations.

It is significant that the prohibition of force is stated in the Charter in the form of a general principle and in words the meaning of which has been controversial among statesmen and international lawyers ever since 1945.

Article 2, paragraph 4 obligates all members to "refrain in their international relations from the threat or use of force against the territorial integrity or political independence of any state, or in any other manner inconsistent with the Purposes of the United Nations." The reference to territorial integrity and political independence and to the purposes of the United Nations has been interpreted to imply that it is the intent rather than the objective character of an action that makes the threat or use of force unlawful. To be sure, such interpretation does not deprive Article 2, paragraph 4 of the Charter of its normative character, but it does suggest the lawgiver's intention to assure that the concrete meaning of the norm should be established in close relation to the particular circumstances of each case in which its violation is alleged. There is another indication to the same effect. Article 39, which charges the Security Council to decide whether enforcement measures are required, does not repeat the formulation of Article 2, paragraph 4. It provides, instead, that "the Security Council shall determine the existence of any threat to the peace, breach of the peace, or act of aggression." Accordingly, the Council is not bound to consider every breach of the prohibition of force as an act calling for enforcement measures. On the other hand, the Council may deem enforcement measures necessary even if Article 2, paragraph 4 has not been violated. In fact, the "threat to the peace," in the meaning of Article 39, need not arise from any contravention, whether of the law of the Charter or of general international law. It is its political and not its juridicial nature that makes a specific act or situation a "threat to the peace" and thus liable to the Council's jurisdiction. It fits into this picture that the Charter knows only measures and no sanctions. In other words, it uses a term with connotations of administrative rather than criminal law to designate all coercive United Nations actions regardless of whether they have been called for by a lawful or unlawful act.

The spirit in which the enforcement system of the Charter was conceived is illustrated most strikingly by another feature of Article 39. It charges the Security Council with the determination of "an act of aggression" but not of the aggressor. The distinction would be too tenuous for any far-reaching conclusions if it had not, from the twenties onward, played a considerable role in the discussions on the definition of aggression. It is a distinction, in fact, to which two legal and political conceptions of collective security, the punitive and the diplomatic, must be related. While the allocation of the legal responsibility for an act of aggression is an essential function of the collective security organization according to the punitive school, the diplomatic school insists that it is not the proper task for an agency of collective security to perform. The restoration of peace, the chief purpose of collective action, and the adjustment of the dispute that has led to armed conflict, will be delayed and made more difficult if the organization assumes the role of prosecutor and judge in addition to its police functions and its conciliatory functions. The wording of Article 39 as well as other features of Chapter VII of the Charter prove that its authors were leaning in the direction of the diplomatic school. Far from constituting a criminal code, the rules of the Charter relating to the enforcement system of the United Nations could rather be called a mere legalization and formalization of the diplomatic conceptions and procedures characteristic of the concert system of collective intervention practiced by the European Pentarchy in the nineteenth century.

Since the political assumption of continued close great-power co-operation proved fallacious, the framers of the Charter failed to receive due credit for what one might call their constitutional realism. The restriction of the enforcement system, practically speaking, to conflicts among minor nations; the limited scope of the substantive interests to be protected; the stress on peace and the dynamic conception of peace; the flexibility of the legal principles to be observed by the organization and its members; the type of enforcement machinery and the legal character of the enforcement system; the importance attached to the conciliatory function—all these features testify to the wisdom of the constitution-maker in setting limits on the obligations of the organization and its members that are consonant with its physical power and with the willingness of its members to co-operate. One may wonder, however, whether the same can be said of the subsequent attempts to develop the constitutional system of the United Nations along lines somewhat closer to Wilsonian concepts of collective security. Ironically, it was the United States, the chief architect of the Dumbarton Oaks Proposals and of the Charter, that took the lead in reinterpreting and remolding the original system.

It is less surprising that the United States assumed leadership in such reinterpretation than that it should ever have become the proponent of the Dumbarton Oaks scheme. American democratic traditions, in general, and traditional espousal of the rights of small nations, in particular, hardly predestined the United States to advocate an authoritarian and oligarchic type of international organization. There is nevertheless a close connection between the promotion of this type of organization and certain traditions of American foreign policy. We know on the authority of the late Harley A. Notter, the official historian of American *Postwar Foreign Policy Preparation,* what dilemma confronted the planners in the State Department when they were preparing draft constitutions of the international organization that was to be established. "While strong pressures toward striving for a federalized international organization—or government—were being exerted," Notter remarks, "there was also at this period a possibility that the dominating American opinion of the years before the war in favor of political isolationism might reassert itself. Uncertainty regarding Senate consent to ratification of any proposed agreement in this field was ever present."[1]

In other words, the task of the draftsmen in the State Department was to be no less than to devise a system legally more advanced toward genuine international government than the League of Nation had been, while ensuring at the same time that this more radically internationalist scheme did not offend anti-internationalists inside and outside the Senate. The task could be performed only by means of a legal construction that would assure to the United States, together with other great powers, a special privileged status within the system of international government and would reduce the residual risks involved in American membership still further by limiting the liabilities of the organization itself. The type of United Nations constitution that the American government promoted and successfully steered past all diplomatic hindrances to its final adoption at San Francisco met those conflicting requirements most satisfactorily. The Charter not only provides for the nucleus of a world government; it also incorporates, as has been rightly observed, virtually all of the Lodge reservations to the ill-fated Covenant of the League of Nations.[2] Thanks to the veto in the Security Council, the United States retained, in particular, the traditional right of a sovereign state to be its own interpreter of its legal obligations, including its obligations under the Charter. In other words, we were to be our own judges, not only of our obligation to participate in collective enforcement measures but also of those rules of conduct by which the Charter tried to control and restrain the actions of all nations.

The realities of United Nations politics in the first years of the organization's existence did not by any means bear out isolationist anxieties about the consequences of American membership in a universal political organization. The leadership that had devolved upon this country as a result of World War II assured it a commanding position in the United Nations. Without exercising undue pressure, the United States, in all of the organs of the United Nations, including the Security Council, could count on sweeping majorities in support of its policies. Ironically, American actions were frustrated only in the Security Council, owing to the very device that was intended to stifle, and actually did stifle, isolationist opposition to the ratification of the Charter. While it had been originally assumed—and, in fact, not by isolationists alone—that for the sake of our national interest we needed some form of minority protection as provided by the veto, we now began to realize that we stood to gain rather than lose by relying on the untrammeled operation of the majority principle in the General Assembly.

However, considerations of expediency alone do not account for our tendency to shift the constitutional balance from the Security Council to the General Assembly. No less decisive was our idealistic urge to apply to international politics, at long last, the principles and procedures of domestic democratic government. Even assuming—as actually one could not assume—that there was a reasonable chance of continued American-Russian co-operation in the postwar period, the two superpowers could have kept such co-operation going only by a policy based upon the mutual recognition of spheres of influence and the give and take of exasperating diplomatic negotiation. How much more than by such devices, always distasteful to us, were we bound to be attracted by the avenue open to us in the General Assembly, where issues on which we could not agree with the Russians could be submitted to the judgment of the world's "town meeting." The submission to the General Assembly of the unsettled question of Korea in 1947 is the most notable and, in terms of its consequences, the most momentous example of such a policy.

Nor were we the only ones who tended to elevate the General Assembly to a status of equality with, if not superiority to, the Security Council. The central position of the Council in the constitutional structure of the United Nations was most strongly opposed by all minor nations at San Francisco. Not satisfied with the concessions to which the Sponsoring Governments finally agreed at the Conference, the minor nations made it clear that they would renew their efforts to broaden the powers of the democratic body once the organization had started to function. They were all the more pleased, therefore, when the United States joined forces with them in trying to assure the ascendancy of the General Assembly. But they soon realized— in fact as early as 1947 and 1948 when dealing with the Korean issue—that there were risks involved in moving the Assembly up to a higher plane of world politics, namely the risk of being drawn into the vortex of power diplomacy.

To paraphrase Canning's famous dictum, the American decision to throw the Korean question into the lap of the General Assembly was an attempt to use the new world organization to redress the balance of the Far East. Or, to put it differently, it was an application of the Concert idea in reverse. To be sure, the judgment on the Korean question was to be handed down by the Assembly as a general representative organ of the United Nations, acting on behalf of the organization. In legal terms, it was the world body as a whole that was to recommend what practically amounted to an authentic interpretation, or rather revision, of the great-power agreement on Korea, concluded at Moscow in 1945. Speaking in political terms, however, the American initiative meant nothing less than calling upon a combination of great and small powers to settle an important question—in fact one of the hot issues of the Cold War between West and East—without the consent of one of the great powers whose vital interests were certain to be affected by the decision of the Assembly.

The 1947 submission of the Korean question to the General Assembly was undoubtedly a well-intentioned attempt to effect the peaceful change of an intolerable political situation the continuance of which threatened to cause grave international friction and that actually soon resulted in armed conflict. But unfortunately it had one drawback; it did not really settle the Korean question. Contrary to the "executive" concert of great powers, the "parliamentary" concert of the General Assembly can only debate and vote but not compel. Scoring parliamentary triumphs is no substitute for the settlement of an issue by the great powers. In fact, it may aggravate matters by deepening the rift between those governments whose agreement is indispensable to the solution of the question. It was for this reason that some members of the Assembly followed the American lead in the Korean case only with unmistakable misgivings. They felt particularly uneasy about the American-sponsored endorsement by the Assembly of the South Korean government as the only lawful government in Korea. This action, they thought, could easily be construed as a moral commitment on the part of the United Nations to preserve the territorial integrity and political independence of South Korea.

If the United Nations was unable to break Russian resistance to a change of the *status quo* in Korea through pacific procedures as sought by the West, it did have a substantial share in successfully preventing the Soviets from changing the *status quo* in their favor through a war by proxy.

In 1950, as the Korean war raised American influence in the United Nations to a point never to be reached again, it also brought about an important change in United Nations law, initiated by the American government. For all practical intents and purposes, the reform measure of 1950 amounted to a far-reaching change of the constitutional character of the United Nations system of collective security, affecting the rights and obligations of its members, although it was enacted in the form of a simple act of the Assembly, the famous "Uniting for Peace" resolution.

The measure, which was hailed in the General Assembly as a "turning point in the history of mankind," did not yield all the results its proponents hoped to attain and had results, which they hardly foresaw, that were not pleasing to them.

According to the resolution, decisions on enforcement measures—so far an exclusive function of the Security Council—were henceforth to devolve upon the General Assembly in cases in which the Council, for lack of unanimity of the permanent members, failed to exercise its responsibility for the maintenance of international peace and security. The purpose of granting conditional enforcement power to the Assembly was obviously to circumvent a Russian veto that would preclude United Nations action against the Soviet Union itself or any country supported by it. But the American government, when initiating the measure, pursued a still more ambitious objective. It was a new attempt to create a collective security system technically more advanced than that of the League of Nations. The resolution envisaged the establishment of military enforcement machinery that would make effective the Assembly system of collective security. In purely technical terms, the new system was devised along the same lines as the stillborn Council system envisaged in Chapter VII of the Charter. But the political character and purpose of the system established by the resolution was to be basically different from that of the Charter. It was to be an instrument in the hands of the parliamentary concert of the General Assembly instead of in the hands of the executive great-power concert of the Security Council. For years thereafter, we were to press the General Assembly to implement the technical provisions of the "Uniting for Peace" resolution. But they remained a dead letter no less than the corresponding provisions of the Charter. The Assembly refused to carry out a policy that it feared would transform the collective security system of the Charter into what in fact would amount to an alliance against the Soviet Union.

Be that as it may, we certainly initiated and sponsored the reform of United Nations law, to be accomplished by the "Uniting for Peace" resolution, primarily with a view to the exigencies of the Cold War. We hoped that an extension of the system of collective security to cover conflicts among great powers as well as those among minor powers would deter the Soviet Union from moving on to a hot war. Therefore, we did not find the price that we had to pay too high for obtaining additional protection against aggressive intentions of our Russian adversary. In order to make possible the circumvention of a Russian veto in the Security Council, we also implicitly abandoned our own veto right and that of our allies. Thus in a sense we extended our obligations beyond what they were under the Charter. We ceased to be our own judges, either of our obligation to participate in collective enforcement measures or of the rules of conduct contained in the Charter. In fact, neither we nor our chief allies were to be protected thereafter from becoming ourselves the object of enforcement measures. This seemed to be a well-calculated risk. After all, contrary to the Security Council, the General Assembly has only recommendatory powers. But what seemed even more reassuring was the fact that, with our commanding position in the Assembly, it was not likely that we would ever be outvoted. It did not take us long, however, to realize that we had underrated the impact of the other Cold War, the one between the colonial and anticolonial powers, both on the operations of the Assembly and on the political dynamics of the collective security system.

The Western proponents of the "Uniting for Peace" resolution found satisfaction in seeing it applied to cases to which it had been tailored, as to the case of Chinese Communist intervention in Korea and to the case of Hungary. The Suez and the Lebanon cases, however, showed that the new system could also be used against the West. The irony of this development is impressively suggested by the change in Soviet attitude toward the "Uniting for Peace" resolution. The Soviet Union, which originally opposed its adoption most violently both on constitutional and on political grounds, has since discovered that the General Assembly system can be made to serve Russian interests too. It has therefore come around to accepting the change of United Nations law, tacitly at least. Thus, if our sponsorship of the reform measure of 1950 actually was intended to span and tighten our particular alliances by an all-embracing American-led alliance in the legal form of an abstract collective security system, the plan has undoubtedly miscarried, and not only because its technical implementation failed to materialize. As the Suez and Lebanon cases show, the operation of the system that we initiated is apt to strain our inter-allied relationships and make us vulnerable to interference by the Assembly with our own actions, lawful as they may be. The fact of the matter is that the Assembly system of the "Uniting for Peace" resolution, which we designed as a means of strengthening the Western defense position against the East, can also be used by the anticolonial powers, and by the Soviet Union, both against the colonial powers and against us. Brief as the history of the organization of collective security is, it clearly suggests that members tend to use the abstract system, contrived as a protection of all against each and every other state, for the purpose of building and cementing an alliance against a concrete state or group of states. But it also suggests that, given the complexity of international relations, such use of the system is not likely to be successful.

This is also borne out by the experience of the Korean war to which we must return once more. The legal and political issues to which the North Korean aggression gave rise in the organs of the world body are important in their bearing upon the whole conception of collective security.

The United States, which apart from South Korea bore the chief military burden of collective action against the aggressors, also determined the policy to be pursued. American political leadership remained un-challenged, except by the Soviet bloc, throughout the war. But it cannot be denied that the United States found it increasingly difficult to maintain the harmony of views that prevailed in the United Nations during the first weeks of the collective action. While practically all non-Communist member governments approved of the decision to repel North Korean aggression, they were at variance as to the ultimate purpose of the United

Nations action.

The chief question on which they disagreed was whether the collective action was to be confined to restoring the *status quo ante* and terminating hostilities—postponing the settlement of the issues underlying the armed conflict—or whether the United Nations was authorized, if not committed, to go beyond a mere police action and employ its enforcement power to solve the Korean question on United Nations terms. In taking the latter view, the United States could claim that the Charter authorized the Security Council, by implication at least, to exercise legislative authority in removing threats to the peace. However, the political presupposition for rendering effective a legislative fiat of the United Nations, namely, agreement among the great powers, was unfortunately lacking in this case. It could therefore be argued—and it was argued by critics of the American policy—that insistence on the farther-reaching objective, a change of the *status quo ante*, would delay the restoration of peace, which according to the Charter was the primary purpose of enforcement measures.

In terms of the Charter, American policy could be questioned for still another reason closely related to the decision to go beyond a mere police action. The Charter system of collective security rests upon the diplomatic conception, as we have called it. In fact, the United States itself had stated at the San Francisco Conference that the United Nations when taking enforcement measures ought not to assume the role of a prosecutor or judge but concentrate its efforts on the restoration of peace. American policy in the Korean case, however, was from the beginning inspired by the punitive notion of collective security. The punishment of the aggressors was declared an objective of the enforcement action and served to justify its continuation beyond the purpose of restoring the *status quo ante*. One may doubt whether this policy actually contributed to the prolongation of the armed conflict. But it certainly did not facilitate its termination. Be that as it may, it is far from surprising, realistically speaking, that enforcement measures, taken in the context of a conflict that was ideological as well as political, should assume a punitive character. The temptation to resort to the punitive notion will always be strong, regardless of the legal conceptions on which a collective security organization is founded. It will be almost irresistible in a case like the Korean war, which was part of a world-wide political and ideological struggle.

It is not surprising, either, that the resistance against being drawn into that struggle should have grown among United Nations members once the aggression was checked. In fact, the formation, in the second half of the fifties, of the third force in the General Assembly, insisting on its neutrality in the ideological and political Cold War between West and East, can be traced back to the later days of the Korean war. The nations that try to stay outside the Cold War wanted the United Nations to deal with the fighting in Korea in terms of a conflict among the actual belligerents only, and to steer clear of involvement in political and ideological warfare against the Soviet Union and communism. They shunned a policy of lining up the organization against Soviet Russia and its ideology, not only on principle but also because they feared this might lead to the widening of the local conflict into a global war. The United States and its close associates in the Korean war were no less conscious of this danger nor were they less eager to avoid it. However, they were firmly convinced that the real aggressor was Russian-led communism, and they therefore felt that it was the task of the United Nations to inflict upon this aggressor a crushing diplomatic defeat.

But the respective positions were to be different when armed conflict arose in the context of the other Cold War being waged between the colonial and anticolonial powers. In the Suez case we did not shrink from meeting our commitments under United Nations law, but we were not inclined, for good reasons, to interpret them as broadly as the anticolonial members felt we should. While the latter wanted the United Nations to deal with the conflict in terms of the political and ideological cause for which they stood and to identify itself with that cause, we confined our efforts in the United Nations to securing the termination of hostilities and the restoration of the *status quo ante*.

The constitutional development of the United Nations reflects and is due to the political pressures brought to bear upon the organization by the two Cold Wars in which the members of the international community are engaged today, the one between the great powers and the one between the colonial and anticolonial powers.

According to the Charter, it was the Security Council, dominated by the great powers, that was to be the center of authority in the organization. Though its collective security functions were limited to minor conflicts, its legal powers within those limits were to be broad and its physical power sufficient to give them effect. When owing to the Cold War between East and West the concept of an executive concert of the great powers failed to materialize, we tried to shift the center of authority and power to a par-liamentary concert of great and minor powers. It was hardly a realistic scheme from the beginning and became even less so when the extension of the collective security system to major conflicts was not followed by the establishment of military machinery commensurate in physical strength with the legal powers of the parliamentary concert. The claim of the General Assembly to speak on behalf of the organization as a whole rested exclusively on its moral authority as a democratic body. But the validity of that claim was not generally recognized; and moreover it was open to the objection that the Assembly was an essentially political body, acting in accordance with considerations of political expediency rather than of moral principles.

The expectation that the concentration of authority and power in a parliamentary concert would enable the United Nations to discharge its functions effectively as a collective security body was not well founded for yet another reason. As the scheme of Dumbarton Oaks and San Francisco was inspired and based upon the pattern of the Grand Alliance of World War II, so was the scheme of the "Uniting for Peace" resolution patterned upon the political constellation in the initial period of the Korean war. Not only was the democratic bloc in the Assembly at that time overwhelmingly strong numerically; it also seemed sufficiently coherent to serve as the foundation for a lasting system of collective security. However, the coherence actually was due rather to the fear of imminent Russian aggression than to a true community of views and interests. The Russian danger at that time overshadowed all other questions, even in the eyes of the anticolonial members of the United Nations. But this is no longer the case. On the contrary a growing number of member nations regards the United Nations today primarily as an instrument to further the emancipation of the colonial peoples and to eradicate the last vestiges of Western power and influence in the world. But quite apart from the colonial issue, the lines of the bipolar structure of the contemporary world are not as clear at the close of the fifties as they were at the beginning.

The weakening of the political coherence of the General Assembly forecloses the hope for an effective system of collective security built upon the Assembly that would permit great and small nations alike to dispense with the traditional devices of power-diplomacy. But it is not likely to end the sway of the collective security ideology and its successful use for diplomatic purposes. For instead of replacing traditional diplomacy, as it was hoped, collective security—or the idea of collective security—has itself become a diplomatic weapon in the struggle for power. This does not detract from the moral value of the idea, which is indeed inspired by man's eternal longing for a peaceful and just international order; it only means that the idea shares the fate of other lofty ideas, namely, employment for combative purposes. It has become part of the art of diplomacy to judge the adversary's actions in the inflexible terms of the idea of collective security while basing one's own actions on the more flexible law of collective security.

There exists no strictly legal obligation for a member of the United Nations to agree to enforcement measures or to participate in them. True, the Security Council was to possess the legal power to order such participation. However, the exercise of this power was made dependent upon the conclusion of special military agreements between the Council and member nations. No such agreements were ever concluded. The General Assembly, on the other hand, was given only recommendatory powers by the Charter and can only recommend action even under the "Uniting for Peace" resolution.

The legal situation scarcely differs with regard to the binding authoritative character of the act by which the Council or the Assembly, respectively, determine the existence of a threat to the peace, a breach of the peace, or an act of aggression. While the determination by the Council must be considered as legally binding upon all members, the Council for political reasons is barely capable of agreeing on such a determination, which requires seven affirmative voles, including those of the five great powers. It might also become increasingly difficult to attain the two-thirds majority required in the Assembly. But in any case a determination by the Assembly can hardly be considered as binding upon the members in a strictly legal sense. It has at best moral and political significance. The distinction between the moral and legal force of United Nations decisions is admittedly tenuous, and the resort to it might not always be helpful. Nonetheless no member nation seems to be ready to dispense with it altogether and thus to recognize implicitly the legal authority of the world body as superior to its own.

At the same time, governments appear to be most eager to cover their acts with the authority of the United Nations and to justify their actions and omissions in terms of the Charter. The Charter has come to play the role that the *Jus Publicum Europaeum* played in the nineteenth century. It has become a matter of respectful reference. There is an increasing tendency to assume what one might call vicarious responsibility for the United Nations. The argument is advanced that if the United Nations proves incapable of maintaining international peace and security, it falls to particular members to do so in its place. The Truman Doctrine of 1947, the Tripartite Declaration of 1950 regarding the Arab-Israeli armistice borders, the Joint Resolution on the Defense of Formosa passed by Congress in 1955, and the Eisenhower Doctrine of 1957 suggest the extent to which we ourselves are ready to assume such vicarious responsibility. Admittedly, in contemplating actions under these doctrines and resolutions we hope they will eventually be approved by the United Nations, explicitly or implicitly. But it is nonetheless significant that the United States, which can claim to be second to none in devotion to the ideals of the United Nations, is finding it ever more necessary in its interpretation of the Charter to go to the very limits of what United Nations law presumably permits.

The same tendency is apparent in the interpretation, or rather reinterpretation, of Article 51 of the Charter, which recognizes self-defense as an inherent right of all members of the organization. Comparatively speaking, the formulation of the right of self-defense in that article is less flexible than the formulation in Article 2 of the principles governing the conduct of the United Nations and of its members. According to the wording of Article 51, the exercise of the right of self-defense was to be permissible only "if an armed attack occurs against a Member of the United Nations." It seemed to preclude the legitimacy of any preventive action against armed attack that was merely imminent but had not yet actually begun. However, by practically accepting in 1947 the First Report of the Atomic Energy Commission, the Security Council itself recognized implicitly that so strict an interpretation was not justified in view of the conditions of nuclear warfare.[3] Moreover, there is a distinct trend among United Nations members today to claim that the term "armed attack" must be interpreted also to cover indirect aggression, in the form, for instance, of foreign support for domestic subversion. As the discussions on the definition of aggression indicate, some members—especially those who have grievances against economically more advanced nations, or think they have—are even inclined to consider economic exploitation as a form of indirect aggression and therefore as a legitimate title for the exercise of self-defense. In other words, in spite of Article 51, self-defense tends again, as was the case in former times, to be held legitimate in practically any case in which a nation feels wronged by the policy of another nation.

In point of fact, international lawyers have posed the question whether and to what extent the United Nations still has the legitimate authority to control its members' exercise of their inherent right of self-defense. It is not surprising that such authority should be questioned. Is it not a time-honored maxim of political philosophy that society may legitimately claim to restrict the right of its members to judge for themselves and to assert their own cause only to the extent of its willingness and ability to afford them protection? It was on this general ground that members of the League of Nations began to deny the validity of the Covenant in the second half of the thirties, after the failure of the League sanctions in the Italo-Abyssinian War. No member of the United Nations, including the Soviet Union, has gone so far as yet. But the tendency among all United Nations members to take advantage of the flexibility of the law of the Charter is unmistakable. Indeed, it is natural enough in view of the undeniable fact that the United Nations cannot be relied upon to protect nations against the perils of international politics, which are infinitely greater today than they have ever been before.

Certain practical conclusions should be drawn from the constitutional and political development of the United Nations. They have been most clearly and convincingly stated by Mr. Dag Hammarskjold, the second Secretary-General of the United Nations, in the "observations" on the Suez crisis with which he introduced his "Annual Report on the Work of the Organization," submitted to the General Assembly in 1957. The United Nations, Mr. Hammarskjold warns, should not persevere in its tendency to claim "a world authority enforcing the law upon the nations." It possesses neither the legal powers nor the physical power to give effect to that claim. The members should rather look upon the organization as "an instrument for negotiation among, and to some extent for, governments." In other words, the United Nations is essentially a diplomatic body and not a government. United Nations procedures, accordingly, should not be conducted upon the pattern of parliamentary procedures but be inspired instead by the spirit of traditional diplomacy. Debate and vote are not intended to supply nations with additional means for displaying and satisfying their pugnacious instincts, but to guide "the development in constructive and peaceful directions" and thus assure the reconciliation of their divergent interests. In sum, the United Nations should not try to act as a legislator but should act as a moderator.

But Mr. Hammarskjold also makes clear that his suggestion that the United Nations serve primarily as a mediator, standing between the parties to a conflict rather than claiming to be their superior, is not meant to imply that it should disregard the rights and wrongs in the conflict it tries to resolve.

In fact, the notion that a mediator has to pretend moral indifference was already rejected by the classical writers on international law at a time when the mediator, as a rule, was an individual state. It would indeed be preposterous to impose moral indifference upon a collective mediator like the United Nations. True, Emmerich de Vattel, who taught the fathers of the American Republic the principles of international law, begins his discussion of mediation by emphasizing that "the mediator ought to observe an exact impartiality; he should soften reproaches, calm resentments, and draw minds towards each other." But he then continues: "His duty is to favor what is right, and to cause to be restored what belongs to each; but he ought not scrupulously to insist on rigorous justice. He is a moderator, and not a judge; his business is to procure peace; and to bring him who has right on his side, if it be necessary, to relax something with a view to so great a blessing."

It is undoubtedly more difficult today than it was in the eighteenth century to act in the gentle spirit of Vattel's words. But, all the same, is it not worth trying?

FOOTNOTES

[1]*Postwar Foreign Policy Preparation 1939–1945.* U.S. Department of State Publication, General Foreign Policy Series 15 (Washington, D. C., 1949), p. 113.

[2]Leo Gross, "The Charter of the United Nations and the Lodge Reservations," *American Journal of International Law,* 41, No. 3 (July 1947), pp. 531 ff.

[3]The report contains the following recommendation: "In consideration of the problem of violation of the terms of the treaty or convention on atomic matters it should also be borne in mind that a violation might be of so grave a character as to give rise to the inherent right of self-defense recognized in Article 51 of the Charter of the United Nations." See United Nations, *Repertory of Practice of United Nations Organs,* II (1955), p. 435.

THE UNITED NATIONS IN CRISIS*

Hardly ever has the prestige of the United Nations soared so high as it did in the initial stage of the Congo crisis last summer. True, the organization had only limited success—and could not reasonably be expected to have more—in its attempt to restore some semblance of law and order in the strife-torn Republic. Nevertheless it could rightly claim that by the promptness of its armed intervention it averted, at least for the moment, possibly very serious international complications. Walter Lippmann's dictum that "the United Nations would have to be invented if it did not already exist"[1] expressed a feeling generally shared in those days. At the beginning of the fifteenth session of the General Assembly, last September, the admission of sixteen new members and the presence of numerous heads of state or government appeared to testify no less impressively to the growing importance of the United Nations in world affairs.

But no sooner had the Assembly session been earnestly under way than the picture changed. With Nikita S. Khrushchev's address of September 23, culminating in the proposal to substitute for the present one-man office of the Secretary-General a directorate of three chief executives, the United Nations found itself plunged into a constitutional crisis. The shock produced by Khrushchev's demand was the greater because—even before the collective action in the Congo, in the planning and execution of which the Secretary-General played the leading role—hope that the world body might at long last become a kind of independent power had been concentrating ever more on the potentialities inherent in the executive office. The draft resolution on disarmament, which the Soviet delegation submitted to the General Assembly on October 13, was hardly likely to soften the shock, for it proposed to change the structure not only of the Secretariat but of the Security Council as well, "so that all three groups of states—the socialist countries, the countries members of the western powers' blocs, and the neutralist countries—may be represented in those organs on the basis of

*Reprinted with permission of *Social Research*, Winter 1960 (Vol. 27, No. 4).

equality."[2]

The pessimistic mood created by the dismal prospect of an organization purposely paralyzed by constitutional devices was yet further nourished by the discouraging development in the Congo, and by the growing difficulties that the United Nations faced in the field and at its New York headquarters in trying to cope with the problems in which it had become involved through its armed intervention. After having displayed surprising vigor in the initial period of the Congo affair, the organization soon proved to be affected with incontestable symptoms of paralysis, arising from political and financial rather than constitutional reasons. The United Nations found itself engulfed not only in a constitutional but in a political crisis as well.

We should be ill advised indeed if we were to take the constitutional crisis lightly. Admittedly, it is not yet clear how resolutely the Soviet Union is going to press its demand for a revision of the Charter along the lines it suggested last fall. But it has undoubtedly chosen a tactically most propitious moment for presenting its demand. Strictly speaking, the constitutional crisis antedates the submission of the Russian proposal. Some adaptation of the Security Council, and of other limited representative organs of the United Nations, to the growing number of member states, requiring amendment of the pertinent Charter provisions, has long been overdue. The question has given rise to heated controversies in the General Assembly for several years, and was one of the chief issues at its fifteenth session. By coming forth with a radical scheme of revision the Soviet Union has strengthened its bargaining power in the impending discussions and decisions on the future composition of those organs.

But obviously we can even less afford to take lightly the political crisis, of which the symptoms have been multiplying in recent months and even longer. The current crisis reveals the precarious nature of both the political and the constitutional conceptions that have been in the ascendant in the United Nations during the last five years. Therein lies probably its true historical significance. The melancholy experience of two earlier periods of United Nations history seems to be repeating itself once more.

There is always something arbitrary about an attempt to constrain the continuous flow of history into separate periods. It appears to be particularly problematic to speak, as I shall here, of three distinct phases of United Nations constitutional history, since the Charter, the basic law of the organization, has so far remained formally unchanged. However, the constitutional history of the world body is as little merely a history of its basic written law as is that of any other political organization. In fact, the law of an international body, like international law in general, is necessarily more amenable to political influences operating on it and continually remolding it than municipal law. It is therefore far from surprising that the constitutional history of the United Nations mirrors more or less faithfully the political and structural changes that have occurred in the international community during the fifteen years of its existence.

These changes are reflected particularly in the shifting balance between the chief constitutional organs, and in the respective roles played by the Security Council, General Assembly, and Secretary-General in three successive efforts to develop the United Nations beyond a mere conference machinery into a body politic capable of taking action, including military action, in the preservation of peace. Before trying to evaluate, in the light of recent experience, the ultimate chances of the third effort, dating from about 1955, we shall do well to recall the preceding attempts.

I

The concentration of military might in a few great powers, combined with the growing importance of smaller nations in world affairs, is perhaps one of the most striking and paradoxical features of the postwar period. It is hardly less paradoxical that the United Nations should have so greatly contributed to the increasing prestige and influence of the small states. Though it could well have been argued from the beginning that the small nations would be the chief beneficiaries of the organization, their share in the exercise of its power was by no means intended to be very substantial. The United Nations was designed as a mixed form of international government with a preponderance of the oligarchic rather than the democratic elements. The minor powers were to be members of the General Assembly, with rights completely equal to those of the great powers, and they also were to be represented in the Security Council, but these democratic elements of the constitution, however important they were, left intact the oligarchic core, the built-in concert of the five great powers.

In the first place, the Security Council—and the Security Council alone—was granted a kind of supranational authority, though only in security matters proper. It was defined in such broad and vague terms that it could be interpreted to include even the right to impose on member states changes of the legal and political status quo. The authors of the Charter also sought to insure the Council's capacity to take military action by obligating the member states to make armed forces available to it, on its call, and to lend it their military assistance in other forms as well. And in the second place, the five great powers were given a privileged position in the Council, as compared with that of its other members, representing the medium and small nations.

The combination of these two constitutional devices—the exclusive, broad, and compulsory powers of the Council under Chapter VII of the Charter and the privileges of the Big Five—made the great powers legal masters and, provided only they were able to take concerted action, was likely to make them also actual masters of the organization. At the same time, because of the veto privilege granted each of the great powers, none of them would in effect become subject to the Council's jurisdiction. Like the members of the European Concert of Powers in the nineteenth century, the members of the World Concert of Powers in the twentieth century were to be only agents, not objects, of international government. The hegemonic position of the five great powers in matters pertaining to Chapter VII was especially obvious in the Charter provisions regarding the composition of the Military Staff Committee, which was to advise and assist the Security Council on all military matters and "be responsible under the Security Council for the strategic direction of any armed forces placed at the disposal of the Security Council." As a matter of principle, the Committee was to consist exclusively of military representatives of the five concert powers, though other member states should be invited by the Committee to be associated with it when it held their participation in its work was required.

In view of the current controversy over the office and role of the Secretary-General, it is particularly pertinent to recall that at the general conference of the founding members held at San Francisco in 1945, the great powers tried to apply the idea of their joint hegemony to the organiza-tion of the Secretariat as well. To be sure, the proposals they had previously agreed on at Dumbarton Oaks provided that only the Secretary-General should be elected by the Security Council and the General Assembly; all other administrative officers were to be appointed by the Secretary-General himself. This proposal was in accord with the conception of the executive office that the United States government had been promoting through all stages of preparation of the future organization.[3] Afterward, however, the great powers reversed their position on the Secretariat. According to the amendment they jointly submitted to the conferees of San Francisco, the Secretariat was to be headed by a Secretary-General and four deputies, all of whom were to be elected by the Council and Assembly. The unmistakable implication of the new proposal was that the deputies should be equals rather than subordinates of the Secretary-General, and that the executive function should be divided among representatives of the great powers. The Soviet government took great pains to secure the adoption of the amend-ment, but the latter ran into heavy opposition from the smaller states, which felt that such a set-up "might jeopardize the international character of the Secretariat."[4] The amendment failed to receive the required two-thirds majority, and the conference of San Francisco endorsed the original Dum-barton Oaks provision for a single chief executive.

The question of the Secretariat played no important role at San Francisco. There the great constitutional issues over which major and minor powers were divided referred to the Security Council and the General Assembly. It makes curious reading today that the middle and small states were so seriously concerned about the danger that the concert powers, dominating the Security Council, might employ United Nations procedures and machinery for effecting "settlements of the Ethiopian, Munich, and Albanian type."[5] Equally unrealistic in the light of subsequent developments, seems to have been the hope of the great powers that they would be able to cooperate with one another. The collective-security system of the Charter was based on the political assumption that the grand alliance of the militarily strongest nations against the Axis powers in World War II could be continued into peacetime and be made the permanent nucleus, military and political, of the system. But no sooner had the United Nations come into existence than the built-in concert of the great powers tended to fall apart. Ironically, the common front that the latter maintained against the minor powers in the constitutional struggles of San Francisco was practically the last manifestation of the concert idea. Whenever on later occasions the great powers found themselves on the same side of the parliamentary battle lines in the councils of the United Nations, as they did recently in the initial stage of the Congo crisis, it was rather the accidental result of a temporary concurrence of interests than the expression of a deliberate coordination of policies.

One may argue nevertheless that the makers of the United Nations Charter were not actually so naive as they today appear to have been. It is true, the political assumption on which they were trying to build was faulty. But they are entitled to some credit for what one might call their constitutional realism. The intention to adapt the legal structure of the future organization to the power structure of international society was constitutionally sound. It also was justified by historical experience. Especially the experience of the European Concert of Powers, the most nearly successful experiment in international government, seems to suggest that the idea of a supranational world executive can be realized, if at all, only in the constitutional forms of a more or less oligarchic system based on its strongest members. Moreover, neither the major nor the minor powers were blind to the precariousness of the assumption that the political alignments of the war period would outlast the termination of the armed conflict. While the smaller nations were genuinely afraid that they might have to suffer unjustly from the irresistible power of an organization directed by the united will of the five permanent members of the Security Council, they were hardly less alarmed about the prospect of an organization paralyzed by lack of unity among them. This possibility was also clearly realized by the major powers. But it was, of course, less disturbing a prospect for them than for the weaker nations that stand most in need of international protection against aggression. One may well say, in point of fact, that the great powers gladly accepted the risk of a paralyzed Security Council as the price to be paid for their protection against being outvoted there.

Such considerations account for the United States government's promotion of a built-in concert no less than for the Soviet government's acceptance of it. The Dumbarton Oaks proposals, after all, were based on plans for the future organization that had been prepared in the United States Department of State. Harley A. Notter, the official historian of American postwar foreign-policy preparation, has pointed out the dilemma that confronted the constitutional draftsmen in the Department. While one wing of American public opinion was urging a security system legally more advanced toward genuine international government than the League of Nations had been, the planners also had to take account of the "possibility that the dominating American opinion of the years before the war in favor of political isolationism might reassert itself. Uncertainty regarding Senate consent to ratification of any proposed agreement in this field was ever present."[6] The dilemma could be solved only by means of a constitutional construction that would assure to the United States, together with its peers, a special privileged status in a legally and physically powerful organization. The Dumbarton Oaks proposals and also the Charter were almost ideally suited to satisfy both internationalists and isolationists.

II

To suggest that the security system of San Francisco has not proved successful would be too euphemistic a way of describing its fate. The truth of the matter is that it has not come into existence at all. Chapter VII of the Charter spelled out some principles relating to the armed forces to be made available to the Security Council, but in effect left their implementation in the hands of the five great powers. It also provided that the member states' actual contributions to the prospective military establishment should be determined by special agreements to be concluded between them and the Council. No such agreement was ever even negotiated, and the attempt of the Military Staff Committee to draft a common statement of principles governing the organization of the armed forces to be put at the Council's disposal ended in failure. Once the leading members of the Grand Alliance of World War II had become adversaries in the cold war following it, and potential enemies in another global conflagration, the very possibility of military cooperation between them was foreclosed. Thus the United Nations remained without the military teeth that were to distinguish it so favorably from the toothless League of Nations.

The more the cold war between West and East unfolded, the oftener were the members of the hoped-for great-power concert the very protagonists in the issues submitted to the Security Council, and the more was the latter impeded from taking even innocuous political action. In fact, the Council, which was looked on by the founding fathers as the chief instrument of the great powers in guiding and directing the organization, became one of the main battlegronds of the cold war they were waging against one another. The General Assembly became another, when around 1947–48, as a consequence of the cold war, its political role began to expand. As the cold war opened a new chapter in the political history of the United Nations, so the ascendancy of the Assembly, resulting from it, opened a new chapter in its constitutional evolution.

The cold war was not the only cause of the constitutional development that moved the Assembly more and more into the political center of the organization. At the San Francisco conference, when the smaller nations finally yielded to pressure and accepted the substance of the great powers' constitutional proposals, they did so in the hope that in the course of time the actual practice and formal amendments of the Charter would blunt its oligarchical characteristics. Accordingly, they could not but favor a de facto revision of the Charter by which the powers of the Assembly were extended. But the chief agent of the constitutional transformation that was to culminate in the Assembly's adoption of the Uniting for Peace resolution on November 3, 1950, was undoubtedly the United States government. In fact, some of the smaller nations followed the American lead only reluctantly. They realized that the elevation of the Assembly would tend to implicate them in the cold war more deeply than they liked.

Nor can the impetus of American revisionism be explained exclusively in terms of the cold war. It was only with a troubled conscience that public opinion in the United States had accepted the relegation of the General Assembly to a secondary political role. The oligarchical features of the Charter could not appeal to a nation that by its idealistic and democratic traditions was inclined to envisage the international governance of mankind in the constitutional form of a parliament of man rather than of a great-power concert based on a European aristocratic pattern. As mentioned before, the American government had promoted and worked for the adoption of a scheme of this type only because it thought it was a highly effective system of collective security and at the same time palatable to isolationist tastes. Both reasons lost their apparent cogency once the United Nations began actually to operate.

As for the effectiveness of the oligarchic system, in the cold-war situation in which the organization soon became enveloped it was not the Security Council but the General Assembly that proved capable of taking action in the preservation of peace. And as for isolationist anxieties about possible encroachment by the organization on American sovereignty, these were disproved by the realities of United Nations politics in the first years.[7] Through the hegemonic world position that had fallen to the United States, as a consequence of war and victory, this country could in all organs of the United Nations count on sweeping majorities in support of its policies. Accordingly, the United States was then in no need of legal protection against the organization. Moreover, the limitation on the operation of the majority principle in the Security Council was bound to frustrate American actions and to work to the advantage of the Soviet Union as a minority power. Thus considerations of interest no longer stood in the way, but on the contrary reenforced the idealistic urge, deeply rooted in American traditions, to rely on the untrammeled operation of the majority principle in international no less than in national politics.

Once this confluence of ideals and interest had taken place, the United States no longer felt any inhibitions about ascribing to the General Assembly, as "world parliament," a democratic legitimacy and a moral dignity that it actually never possessed. We also succeeded in strengthening the legal authority of the Assembly, through our initiation in 1950 of the Uniting for Peace resolution. The reform was intended to break the monopoly of the Council in security matters, and to extend to the Assembly the right to decide on enforcement measures. Thus it made it possible to circumvent the veto in the Council, and to institute collective-security measures also against any of the great powers. Though enforcement decisions of the Assembly, unlike decisions of the Council, were to be mere recommendations, not legally binding on members, it was hoped that their moral weight would be greater than that of Council decisions.

The Uniting for Peace resolution, like Chapter VII of the Charter, provided for organs and procedures for military implementation. Like the Security Council, the General Assembly was not to be confronted in a time of international crisis with the staggering task of improvising an armed establishment, but was to be in a position to utilize military units that member states would have undertaken beforehand to put aside and prepare for United Nations service. But the military provisions of the resolution, notwithstanding strong and persistent efforts by the United States government to secure their implementation, remained as much a dead letter as the corresponding provisions in Chapter VII of the Charter. This American defeat was one of the first indications that the political assumption on which the Uniting for Peace system was based was hardly less problematic than that of the San Francisco system. Just as the collective-security scheme of 1945 was patterned on the model of the Grand Alliance in World War II, the fathers of the Uniting for Peace resolution expected the political alignments in the initial period of the Korean war to continue beyond its termination. In fact, however, they tended to change even before the armistice was concluded.

The leadership that the United States government assumed in organizing and executing the United Nations action in Korea had originally the full moral support of practically all non-communist member states of the organization, though only fifteen of them actually participated in some form or other in the military operations of American and South Korean forces. They rightly saw in the North Korean aggression a case that would test the worthiness of the United Nations, and they realized that the organization met the test only through American sacrifices in blood and treasure. The fact that the United States was also prompted by its own national interest did not diminish their appreciation of American policy. However, the longer the Korean war dragged on, the more strongly did India and some other member states feel that the United States shared in the responsibility for its prolongation. Instead of contenting itself with repelling the North Korean aggression, the United States, its critics suggested, tended to transform what should have been kept within the purposes and limits of a collective-security action into an ideological and power struggle against communism in general and the Soviet Union in particular. Thus in the early 1950s there already began to appear the first traces of what was later to grow into the so-called third force, consisting of nations that tried to keep neutral in the cold war between the two super-powers.

But it was only in the latter half of the 1950s that this force became numerically strong enough to assert itself actively in the councils of the United Nations. In 1955, with the admission of sixteen new members, the membership rose to seventy-six; it increased by six more in the following years, and made another jump to a total of ninety-eight and then ninety-nine at the fifteenth Assembly session last fall. The rapid approximation to universality of membership and its effect on the political complexion of the United Nations could not but exert a profound influence on its constitutional character as well. Indeed, one is entitled to date from about 1955 a third period in the political and constitutional history of the world body.

III

The cold war continued, to be sure, but its nature and forms somehow changed in this period. The danger of an immediate armed clash between West and East decreased, and the lessening of international tension also lessened the rigidity of the international alignments. The bipolar structure that characterized international society in the first postwar decade gave way to a more flexible structure, and the third, or neutralist, force emerged into full prominence. In this relatively fluid situation the two super-powers' "peaceful competition" for influence and power in the uncommitted areas was bound to gain ever more momentum.

Anxious to maintain and possibly improve the global balance of power to its own advantage, each of them began to woo the smaller nations, unborn as well as born. Currying their favor, from 1955 onward they promoted and supported rather than obstructed the admission of new members to the United Nations. During the first decade of its existence only nine states were permitted to join the founding members. During the following five years no less than thirty-nine states, many of them newly born, were admitted. The pertinent Charter provisions notwithstanding, the admission procedures have become in practice a mere formality. Significantly, the exceptions to the current practice of opening the doors of the organization to every applicant are the cases in which the cold-war positions of the first postwar decade have remained frozen.[8]

Another factor that had a decisive effect on United Nations policies in the latter half of the 1950s was the deepening antagonism between the colonial and anticolonial powers. Three of the four major cases of this period in which the organization intervened in some form or other were related to the colonial question: the Suez case of 1956, the Lebanon issue in 1958, and the Congo crisis of 1960. Only the Hungarian case was an issue of the West-East conflict. Just as the protagonists of the latter had from the beginning used the institutions and procedures of the United Nations for the purposes of the cold war they were waging against each other, so did the anticolonial powers utilize them for the purposes of the cold war they were waging against the colonial powers. The world organization was in their eyes primarily an instrument for the liquidation of colonialism. Moreover, just as the West-East conflict had resulted in the formation of two blocs in the deliberative bodies of the United Nations—the American-led democratic and the communist—so did the other cold war lead to the consolidation of the Afro-Asian bloc.

Though the anticolonial struggle became ever more intense, and at times overshadowed all other questions, it never superseded the cold war waged in the United Nations between the Western and Eastern alliance systems. One might rather say that the two cold wars became increasingly intertwined. Interest considerations pertaining to the one influenced the members' tactics in the other. The degree to which the front lines of parliamentary battles are cutting across each other in the General Assembly is indicated by the fact that the Afro-Asian bloc comprises members that belong also to Western military alliances or Western political associations. Both India and Pakistan, for example, are members of the Commonwealth, and Pakistan is also part of the Southeast Asia Treaty Organization. The complexity of the loyalties and interests that bear on the policies of United Nations members accounts for the comparative fluidity that has characterized the political structure of the General Assembly during the last five years, in striking contrast to its rigidity in the first decade. Of the three blocs in the Assembly only the communist bloc of nine members (Yugoslavia not included) is held together with iron discipline. The cohesiveness of the Afro-Asian bloc, which in the latter 1950s numbered twenty-nine and in 1960 went up to forty-six members, is comparatively loose, and even more so is that of the American-led Western bloc, with its more than forty members. Each of these two blocs is likely to fall apart when it votes on questions that from its point of view are related to the other cold war, but there have even been defections from the American bloc on issues of the West-East conflict and from the Afro-Asian bloc on questions of colonialism.

The change in the political complexion of the United Nations could not fail to affect the two super-powers' positions within the organization. But basically, in this respect too, the development only mirrors the development outside. Both the increase of Russian and the decline of American influence in the councils of the United Nations are ultimately due to political, military, and economic factors that have been changing the global balance of power to the advantage of the East and the disadvantage of the West. Since the United States government, in spite of its loss in prestige, has so far been able to prevent the seating of the Peking government in United Nations organs, it has succeeded for the time being in making the realities reflected in the mirror look to Western eyes less unpleasant than they actually are.

There is no danger that the Soviet Union may attain in the United Nations a hegemonic position similar to that in which the United States found itself in the first postwar years. Its current promotion of changes that would weaken rather than strengthen the constitutional structure of the organization seems to indicate that the Soviet government itself does not believe in such a possibility. Though the Soviet bloc in the Assembly has grown in absolute numbers, the proportion of communist to con-communist members is even somewhat smaller today than it was about ten years ago. Now, however, there are opportunities for political maneuvering in the Assembly which then were foreclosed to the Soviet Union.

In those years its spokesmen used to ridicule and complain about the "mechanical majority" produced by American pressure on Assembly members outside the Soviet bloc. They overlooked, or probably did not want to realize and even less to concede, that fear produced by Russian policy was what induced the members of the Western bloc to subject themselves to strict parliamentary discipline. But the fact remains that the Soviet Union did find itself relegated to the not very enviable position of a permanent minority power with little actual influence on parliamentary decision-making, especially in the General Assembly. Indeed, one might have wondered in the earlier years why the Soviet Union cared at all to remain a member of the United Nations. It is by no means difficult, however, to surmise the motive for its policy. From the beginning of its revolutionary career, Bolshevism has been inclined to adopt a pragmatic attitude in institutional and tactical questions. After 1905 Lenin, asserting that the parliamentary forum offers even to the smallest group, provided it is resolute enough, the possibility of successful revolutionary agitation and propaganda, pled for socialist participation in the Imperial Duma. Similar considerations can be assumed to have prompted Stalin to agree to and maintain Russian membership in the various newly established international organizations. Being fully conscious of the dynamic force in anticolonialism, the Soviet government was unlikely not to realize the chance United Nations membership offered it, as the champion of colonial liberation, to enhance its own prestige and influence.

The Soviet Union was fortunate in that its promotion and support of colonial emancipation was bound to strengthen its position in the cold war between West and East. The very powers against which the anticolonial movement is directed are its adversaries in the cold war. Unfortunately the opposite applies to the United States. Having been a sincere opponent of colonialism throughout its national history, it is today inhibited in its support of the anticolonial drive by being allied against the Soviet Union with countries that are the chief targets of that drive. Recently, in the Congo crisis, the United States again found itself in the embarrassing position of having to reconcile its anticolonialist sympathies with the consideration due an ally. The dilemma is the more painful for American policymakers since any failure to give all-out support to the anticolonial cause is likely to redound to the Soviet Union's advantage.

Nothing illustrates more strikingly the effect of the colonial question on the respective positions of the United States and the Soviet Union than the use to which the Uniting for Peace resolution has been put. When the United States government initiated the measure in 1950, it hardly tried to conceal that communist aggression was its object. But the authorization of the General Assembly to intervene in case of a threat to or breach of the peace has turned out to be a double-edged weapon. In actual fact the procedure provided for in the resolution has been set in motion against democratic nations (the Suez crisis of 1956 and the Lebanon case in 1958) as well as against communist states (the Chinese aggression in Korea in 1951 and the Hungarian crisis in 1956). The lesson taught by the Lebanon case is in a sense more significant than the experience of the Suez crisis, though the latter was politically the more serious. In both, the Western powers involved had to change their course of action under the pressure brought to bear on them by the General Assembly; but while in the Suez case the

216

United Kingdom and France undoubtedly committed a prima facie violation of the Charter, the United States, in complying with the request of the lawful government of Lebanon to lend it military assistance against domestic subversion, could very well claim that its action was legally permissible.

The respective parliamentary strengths of the United States and the Soviet Union are functions of the question with which the Assembly is dealing at the time, rather than of the size of the three blocs, and accordingly vary from case to case. In fact, voting results in the world parliament have become almost as difficult to predict as they were in the Chamber of Deputies of the Third French Republic. The variableness, like the complexity, of Assembly voting patterns is due, in the first place, to the loose coherence of the Western and the Afro-Asian blocs. But it also is a consequence of the voting rules. Most politically important resolutions require for their adoption a two-thirds majority of the members present and voting. Since "members which abstain from voting are considered as not voting,"[9] when there are numerous abstentions a relatively small number of affirmative votes is sufficient to carry a motion. On the other hand, the smaller the number of abstentions, the more affirmative votes are required in order to obtain the two-thirds majority. While this rule tends to increase the liability of majority formation in the Assembly, it also furthers the expression of different shades of opinion.

The structural development that has accompanied the increasing size and changing political complexion of the United Nations General Assembly has been a curious one. As we have seen, the rigid, strictly bipartite structure of the late forties and early fifties has given way to a tripartite structure. But at the same time there has been taking place, apart from the Soviet bloc, a loosening up of the political groups within the Assembly, evidenced by its increasingly flexible voting pattern. To speak in terms of Rousseau's discussion of the general will and the effect exerted on it by partial associations,[10] in the earlier period of the Assembly's history there were not as many votes as there were member states, but only as many as there were associations—which means two, the vote of the Western and the vote of the Eastern bloc. Accordingly, there was no general will, and the opinion that prevailed was purely particular. From that state the General Assembly has lately been moving in the direction of a body in which differences are more numerous and give therefore a more general result. The United States, having been practically uncontested master of the Assembly in the initial period of its history, has badly suffered from its recent trend toward what Rousseau regarded as the ideal structure of a political body if the general will is to express itself. Conversely, the Soviet Union, commanding then and still today only a small minority bloc, could not but greatly profit by an evolution that made the Assembly more malleable and more susceptible to

Soviet influence than it originally had been. However, the Soviet Union has by no means gained as much as the United States has lost. The chief beneficiaries of the constitutional ascendancy of the General Assembly and of its internal changes have been the smaller and even the smallest member states—those that, according to the oligarchic conception of Dumbarton Oaks and San Francisco, were meant to play only a subordinate role in the political processes of the United Nations.

IV

The political factors that in the course of the last five years have added to the prominence and changed the character of the General Assembly have affected the constitutional development of the United Nations in other respects as well. Their effect on the constitutional position of the Secretary-General has undoubtedly been the most significant.

In view of the height to which the influence and prestige of Mr. Dag Hammarskjold, the second holder of the Secretary-Generalship, have risen in recent years, we are inclined to underrate the political role that Mr. Trygve Lie, the first occupant of the office, played in the initial period of the United Nations. Admittedly, one might question whether Mr. Lie exploited the potentialities of his high office to the full.[11] But certainly he was very far from considering himself merely an international civil servant and confining himself to the performance of administrative duties, or even from denying himself the right to diplomatic initiative. His bold attempt in 1950 to promote a settlement of the issue of Chinese representation—the question is still plaguing the United Nations today—impressively suggests that it was the political conditions under which he was operating, rather than his conception of the office, that prevented him from assuming a still more active part in United Nations politics than he did.

During Mr. Lie's tenure, issues directly related to the cold war between West and East were predominant, and United Nations membership was rigidly divided into the two parties to that conflict; during Mr. Hammarskjold's tenure, on the other hand, new international problems have emerged, and a third force in the United Nations has acquired increasing strength. The one situation was as unfavorable to a potent and independent political role of the Secretary-General as the other has been propitious to it. It is not an accident that the highest points in the rise of the Secretary-General—the 1956 Suez crisis and the first phase of the 1960 Congo crisis—found the United States and the Soviet Union, the two super-powers, on the same side of the political fence, even though for only a short while.

These two cases of armed intervention not only illustrate the powerful position that the Secretary-General has attained in the third period of United

Nations history. They also bring out in bold relief the new constitutional and political conceptions of collective security that came to the fore when those of the first and second periods failed to materialize.

The United Nations Emergency Force and the United Nations Force in the Congo, improvised in 1956 and 1960 respectively, are occasionally held to be essentially similar to the military establishment envisaged in Chapter VII of the Charter. In actual fact, however, they differ basically from the latter in purpose, nature, and internal organization. The armed forces of the Charter, to be put at the disposal of the Security Council, were to be an army proper, employed for repelling aggression and for other military actions, offensive or defensive, related to the task of enforcing international peace. Neither the United Nations forces along the Israeli-Egyptian frontier nor those in the Congo were assigned any enforcement functions in the sense of Chapter VII. Rather, their purpose was politically to facilitate the termination of the military action of the United Kingdom, France, and Israel in the first case, and of Belgium in the second, and thus bring into play the pacific procedures under Chapter VI of the Charter. In both cases it was clearly understood, as the Secretary-General put it in a 1958 analysis, that, "the Force should not be used to enforce any specific political solution of pending problems or to influence the political balance decisive to such a solution."[12] Accordingly, the Force was not intended, in fact it was not permitted, to engage in combat activity, least of all to take offensive action. Its use of armed force was strictly limited to the exercise of a narrowly defined right of self-defense. Thus, in both cases, the Force was to be a para-military formation restricted to para-military operations.[13]

In the first case, the United Nations Emergency Force, once it had performed its initial task of assisting in the termination of hostilities between the contending parties, was charged with the function of maintaining peaceful conditions in the critical frontier area of Gaza. The United Nations Force in the Congo played a dual role from the beginning of its intervention, and continued to maintain, or rather tried to restore, law and order throughout the vast territory of the Republic after the Belgian military units had been withdrawn from it. Nevertheless, the principle that the Force should abstain from influencing not only the military but also "the political balance affecting efforts to settle the conflict"[14] was to apply in both cases to the police function as well. As regards the latter function, the discharge of the mandate gave rise to no difficulties in the Gaza Strip, where the local authorities charged with the internal administration of the territory were operating normally under more or less normal conditions. More awkward were the problems that the United Nations Force faced in the Congo. There the violent civil dissensions and the absence of an effective administrative machinery, national and local, were bound to involve the United Nations

Force, against its mandate and its own intention, in the domestic and foreign affairs of the Republic, now on the one side and now on the other.

The character of the two para-military bodies differs in still another important respect from that of the military establishment provided for in Chapter VII of the Charter and envisaged by the Military Staff Committee. That Committee, in its report submitted to the Security Council in 1947, proposed that "all Member Nations shall have the opportunity as well as the obligation to place armed forces. . .at the disposal of the Security Council on its call"; the Committee further recommended that the permanent members of the Security Council—that is, the five great powers—"shall contribute initially the major portion" of the armed forces to be made available to the Council.[15] But when the General Assembly in 1956 and the Security Council in 1960 decided to improvise a United Nations Force, it was at the same time agreed that military personnel belonging to any of the permanent members of the Security Council should be excluded from the Force.[16]

The principle of great-power exclusion is suggestive of the nature of the international conflict to which this form of United Nations military intervention is adapted, as well as of the political purpose that the intervention is intended to serve. Both in the Suez and in the Congo case the local conflict turned on a colonial issue, and hence had no direct bearing on the global conflict between the Western and Eastern power blocs. Even so, the close interdependence in the present world of all political issues, international and national, made it very likely that the local conflict would finally implicate the two super-powers, thus adding to the existing global tensions and to the danger of a worldwide conflagration. In fact, it was for the purpose of averting this very danger—by securing a quick termination of the locally limited armed conflict—that the United Nations undertook its political-military intervention in the Near East and in Africa. The attempt to make a built-in concert of the great powers the legal and actual core of the world body had been based on the assumption that international conflicts, including local conflicts, necessarily affect the interests of the major powers so closely as to require, in all cases, their leading participation in settling them. In contrast, the conception of "preventive diplomacy," as Mr. Hammarskjold has called it,[17] is founded on the hope that some issues can be kept out of the great-power sphere and, with those nations' forbearance rather than under their leadership, brought to a solution by the minor powers.

There has been throughout United Nations history a close correspondence between the political conceptions of collective security and the methods of military planning and types of military organization intended to give effect to those conceptions. According to Chapter VII of the Charter, it was the Military Staff Committee, acting under the Security Council, that was to plan the size and character of the armed forces to be made available to the Council in advance of any possible case of employment. The Committee was also charged with the strategic direction and command of those forces. In its report of 1947 it made provision for an "overall" or "supreme" commander to be appointed by the Council on the advice of the Committee.[18] Thus the joint hegemony of the members of the great-power concert in the political affairs of the United Nations was to have its counterpart in their joint hegemony in military matters.

Since the military system envisaged in Chapter VII failed to materialize, another had to be improvised when the Security Council decided on June 27, 1950, that United Nations members should furnish military assistance to the Republic of Korea in defending itself against armed attack. The system finally adopted was planned and set up by the United States government; actually the Security Council only ratified an American decision. It provided for a Unified Command under the United States, with the United States entitled to designate the commander of the forces made available to the Command. Throughout the Korean war, American military action was independent of any continuing military control by United Nations organs. This grant to the United States of supreme military authority in conducting what was formally a collective enterprise was a recognition of the fact that the United States was actually carrying the main burden of the United Nations action in Korea. But it also reflected the political character and structure of the United Nations at that particular period. It indicated, in other words, that the unrealized plan of a joint great-power hegemony had given place under the pressure of circumstances to the reality of a single-power hegemony.

Very different indeed is the imprint that the political and constitutional context of the later fifties put on the organization of the United Nations military interventions in 1956 and 1960. Both the plan for the United Nations Emergency Force in the Near East and that for the United Nations Force in the Congo were worked out in the Secretariat; the first was then formally approved by the General Assembly, the second by the Security Council. For all practical purposes the Secrerary-General, especially in the Congo crisis, was authorized to do what he himself had proposed to do. Moreover, he played an important role in regard to the Commander of the Force. In 1956 the Commander, though appointed by the General Assembly, operated "under the instructions and guidance of the Secretary-General on the basis of executive responsibility for the operation entrusted to him by the Assembly"; in other words, he was responsible politically to the Assembly, but administratively to the Secretary-General.[19] The latter's leading role in rnilitary matters was even more conspicuous in 1960, when it was he, rather than the Security Council, that appointed the Supreme Commander of the United Nations Force in the Congo.[20] In this case the Secretary-General held the Supreme Commander responsible to himself politically as well as administratively.

Even more remarkable was the political role played by the Secretary-General. In the Suez and Congo crises he was entrusted respectively by the Assembly and the Council with the task of implementing their resolutions; the interpretation of their rather broad terms was left entirely to him. A most important part of this function consisted of diplomatic negotiations and the conclusion of agreements on behalf of the United Nations—agreements with member governments participating in the collective actions, with the governments against which the actions were directed, and, in particular, with the governments of the host countries in which the Forces were stationed. The significance and the scope of this diplomatic and legal activity can hardly be overrated.

V

In the ascendancy of the office of the Secretary-General the climax was reached in the initial period of the Congo crisis last summer. It was primarily the pressure of events and the uniquely involved nature of the Congo case that accounted for the central and decisive role Mr. Hammarskjold assumed in those critical weeks. His actions, brilliantly conceived and executed with consummate skill, were a brave and noble response to an awesome challenge. Clearly, however, his policy was also an expression and application of personal conceptions concerning the character and function of the United Nations and its executive officer, which can be traced back in his thinking. This is by no means meant to imply a doctrinaire inclination on the part of the present Secretary-General. On the contrary, his approach to political problems is essentially pragmatic, as is attested both by his official acts and by his public statements inside and outside the United Nations. His conceptions do not arise from preconceived ideas, but reflect, rather, the influence of the political development during his tenure of office. For this very reason they have undergone significant changes in the course of the years.

Mr. Hammarskjold's earlier views on the nature and function of the United Nations can best be stated in the words of the Annual Report that he submitted to the General Assembly in the fall of 1957. "The Charter, read as a whole," he affirmed, "does not endow the United Nations with any of the attributes of a super-state or of a body active outside the framework of decisions of Member Governments. The United Nations is, rather, an instrument for negotiation among, and to some extent for, Governments. It is also an instrument added to the time-honored means of diplomacy for concerting action by Governments in support of the goals of the Charter. This is the role the Organization has played, sometimes successfully, sometimes with disappointing setbacks, throughout its life."[21] This conservative interpretation of the Charter is the more noteworthy as the latter undoubtedly lends itself to an interpretation less restrictive of the Security Council's legal authority when acting under Chapter VII. The fathers of the United Nations did conceive of the Council as a body that in international emergency situations could, and should, become "active outside the framework of decisions of Member Governments" and exercise supranational governmental powers.

It is also significant that the Secretary-General chose that particular moment for offering his moderate counsel in an official communication. The problem of the authority of the United Nations and its chief organs had been weighed by him the year before, in a February 1956 address to an Indian audience. His conclusions then were that the General Assembly was not basically a parliament but rather "an organ for multi-lateral negotiations with a few of the elements of parliamentary life reflected in it"; that the Security Council, whatever the original intentions of the founding fathers at San Francisco might have been, was actually "neither a government nor a court"; and, finally, that the Secretariat was "not a kind of super-diplomacy or super-Foreign Office," was "not even a coordinated organ of that kind," and "the Secretariat, or the Secretary-General, never tries and never should try to tell any country, any Government, what it should do."[22] But when Mr. Hammarskjold returned to the problem of United Nations authority, in his 1957 Report, the experience of the Suez crisis lay behind him. In fact, that Report was intended to summarize the lessons suggested by the part the organization had played in the solution of the Near Eastern conflict. Having acted as the main catalyst in the laborious work of resolving the conflict, the Secretary-General wanted to testify to the fact that the success of the intervention was due to the combined use of United Nations mediatory procedures and methods of traditional quiet diplomacy, rather than to the assertion of superior legal authority and coercive powers.

The Secretary-General also made it clear, in 1957, that he did not indulge in a hope that the limitations on the organization's power could be substantially corrected or even eliminated by means of constitutional reform. The United Nations, he suggested, whatever its constitutional system, is bound to reflect the political realities of the world in which it is operating. While "the dynamic forces at work in this stage of human history have made world organization necessary," it remains true that "the balance of these forces has also set the limits within which the power of world organization can develop at each step and beyond which progress, when the balance of forces so permits, will be possible only by processes of organic growth in the system of custom and law prevailing in the society of nations." Accordingly, Mr. Hammarskjold recognized, as indeed he always has, that the United Nations' usefulness in conflicts that fall within the orbit of the cold war between the great powers of West and East is strictly limited, and that therefore systems of defensive alliance, maintained side by side with the United Nations and expressing the prevailing balance of forces, are still indispensable and legitimate devices of international politics. Especially, as he put it in his 1960 Report, in case of conflicts between the power blocs of West and East it is "practically impossible for the Secretary-General to operate effectively with the means put at his disposal, short of risking seriously to impair the usefulness of his office for the Organization in all the other cases for which the services of the United Nations Secretariat are needed."

Mr. Hammarskjold was the less eager to take such risks as the political development seemed to increase the chance that the organization and its chief executive could render valuable service even in a deeply split world. In view of the growing number of "uncommitted," "neutral," or "neutralist" countries that refused to "tie their policies, in a general sense, to any one of the blocs or to any specific line of action supported by one of the sides in the major conflict," the Secretary-General felt that the areas outside the orbit of the West-East cold war were extending rather than shrinking. Also he tended to assume that the great powers themselves might become mutually interested in avoiding an outcome in which "a regional or local conflict" was "drawn into the sphere of bloc politics." In sum, it seemed to him that the changing political context offered the opportunity of supporting and furthering, by ingenuity and effort, slow processes of organic growth that could finally bring into being a more just and secure world order.

The success of "preventive United Nations diplomacy" in such cases as Suez and Gaza, Lebanon and Jordan, and Laos made Mr. Hammarskjold inclined to think and suggest that the United Nations was somehow beginning to outgrow the stage of development in which the possibility of action depended more or less exclusively on the will and the policies of the member governments.[23] "It is possible to say," he told a Danish audience in May 1959, "that increasingly, although in a way difficult to define, something like an independent position for the Organization as such has found expression both in words and deeds. The roots of this development are, of course, the existence of an opinion independent of partisan interests and dominated by the objectives indicated in the United Nations Charter. This opinion may be more or less articulate and more or less clear-cut but the fact that it exists forms the basis for the evolution of a stand by the Organization itself, which is relatively independent of that of the parties."

Moreover, said Mr. Hammarskjold, the tendency of the organization "to gain a certain independent position" has "led to the acceptance of an independent political and diplomatic activity on the part of the Secretary-General as the 'neutral' representative of the Organization." He emphasized that the Secretary-General, owing his position to election by both the Security Council and the General Assembly, is pointed out by the Charter itself as "an independent opinion factor," able to speak and act on behalf of the entire organization as long as he has "the full confidence of the Member States, at least as to his independence and his freedom from personal motives." Mr. Hammarskjold conceded that some of the procedures introduced by the Secretary-General into United Nations practice and "perhaps combined with a modified balance in the use of various organs" were a strain on the letter of the Charter. He felt confident, however, that the freer interpretation was justified by the spirit of the Charter, since it was conducive to attaining the Charter's objectives.

Recently Mr. Hammarskjold has also mentioned what he regards as a distinct trend toward a broadening of the legal powers of the United Nations. In the concluding words of his Copenhagen address he suggested that we need the United Nations "as a foundation and a framework for arduous and time-consuming attempts to find forms in which an extra-national—or perhaps even supra-national—influence may be brought to bear in the prevention of future conflicts." A year later, in Chicago, he resumed his discussion of the legal powers of the world body and presented his view thereon in terms of an evolutionary theory of international law and organization. We are living, he remarked, in a stage of transition from "institutional systems of international coexistence" to "constitutional systems of international cooperation"—terms that seem to correspond to the traditional notions of international as compared with supranational law and organization. His examples of the latter are the attempts toward integration of Western Europe and the points where the Charter of the United Nations "reaches into the constitutional sphere," as it does in Chapter VII with its grant of mandatory governmental powers to the Security Council.

Thus Mr. Hammarskjold has abandoned his original interpretation of the nature of the United Nations, as presented in his 1957 Report to the Assembly, and has reverted to the conception of the founding fathers. He endeavors, in particular, to refute the view that the Chapter VII provisions that have not yet been implemented are therefore a dead letter. His criticism of this view is obviously prompted by his observation that current discussions on the principles and methods of policing a disarmament agreement, if it should ever be concluded, have completely disregarded the provisions of Chapter VII suitable to such a task. But this makes his present position no less indicative of the changes in his thinking on the political and legal nature of the organization.

Equally significant in his Chicago speech, which at a subsequent press conference he called his "creed" or "confession of faith,"[24] is the "socio-logical perspective taken over from theories of biological evolution" in which he sees the present and the future of the United Nations. Each social and political organism, Mr. Hammarskjold believes, carries within it seeds for the growth of higher forms, covering ever wider areas and groups of peoples. Such an institutional system as the United Nations, "stage by stage, may be developed and enriched until, on single points or on a broad front, it passes over into a constitutional system of cooperation." He concludes with the words, moving indeed in view of the crisis into which the United Nations and its Secretary-General were shortly afterward plunged: "Working at the edge of the development of human society is to work on the brink of the unknown. Much of what is done will one day prove to have been of little avail. That is no excuse for the failure to act in accordance with our best understanding, in recognition of its limits but with faith in the ultimate result of the creative evolution in which it is our privilege to cooperate."

It was in this spirit that the Secretary-General responded to the challenge of the turbulent and frightening events in the newly independent Republic of the Congo. His policy there was determined by the conception he had come to adopt in the immediately preceding years concerning the nature and powers of the United Nations, as well as by the pressure of circumstances and the necessities of the case. It was symptomatic of Mr. Hammarskjold's approach to the Congo crisis that it became the first case in the constitu-tional history of the organization in which there was full application of Article 99 of the Charter, according to which "the Secretary-General may bring to the attention of the Security Council any matter which in his opinion may threaten the maintenance of international peace and security."[25] Since the Council proceedings had been initiated under this article, the Secretary-General felt entitled to consider Chapter VII applic-able to the Council's decisions, although they had not been made explicitly under that chapter, and accordingly to interpret them as mandatory rather than recommendatory.[26]

Therein lies the most important legal difference between United Nations policies in the Congo case and in the Suez case. In the Near East the military intervention was decided on by the General Assembly, which has only recommendatory powers; therefore in all United Nations dealings with individual governments the principle of voluntary cooperation prevailed. In the Congo case, too, contributions of national contingents to the para-military Force were, of course, entirely voluntary; and there too it was clearly understood that the Force should not be used to enforce any specific political solution of pending problems, international or domestic. However, as regards the implementation of what Article 40 of the Charter calls provisional measures, there was in the Congo case a distinct tendency to assert the superior legal authority of the Security Council and the legal obligation of member states to comply with its decisions, rather than to rely exclusively on the conciliatory powers of Chapter VI.

VI

In Mr. Hammarskjold's terminology, one might describe his policy in the Congo crisis as an attempt to make full use of the "constitutional" elements contained in the United Nations Charter. Indeed, the political and legal potentialities inherent in his office had never before been put in such bold relief as in the initial stage of the Congo case. It is true, the Secretary-General acted under the authority of the Security Council and submitted to its judgment whenever his interpretation of the mandate given him was challenged. But the fact remains that actually it was he rather than the Council that was the chief organ of the United Nations through the hectic weeks of summer 1960.

Mr. Hammarskjold's personal prestige and his managerial efficiency do not alone account for the strength of his position in the organization during the Congo crisis. Admittedly, they were important contributing factors, but the decisive factor was the constitutional authority his office acquired in the political and constitutional constellation of the later 1950s. The constitutional standing of the Security Council suffered badly, in the first place, from its practical ineffectiveness as the executive body it was originally intended to be. After several years of a rather shadowy existence, the Council again played an important role only in 1960. Moreover, its oligarchic character could not but weaken its authority in an organization that was developing toward more democratic forms than those outlined by the founding fathers. In fact, with the steady growth of membership, the Council's representative character became ever more dubious. On the other hand, the General Assembly, with its increasing size, became necessarily less and less able to cope effectively with the executive tasks that fell to it as its powers increased. Under those conditions the Secretary-General almost automatically moved up into an unrivaled position of executive leadership.

Since the Secretary-General, unlike the privileged members of the Security Council, derives his executive authority from a democratic process of election by Council and Assembly, he can rightly claim that his authority has a democratic basis and turn this fact to his advantage. Indeed, he did so last fall in a statement to the Assembly that may well be characterized as an expression of the parliamentary conception of the Secretary-Generalship. Rejecting Mr. Khrushchev's demand for resignation, he asked the Assem-

bly, in effect, for a vote of confidence. "I have no right to do so [to resign],"
Mr. Hammarskjold said, "because I have a responsibility to all those states
members for which the organization is of decisive importance, a
responsibility which overrides all other considerations. It is not the Soviet
Union or, indeed, any other big powers who need the United Nations for
their protection; it is all the others. In this sense the organization is first of all
their organization, and I deeply believe in the wisdom with which they will
be able to use it and guide it. I shall remain in my post during the term of my
office as a servant of the organization in the interests of all those other
nations, as long as they wish me to do so."[27]

This statement reveals, as in a flash, the political and constitutional
changes that the United Nations has gone through, from the days of its
conception at Dumbarton Oaks through the days of the Congo crisis: the
shift of emphasis from the great powers' role in the organization to that of
the smaller nations, and the accompanying shift of balance among its chief
constitutional organs. The statement also may very well have been the
epilogue to the third period in the political and constitutional history of the
world organization.

The threat to the office of the Secretary-General and thereby to the United
Nations itself, implicit in the Soviet Union's demand for the replacement of
the present one-man office by a triumvirate, is serious enough. But the
danger of paralysis for political reasons is probably more imminent than that
of paralysis effected by means of constitutional reform. During its fifteen-
year history the United Nations has moved ever closer to the ideal of a
universal democratic organization. Still, a democratic constitution, actual
or legal, is not necessarily more conducive to the effectiveness of a peace
organization than an oligarchic constitution. As the history of domestic
politics shows, the relationship between liberty and order is unfortunately
more complex than we would like it to be. At any rate, the danger that the
General Assembly will become less and less capable of taking action is a
real one. And the validity of yet another presupposition of successful
United Nations preventive diplomacy is becoming increasingly doubtful,
for the development of the Congo crisis and other symptoms impressively
indicate how tenuous is the line separating the two types of conflict that are
today dividing mankind.

FOOTNOTES

[1]New York *Herald Tribune*, July 21, 1960.

[2]United Nations, General Assembly, A/C, 1/L249, 13 October 1960.

[3]See Stephen M. Schwebel, *The Secretary-General of the United Nations* (Cambridge, Mass.,
1952) pp. 17 ff.

[4]United Nations Conference on International Organization, *Selected Documents* (Washington
1946) pp. 220, 514 ff.

[5]*Ibid.*, p. 485.

[6]U. S. Department of State, General Foreign Policy Series 15, *Postwar Foreign Policy Preparation 1939–1945* (Washington 1949) p. 113.

[7]For an elaboration of these remarks see Erich Hula, "The Evolution of Collective Security under the United Nations Charter," in Arnold Wolfers, ed., *Alliance Policy in the Cold War* (Baltimore 1959) pp. 88 ff.

[8]Some weeks ago the United Nations unexpectedly relapsed into the admission, or rather non-admission, practice of the early fifties. On December 3–4, 1960, when the Security Council refused to consider the membership application of the Mongolian People's Republic, the Soviet Union vetoed a French-Tunisian resolution recommending to the General Assembly the admission of Mauritania, youngest of the newly independent African states.

[9]Rule 88 of the Rules of Procedure of the General Assembly. According to Rule 69 "a majority of the Members of the General Assembly shall constitute a quorum."

[10]Jean Jacques Rousseau, *The Social Contract*, Book II, Ch. 3. Though Rousseau's argument is related to direct democracy, his analysis of the effect of factions on the formation of the general will fits also the case of parliamentary bodies.

[11]See Schwebel (cited above, note 3) p. 206.

[12]United Nations, General Assembly, A/3943. Report of the Secretary-General, *United Nations Emergency Force: Summary Study of the Experience Derived from the Establishment and Operation of the Force*, 9 October 1958, par. 167.

[13]*Ibid.*, pars. 175–79.

[14]*Ibid.*, par. 12.

[15]General Principles Governing the Organization of the Armed Forces Made Available to the Security Council by Member Nations of the United Nations, Articles 9, 10; see United Nations, Lake Success, *Yearbook of the United Nations, 1946–47* (New York 1947) p. 425.

[16]*United Nations Emergency Force* (cited above, note 12) pars. 13 and 16. First Report by the Secretary-General on the Implementation of Security Council Resolution S/4387 of July 14, 1960; see *United Nations Review*, vol. 7, no. 2 (August 1960) p. 9.

[17]United Nations, General Assembly, *Official Records*, Fifteenth Session, Supplement No. 1A (A/4390/Add 1), Introduction to the Annual Report of the Secretary-General on the Work of the Organization 16 June 1959—15 June 1960 (New York 1960) pp. 4 ff.

[18]Article 41; see *Yearbook . . . 1946–47* (cited above, note 15) p. 428.

[19]*United Nations Emergency Force* (cited above, note 12) pars. 76, 169.

[20]First Report . . . in *United Nations Review* (cited above, note 16) p. 10.

[21]United Nations, General Assembly, *Official Records*, Twelfth Session, Supplement No. 1A (A/3594/Add. 1), Introduction to the Annual Report of the Secretary-General on the Work of the Organization 16 June 1956—15 June 1957 (New York 1957) p. 3.

[22]United Nations, Department of Public Information, "The United Nations—An Appraisal," Text of an Address Given by Secretary-General Dag Hammarskjold before the Indian Council of World Affairs in New Delhi, India, February 3, 1956.

[23]The following remarks and quotations are based on two addresses made by the Secretary-General in 1959 and 1960: "Do We Need the United Nations?" delivered before the Students Association, Copenhagen, May 2, 1959, United Nations Press Release SG/812, 1 May 1959; and "The Development of a Constitutional Framework for International Cooperation," delivered at the University of Chicago Law School, May 1, 1960, and published by the United Nations in 1960.

[24]See *United Nations Review*, vol. 6, no. 12 (June 1960) pp. 30 ff.

[25]Mr. Trygve Lie's claim that he invoked Article 99 in the case of Korea is controversial. See Schwebel (cited above, note 3) pp. 23 ff., 90, and 104 ff.

[26]See Mr. Hammarskjold's statement to the Security Council on August 8, in *United Nations Review, vol. 7, no. 3 (September 1960) p. 17.*

[27]New York *Times*, October 4, 1960, p. 19.

THE UNITED STATES AND THE UNITED NATIONS*

The United Nations policy of the United States has been a matter of increasing concern in recent years. This concern has become manifest especially in the national debate, inside and outside the United States Congress. Several participants in the discussion, men whose public record qualifies them as sincere supporters of the world organization, have asked for, or undertaken themselves, a reconsideration of the United Nations and of the policy that the United States should pursue toward and in the world body.[1]

A sober reappraisal of the United Nations, as it is today, in the light of the foreign policy interests of the United States, is indeed well warranted. Admittedly, the United Nations owes its existence primarily to American efforts; the United Nations Charter is largely the product of American planning, and the actual development of the Organization *praeter* and *contra legem* has been decisively influenced by United States actions. But all this does not deprive us of the right to ask whether and to what extent the United Nations still deserves American support. The special relationship of the United States to the United Nations merely obligates us, when reassessing our United Nations policy, to be duly conscious of the special responsibility which the United States has assumed toward the Organization.

I

There are a great many variants of criticism in this country of the United Nations and its policies. There are in fact about as many as there are cases in which the United Nations has, or has not, taken action and as there are

*Reprinted by permission of the Public Affairs Conference Center from *Beyond the Cold War*, ed. Robert A. Goldwin, (Chicago: Rand McNally & Co., 1966).

231

views, valid and invalid, on what the United Nations can, and what it should, do. The criticism ranges from the charge that the Organization has no practical relevancy in the real world of international politics, to the accusation that it is a serious threat to the sovereignty and security of the United States. These extreme contentions are suggestive of the two main trends of criticism to which the United Nations has been, and is, subjected.

During the first decade of its existence the United Nations was chiefly reproached for not doing things, for not going far enough in what it was supposed to do, for not making full use of the legal powers conferred on it. Complaints of this type were probably strongest in the Greek case, but were leveled at the Organization also in the Indonesian, the Palestine, the Kashmir, and, last but not least the Korean case. True, as the United Nations, contrary to what this critcism would seem to suggest, took in general a rather broad view of its legal authority, even in those earlier years, it was occasionally also blamed for exceeding its powers. But the trend favoring a loose construction of the Charter definitely prevailed in American public opinion during the initial period of the United Nations.

Owing to the emergence and the growing influence of new political forces in the United Nations, still another type of criticism gained momentum in American public opinion during the second decade of the Organization's existence. More and more often the United Nations was reproached not for what it did not do but, on the contrary, for what it did do, for going too far in its actions, for arrogating and exercising powers that under the Charter it did not possess, particularly for intruding into the domestic jurisdiction of member states, expressly recognized by the Charter as falling outside United Nations control. These complaints were chiefly related to the activities of the world body in the rapidly shrinking colonial field and were vehement in the cases of the Congo, West New Guinea, South Africa, Southern Rhodesia, and the Portuguese African territories.

This criticism of United Nations policies poses the problem of the current policy and position of the United States in the world Organization. Insofar as the United States government wholeheartedly supported, or even initiated, those policies, it clearly shares in the responsibility for them, as is the case in the issues of the Congo and West New Guinea. If, as in the other cases mentioned, the United States obviously only yielded to political pressures brought to bear upon its decisions, the question arises as to how strong the United States still is in the councils of the United Nations. How long, critical voices ask, will it still be possible to assume more or less dogmatically that the interests of the United Nations and the United States are necessarily identical? In fact, has not the assumption already been invalidated by trends and events beginning with the Suez crisis in 1956, if not earlier?

II

The assumption underlies the Uniting For Peace Resolution of 1950 rather than the United Nations Charter of 1945. Since the essentials of both instruments are of American origin, the difference indicates a significant change during those five years in the attitude of the United States toward the United Nations.

Harley A. Notter, the official historian of United States *Postwar Foreign Policy Preparation,* vividly describes the dilemma that confronted the planners in the State Department when they set out to draft the constitution of the peace organization that was to replace the defunct League of Nations. The prospective constitution had to win the approval of the internationalist wing of American public opinion and had to be acceptable to the isolationist wing as well. "Uncertainty," remarks Notter, "regarding Senate consent to ratification of any proposed agreement in this field was ever present."[2] In other words, the future organization was to be more akin to genuine international government than the League of Nations, but the restrictions on United States sovereignty less far reaching than supposedly they would have been under the Covenant. The only solution of this dilemma was a constitutional construction that would provide the nucleus of a supranational world government and at the same time assure the United States, and necessarily other major powers as well, a special privileged status within the system. The United Nations Charter fully meets these requirements. The Security Council was to have supranational powers, though only as peace-enforcing agency acting under Chapter VII of the Charter. Moreover, the United Nations procedures were to be governed by the majority instead of the unanimity principle which prevailed in the League. But thanks to the rule of the Charter that majority decisions of the Security Council shall require the concurrent votes of the five permanent members of the Council, which implies their veto right, the United States would virtually be exempt from the supranational authority of the Council. It could not be compelled to participate in any sort of enforcement measures and, by the same token, could prevent their application against itself. In regard to the very questions of war and peace that affect its interests most closely, the United States, together with the other major powers and contrary to all other United Nations members, would retain the traditional right of sovereign nations to be their own judges of their rights and obligations under international law, including those under the Charter. As Senator Arthur H. Vandenberg, when advocating the ratification of the Charter, assured his colleagues, the flag would stay on the dome of the Capitol.

The grant to some members of a privileged position in the United Nations was hardly consistent with the idea of equality of states, affirmed in the Charter, or, for that matter, of collective security as a generally applicable system. The device of a built-in concert of the leading powers in an otherwise democratic organization is reminiscent, in fact, of the European Concert of Powers in the nineteenth century, though this was a purely aristocratic model of international government. The ingenious construction, however, not only was apt to assuage isolationist fears but recommended itself and was justifiable on other grounds as well. In the first place, to require for the operation of the United Nations peace system agreement among its most powerful members was only a formal recognition of the fact that the maintenance of international peace depends ultimately upon their cooperation. Secondly, to rule out the application of the enforcement system against one of the great powers, and particularly one of the two then emerging superpowers, was intended not to burden the United Nations with a task that would most certainly go beyond its physical capacity. Moreover, such enforcement action would practically mean the very kind of global war that the United Nations was founded to avert.

The rapidly unfolding Cold War made it soon clear that the political assumption on which the Charter system of collective security was based did not stand the test of reality. The very powers that were expected to cooperate in the direction of United Nations affairs were pitted against one another in and outside the United Nations and began to look upon each other as potential adversaries in another world holocaust. It soon also became clear that the veto shielded not only the great powers themselves but also their allies and satellites against United Nations intervention. But if we thus found out to our dismay that the Security Council would not be able to cope with the very questions that affected us most closely, we also discovered that we had overrated the risk of United States membership in the world body.

The hegemonic position that had fallen to the United States as a result of World War II secured it the leading role also in the United Nations. In fact, we commanded in all of its councils sweeping majorities in practically all important issues that were raised in them. The feeling that United States interests were in need of protection by constitutional devices against United Nations policies, therefore, began to yield to the belief in a preordained harmony of the United States and United Nations interests. Ironically, the protective shield of the great-power veto proved to be the only obstacle we encountered in trying to make full use of United Nations procedures for furthering American interests. Thus we forgot that only a short time ago we considered the veto an indispensable guarantee of "our perpetuated independence of international dictation," as Senator Vandenberg put it in 1945, and disparaged with its alleged abuse by the Soviet Union the device itself. In order to circumvent the Soviet veto in the Security Council, we now favored, and became instrumental in effecting, a gradual shift of the constitutional center from the Council to the General Assembley. Finally, in 1950, at the height of the Korean crisis, we sponsored the Uniting for Peace resolution which terminated the monopoly of the Council in dealing with threats to the peace, breaches of the peace, and acts of aggression.

By initiating a constitutional reform that was intended to circumvent the Soviet veto in the Council and subject the Soviet Union in the last instance to majority decisions of the General Assembly, we also implicitly submitted our own policies to the ultimate control of the Assembly. In strictly legal terms, admittedly, we thereby did not extend our obligations beyond what they were under the Charter, for, unlike the Security Council, the General Assembly has no compulsory but only recommendatory powers. But such distinctions do not weigh very heavily in United Nations politics. Moreover, what the Assembly is lacking in legal authority it makes up for by the greater prestige it enjoys as the democratic organ of the United Nations. It was, in fact, part of our own policy, both for reasons of ideological predilection and of expediency relating to the Cold War, to extol the Assembly and attribute to it a democratic legitimacy and moral authority that it actually does not possess, either by its composition or by the spirit of its proceedings. The risk we ran thus by sponsoring the Uniting for Peace resolution was not altogether negligible. However, it seemed inconceivable then that we would ever be unable to sway the deliberations and decisions of the world parliament.

Just as the collective security scheme of the Charter was patterned on the model of the Grand Alliance of World War II, the system of the Uniting for Peace resolution was based on the assumption that the political alignments in the initial period of the Korean War would continue beyond its termination. But the second assumption proved as faulty as the first. The political constellation of 1950 tended to change even before the Korean hostilities ended.

The Assembly system of the Uniting for Peace resolution, as we never tried to conceal, was designed as a means of strengthening the Western defense position against the East; it was aimed at the Soviet Union. To all practical intents and purposes it was an attempt to span and tighten our particular alliances by an all-embracing American-led alliance in the legal form of an abstract collective-security system. The tendency of the members of a collective security organization to use the abstract system, contrived as a protection of all against each and every other state, for the purpose of building and cementing an alliance against a concrete state or group of states, will always be very strong indeed. But, given the complexity of international relations, the use of the system for such purpose is also likely to be strongly resisted, as the United States soon found out. The Uniting for Peace resolution provided for military means, similar to those envisaged in Chapter VII of the Charter, which were to assure the effectiveness of the new system. However, the General Assembly persistently refused to implement the military provisions of the resolution. The latter remained a dead letter no less than the corresponding provisions of the Charter.

The result of the reform of 1950 differed from the expectations of its sponsors in still another respect. The authors of the Uniting for Peace resolution found satisfaction in seeing it applied to cases to which it had been tailored, as to the case of Chinese Communist intervention in Korea and to the case of Hungary. The Suez and the Lebanon cases, however, showed that the new system was a double-edged weapon that could be used against the West as well. Moreover, the reluctance of the smaller member nations to become involved in the power struggle of the giant members— traces of this reluctance were already discernible prior to and during the Korean War— strongly increased with the rapid growth of United Nations membership and the formation of a neutralist faction in the latter half of the fifties. We soon also realized that we had underrated the impact of the other Cold War, the one between the colonial and anticolonial powers, both on the operations of the Assembly and on the political dynamics of the Organization in general. Ever since the middle of the fifties the colonial issue, in one form or another, has been in the center of United Nations politics, and the tendency of the anticolonial members to view and use the United Nations primarily as an instrument for terminating the colonial system has become ever stronger.

III

The failure of the United Nations members to implement the military provisions of Chapter VII of the Charter and of the Uniting for Peace resolution has so far not been understood to imply the abandonment of the very principle of collective security that to prevent and repel aggression, if necessary by armed force, is the most significant task of the world body. Rather, the assumption was that the principle itself was still valid, though its application would have to be improvised in each case of need. The validity of the principle was recently contested, however, by none other than Secretary-General U Thant in his Harvard address of June 13, 1963, [3] and in later statements as well. "There has been," the Secretary-General said, "a tacit transition from the concept of collective security, as set out in Chapter VII of the United Nations Charter, to a more realistic idea of peace-keeping. The idea that conventional military methods—or, to put it bluntly, war—can be used by or on behalf of the United Nations to counter aggression and secure the peace seems now to be rather impractical." As the Secretary-General emphasized, the peace-keeping forces of the United Nations in the Middle East and in the Congo were essentially different from the military forces envisaged in the Charter and the Uniting for Peace resolution. Their task was not to enforce peace, but to support the Council and the Assembly in attempts to terminate an international conflict by the pacific procedures outlined in Chapter VI of the Charter. "They are essentially peace and not fighting forces, and they operate only with the consent of the parties directly concerned." They also are composed of military forces supplied by the smaller nations and not, as the Charter provided, by the great powers, "which has the advantage of not entangling United Nations actions in the antagonisms of the cold war."

The Secretary-General's statement undoubtedly was motivated by his neutralist leanings, but it would be difficult to deny that it is a realistic appraisal of current trends in the United Nations. We had better accept the fact that the emergence in the General Assembly of a strong neutralist faction has undone what the United States tried to accomplish by initiating the Uniting for Peace resolution. At any rate, it is most unlikely that in case of Soviet aggression the two-thirds majority required for recommending or authorizing military enforcement measures could be attained. It is doubtful, in fact, whether sufficient votes might be available in the Assembly for recommending economic or diplomatic sanctions or even for a mere condemnation of the aggression. At best, the Assembly might agree on a colorless, politically meaningless resolution.

The situation is not likely to be different, as the experience of the Goa case has taught us, if a colonial power, or, for that matter, a state pursuing domestic policies giving offense to anticolonialist members, should become the victim of aggression; for instance, to put it bluntly, if African or Asian member states, in violation of the Charter, should resort to force for the purpose of securing the independence of the few remaining colonial possessions or the termination of South Africa's discriminatory domestic policies. The situation might be about the same in case of Arab aggression against Israel, which in Arab eyes is a colonial power. The balance of physical forces in Africa being what it is today, the immediate danger to peace on that continent is not so much direct as indirect aggression by the time-honored method of subversion from outside. But even direct aggression is within the realm of possibility.

The sweep in and outside the United Nations of the anticolonialist movement is due to a combination of several favorable factors. The movement has benefited, and still does, by the competition of the two superpowers for influence and power in the uncommitted areas of the world. Anxious to maintain and possibly improve the global balance of power to its own advantage, each of them began to woo the smaller nations, unborn as well as born. Currying their favor, from 1955 onward, they promoted and supported rather than obstructed the admission of new members to the United Nations. The pertinent Charter provisions notwithstanding, the admission procedures have become a mere formality. The notion that membership implies obligations toward the Organization which applicants for admission have to prove to be willing and capable of meeting has become obsolete.

Both superpowers, moreover, for reasons of their political traditions, are morally committed to an anticolonialist course, which, of course, is not to say that their ideas of self-determination of peoples under colonial rule have the same meaning and practical implications. At any rate, the Soviet Union and the United States, in pursuing their anticolonialist policies, find themselves in almost opposite positions. The one is as fortunate for the former as the other unfortunate for the latter. For while the Soviet Union can always be certain that its policy is not only compatible with but actually furthering its national interest, the United States is always plagued by doubts about the effect of its policy on the strength of the Western world, with which it is bound by common interests and ties of a military-political alliance. Long-range interests seem to suggest full support of decolonization, but more immediate interests relating to the West-East conflict pull in the other direction. This accounts for the Hamlet-like attitude of the United States in colonial questions that has manifested itself as far back as the Conference of San Francisco. It was not the United States but the Soviet Union that proposed to the Conference to make it an express purpose of the United Nations "to develop friendly relations among nations based on respect for the principle of equal rights and self-determinations of peoples."(Article 1, paragraph 2).

The endorsement by the Charter of the principle of self-determination has proved a powerful ideological weapon in the anticolonialist struggle. So has the fact that the Charter proclaims as another purpose of the United Nations "to achieve international cooperation. . .in promoting and encouraging respect for human rights and for fundamental freedoms for all without distinction as to race, sex, language, or religion" (Article 1, paragraph 3). The very provisions of the Charter which deal directly with colonial matters have been no less effective in strengthening the cause of colonial emancipation. Both Chapters XI and XII envisaged a radical transformation and the final termination of the colonial system, with the United Nations assisting in the process.

Article 1 of the Charter establishes a hierarchy of the purposes that the United Nations is to pursue. The purposes stated in the second and third paragraph are clearly subordinate to the purpose "to maintain international peace and security" stated in the first paragraph of Article 1. In fact, one can speak of a Hobbesian tendency among the fathers of the Charter to absolut-ize the value of peace. When at San Francisco some smaller nations proposed to make, in addition to the maintenance of international peace and security, the maintenance of international law and justice an express United Nations purpose, the conferees, following the lead of the United States, rejected the proposal. According to the intention of its founders, the United Nations, in promoting self-determination of peoples and human rights, must go no farther than is conducive to the cause of peace.

But whatever the original intention might have been, the very endorse-ment by the Charter of these principles tends to cast a shadow of doubt on the legitimacy of any conditions that are inconsistent with them. It lends itself to the interpretation and, in fact, has been interpreted to imply that only a political order, international or national, founded on those principles is legitimate. Or, in negative terms, states, governments, possessions, boundaries, or international treaties that supposedly do not conform to them are lacking in legitimacy. The solemn affirmation of these principles, by the same token, does seem to sanction policies and actions, including revolu-tionary policies and actions, that try to reshape the world according to those political maxims. It is no accident that the Charter outlaws war but not revolution.

Admittedly, the fact that the Charter lends support to the anticolonialist cause cannot be understood to imply a qualification of the obligation of United Nations members, stated in Article 2, paragraph 4 of the Charter, to "refrain in their international relations from the threat or use of force." The prohibition of force, often called the most essential provision of the Charter, is meant to be absolute and leaves no room for a legally permissible "war of liberation" of any kind. But the very fact that the Charter favors so strongly the end, liberation (if liberation it is), cannot but lessen the effectiveness of the limitations it places on means for attaining that end. Nor is it likely that the United Nations will take strong action against aggression if it considers the cause for which it has been undertaken legitimate, as we know from the attitude of United Nations members in the Goa case.

The contingency of Goa need not actually repeat itself, however. What we have experienced so far, and must expect to meet with more and more often in the near future, is the exploitation by African and Asian members of our fear that they will use force unless we help them to mobilize the machinery of the United Nations for the attainment of their particular ends. The threat to the peace, caused by those states, is used by them as an argument in urging the United Nations to take collective action against the very states they themselves are threatening. The pressure brought to bear by African and Asian members both on the Security Council and the General Assembly to take coercive punitive measures of one kind or another against

Portugal and South Africa has been mounting in recent years, and indications that we are yielding to the pressure have been multiplying. One wonders whether the time has not come for the United States to reassert the primacy of peace in the hierarchy of United Nations purposes, recognized in the Charter, thanks primarily to its own efforts. True, our national traditions are not apt to arouse in us sympathies for historic rights, but prudence and forbearance in applying abstract principles *are* part of our national heritage.

One can think still of another type of international conflict with which the United Nations might have to deal in the future: conflicts between the emancipated heirs to the former empires. The tensions between Indonesia and the Federation of Malaya and border disputes between African states are cases in point. The fluidity of the political constellations in the Council and the Assembly can in such cases be expected to be greater than in those relating to the two cold wars. It is also possible that the rift within the formerly monolithic world Communist movement will have similar effects on the dynamics of United Nations politics. The structure, the political capacity, and the functions of the United Nations are likely to be subject to rapid changes in the future as much as they have been in the past.

IV

The failure of the United Nations to develop an effective system of collective peace-enforcement, on the pattern either of Chapter VII of the Charter or of the Uniting for Peace resolution, was bound to affect the members' conceptions of their rights and obligations under the Charter.[4] They probably were still more powerfully influenced by the prospect of nuclear aggression, which was not yet anticipated at the time the Charter was drafted. Both factors combined to revive the notions of self-help that were dominant in international society prior to its institutionalization and lingering on still in the Covenant of the League of Nations, but exorcised from the United Nations Charter. Thrown back on their own resources and facing the possibility of a type of aggression which could spell their very annihilation, United Nations members in general and the nuclear powers among them in particular have increasingly tended to apply to their rights under the Charter, and especially "the inherent right of individual or collective self-defense" recognized in Article 51, an extensive interpretation and to interpret restrictively their obligations, particularly the obligation of Article 2, paragraph 4, to refrain from the threat or use of force. The experience of the League is repeating itself in the United Nations: Members of a political society are ready to recognize limitations on their right to judge for themselves and assert their own cause only as long and to the extent that the public authorities are willing and able to afford them protection.

It would be difficult to say whether the erosion of Article 51 or that of Article 2, paragraph 4, set in first, and which of the two processes is more advanced today. At any rate, the erosion has progressed pretty far in either case, although the United Nations has not yet reached, and perhaps never will reach, the stage the League of Nations entered in the second half of the thirties, when the members began to deny officially the validity of the most important provisions of the Covenant. United Nations members so far try rather to present their deviations from the Charter as consistent with its spirit, if not its letter. The reinterpretation to which the Charter has been subjected since 1945 is the more ominous as the United States, too, which can claim to be second to none in devotion to the ideals of the Charter, has substantially contributed to the modification of its original meaning.

The reinterpretation of Article 51 was begun by the Security Council itself. By accepting in 1947 the First Report of the Atomic Energy Commission, it recognized implicitly that the strict interpretation of the words, which seem to limit the permissible exercise of the right of self-defense to the case of an actual armed attack, was not justified in view of the conditions of nuclear warfare. In other words, preventive action against an imminent nuclear attack, the Security Council implied, was to be considered as lawful. Soon there also developed among United Nations members a trend to claim that the term "armed attack" must be understood to cover indirect aggression as well, in the form, for instance, of foreign support for domestic subversion. Thus, in spite of Article 51, self-defense again tends, as was the case in former times, to be held legitimate in practically any case in which a nation feels seriously wronged by the policy of another nation. United Nations members, moreover, did not hesitate to tell the Security Council that it had no right to control their exercise of self-defense unless the Council could assure them of effective protection by its own means of their vital interests.

The reinterpretation of Article 2, paragraph 4, also began at an early date. It was encouraged by the wording of the provision which seems to imply a qualification of the no-force rule that actually, however, was not intended by the fathers of the Charter. Mention was already made of the doctrine of the justness of wars of national liberation. Before it was adopted by anticolonialist members and applied by India in the Goa case, the doctrine was advocated by the Soviet Union and put to use by the Soviet bloc in the Korean War. Ineffectiveness of the United Nations as a reason warranting disregard of the prohibition of force played a great role particularly in the Suez crisis. "If the United Nations proves ineffective," the Australian Premier declared, "we must, in the absence of willing and proper negotiations, be ready to impose sanctions ourselves. The doctrine that force can never be employed except pursuant to a decision of the Security Council is a suicidal doctrine."[5] The most dramatic case involving the interpretation of the Charter's rules on the use of force and the right of self-defense was, of course, the Cuban crisis of October 1962. The legality of the United States quarantine against Cuba is still a matter of heated controversy among American international lawyers. It is indeed most difficult to prove the legality of the American action in terms of the Charter as it was originally understood and as the United States itself repeatedly interpreted it. But this makes the Cuban case yet more significant as an indication of current interpretations of the law of the United Nations. The case suggests most impressively indeed the persistency of the notion, supposedly discarded a long time ago, that resort to force for the purpose of maintaining the balance of power is legitimate. United States policies in Viet Nam and in the Dominican crisis are more recent manifestations of the process of erosion suggested above.

V

Tested by the most ambitious intentions of its founders, the United Nations undeniably is in default. It has failed to create an effective system of peace enforcement and, therefore, has also failed to secure unqualified acceptance of legal principles meant to eliminate from international society recourse to self-help and thus approximate the relations among its members to those among members of a national community. But the League of Nations and the United Nations have both also been assigned tasks that were performed in international society before. Moreover, not all legal principles of the Covenant and the Charter are novel principles, untried prior to the establishment of these organizations. The rules of Chapter VI of the Charter governing the pacific settlement of disputes by the Security Council and the General Assembly are in fact of a rather conservative nature. What, then, is the record of the United Nations as an agency of mediation and conciliation?

There seems to be almost general agreement that on the whole the performance of the world body in this field has been far from poor. Needless to say, the record at the same time has been rather uneven, the success of the United Nations in resolving disputes and terminating armed conflicts necessarily depending upon the character of the issues involved in each case. There are intractable issues that even the most skillful mediator cannot settle. Moreover, he can only advise the parties but not compel them to comply with his advice. Mediation and conciliation are procedures based on the principle of consent.

The most intractable issues that the United Nations have faced have been those relating to the Cold War between East and West. The Organization certainly was not able to resolve them, but its mediatory efforts have nonetheless been useful, at least in some cases. The United Nations admittedly played in the Cuban crisis of October 1962 only a minor role, but there can be no doubt that its very existence and the services it actually offered facilitated the resolution of the conflict. It was in areas outside the orbit of the Cold War, however, where what the late Secretary-General Dag Hammarskjold called "preventive United Nations diplomacy" scored its greatest successes. True, even in such cases as Suez and Gaza, Lebanon and Jordan, Laos and the Congo, the effectiveness of the United Nations depended ultimately upon the attitude of the two superpowers. If they were not ready to support the policy of the United Nations, they had at least to acquiesce in it.

The successes of the United Nations in these cases were also due to the political and constitutional development of the Organization itself. The emergence of a tripartite, instead of the bipolaristic structure that prevailed in the first decade of United Nations history, prepared the ground for the rise in the Organization of the Secretary-General to the position of a leading diplomatic figure and powerful executive. Mr. Hammarskjold could claim ever more forcefully, even vis-a-vis the great powers, that, owing his office to election by both the Security Council and the General Assembly, he was set apart by the Charter itself as "an independent opinion factor" able to speak and act on behalf of the entire Organization as long as he had the confidence of the member states. Making full use of the moral and legal authority he had acquired, the Secretary-General organized in the Suez and Congo cases what in the diplomatic language of the nineteenth century can be called armed mediation. While the United Nations is generally given credit for its armed mediation in the Middle East, its action in the Congo, especially in its later stages, aroused much criticism.

The usual kind of criticism any mediator, individual or collective, must expect to be subjected to is that he has yielded to the power realities and disregarded the rights and wrongs in the conflict he has tried to resolve. This criticism was leveled, for example, at the settlement by the United Nations of the conflict between the Netherlands and Indonesia over West New Guinea. The criticism of United Nations policy in the Congo went much farther. It consists in fact of three indictments: first, that the United Nations enforced a settlement of the internal conflict in the Congo, though the mediator is only entitled to advise and recommend; second, that the settle-ment was unjust because it violated the right of Katanga to self-determination, a right which is affirmed in the Charter; third, that the enforcement of the settlement, regardless of its content, violated another basic principle, recognized in Article 2, paragraph 7 of the Charter, accord-ing to which the United Nations has no authority "to intervene in matters which are essentially within the domestic jurisdiction of any state."

It is, indeed, true that the United Nations overstepped the limits set to the mediator. Its action in the Congo began as armed mediation, but ended as armed intervention. The experience of former times repeated itself in the Congo: The line of distinction between armed mediation and armed intervention is very thin and likely to be disregarded when mediation of a conflict runs into insuperable difficulties. This must be expected to happen particularly in the case of a collective mediator such as the United Nations. But one may seriously doubt whether the charge of a violation of the principle of self-determination is equally well founded, or, rather, whether the principle was applicable to the Katanga case at all. The principle of self-determination makes no sense where, as in Katanga, there is no homogeneous collectivity recognizable as the subject of the right. Moreover, is the policy of most African states to recognize the boundary lines established during the colonial era not more likely to conduce to the stabilization and consolidation of the continent than the application of the abstract principle of self-determination? "The circumstances," Edmund Burke has wisely remarked, "are what render every civil and political scheme beneficial or noxious to mankind."

There is, on the other hand, again some truth in the third indictment of United Nations policy in the Congo. In terms of Article 2, paragraph 7, of the Charter, as originally conceived, the exception to the nonintervention principle hardly applied in the Congo case for the very reason that the action of the United Nations was meant to be mediation under Chapter VI, but not enforcement under Chapter VII, of the Charter. In fact, the United Nations action in the Congo is difficult to fit in with the original scheme of the Charter in general.

When the newly founded Republic of the Congo turned to the United Nations with the request for military assistance, it claimed that it was the victim of external aggression. In actual fact, the dispatch of Belgian armed forces when public peace and order broke down in the infant republic was intended to serve no other purpose than the urgently required protection of life and property of Belgian citizens. It was none other than Mr. Hammarskjold who frankly recognized that it might be doubtful whether "the United Nations faced a conflict between two parties." The Secretary-General held that the question was not legally essential for the justification of the United Nations action. He saw its legal basis in the explicit request of the Congolese Government for military assistance and in the implied finding of the Security Council that the consequences of the breakdown of internal law and order in the Republic constituted a threat to international peace and security. The restoration of domestic law and order was thus from the beginning one of the objectives, if not the primary objective, of the United

Nations action.

In trying to define the legal and political nature of the Congo case, one is reminded of the suggestion General Smuts made in 1918 that the future League of Nations should assume the guidance and control of the new states that were then arising from the breakup of the Austrian, Russian, and Turkish empires. The same idea that the ordering hand of an international organization should, if need be, assist formerly dependent peoples in the early days of statehood inspired Secretary-General Hammarskjold when he proposed the United Nations action in the Congo.

The record of the United Nations as an essentially diplomatic body, charged with the traditional functions of mediation and conciliation, thus shows a picture that is the very opposite of its record as a collective security system proper. It is at least prior to the financial crisis that incapacitated the Organization, a picture of expansion and not of retraction. From the mere conference type of international organization the United Nations has developed into a body capable of "executive action, undertaken on behalf of all members, and aiming at forestalling conflicts and resolving them, once they have arisen, by appropriate diplomatic or political means," to describe this transformation in the words of Mr. Hammarskjold's last annual report to the General Assembly. Admittedly, the concomitant of this development has been an increasingly loose interpretation of the pertinent powers of the Organization. The limitation on the authority of the United Nations in Article 2, paragraph 7 of the Charter has been exposed to the same process of erosion as the limitations on the rights of United Nations members in Article 2, paragraph 4 and article 51. No sooner had the Organization started to operate than a restrictive interpretation of the nonintervention principle came into use. This tendency was the stronger as the Charter principles of self-determination and human rights actually invite United Nations intervention in domestic affairs. But the chief reason for this development was political. The boundary line between domestic and international matters is always difficult to draw with precision and is bound to be even more so in a revolutionary age when the front lines of ideological warfare are cutting across all geographical and political boundaries and acts of indirect aggression are a daily occurrence in international politics.

If we complain today about the tendency of the United Nations to arrogate and exercise powers that under the Charter it does not possess, we should also remember the record of the founding Conference at San Francisco. It shows that the United States was foremost among those conferees who rejected the legal guarantees for which smaller nations were pleading as a protection against the virtually unlimited powers of the Security Council under Chapter VII of the Charter. Such restrictions on the Council's authority, the United States felt, would lessen its effectiveness as an instrument of peace.

VI

That we are today increasingly concerned about loose interpretations of the Charter is, of course, an expression of our growing uneasiness about our diminishing strength in the councils of the United Nations. But do we actually need to be alarmed about our position in the Organization?

Undoubtedly, the ease with which the United States influenced and controlled United Nations policies during the first decade of its history is a matter of the irretrievable past, as much as is the commanding position the United States held outside the United Nations during those years. But, speaking in general terms, one is entitled to say that ours is still the most influential voice of any single nation in the halls of the world organization. With equal assurance one may assert that the Soviet Union has no chance to attain in the United Nations a hegemonic position similar to that of the United States in the first postwar years. The Soviet Union has not gained as much as the United States has lost through the recent evolution of the United Nations. The chief beneficiaries of the ascendancy of the General Assembly and of the open-door policy in matters of admission have been the small and smallest nations of Asia and Africa. "The fact is," as Ambassador Adlai E. Stevenson remarked in 1963, "that in 17 years the Soviet Union has never once—never once—succeeded in building a majority for any proposition of substance against the opposition of the United States."[6] The statement is as valid today as it was in 1963. Nor must we judge the voting chances in the General Assembly exclusively by the numerical strength of the several blocs. In actual fact, the voting pattern is surprisingly flexible today, owing to the curious way in which the two cold wars are intertwined and to the resulting complexity of loyalties and interests that bear on the policies of United Nations members. Both the Western and the Afro-Asian blocs are likely to fall apart when they vote on questions that, from their point of view, are related to the other cold war, and there are often even defections from the Western bloc on issues of the West-East conflict and from the Afro-Asian bloc on questions of colonialism. Only the coherence of the Soviet bloc has so far been absolute.

To judge from the voting record, there is thus no reason for being alarmed about our position in the United Nations. The voting record, however, does not tell the whole story about our actual weight in the Organization. The record does not cover the cases in which we refrained, as we did in the Goa case, from submitting a question to the General Assembly, or, for that matter, to the Security Council. Nor does it reveal the scruples we might in many cases have felt in going along with the majority for reasons of expediency. If we want to find out whether and to what extent United States and United Nations interests are still running parallel, we, rather, must ask and answer the questions: What can we reasonably expect to be able to prevent it from doing, in matters that are of vital concern to us?

If we ever had illusions about the contribution the United Nations could make to our military security, they were soon dissipated by the stark facts of postwar international politics. Since the end of the forties we have been relying exclusively on our system of alliances and on our armaments as means for protecting our national interest. This policy has so far not been seriously impaired by the United Nations. Is there any danger that it will in the future? Two possibilities, in particular, immediately come to mind; mounting pressure of the United Nations in questions of disarmament, exerted in a direction which seems to us to run counter to the requirements of our national safety, and opposition in the United Nations to actions we might feel compelled to take in the Western hemisphere. If need be, the one would have to be resisted as the other disregarded. The more difficult case for us to handle would be the second, as we know from recent experience in the Cuban and Dominican cases. Assuming armed intervention in some part of the Western hemisphere once more would become necessary in our view, the hostile reactions to it in the United Nations might very well be formidable. But this prospect would hardly be decisive in deterring us from taking the action. The decisive consideration in weighing the pros and cons of the measure undoubtedly would be the likely reaction to it of the Soviet Union; our second consideration would be its effect on our Latin American allies; and the attitude of the United Nations would be our third concern only. In other words, the United Nations would not and could not prevent us from doing what we, rightly or wrongly, hold to be absolutely essential for the protection of our vital interests; it would operate only as a restraining influence on our decision. But, then, is not the exercise of restraining influence on the actions of its members the most significant task of the United Nations?

What about the policies we would like the United Nations to pursue? The preceding discussion on the United Nations as a novel system of collective security and as a diplomatic body, applying and developing traditional methods of mediation and conciliation, has shown the range and the limits within which the United Nations can reasonably be expected to be useful, within which, in fact, it is indispensable. To improvise in each and every case of international crisis the methods and procedures of mediation and conciliation might have satisfied the simpler needs of international society in former times. But the deficiencies of this system, or, rather, lack of system, were felt strongly already in the nineteenth century and led to the formation of the European Concert of Powers, the first modern model of international government. But the Concert still was an occasional rather than a permanent institution. In the complex conditions of world society in the twentieth century, the need for permanent global international institutions of mediation and conciliation has become imperative. It is inconceivable that the United States could, nor is there any reason why it should, discontinue its cooperation in such institutions within the United Nations and withdraw its support from the Organization.

But in view of possible divergencies today between United States and United Nations interests, the United States would do well to reconsider the constitutional policy it has been pursuing during the last fifteen years. Admittedly, we cannot return to the conceptions we advocated at Dumbarton Oaks and San Francisco. Equalitarian tendencies within the international community are today too strong to make the reversion of the constitutional development which has transformed the United Nations feasible, even if we felt it to be desirable. But one wonders whether it would be wise on our part to try to extend the powers of the General Assembly still further. Our attempt, stubbornly pursued during recent years, to secure the recognition of the Assembly's budgetary authority in peace-keeping operations is a case in point. Considering the strength of the political forces opposed to its objective, the attempt was bound to be futile. But it also was ill-advised from the point of view of United States interests. It cannot be ruled out, after all, that the General Assembly one day might engage in peace-keeping operations of which we could not approve, to which, in fact, we might be opposed. The risk of United States membership in the world body cannot any longer be taken lightly.

FOOTNOTES

[1]See the collection of essays on the United Nations in Raymond A. Moore, Jr., ed. *The United Nations Reconsidered* (New York: Columbia Univ. Press, 1963)

[2]U. S. Department of State, General Foreign Policy Series 15, *Postwar Foreign Policy Preparation* 1939–1945 (Washington: U. S. Government Printing Office, 1949), p. 113. For the following see also Erich Hula, "The Evolution of Collective Security under the United Nations Charter," *Alliance Policy in the Cold War*, ed. Arnold Wolfers (Baltimore, 1959), pp. 88ff.

[3]See *United Nations Review*, X (July, 1963), pp. 54ff.

[4]See Hula, *op. cit.* pp. 99ff.

[5]Quoted by B. V. A. Roeling, "The Question of Defining Aggression," *Symbolae Verzijl*, ed. (La Haye, 1958) p. 325.

[6]The statement was made before the Subcommittee on International Organization Affairs of the Senate Committee on Foreign Relations on March 13, 1963. See *The Department of State Bulletin*, XLVIII, No. 1241 (April 8, 1963), p. 527.

FIFTY YEARS OF INTERNATIONAL GOVERNMENT
REFLECTIONS ON THE LEAGUE OF NATIONS AND THE UNITED NATIONS*

Hans J. Morgenthau came into prominence as a student of international relations at a time when the illusions of Wilsonian internationalism, only slumbering since the Covenant of the League of Nations was defeated in the United States Senate, were once more awakened in this country by the outbreak of World War II. The new wave of hope rose particularly high in the academic community. Morgenthau was one of the few scholars who was not swept along by it. His realistic approach to the problems of international politics in general, so characteristic of *Politics Among Nations,* his *magnum opus* published in 1949, also determined his assessment of the potentialities of a global, political, international organization as a peace-preserving instrument. Morgenthau's sober realism, unfortunately, has stood the test of time only too well.

The idealistic peace strategists of the forties were convinced, and anxious to convince others, that the establishment of the United Nations would inauguarate a new era of human history. They could not altogether avoid references to the defunct League of Nations, but they insisted on the superiority, for constitutional and political reasons, of the new over the old organization. There were indeed differences, legal as well as political, between the two bodies, including differences seemingly speaking in favor of the future world body. Its sponsors failed to see, however, or did not want to see, that the United Nations, like the League of Nations preceding

*Reprinted with permission of The New Republic Book Company from Kenneth Thompson and Robert J. Myers (eds.), *Truth and Tragedy. A Tribute to Hans J. Morgenthau,* 1977.

it, was after all only another variant of the same type of government—if government it can be called—the confederate system. The inherent weaknesses of this form had already been demonstrated, once and for all, in the Federalist Papers.

The disappointing record of the United Nations hardly justifies any claim of superiority over the peace organization of Geneva, notwithstanding the fact that it has already surpassed the lifespan of the League. While the latter ceased to play an active, politically significant role after merely eighteen years of existence, the United Nations has now been operating for more than three decades. In the light of the experience of these thirty years, we begin to wonder whether the performance of the organization on Lake Geneva was not perhaps in some respects more commendable than that of its successor on New York's East River.

To weigh with some accuracy and fairness the respective merits and demerits of the two bodies would be difficult, if not impossible, for it would also require balancing the political forces and differences with which they were contending. Nor is so ambitious an attempt intended in the following pages. But it might be possible and worthwhile to point out and ponder on some basic similarities and dissimilarities in the records of the two world bodies. A clearer awareness of the continuity of issues and problems in the history of general political international organization should help us to see that there is more coherence and unity in it than we might be inclined to assume, and thus gain a better insight into the actual and potential role of international organization in contemporary world politics.

When claiming for the United Nations constitution superiority over that of the League, its proponents primarily meant that the Charter provided for a legally stricter and technically more advanced system of collective security. Not that they did not see that the first requirement for preserving peace was a machinery for the pacific settlement of international disputes that, if properly functioning, would save the organization from having to resort to enforcement measures. But they did indeed feel very strongly that the establishment of a truly effective system for the enforcement of peace was the best means for ensuring the successful operation of mediatory and conciliatory procedures.

Leaving aside for the moment the much more important question of whether the political assumptions on which the collective security system of the Charter was based were more realistic than those underlying that of the Covenant, the claim of superiority was not entirely unjustified.

The two fundamental principles of collective security—the restriction of

250

the lawful resort to war by sovereign states to the case of self-defense and the legal obligation of the international community to render assistance, possibly military assistance, to the victims of aggression—were utterly alien to the traditional notions of international law and politics. It is therefore hardly surprising that the first step in so radical a departure from time-honored maxims and practices was taken with some hesitation. The Covenant imposed upon the members of the League the duty to try to settle disputes likely to lead to a rupture by peaceful means, political or judicial, but it did not yet abolish unconditionally the *jus ad bellum* of the sovereign state, practically uncontested before World War I. That the League was conceived as an institution promoting cooperation among its members, rather than arrogating to itself supranational coercive powers, found expression also in the famous Article 16 of the Covenant relating to the diplomatic, economic, and military sanctions to be taken in the case of a member's unlawful resort to arms. The article left to the discretion of the several members the decision on the *casus foederis* and on the coercive measures to be applied.

The conviction that the collective-security provisions of the Covenant required some strengthening was already held by League members themselves. The Assembly and Council of the League—prompted by the members' conviction that the collective-security provisions of the Covenant required strengthening—soon became engaged in frantic, although ultimately futile, efforts to tighten the rules prohibiting the resort to war and to centralize the procedure on sanctions in the hands of the League organs. This was to be attained by separate international agreements supplementary to the Covenant, such as the Geneva Protocol of 1924, or by an outright revision of the Covenant itself, or by a combination of both methods. The efforts were inspired by various convergent motives.

France and nations close to her wished to strengthen the security provisions of the Covenant because they saw in the League an instrument capable of being used in a grand alliance against defeated Germany. The tendency to employ the abstract system of collective security, contrived as a protection for all against any aggressor state, for the purpose of building and cementing an alliance against a specific state or group of states, will always be very strong and reveals itself in the history of both the League and the United Nations. Other nations, particularly minor ones, felt they could only benefit from an effective protective system against aggression in which the greater powers were supposed to carry the main burden. In the parlance of Geneva, they were the consumers of collective security, in contrast to the great powers, its producers. Last but not least, collective security was in the twenties a most powerful idea, with a worldwide appeal difficult to realize some fifty years later.

Looking back at those efforts inside and outside the League, made at a time when the prestige of the organization was at its height, one is struck by the close interplay of political forces in the old and the new world. The Geneva Protocol and similar international agreements considered by the League were as much an incentive to the negotiation and conclusion of the Kellogg Pact outlawing war as the latter was to the reformers of Geneva. No less striking is the extent to which the principles and techniques of collective security, as formulated and devised in the Charter of the United Nations, were formulated and devised in the proposals that had been worked out by the organs of the League. Certain conceptions of the reformers of Geneva were even more radical in part than those of the founders of the United Nations.

As a matter of fact, the system of collective security incorporated in the Charter was in one highly important respect less ambitious than that of the Covenant itself. The sanctions of Article 16 were, on principle, applicable against any member of the League, including the great powers holding a permanent seat in the Council. In the Italo-Ethiopian conflict of 1935, the only case in which the procedure of sanctions was actually set in motion, it was directed against one of the then great powers, Italy. The subjection of all members of the League to coercive measures fit in with the egalitarian structure of the organization of Geneva. The enforcement system of the United Nations was, on the contrary, originally intended to be restricted to conflicts among smaller nations. One of the reasons the new organization was given an oligarchic structure by its founders was to rule out its universal applicability. The collective-security system of the United Nations, allegedly a great improvement upon that of the League, was, in fact, intended to operate within a constitutional framework similar to the European Concert of the Powers of the nineteenth century rather than to that of the organization of Geneva.

This construction seems somewhat surprising, considering the preponderate influence of the United States upon the formation of the new organization from the days of the preparatory work in the State Department through the deliberations at Dumbarton Oaks and San Francisco. American democratic traditions in general, and America's traditional espousal of the rights of small nations in particular, hardly predestined the United States to advocate an authoritarian and oligarchic type of international organization, confining smaller nations to a minor role. The explanation of this American policy is not difficult to find, however. The scheme of the future world body had to satisfy both American internationalists, who were pleading for an organization approximating world government, and American isolationists, who were still opposed to an international organization, even one no stronger than the defunct League of Nations. The only solution to the dilemma was a scheme of supranational government in the operation of which the United States and the other great powers of the day would be assured a leading role without being subject themselves to its coercive powers. The means for attaining this end were to be the centralization of all pertinent powers, including the decision on whether a breach of the peace had been committed and what coercive measures should be taken, in the hands of a Security Council alone, and the exemption of the five great powers, who held permanent seats on the Council, from the operation of the majority principle by requiring their concurrence in an affirmative vote. With such a privileged position guaranteed to the United States, the isolationists, so the planners in the State Department calculated, would not block the road toward a security system superior to that of the League both in terms of the rules limiting the *jus ad bellum* and in terms of the enforcement machinery to be set in motion against a future aggressor. The Charter, incorporating as it did this ingenious legal construction, had indeed smooth sailing in the Senate. Senator Arthur H. Vandenberg, when advocating American membership in what apparently promised to be a powerful peace organization, could at the same time assure his colleagues that the flag would stay on the dome of the Capitol.

American insistence on this constitutional scheme seems to be open to the charge of cynicism. Realism in politics is often mistaken for cynicism even if it is as sound as it undoubtedly was in this case. In the first place, the privileged members of the system, the great powers, were also to carry its main burden, especially if and when military enforcement measures were required. They were to be the chief producers of collective security. Second, and more important, ruling out the application of the enforcement system against one of the great powers, and particularly one of the two then emerging superpowers, meant not to charge the United Nations with a task that would most certainly go beyond its physical capacity. Indeed, such enforcement action would, practically, mean the very kind of global war that the United Nations was founded to avert. The failure of the League to impose sanctions in the Sino-Japanese conflict or truly effective economic sanctions in the Italo-Ethiopian case had already clearly indicated the limits within which a system of collective security might possibly work.

Commendable as the constitutional realism of the fathers of the Charter was, they proved less farsighted in regard to the political assumptions on which they were trying to build permanent peace. To put it more generously, their ability to divine the future was no greater than it usually is in human, and particularly political, affairs.

It was only natural that Americans, when weighing the political reasons for the League's failure, were more inclined than others to attibute it to the fact that in the end the United States had refused to join the organization that owed its very existence largely to Wilson's statesmanship and that was based upon conceptions of international politics more deeply rooted and more widely held in this than in other countries. It is easier to understand the optimistic political expectations of 1945, insofar as they were based upon American participation and leadership in the future United Nations, than it is to understand the optimistic assumption of the five members of the world concert of powers, which were to form the nucleus of the organization, that they would be willing and able to cooperate closely with one another. The deep ideological rift within the Concert made it very unlikely that the military Grand Alliance of World War II could be continued and sustained as a political instrument into the period of peace.

The explanations of the badly misplaced optimism clearly lie in the tenets of the liberal creed ingrained in the American political mind, such as the belief in the fundamental harmony of divergent interests and opinions, the potency and justness of public opinion, and the effectiveness of rational procedures in resolving conflicts in the international, no less than in the national, community. Americans believed in the general efficacy of the ideas, institutions, and procedures of liberal democracy and in their suitability for ordering international affairs, since their domestic political creed, after the termination of the Civil War, had not had to stand the test of political forces that were hostile to the democratic faith or state.

The Soviet Union, on the other hand, can be safely assumed to have not held such liberal tenets. Least of all did it expect that their application in international affairs would render the game of power politics obsolete. That the Soviet Union joined the United Nations, and even more that it remained in it throughout the long period of American predominance while it was itself relegated to the unenviable position of a seemingly permanent minority power with little actual influence on United Nations policies, was a result of other motives. Bolshevism, from the beginning of its revolution-ary career, has been inclined to adopt a pragmatic attitude in institutional and tactical questions. After 1905, Lenin, asserting that the parliamentary forum offered even to the smallest group, provided it was resolute enough, the possibility of successful revolutionary agitation and propaganda, pleaded for socialist participation in the imperial Duma. Similar con-siderations can be presumed to have prompted Stalin in 1945 to agree to and maintain Russian membership in the various newly-established inter-national organizations. Being fully conscious of the dynamic force in anticolonialism, the Soviet Union from the beginning realized the chance United Nations membership offered it, as the champion of colonial libera-tion, to enhance its own prestige and influence. It was no accident that it was the Soviet Union that in 1945 insisted on an endorsement in Article 1 of the Charter of the principle of national self-determination.

Considering the heterogeneous composition of the built-in concert of the great powers, it is hardly surprising that it tended to fall apart from the moment the United Nations began to operate. Ironically, the common front, which the members of the pentarchy maintained at San Francisco against the minor powers in order to secure their acceptance of the authoritarian-oligarchic features of the Charter, was practically the last manifestation of the concert idea. Whenever on later occasions the five great powers found themselves on the same side of the parliamentary battle lines in the United Nations organs, it was the accidental result of a temporary concurrence of interests rather than the expression of a deliberate coordination of policies.

The incipient cold war and, resulting from it, the emergence of its chief protagonists, the United States and the Soviet Union, as potential adversaries in a hot war, had a profound effect on the security as well as the constitutional system of the United Nations as devised at Dumbarton Oaks and enacted at San Francisco. The Security Council, which was intended to act as a kind of supranational government, soon became the main battlefield of the cold war and therefore proved unable to fulfill the task the Charter had assigned to it—to accomplish the military implementation of the security system envisaged therein. The military machinery that was to supply the organization with teeth, to speak in the language of the forties, and that was the most highly praised advance over the Covenant of the League, was never actually created. The military enforcement measures employed in 1950 in Korea were improvised on the spur of the moment and could be set in motion with some semblance of legality only because the Soviet Union was, at the critical moment, engaged in a boycott of the Council and thus deprived of the chance to control its policy, a blunder it was not likely to repeat. Moreover, the military action of the United Nations was collective in appearance rather than in reality, insofar as the United States' military assistance to South Korea, the victim of aggression, was supported only by token forces of other members. The great majority of United Nations members, with the exception of the members of the Soviet bloc, by and large contented themselves with backing the American government morally and politically.

The unfolding of the cold war had prompted the United States, before 1950, to seek other means for protecting its national interests. President Wilson conceived of the League of Nations as the negation of the traditional European balance of power game, with military alliances as its instrumentalities; in his opinion, this was one of the main reasons for the recurrent wars in the old world. Nor did his heirs who built the United Nations hold these devices in high esteem. The more remarkable, therefore, was the speed with which they became converts to the notions and devices of old-world diplomacy when the concert scheme of 1945 failed to material-ize. The initiation and conclusion in 1949 of the Atlantic Pact was the first, but by no means the last, step in building up a worldwide system of alliances under American leadership.

This did not mean, however, that American fervor for the idea of collective security was spent. Thanks to the hegemonic world position that had fallen to the United States as a consequence of victory in World War II, it could count on sweeping majorities in all organs of the United Nations in support of its policies. Isolationist anxieties about possible encroachments by the organization on American sovereignty, disproved by the realities of United Nations politics in the initial years, began to yield to a belief in a preordained harmony of United States and United Nations interests. Ac-cordingly, there no longer seemed to be a need to withhold from the General Assembly the power to decide on whether and what kind of enforcement measures, military or otherwise, should be taken in case of an alleged breach of the peace. In the fall of 1950, the United States prevailed upon the General Assembly to adopt the Uniting for Peace resolution that was intended to break the monopoly of the Security Council in security matters, established by the Charter, by conferring on the Assembly conditional enforcement power.

The irony of the reform of 1950 that, to put it mildly, effected a *de facto* revision of the Charter, was that the security system inaugurated by the Uniting for Peace resolution was essentially a replica of the Geneva system. It was technically as defective as the League system had been, insofar as the purely recommendatory powers of the Assembly, unlike the mandatory powers of the Council, practically amounted to a decentralization of the enforcement system. And it was politically as ambitious as the Geneva system, insofar as it was meant to be universally applicable, against great powers no less than minor powers. The authoritarian-oligarchic pattern of the European Concert of Powers of the nineteenth century was replaced by a democratic pattern more akin to American political traditions.

The reform scheme of 1950 owed its origin to a confluence of ideals and pragmatic considerations. The United States government never had felt quite at ease when defending the design of Dumbarton Oaks and San Francisco against domestic and foreign critics. When it became clear that the limitation on the majority principle in the Security Council actually tended to frustrate American policies and to work to the advantage of the Soviet Union as a minority power, and the untrammeled operation of majority rule in the Assembly did not seem any longer to threaten American interests, the United States welcomed the chance to bring its constitutional policies in the United Nations into line with the principles and procedures of domestic democratic government. It no longer had any inhibitions in ascribing to the General Assembly, as "town meeting" or "world parliament," a democratic legitimacy and moral dignity that the Assembly never actually possessed. Pragmatic considerations relating to the exigencies of the cold war between West and East played no less a role in Washington's decision to promote a new security system that made enforcement measures as legally applicable against great powers as against small powers and hence against the Soviet Union. Sponsorship of the Uniting for Peace resolution by the United States was no doubt ultimately intended to span and tighten its particular alliances by an all-embracing, American-led alliance against the threat of Soviet aggression in the legal form of an abstract system of collective security.

It soon turned out, however, that the political foundation on which the security system of 1950 was based was no more solid than that of the system of 1945. The political constellation inside and outside the United Nations in the initial period of the Korean conflict began to yield to new political alignments even before the armistice was concluded. The fifties did not bring about the end of the cold war between West and East, but its nature and form somehow changed in those years. The danger of an immediate armed clash between its protagonists decreased, and the lessening of international tension also lessened the rigidity of the international structure. The bipolar structure that characterized international society in the first postwar decade gave way to a more flexible structure, and a third, or neutralist, force emerged into full prominence. In this relatively fluid situation the two superpowers' "peaceful competition" for influence and power in the uncommitted areas was bound to gain ever more momentum.

Anxious to maintain and possibly improve the global balance of power to its own advantage, each of them began to woo the smaller nations, unborn as well as born. Currying their favor, from 1955 onward they promoted and supported rather than obstructed, as they had originally done, the admission of new members to the world body. With their steady influx and the organization's changing political complexion resulting therefrom, the antagonism between colonial and anticolonial members tended to overshadow the cold war between West and East without, however, superseding it altogether. Rather, the two cold wars became ever more intertwined with one another. Interest considerations pertaining to the one influenced members' tactics in the other, which made for a fluidity in the Assembly's alignments that sharply contrasted with the rigidity of the earlier years. The development could not fail to weaken American influence in the United Nations organs on the one side and strengthen the influence of the Soviet Union on the other.

A striking illustration of the effect of the change in the political complexion of the United Nations, and of the emergence of the colonial question in its various forms as its chief concern, is the use to which the Uniting for Peace resolution has been put. When the United States government initiated the measure in 1950, it hardly tried to conceal that communist aggression was its object. But the authorization of the General Assembly to intervene in case of a breach of the peace has turned out to be a double-edged weapon. The procedure provided for in the resolution has been set in motion against democratic nations as well as against communist states.

A more significant result of the developments in the fifties and in subsequent years was the tacit abandonment by the United Nations of military enforcement measures as a means for giving effect to the idea of collective security. The failure of strong and persistent efforts by the United States government to secure the Assembly's approval of its proposal to implement the military provisions of the Uniting for Peace resolution in a way similar to the military measures envisaged in Chapter VII of the Charter was a clear indication that the members of the organization simply were not ready to assume in advance the obligations implicit in a promise of military assistance to the victim of aggression. Indeed, the failure of the measures taken by the Security Council against Southern Rhodesia in 1966 indicated that the members were hardly less reluctant to participate, even in merely economic and financial sanctions, unless their own national interests prompted them to do so. It must be admitted, though, that the reluctance in this case might also be attributable to the feeling of member states that they were going to be entangled in another attempt, this time for the purpose of liquidating colonialism, to turn the abstract system of collective security into a concrete political alliance.

The refusal of the United Nations members to provide the military means required for the operation of the system of collective security is not the only symptom that the validity of its basic principles is no longer recognized. Another more ominous symptom is that they have reclaimed, the spirit and the letter of the Charter notwithstanding, their right to go to war whenever they deem it necessary.

The cold war between West and East soon led to a revival of the notions of self-help as they prevailed in international society before its institutionalization in the twentieth century. Nor was it surprising that United Nations members in general, and the nuclear powers among them in particular, when thrown back on their own resources and facing the possibility of a type of aggression that, owing to modern weaponry, could mean their annihilation, have increasingly tended to apply an extensive interpretation to the "inherent right" of self-defense recognized in the Charter. Nor is it too surprising that the Charter provisions prohibiting the use of force in international relations became the victim of the revolutionary forces unleashed in the anticolonial struggle. Led by the Soviet Union, anticolonial members of the world body did not hesitate to justify wars of so-called national liberation by restrictive interpretations of the Charter limitations of the *jus ad bellum*.

Given the fact that, from a realistic point of view, the system of collective security always was at best a chimerical project and at worst a remedy more pernicious than the disease, insofar as its actual application would tend to transform a particular war into a general war, and thus, by widening war, increase its evil effect, we shall do well to resign ourselves to the final abandonment of the scheme. As far back as the early thirties, when the fascination of the idea of collective security was still at its highest, an Italian author succinctly summarized the reasons for its futility: It obligates its members to make war against nature, that is, for reasons they do not hold to affect their national interests, and it forbids them to make war according to nature, that is, for their own national interests. The dictum, rightly or wrongly, was attributed to fascist inclinations of its author. Be that as it may, the history of the League of Nations and the United Nations has not disproved him.

Being based on conceptions of international law and politics alien to earlier times, the collective-security system built into the League of Nations and United Nations was undoubtedly one of their most striking features. Indeed, those who truly believed it was *the* means for ensuring permanent peace could not fail to see in it the very *raison d'être* of general political international organization. But there were always others who held that the main task of the organized international community was to develop and improve upon the mediatory and conciliatory methods for the pacific settlement of international conflicts, already devised and practiced within the framework of bilateral diplomacy prior to World War I. Admittedly, the performance of this task would be less spectacular than ambitious attempts to break new ground, but it promised in the long run to be more rewarding. As a matter of fact, in the histories of the League and the United Nations, periods of emphasis on their coercive powers alternated with periods of stress on their mediatory and conciliatory functions.

The expectation that the collective mediator or conciliator, operating as an organ of the world community, would necessarily benefit from the moral and political authority of the world body he was representing and, therefore, have a better chance than the mediator, operating within the framework of bilateral diplomacy, to achieve an agreement of the parties to the dispute on the terms of settlement was somewhat too optimistic to come true in all cases. Not only were the authority and the prestige of the organization itself continuously fluctuating, but it was also unlikely that the particular circumstances would fail to assert themselves in each and every conflict. But the permanent availability of political and judicial agencies, ready to intervene at any moment if and when called upon, nevertheless proved to be an advantage that can hardly be overrated.

The pacific settlement procedures provided by the Covenant and the Charter, as well as the powers granted to the organs of the League and the United Nations in resolving international conflicts, differ from one another in quite a few respects. But both organizations, naturally, were plagued by the same problems that have time and again emerged in the history of diplomatic mediation. By far the most difficult one, undoubtedly, was how to balance against one another considerations relating to peace and to law and justice. It was repeatedly and rightly said that, while the Covenant leaned toward the paramountcy of law and justice, the Charter, with its Hobbesian touch, most values peace. But one wonders whether both organizations in their actual practice did not yield to the political exigencies of the case at hand rather than act in strict accordance with abstract precepts.

In spite of these reservations, the fact remains that the records of the League and the United Nations as essentially diplomatic bodies performing the traditional functions of mediation and conciliation are, in terms of achievement, the very opposite of their records in the field of collective security. The United Nations even surpassed the League by creating, with the so-called "peace-keeping forces," an instrumentality that greatly strengthens its position and thus considerably enhances its usefulness.

True, this device of what Hammarsjkold called "preventive United Nations diplomacy" is not, and was never understood to be, applicable in each and every case of international conflict. Its suitability is limited to local conflicts among minor nations, provided the great powers, and especially the two superpowers, have a common interest in keeping the conflict localized. But these limitations notwithstanding, the successful application of the scheme in highly explosive situations impressively shows how much the United Nations, without asserting superior legal authority and coercive powers, can achieve by making skillful use of the subtle methods of multilateral diplomacy for securing the voluntary cooperation of its members.

The question of the extent to which a political international organization patterned upon the institutions of democratic national government should rely on the methods of classical diplomacy for attaining its purposes was, by and large, answered more conservatively in the League of Nations than in the United Nations, for legal as well as political reasons.

The League was conceived by its founders as an institution for coordinating the policies of its several sovereign member states rather than as a coercive body claiming authority over them. Moreover, substantive decisions of the League organs in general required unanimity for their adoption—in other words, a consensus that could be attained only by negotiation among members. More important yet, the political climate in the League, hardly disturbed by ideological rivalries, was conducive to the employment of diplomatic methods. Not that there was any lack of ideological conflicts in the world of the twenties and thirties, but they played a lesser role within the League than they do within the United Nations today. Mussolini's Italy displayed no ideological fervor inside the League and only became involved in a conflict with it because of a belated experiment in imperialist policy in no way typical only of fascist ideology. Hitler, as soon as he came to power, decided to take Germany out of the League. And when the Soviet Union finally joined the League in 1934, it wanted to be instrumental in transforming the abstract system of collective security into a concrete alliance against the threat of Nazi aggression and accordingly toned down, rather than emphasized, its ideological differences with the liberal-democratic members of the organization.

In the light of United Nations experience, the League was indeed a model of old-time diplomacy. Paul-Henri Spaak, the Belgian statesman who had represented his country in the League before representing it in the United Nations, has drawn a highly revealing picture of the rational procedures in the defunct League. "The public debates," he wrote in 1948, "in which the opposing theses were represented, were quite carefully prepared in the corridors, and . . . in reality every one there was playing a role which he had learned in advance. When anyone deviated from the role which had been written by the authors, he was immediately considered to be a very bad character."

The founders of the United Nations, contrary to those of its predecessor, liked to emphasize its supranational and coercive powers. Furthermore, the adoption of the majority principle, claimed to be one of the progressive features of the Charter, made it no longer necessary to strive for a consensus of the members nor to engage in negotiations for achieving it. But by far the most decisive factor accounting for the tendency in the United Nations to relegate diplomatic methods to a secondary place and to give free play to parliamentary procedures was and still is the involvement of the world organization in the two intertwining cold wars. Their participants soon discovered that the presumably more rational procedures of international parliamentarism lent themselves more easily than the principles and techniques of old-time diplomacy to the combative purposes the United Nations members were and are pursuing against one another. To embarrass and revile the adversary in public so-called debate and to score, thanks to the majority principle, parliamentary triumphs over him, does not solve any question. It merely heightens international tension instead of lessening it. But it might, and often does, have the effect of weakening the adversary's political position. No wonder, then, that from the beginning of the United Nations operation there has never been a shortage of "bad characters." Some have proved to be particularly skillful in using the question of human rights as a weapon in ideological warfare.

The United States was for a long time on the winning side of the parliamentary skirmishes and battles waged in the halls of the United Nations. Being certain of majority support in the Security Council, the United States did not care to prearrange discussion and voting with the Soviet Union. In fact, it would occasionally provoke a Soviet veto only in order to utilize another alleged or real abuse of the veto right for propaganda purposes. The proceedings in the General Assembly offered even better opportunities for outmaneuvering the Soviet adversary in the propaganda war. The preponderate influence of the United States in the councils of the United Nations began to decline only in the latter half of the fifties, owing to the growth of the third force, neutralist in its attitude to the cold war between West and East, but intent on employing parliamentary procedures, both in the Council and in the Assembly, for its own combative purposes.

The weakening of United States power in the United Nations, reflecting the weakening of its hegemonic position outside it, was for some time hardly perceptible, but it has become increasingly obvious in recent years. It is not likely, however, that American influence will sink to the level of that of the Soviet Union in the first decade of the organization's existence. American parliamentary strength in the General Assembly can be expected to remain a function of the concrete question with which the Assembly is dealing at the time, rather than of the mere numerical size of the three blocs and, accordingly, to vary from case to case. Communist China's entrance into the world body will, in the long run, probably weaken rather than strengthen the coherence of the Afro-Asian and perhaps even the Soviet bloc, and hence help to maintain, if not increase, the fluidity of the political alignments in the Assembly. A permanent merger of the Soviet and the anticolonial blocs is indeed not in sight. The record of recent proceedings in the Security Council leaves no doubt that the days of American supremacy are over in this body, too. However, although the United States is no longer able to count on majority support of its policies, in the Council its veto right still makes it possible for the United States to nullify majority decisions not agreeable to it, provided they are of a substantive and not merely procedural nature. It is indeed a bitter irony that the United States finds it ever more necessary to resort to this defensive negative device. It was, after all, the Security Council that, in the conception of its American architects, was to be the chief instrument of an advanced system of international government. It also is a clear symptom of the profound change in the political character of the world organization, reflecting the changing political realities outside it.

The concentration of military might in a few great powers, combined with the growing importance of smaller nations in world affairs, is perhaps one of the most paradoxical features of our time. Both the League of Nations and the United Nations have contributed greatly to the increasing prestige and influence of the small states. In fact, the rise of the latter antedates the establishment of international organization. It begins, not accidentally, with the decline of the European Concert of Powers toward the end of the nineteenth century. The Covenant of the League was an affirmation of the revindication of the principle of legal equality of states accomplished before World War I.

The Covenant granted to the five great powers of those days the privilege of permanent representation in the Council, but their voting rights were, under the unanimity rule, no different from those of the four minor Council members. Moreover, the powers of the Council and the Assembly, the general representative body, were, under the Covenant, concurrent powers. In the actual practice of the League the smaller member states were able to strengthen their constitutional and political positions still further. Under their pressure there was created not only a new category of semipermanent Council members but the number of nonpermanent Council members was increased as well. In addition, the influence of the Assembly often tended to eclipse that of the Council. Smaller states, accordingly, became increasingly inclined to consider membership in the League a status symbol.

The constitution of the United Nations, as originally conceived, caused a setback in the ascendancy of the minor states. True, they were intended to be the chief beneficiaries of the new world body but, owing to the built-in concert of the great powers, their share in the exercise of the organization's powers was not meant to be very substantial. However, the egalitarian trend was only arrested for a brief time. From a mixed form of international government with a preponderance of oligarchic elements, the United Nations, from 1950 onward, rapidly developed into a preponderately democratic body. ("Democratic" as regards the constitution of the United Nations itself, but not, of course, as regards the domestic constitutions of its several members. Domestic democracy is the exception rather than the rule with United Nations members.)

Considering the uneven balance in the United Nations that has resulted from the admission of many miniature states, if states they can be called, covering in some cases an area and comprising a population no larger than those of a small urban district in a middle-sized American state, one wonders indeed whether the process of democratization has not gone too far or, more precisely, whether it has been accomplished in accordance with sound democratic notions.

It is not only the numerical preponderance of smaller member states in the United Nations that poses political problems. It is indeed more portentous that the influx of new members, due to the dismantling of the Western-ruled empires, has greatly strengthened the dynamic forces in the world body. In a statement to the General Assembly in 1960, Secretary-General Hammarsjkold, emphasizing that it was not the big powers but "all the others" who need the United Nations for their protection, declared: "In this sense the organization is first of all their organization, and I deeply believe in the wisdom with which they will be able to use it and guide it." One would like to share Hammarsjkold's belief, if historical experience did not rather suggest that revolutionary forces, bent on political and social change, are impelled by passion rather than reason.

In this case, too, the United Nations does not create the political realities of the present-day world but serves rather as the mirror in which they are reflected. One can surely break the mirror if one does not like the image one sees in it, but one must all the same go on contending with the forces and problems it unpleasantly reveals. The picture the mirror shows today is indeed most unpleasant to the American beholder who, impelled by the combination of idealistic and egotistic motives that usually determines the behavior of men and nations, has probably indulged in more illusions about the effect of general political international organization than citizens of most other nations. If the United States should decide to break the mirror, it would only yield to yet another illusion, more dangerous perhaps than those it previously entertained. The confrontations with its adversaries in the councils of the United Nations, which it had tried to escape by abandoning the world body, would only become more violent if they were continued, as they unavoidably would be, outside a common institutional framework, tenuous and problematic as it undoubtedly is. Looking back upon the fifty years of so-called international government, one cannot fail to be impressed by the fact that, owing to the ever-growing interdependence of areas, issues, and problems in the present world, political international organization, in some form or other, has become an integral part and permanent feature of contemporary international society. The grand designs are dead, but the more modest functions of international organization, only partly mentioned in these pages, still need to be served.

III(C)

HUMAN RIGHTS

INTERNATIONAL LAW AND THE PROTECTION OF HUMAN RIGHTS*

The difference of subject matters regulated by national law on the one side and international law on the other, has been one of the principal arguments the proponents of the dualist doctrine have been employing in support of their position. National law, the dualists have been maintaining, is concerned with relations among individual persons and between the state and its subjects. The concern of international law are relations between states. The argument, no doubt, carried some weight as long as the actual contents of the typical rules of international law corresponded more or less closely to the theoretical assertion.

Even at the time when the weight of evidence seemed to be against him, Hans Kelsen refused to accept the dualist thesis. As his first treatise on the theory of international law proves, Kelsen realized from the very beginning the contingent character of the contents of nineteenth-century international law. Ever since then, he has been insisting that "there is no matter that cannot be regulated by a rule of customary or contractual international law." The potential transformation of any domestic matter into an international matter, by making it the subject of an international treaty, has been used by Kelsen as one of the main arguments in support of the unity of national and international law.[1]

The development of the law of nations in the twentieth century has been a full justification of Kelsen's theoretical position. An ever-growing number of relations within each single state, relations between the state and its subjects as well as among individuals, has in the last decades actually been made, or proposed as the subject matter of international treaties, particular

*Reprinted from George A. Lipsky (ed), **Law and Politics in the World Community,** University of California Press, 1953. Reprinted by permission of the publisher.

and general. No less striking is the tendency to extend international law to domestic matters of highly political complexion, including those that are internally regulated by constitutional law. The most important manifestation of this tendency is the attempt of the United Natons to secure the protection of human rights by means of international law. Limitations on constitutional autonomy, formerly the mark of inferior rank in the community of nations, will, it is hoped, be accepted by all nations in the future.

The recent history of international law has thus been a telling refutation of the dualist thesis that the subject matters of the rules of national and international law are necessarily and always different, and has corroborated the monistic assertion of the unity of law.

However, it is one thing to maintain that an internal relation within states can be made the subject of international norms, and an entirely different matter to decide in a concrete case *de lege ferenda* whether it should be regulated by international law. The latter question is a problem of legal policy, and, as in any other question of policy, the answer to it involves a decision on ends and means, unrelated to legal theory proper.

Accordingly, international regulation of internal matters must, in each concrete case in which it is proposed, be justified first of all in terms of the objective which it is intended to serve. In view of the complexity of human affairs, however, it is not sufficient to weigh an objective in terms of its absolute merits alone. The question must therefore be asked how the adoption of a suggested scheme might affect other vital interests of international society, and, especially, whether it is likely to further or impair peaceful relations among its members. Moreover, extension of international law to domestic affairs means a change in the division of powers between the community of nations and the several states. Does the end to be attained by international regulation justify such limitations upon internal independence as are involved in the proposal?

Finally, it must be asked whether the objective of establishing uniformity is a feasible one considering the diverse conditions to which uniform regulation is recommended to be applied. Is agreement on uniform rules possible at all, and, if it is, how effective is it going to be? After all, international regulation of internal relations within states does not mean that those relations cease to be shaped and determined primarily by national factors, moral, political, economic, and social. Is it reasonable to expect that the latter can be made to yield to the force, persuasive rather than coercive, of international law? What influence is the structure of international society likely to have upon attempts to give effect to the uniform regulation? As a matter of fact, from a realistic point of view the question of the limits within which the purpose of international regulation of domestic policies stands a reasonable chance to be achieved is of decisive importance. For a rational policy will carefully avoid aiming at unattainable ends.

The attempt to secure the observance and protection of human rights and freedoms everywhere by an international covenant must therefore not be judged in terms of the worthiness of the objective alone. The latter can be granted, and at the same time the wisdom of the undertaking doubted. The question which comes first to mind when one tries to pass judgment on the efforts of the last five years to internationalize human rights is, of course, whether and to what extent it is a realistic scheme. The covenant on human rights is not intended to be *un text simplement dogmatique,* as the French Declaration of the Rights of Man and the Citizen of 1789 was.[2] It is planned to be a legal instrument which is not only to give additional protection to rights and freedoms already enjoyed by citizens of free countries, but to establish government by internationally guaranteed law where it does not exist. To extend the range of freedom and justice is the very *ratio legis,* but it is also the most ambitious part of the project.

The goal set—uniformity of constitutional relations between state and citizen throughout the world—is higher and to be attained on a wider scale than the objective of any other international instrument that has ever been contemplated or enacted. But the idea of subjecting domestic affairs to international control has been tried before, though for more modest purposes. The most important examples of devices for regulating internal relations by international treaties with a view to securing human rights and freedoms are the system of international labor conventions, the system of international minorities protection and the mandates system. An examination of the first and second instances, especially, might enlighten us on the legal and political problems involved in the internationalization of human rights. The one is significant by its intended world-wide scope, the other as an attempt at guaranteeing constitutional rights. We shall therefore do well to consult "that best oracle of wisdom, experience."

I

The most striking feature of the constitution of the International Labor Organization is the combination of far-reaching ultimate objectives with gradualism in attaining them.

By promoting international labor conventions the organization is not only to strengthen the legal guarantees of humane conditions of labor already gained by workers in advanced industrial communities, but to extend their benefits to the working people of economically and socially backward countries as well. In fact, the constitution states as the aim of the organization the general improvement of conditions beyond the standards already achieved in any one of the member states. However, this task is to be accomplished by stages. The constitution itself establishes the necessary machinery, but refrains from laying down any uniform rules immediately binding upon the members. The statement of general principles of labor legislation in the original constitution and especially in the Declaration of Philadelphia of 1944 anticipates, it is true, the catalogue of economic and social rights to be incorporated, according to present plans, in the future covenant on human rights. Those principles lack, however, as those of the economic and social rights proclaimed in the Universal Declaration of Human Rights of 1948, the force of positive law. They are common standards to be aimed at by future international and national action. The constitution recognizes expressly "that differences of climate, habits and customs, of economic opportunity and industrial tradition, make strict uniformity in the conditions of labor difficult of immediate attainment." It therefore provides for various gradual processes through which the general conference, the quasi-legislative agency of the organization, should try to arrive at the ultimate goal.

The conference is to proceed by consecutive acts. Each of them is to be limited to the regulation of a particular matter of clearly defined scope. If the circumstances are such that the subject, or an aspect of it, being dealt with by the conference is considered to be not yet suitable or appropriate for a convention legally binding upon ratifying states, the conference is to confine itself to a mere recommendation without obligatory force. It may adopt conventions embodying general principles rather than providing for specific obligations. It may limit itself to establishing minimum standards instead of decreeing maximum standards. Moreover, in framing a convention or recommendation of general application the conference shall have due regard for special national conditions and shall suggest the modifications, if any, which it considered may be required to meet the case of such members. Finally, the constitution rules out any attempt to effect by conventions a deviation from the domestic constitutional division of powers between central government and self-governing units, be they component parts of a federal state or nonmetropolitan territories.

Thus the system has been designed with a view to securing the widest acceptance of conference decisions at the risk of rendering them practically meaningless. For only general, more or less precise, rules, generally applicable and applied, can effect the improvement and the equalization of unequal conditions that form the very task of the organization.

The conference is composed not only of government delegates, but of representatives of industrial organizations of workers and employers as well. No doubt, it is in the history of international organization the closest approximation to a parliament of man. It would, however, be difficult to maintain that the conference has ever displayed a revolutionary mood. Nothing is more characteristic of its conservative attitude than its reluctance to regulate by conventions relations that traditionally belong to the province of domestic constitutional law. To assure freedom of association has from the beginning been one of the main objectives of the organization. In fact, the principle forms the very foundation of its tripartite structure. But the conference did not incorporate it in a convention earlier than 1948, and apparently then only in response to competitive efforts of the United Nations Commission on Human Rights.

All the same, the unsatisfactory number of ratifications of conventions indicates that the conference has, frequently under the pressure of organized public opinion, gone further than the realities of the situation have warranted. In discussing the prewar experience of the International Labor Organization, an official report of 1946 concedes "the very unequal extent to which the Conventions have been ratified by different Members of the Organization, and the large number of cases in which Conventions have not been ratified by Members the government representatives of which voted for their adoption."[3] Since World War II the record of ratifications has been poorer still.[4]

What is, however, more revealing than the inadequate number of ratifications, especially in the post-war period, are the reasons tentatively suggested in the report of the director general of 1949. The explanation of the disappointing results is, according to the view of "experienced observers" "that certain conventions were drawn up in too much detail, or that the standards set are too high for the majority of States Members." The director-general confessed that the organization "would fail in one of its essential tasks," unless the basis could be laid for an ever wider acceptance of conference decisions.[5]

However, one may wonder whether the lessening of the practical social significance of conventions is not the only price for which a large number of ratifications can be bought. The reasons that seem to account mainly for the frequent failure of states to ratify conventions for which they voted at the conference cannot be remedied by mechanical devices, but suggest rather the unrealistic objectives and assumptions of what is called international legislation.

The labor conference borrows its procedures from national parliaments and adopts decisions that are by their subject matter measures of domestic legislation. All the same they are international treaties, so far as their legal validity depends upon the voluntary act of ratification. It is not the same thing to vote for a convention at Geneva, where purely tactical considerations of the international parliamentary game are allowed to sway the decision, and to give legal effect to it at Washington, Paris or New Delhi where the stubborn facts of domestic politics are bound to be decisive. The convention being substantially, though not formally, internal legislation, any burden and risk to be assumed under its terms will be weighed most carefully with a view to the domestic political, economic, and social consequences of the measure proposed.

Moreover, labor conventions are not and cannot by their very nature be founded on that actual mutuality of interests which induces independent states to become voluntary partners in binding international treaties of the usual type, as, for example, treaties regarding the intercourse between states and among their nationals. This mutuality of interests is lacking especially whenever a labor convention is considerably more than a least-common denominator of standards, or than a statement of vague and flexible principles. Conventions setting high goals or formulating precise rules are by their very purpose bound to affect some countries more severely than others, be it with regard to the conditions of international competition or the state of domestic social legislation in general. What is for some states only formal confirmation of actual policies means for others the acceptance of the obligation to change their policies without receiving reciprocal benefits for the burdens and risks involved in ratifying conventions.

The inherent qualities of labor conventions account also for their unsatisfactory observance by states that have ratified them. In their annual reports to the organization on the application of ratified conventions, some governments state with disarming frankness that their national legislation and administration are not, or only partly, in harmony with the conventions accepted by them.[6] Time and again various agencies of the organization have found it necessary to emphasize "that the ratification of an international labor convention is as solemn and binding as the ratification of any other international treaty, and that ratification thereof imposes a definite obligation upon the ratifying Member States to give effect to the terms of the Convention completely and punctually."[7] The inadequate performance of labor conventions is the more noteworthy as the fathers of the organization have taken very bold steps in trying to secure it by an elaborate system of implementation and enforcement procedures.

By mutually accepting limitations on their traditionally unlimited legislative authority over their own nations, states parties to labor conventions acquire on the other hand the mutual right to interfere in the labor policies of the other parties, so far as those policies are regulated by the conventions. What formerly would have been intervention in domestic affairs is legally now a means of requesting performance of international treaties. Accordingly, under the constitution of the organization any one of the members may file a complaint with the International Labor Office "if it is not satisfied that any other Member is securing the effective observance of any Convention which both have ratified." In other words, this right is in no way dependent upon an actual interest of the complaining state in the observance of the convention by the party against which the complaint is directed.

Nor is the compliance with labor conventions the concern only of the particular states that have ratified them. By authorizing the delegates to the general conference to complain to the governing body about infractions of a convention, the constitution recognizes indirectly a right of third states and nongovernmental organizations as well to set in motion the machinery of implementation by issuing to their respective conference delegate the pertinent instructions. Nongovernmental organizations in addition are entitled to make to the governing body so-called "representations" that any of the member states has failed to give effect to a convention to which it is a party. Last, but not least, the governing body may also initiate implementation proceedings of its own motion.

The separation of the lawful concern in the performance of a treaty from the status of party is the legal expression of the idea that the observance of an international agreement is an interest of the community as a whole and of each of its members as much as of the parties to the agreement. The constitution of the International Labor Organization therefore establishes objective procedures of implementation and enforcement for protecting this interest. The preliminary decision whether a complaint should be investigated rests with the governing body. If the body decides in the affirmative, it shall appoint a Commission of Enquiry for establishing the facts relevant to the alleged nonperformance of a convention, and for making such recommendations as it may think proper as to the steps which should be taken by the defaulting government to meet the complaint. Each of the governments concerned in the complaint has the right to refer the complaint to the International Court of Justice, which has compulsory jurisdiction with regard to the interpretation of all labor conventions. Finally, if the defaulting member fails to carry out the recommendations of the commission or of the court, as the case may be, it may be subjected to collective enforcement measures, possibly economic, aiming at securing its compliance with the recommendations.

The implementation and enforcement provisions of the constitution have suffered a strange fate. Their practical effect has been to deter the members of the organization from ratifying labor conventions rather than to induce them to give effect to conventions they have ratified. What is stranger still, in spite of the inadequate performance of labor conventions, officially attested, the history of the organization records only one case of a complaint and three cases of representation.[8] The lesson we receive from this history is highly instructive all the same.

The conference of 1945 appointed a delegation on constitutional questions with a comprehensive mandate to review all outstanding questions relating to the constitution and constitutional practice of the International Labor Organization. The suggestions made by this delegation were adopted by the conference of 1946 with a view to amending the original constitution of 1919.

Needless to say, the delegation has not failed to examine the possibility of supplementing "the procedures of representation and complaint already provided for in the Constitution, by further measures of international supervision designed to secure a higher standard of observance of the obligations of Conventions." However, the delegation has finally decided against any revision of the implementation procedures. The reasons for this decision, stated in the report of the delegation, are worth quoting:

"The conclusion which [the delegation] has reached is that the problem is primarily one of national standards of law enforcement and that international action must therefore be directed towards promoting the progressive development of more effective national administrative machinery, a more vigorous insistence on the part of trade unions on the strict enforcement of the law, and a whole-hearted willingness on the part of employers to cooperate fully in maintaining the standards agreed upon in the common interest rather than towards measures which would inevitably be regarded as unwarranted international interference with national affairs. The influence of international action of this type will necessarily be slow, since national standards of law enforcement are an expression of a complex of political, social and economic conditions which are rarely susceptible of rapid improvement."[9]

The counsel, to expect no quick results from such action, has in the meantime been fully justified. The Labor Inspection Convention of 1947, intended to promote the "development of more effective national administrative machinery," has so far been ratified by only ten member states, most of them countries of high social and administrative standards.

Similar considerations account for the fact that the constitutional revision of 1946 has toned down the original provisions on enforcement proper. Indeed, collective enforcement of labor conventions by economic or other measures is practically out of question whatever the provisions of the constitution might be. For the international and national risks involved in taking effective actions would be out of all proportion to such advantages as can reasonably be expected to result from them. It would be absurd for an organization designed for attaining social justice as a guarantee of universal and lasting peace to pursue policies likely to disturb international relations.

Thus the organization and its members have apparently resigned themselves to dispensing with the international machinery of implementation and enforcement provided for in the constitution. To the extent to which they actually try to secure the performance of labor conventions, they resort instead to the more informal and more flexible methods of open and secret diplomacy.

The limits, indeed, have proved to be very narrow, within which uniform international regulation of domestic social policies has a fair chance of being accepted and made effective with a view to securing economic and social rights of the workers. The relevancy of this experience for the idea of an international bill of economic and social rights is obvious. If the International Labor Organization has, according to the testimony of its highest officer, so far failed to fulfill its legislative task satisfactorily by successive acts of strictly limited scope, and if it has been unable to secure the adequate performance of the treaties it has promoted, it is not very likely that the United Nations, a body more heterogeneous than the organization of Geneva, shall succeed in agreeing on and giving effect to an elaborate system of precisely formulated economic and social rights by which working people in all countries would actually benefit. But the lesson seems to be pertinent to the idea of an international bill of civil and political rights as well.

II

The system of international minorities protection, established after World War I for securing certain basic rights of members of racial, linguistic, and religious minorities against their own state, has been less of an innovation than the system of international labor conventions. Treaty stipulations designed for such purpose have figured in the public law of Europe throughout modern history. Especially in the nineteenth century they were characteristic of arrangements imposed by the Concert of Powers upon small newcomers to the society of nations.

The stigma of inequality was attached also to the minorities system of Versailles. It was a special regulation applying to special states, and not a general system for the protection of minorities everywhere. In fact, not even all of those states whose dominion has been extended by the peace treaties had to accept international control over their relations with their newly acquired minorities. That the number of countries subject to the special regime was comparatively large, and that there were among them countries of considerable size and importance, could hardly be a consolation for the states affected, particularly not if they were or felt themselves entitled to a significant role in international politics. Nor was the main feature of the new system, the guarantee of the League of Nations, apt to lessen their resentment. It is true that they, themselves, formed part of the supervising international organization. But the very purpose of the collective guarantee, to make international control more effective than it had proved to be in similar cases before, could hardly endear it to them.

If the system of international minorites protection was less novel than the extension of international law to domestic labor relations, its political significance was so much the greater. For it was to regulate "what constitutes the most sensitive sphere of the political life of a country,"[10] the constitutional relationship between states and citizens with potentially centrifugal tendencies. The subject matter of the international regulation was the most explosive political issue in eastern and southeastern Europe, the region to which it was to be applied. No wonder that the system has had such a stormy and short-lived career.

The far-reaching political implications of the scheme, which the principal Allied and Associated Powers, boasting of "the success of their arms," imposed after 1918 upon some fifteen states, are impressively suggested by the elimination of international minorities protection from the present plans for a covenant on human rights. What has been accepted under duress as a special regime is not voluntarily acceptable even as a general scheme. The universality of the covenant has to be bought at the price of omitting from it any provisions specifically aiming at the protection of minorities of any kind. To be sure, so far as the covenant is going to secure the equality of all men before the law, it will rule out any legal discrimination on racial, linguistic, or religious ground, and thus uphold one of the main principles of the system of international minorities protection. But it will not guarantee in any form the differential treatment to which members of minorities feel entitled with a view to the preservation of the group to which they belong as a distinct cultural entity. The guarantee of positive equality and its implementation by public services to be provided by the state for the benefit of its minorities was undoubtedly the most radical feature of the system of 1918.[11]

On the other hand, the political conditions seemed then to be propitious to the bold undertaking. The system was established and to be maintained by a politically homogeneous body of great powers and was to be applied to countries desiring, to put it in the words of the preamble of the minorities treaties, to make their institutions conform with "the principles of liberty and justice." Moreover, at least some of the states, subject to the regulation, entered upon their new political career with legal traditions that qualified them well for conducting a government by law. Accordingly, each of the treaties contained a bill of rights immediately binding upon the so-called minorities states, whereas the constitution of the International Labor Organization formulated merely guiding principles for the future attainment of economic and social rights by subsequent acts of international legislation.

An objective attempt at appraising the actual results of the system of international minorities protection requires a clear realization of the basic conceptions underlying it and of the principal purposes which it was intended to achieve. In the words of one of the best experts in the field:

> . . .the primary objective is the peace of the world; the means through which this is to be attained, and thus the indirect objectives of the Treaties is the internal stability of the Treaty states; and the means through which this, again, is to be achieved is the well-being of the minorities, which shall make them contented and loyal citizens of the states of which they form part. The welfare of the minorities is thus, in a sense, relegated to the third place. It is, however, the foundation upon which the whole system is built up, and is thus, in practice, the first of the three objects to be attained.[12]

In accepting this statement of the philosophy of international minorities protection, we must, however, be careful not to overlook the subjective element involved in the question whether the third purpose of the system has been realized. For the contentment and loyalty of the members of minorities are not a mere function of the degree of their well-being. The attitude of citizens toward their state is never exclusively dependent upon their objective situation, political, cultural, or economic. Particularly, the fervor of modern nationalism is due to the impact of political ideas and sentiments rather than to unsatisfied needs, objectively justified. In short, the degree of well-being is only one of the factors that determine the attitude of minorities toward their state. Nevertheless, it is an important factor.

There is, of course, no way of assessing accurately the extent to which the minorities treaties have actually contributed to the welfare of the minorities in the several states. But we may draw certain conclusions relevant to this question from the way in which the treaty states have tried to conform their laws and institutions to the legal obligations undertaken by them.

The authors of the treaties have refrained from spelling out in detail the fundamental rights to be respected. Apart from the provisions stipulating positive services and special privileges for the benefit of the minorities each of the instruments merely obligates the respective minorities state to assure full and complete protection of life and liberty to all inhabitants without distinction of birth, nationality, language, race, or religion, as well as the equality of all before the law and their equal enjoyment of the civil and political rights. If those minimum obligations are stated in terms that lack precision where no traditional body of jurisprudence can be resorted to for defining their meaning, they are on the other hand not qualified either by an emergency clause, or by a blanket limitation or any specific limitations. Only the right to the free exercise of religion is qualified by the provision that its practice must not be inconsistent with public order or public morals. Furthermore, the treaties provide that their stipulations "shall be recognized as fundamental laws, and that no law, regulation, or official action shall conflict or interfere with these stipulations, nor shall any law, regulation or official action prevail over them."

It seems that the attempt at imparting by international treaty to treaty law the standing and force of municipal constitutional law has been least successful. According to Dr. Robinson's painstaking study on the operation of the minorities system, the minorities states, basing themselves on traditional views of legal theory, have maintained, on the one side, that the treaties required, for becoming applicable to their individual beneficiaries, transformation into domestic law. On the other side, most of them have deliberately failed to effect their outright transformation.[13] This attitude disposed in a convenient way of the ticklish question whether the national courts were under the constitution of the respective country authorized to test the alleged conformity of a municipal law, constitutional or other, with what according to the treaties were to be the fundamental laws overriding all other legal norms and acts.

The degree to which municipal law—constitutional and statutory law—was actually in conformity with the treaty stipulations varied a great deal from country to country. Even strict conformity, however, did not necessarily mean that the administration of the laws was consistent with the obligations of the treaties. After all, in every country of the world, laws, including constitutional laws, are often honored by breach rather than observance. Conversely, the administration of laws was in some cases more in conformity with the treaties than the laws themselves.[14]

Thus the effectivenss of the international regulation was in each state dependent primarily and fundamentally upon factors which the minorities treaties did not, and could not, reasonably undertake to regulate: the general legislative and administrative standards and the specific legal remedies, judicial and administrative, by which citizens can assert the rights and privileges due them under general rules.

However, contrary to the development under the constitution of the International Labor Organization, the implementation of the minorities treaties has not remained a matter of national agencies alone. In fact, efforts to secure the performance of the "obligations of international concern," as the treaties characterized the provisions concerning the rights of the members of minorities, formed an essential part of the activities of the League of Nations, and especially of the Council. The protective stipulations having been placed by the treaties under the guarantee of the League of Nations, the Council declared it not only its right, but its duty as well, to "ascertain that the provisions for the protection of minorities are always observed."[15]

The tacit assumption of this declaration was that the performance of the treaties was an interest of the organized international community as a whole rather than of the individual parties to the treaties. Accordingly, the Council rather than the respective parties had to secure the observance of those instruments. In fact, the separation of the function of guarantee from individual states and its transfer to the central organ of the international community have been considered to be the principal advantage of the new system as against similar devices of the past. They would, it was hoped, effect the de-politicalization of the procedures intended to secure the performance of the protection clauses. Quasi-judicial proceedings rather than political procedures should effect the observance of the minorities treaties.

The Council has made serious efforts to protect the interest of the international community in the contentment of the minorities, and to guarantee objective modes of dealing with their complaints. This is the more notable as the treaties themselves were not entirely propitious to such attempts. All of them stipulated that only member states of the Council "shall have the right to bring to the attention of the Council any infraction or any danger of infraction" of the obligations undertaken by the minorities states. This provision limited the possibility of venting grievances as much as it endangered the impartiality of international implementation. The Council tried to remedy these defects by granting to states not represented on the Council as well as to the minorities themselves the right to petition the League with a view to inducing a member of the Council to put the subject matter of the respective communication before the Council and call upon it to intervene. Moreover, by establishing the Committee of Three and charging it with the examination of the petitions, the Council succeeded in practically substituting for the individual action of a Council member the concerted action of three of its members. In fact, most of the issues raised in petitions have actually been settled definitely one way or the other by the Committee of Three without ever reaching the Council itself.[16]

Impartial decisions in accordance with the treaties on the legal claims of members of minorities seemed to be assured, especially thanks to a provision of the treaties by which the minorities states agreed to accept in advance the jurisdiction of the Permanent Court of International Justice for settling between them and a member of the Council any difference of opinion as to questions of law or fact that might arise out of the treaties. In addition, the Council was authorized to refer to the court any dispute or question related to minorities matters, in order to obtain an advisory opinion on the legal issues involved.

However, in spite of all legal provisions for impartial procedures, the approach of the League to minorities matters throughout the years of its existence was a political and not a juridical one. Nothing is more suggestive than the fact that the Permanent Court of International Justice has had the opportunity to render altogether only three advisory opinions and one judgment. The settlements actually reached either by the Committee of Three or by the Council itself were political compromises rather than applications of the pertinent treaty law.

It would be a mistake to attribute the attitude of the Council to the lack of specific enforcement powers under the treaties. Governments, regardless whether they act on their own behalf or that of the international community, are always inclined to resign themselves to the infraction of treaties rather than to take extreme measures, unless vital national interests compel them to run the risks involved in such steps. Therefore the Council, or, more correctly, the members of the Council would not have acted differently, if armed with legal enforcement powers. The fact is that the prevalence of political over legal considerations, evidenced by the practice of the Council in dealing with complaints of minorities, reveals an inherent weakness of the system of international minorities protection.

The practice has affirmed what is hardly surprising. States, as members of an international organization, entrusted with the collective guarantee of the rights of foreign citizens against their own governments, act fundamentally in the same way as they do as individual guarantors. In either case, they interpret their legal obligation as well as their legal right to protect citizens of another country in accordance with their own national political interests, rather than with the spirit and letter of the pertinent rules of international law. In short, the attempt to internationalize the protection of minorities did not result in the de-politicalization of the minorites question. Instead the system became itself an object of international strife. If the system was characterized in its first period by the tendency of the Western powers to restrict their obligations of protection, in the second period Germany tended to abuse such rights of protection as she had acquired as a member of the Council.

The inclination of the Council members to limit the responsibilities and risks involved in implementing the collective guarantee of the League had a paradoxical consequence. The energy displayed by the Council in settling minorities matters in accordance with the treaties has been in inverse proportion to the relative importance of the issues at stake. Minor cases were more likely to be decided in conformity with the treaties than cases of great legal and political significance for the minorities concerned, because they were of great relevance for their respective governments as well. The melancholy truth is that the Council was least energetic and successful when faced with flagrant treaty violations of the most serious kind, "measures of violence, repression and terror applied by the authorities against minorities."[17]

Nonetheless, the Council could plead attenuating circumstances even in cases that seemed to call for its outright condemnation. It was, first of all, often difficult to ascertain whether the hostilities between governments and minorities were caused by one side or the other. There are ruthless governments, but there are seditious, intractable minorities as well, often incited by outside influences for selfish purposes. Moreover, the protection of minorities was conceived to be only a means for assuring the internal stability of the treaty states with a view to securing through such stability international peace, the primary objective of the system. Thus whenever there was uncertainty about the respective guilt of governments and minorities, the Council was strongly tempted to give the benefit of doubt to the former rather than to the latter.

But even assuming that in a particular case all indications pointed to the full responsibility of the government, one may sympathize with the Council. For it found itself confronted with the formidable task of reconciling in practice what cannot easily be reconciled in theory: peace and justice. That the interests of peace and justice always necessarily coincide is a pious wish rather than a fact. In domestic as well as in international politics we are constantly compelled to weigh their respective merits, the one against the other, and we constantly sacrifice on one occasion justice in order to save peace, and on another peace in order to attain justice. In fact, time and again we have to establish an uneasy balance between them even in our daily private life.

No doubt, the interests of peace often were only a pretence of the Council when neglecting its duty to secure the rights of minorities, confided to its care. But we would fail to realize the complexity of political and human affairs, if we should interpret all of the Council's omissions in opportunistic terms alone. There is an impressive ring of sincerity in the words Briand once exclaimed in a discussion on the minorities problem. He said:

No movement must be allowed to persist which, under cover of unexceptionable sentiments, would lead to widespread unrest in the world or breed fresh insecurity. However worthy of respect certain doctrines and propaganda may be, one thing stands before them all—peace. No special circumstances, no individual aspirations, however justifiable, can be allowed to transcend the interest of peace. Peace must prevail, must come before all. If any act of justice were proposed which would disturb world peace, and renew the terrible disasters of yesterday, I should be the first to call upon those prompting it to stop, to abandon it in the supreme interest of peace.[18]

The complexity of the undertaking to secure domestic justice by international treaties and by their international implementation has been illustrated also by the effect of the minorities system upon the relationship between the governments of the treaty states and their minorities.

The system exposed the treaty states to the lawful interference by the agencies of the League in their dealings with part of their own citizens. The liberal rules on the right of petitioning the League tended to make this interference a more or less regular feature of the public life of those countries. By introducing into it a neutral, outside element, the fathers of the treaties hoped to further the final political reconciliation between the several governments and their respective minorities. But one may wonder whether the actual results corresponded to those expectations.

Contrary to the intentions of its authors, the system, first of all, made it possible for single powers to clothe with the semblance of legality attempts at fostering for their own national purposes the discontent of minorities. To that extent it rendered the adjustment of the relations between governments and minorities more, rather than less, difficult. In fact, it encouraged disloyalty of the members of minorities towards their governments and made, conversely, those governments more reluctant to forego discriminatory policies against their minorities. However, the introduction of a third element has very likely, in other cases as well, lessened rather than increased the chances of an honest compromise on the fundamental issues between the contending nationalities. The readiness of opposing groups to come to an agreement by mutual concessions depends upon a realistic appraisal by them of their respective strength. The hope of the minorities to redress in their favor by international outside support the balance of the internal political forces was a futile one. All the same it blurred the realization that their fate would and could be decided ultimately by the normal procedures of domestic politics alone. Nor, on the other side, were the governments of the treaty states ready to trust the good faith of their minorities, as long as the latter were inclined to turn at any moment internal issues into foreign issues.

There was, therefore, much force in the argument set forth by the representatives of the treaty states from the very beginning that the system of international minorities protection was apt to render their internal consolidation more difficult, and thus not likely to further international peace as its primary objective.

The relevancy of the attempt to internationalize the protection of minorities to the idea of internationalizing human rights is self-evident. Already at the time when the minorities system was not yet buried under the ruins of World War II, the establishment of a universal system of human rights, intended to protect all men against all governments, was looked upon by statesmen and publicists as the logical culmination of the idea launched by the peacemakers of Versailles. However, the lessons we can learn from the minorities sytem are somewhat more involved. It is probably more correct to characterize its actual result as limited failure than as limited success. Be that as it may, from the point of view of international politics and international law its main significance lies undoubtedly in what has been the most novel feature of the system, the operation of a collective guarantee by an international organization. Whereas the constitutional provisions for the implementation of labor conventions have remained a dead letter, the implementation machinery improvised by the Council of the League for securing the observance of the minorities treaties has been utilized fully. But the use of this machinery has not only yielded meagre results in absolute terms; it has had adverse effects on international and national politics as well. Thus the system has raised more problems than it has solved.

III

Throughout human history periods of devastating wars have been productive of great designs, intended to redeem mankind once and for all from the curse of bloody and ruinous strife by devising a more just and stable international order. Revulsion against the horrors of World War II has brought into existence the United Nations of today. Its primary and paramount purpose is to maintain international peace and security by collective actions of the organized international community. To the United Nations has, however, been assigned the still more ambitious task of attaining domestic justice in all its member states as well. The origin of World War II in infamous tyranny seemed to confirm the democratic belief that to end tyranny was also a means for ending war. Thus the conference of San Francisco has charged the organization with assuring the conditions of peace by promoting "universal respect for, and observance of human rights and fundamental freedoms for all without distinction as to race, sex, language, or religion." Complying with this mandate, in 1946 the United Nations Commission on Human Rights went to work on a covenant on human rights.

The United Nations embarked upon its formidable undertaking in the temper of revolutionaries who refuse to accept any lessons from the past. Neither the experience of the International Labor Organization in the field of economic and social rights nor the experience of the League of Nations in trying to secure civil and political rights of minorities was held to have any bearing upon what the United Nations Commission on Human Rights was expected to accomplish. Nevertheless, the members of the commission were soon faced with problems and difficulties of the same nature as those organizations that had before more or less vainly been struggling with them.

In fact, the magnitude of the problems and difficulties the commission was to encounter proved to be the more terrifying, as its goal was set even higher than the objectives of the International Labor Organization and of the League. In addition, contrary to both of them the United Nations harbors under its wings antagonistic political ideologies. They are split over the very questions a covenant on human rights is designed to regulate uniformly. Thus, what was to be made the subject matter of a treaty for establishing a universal system of basic rights was bound to become in the very process of negotiating the treaty the means of ideological warfare.

This more than anything else accounts for the apparently sweeping character of the Draft First International Covenant on Human Rights, which the commission submitted to the General Assembly in 1950.[19] Any attempt of one side to adapt the covenant to the political realities of today was liable to be exploited by the other side as a betrayal of the ideal set up by the Charter of the United Nations. Considerations of this kind account also for the decision of the General Assembly at its fifth session directing the commission to reconsider the draft with a view to inserting into it economic and social rights, assuring its application to federal states as well as to trust territories and nonselfgoverning territories, and improving the methods of implementation.

But tactical reasons alone do not explain the policy of the member states of the United Nations. A covenant which is merely a least common denominator of existing constitutional standards would, first, not fulfill its main purpose of extending the range of freedom and justice. Moreover, and still worse, it might appear to be an endorsement by the world organization of the lowest standards and lack any inspirational value. This consideration speaks in favor of a more ambitious goal. However, there arises immediately another question, familiar to the authors of international labor conventions. Is such a covenant going to be ratified by the very states whose domestic policies it is intended to amend? And if it is ratified by them, are they going to give effect to it?

It is true, the draft covenant fails to include, not only the economic and social rights, but some of the civil and political rights as well that are proclaimed in the Universal Declaration of Human Rights of 1948. However, the declaration is only *un text simplement dogmatique* without obligatory legal force, whereas the covenant is intended to be an instrument of international law binding each state party thereto "to respect and to ensure to all individuals within its territory and subject to its jurisdiction the rights recognized in this Covenant." It corresponds as to content and scope more or less to the traditional municipal bills of rights, and is more comprehensive than the enumeration of civil and political rights of the usual type in the minorities treaties. As a matter of fact, it even stipulates "effective remedies" for securing the internal enforcement of the various substantive rights. Nonetheless, the covenant lacks, and is in view of its subject matter bound to lack, the character of a genuinely uniform regulation. Nor does it provide for an international machinery of implementation that might reasonably be expected to develop uniform rules in applying the covenant.

Whatever the philosphical foundation of a municipal bill of rights is considered to be, and regardless whether a constitution states the rights of individuals in absolute or relative terms, there is practically no right whose exercise is not subject to limitations. It is the very function of the state to adjust conflicting rights among its citizens as well as to reconcile with one another conflicting claims of society and individual. Indispensable as such limitiations upon the rights recognized or granted by the constitution are, they are, on the other hand, liable to render those rights illusory. In fact, to deprive by more or less lawful limitations a bill of rights of its reality, and yet maintain its semblance, is the time-honored technique of arbitrary government under constitutional disguise. It is therefore essential for securing freedom that the ultimate determination of the compatibility of limitations upon rights with the purpose and spirit of the constitution guaranteeing rights should rest in each case with an impartial authority. The system of judicial review of legislation is undoubtedly best suited for effecting this control, unless a country may, as Great Britain, expect its parliament to exercise its legislative functions with the circumspection a High Court would use.

Limitations forming an indispensable part of any municipal system of rights, it was then practically out of the question to internationalize human rights without internationalizing exceptions as well.[20] The great struggle in the Commission on Human Rights was not over the principle of limitations, but over their form and scope. The draft covenant on human rights contains three types of limitations. To the first category belong the limitations incorporated into the formulation of the several rights. They are specific limitations insofar as each of them is related to a particular right, but they are rather general in their scope, as can, for example, be seen from Article 15 of the draft: "The right of peaceful assembly shall be recognized. No restrictions shall be placed on the exercise of this right other than those imposed in conformity with the law and which are necessary to ensure national security, public order, the protection of health or morals or the protection of the rights and freedoms of others." The second type of limitations is represented by Article 2, the co-called derogation article. It authorizes the signatories in a state of emergency or of public disaster to take measures derogating, to the extent strictly limited by the exigencies of the situation, from the obligations stipulated in about half of the articles of the covenant. The third limitation, the antifascist clause of Article 18, is also general and is a legal formulation of the principle that the guarantee of rights stated in the covenant does not imply the recognition of a right to destroy rights.

No doubt, the nature and scope of the exceptions internationalized by the covenant are no less sweeping than those of the rights themselves. It is true, the first and second type of limitations are either expressly stated or tacitly implied in practically all democratic constitutions. But it is true also that they have time and again been employed for destroying democratic constitutions, and are making sweeping bills of rights satisfactorily workable in totalitarian countries. More ominous still is the antifascist clause, a novel feature in what is intended to be a constitutional document of democracy. Be that as it may, a covenant on rights without limitations of this kind or another would not be likely to be ratified even by the most advanced democratic nations. For, however easily the powers impliedly granted by those stipulations lend themselves to political abuse, they are at the same time essential requirements of the governance of states and men.

Thus the task to be solved by the authors of the draft covenant would have been to prevent possible abuse by providing for the establishment in each state of adequate institutional safeguards against it. However, compliance with such obligations would require far-reaching changes in the constitutional machinery of states that lack institutions of this kind, and they are therefore not acceptable to them. As a matter of fact, the practical value of uniform procedural safeguards provided for by an international treaty must not be overrated. For their actual operation would in each country be an expression of a complex of traditions, habits, and conditions beyond the reach of international legislation. At any rate, according to the draft covenant, the question whether a person may test through constitutional procedures the conformity of laws limiting his rights with the stipulations of the covenant, is a question to be answered solely by municipal law. Similarly, the covenant leaves it to the organ authorized by the municipal constitution of the respective state to determine the conditions under which the article of derogation may be applied, without subjecting the agency to any control, legislative or judicial. Such "effective remedies" as the covenant stipulates, are at best apt to secure the conformity of administrative acts with statutory law, but not of statutory law with the covenant itself.

If the adaptation of the covenant to the political realities of today fails to find expression in the number of rights, it is the more conspicuous in the qualifications of rights expressly stated or tacitly admitted by the covenant. The covenant, if ever adopted, is therefore to all practical intents and purposes very likely to be another more or less pious declaration of guiding principles rather than a genuinely uniform legal regulation effecting the equalization of constitutional practices on a high level. This character of the covenant is more strikingly suggested by the provisions concerning its implementation by international procedures.

The objective of the draft covenant on human rights is infinitely more ambitious than the purposes of the systems of international labor conventions and international minorities protection. But its provisions for international implementation are far from betraying even an equal zeal in securing its performance. Like those two devices, the system of internationally guaranteed human rights presupposes and is intended to protect the interest of the international community as a whole in attaining its objective. However, in opposition to the implementation provisions of the constitution of the International Labor Organization as well as to those laid down by the Council of the League, the covenant recognizes only the states parties to the covenant as legitimate representatives of the community interest. Neither states that have not ratified the covenant nor nongovernmental organizations or, least of all, private persons are to be granted by the covenant a legal standing in the proceedings of implementation. As a matter of fact, the covenant assigns not even to the United Nations as a whole the collective guarantee of its stipulations. The tendency to restrict the implementation of what is by its contents a revolutionary document in the history of international law to traditional procedures of old-time diplomacy is revealed by one more symptom. The covenant does not speak of complaints, but merely of matters one state may bring to the attention of another state which is not giving effect to a provision of the covenant both of them have ratified.

No less conservative are the other features of the third part of the draft covenant. The Human Rights Committee, composed of seven members, nationals of the treaty states, is authorized to deal with a matter, referred to it by the one or by the other of the parties to the dispute, only after adjustment by bilateral negotiations between them has failed. The committee is primarily a fact-finding body with the right to call upon the states concerned to supply any relevant information, but without the right to make investigations on the spot. Article 41 of the draft covenant purposely directs the committee only to make available its good offices to the states concerned, and confines the report the committee shall draw up to a statement on "its conclusions on the facts." The Commission of Enquiry, provided for by the constitution of the International Labor Organization, shall make "such recommendations as it may think proper as to the steps which should be taken to meet the complaint." Similarly, the Council of the League was entitled to propose concrete terms of settlement of minorities matters. But no right of recommending a specific solution is granted by the draft covenant to the Human Rights Committee. It is, in addition to its fact-finding function, an agency of mediation rather than of conciliation. It is the clear implication of the draft covenant that human rights are, to the extent to which they are regulated by it, a matter of international concern. Nonetheless, they are, as regards their implementation, treated as matters which are essentially within the domestic jurisdiction of the parties. Accordingly, the draft covenant fails to make provisions for settling issues arising out of its application, or nonapplication rather, by the International Court of Justice or any other international judicial tribunal. The Human Rights Committee being merely empowered to establish facts and mediate between the contending parties, the proceedings of implementation do not result in a legal decision of a superior authority which would lend itself to collective enforcement.

It is true, the provisions of the draft covenant concerning the composition and the procedures of the Human Rights Committee are intended to guarantee the impartiality of the body to which it proposes to entrust its international implementation. All the same one fails to see how the committee should be able to accomplish what is one of the most essential purposes of the internationalization of human rights, namely to remedy the ineffectiveness of their national protection by an effective system of international protection. For the only weapon with which the committee is armed by the draft covenant is the publication of its factual report. This brings up historical recollections. In 1914 Secretary of State Bryan was busy propagating his cooling-off treaties which provided for commissions of inquiry and conciliation as means of preventing war. "The sum and substance" of these treaties, said President Wilson at that time, was "that whenever any trouble arises the light shall shine on it for a year before anything is done; and my prediction is that after the light has shone on it for a year, it will not be necessary to do anything; that after we know what happened, then we will know who was right and who was wrong."[21] The Human Rights Committee of the draft covenant not only resembles the commissions of inquiry and conciliation of the Bryan treaties, but is founded upon their philosophy as well.

The international implementation, envisaged by the draft covenant on human rights, is thus a combination of old-fashioned mediation with the main instrument of twentieth-century diplomacy, the appeal to what is called the world court of public opinion. If this is hardly an adequate way of enforcing human rights, it is the more suitable for turning their protection into a weapon in the struggle of ideas which today threatens the peace of the world. Negligible as are the accomplishments of such a system in terms of its very objective bound to be, its effect upon international relations is considerable.

IV

Noninterference in the domestic affairs of foreign nations is a concomitant of the doctrine of sovereignty. The disrepute into which this notion has in recent times fallen—not unjustifiably to the extent to which sovereignty has been interpreted and used excessively—has therefore affected also the appreciation of the principle of nonintervention. However, it is the only principle which can secure the peaceful coexistence of different groups in international society no less than in national society. Only the recognition and clear delimitation of their autonomous spheres makes possible their cooperation with one another in the pursuit of common interests. For these reasons modern international law, essentially a law between collective entities, has abhorred dictatorial interference of one state in the internal affairs of another state and has tended to restrict the milder forms of interference, too. The more eager a state has been to maintain friendly relations with other states, the more anxious it has been not to burden its international relations with matters extraneous to foreign policy proper. The validity and the wisdom of the principle of noninterference have been challenged only by religious and political movements that were inspired with the missionary zeal to extend their ideas and systems beyond the confines of their own states.

The current tendency to transform domestic matters into international matters by making them the subject of international treaties is therefore the very negation of the conceptions that have been prevailing in international law and diplomacy throughout the last centuries. Whatever the subject of international regulation might be in a concrete case, all these schemes have one thing in common. To the extent to which they narrow the scope of legally internal matters, they enlarge the sphere of lawful mutual interference in what in legal terms are not any longer domestic matters. Thus they widen at the same time the range of possible international frictions by blurring the comparatively sharp lines of demarcation which separated the internal spheres of states from one another in former times.

To be sure, this trend is largely the mere expression of the growing interdependence of the nations of the world. We are rejoicing at the beneficial results of this process, and we have therefore to accept its untoward effects as well. However, the tendency also has purely ideologic-. al roots. In particular, the idea of internationalizing human rights is a manifestation of the universalism characteristic of the dominant political religions of the day—democracy and communism. It would be naive to expect that we could eliminate from current world politics its explosive ideological ingredient by forsaking the ideal of international protection of human rights. But it would be most dangerous on the other hand not to beware of the effect this pathetic effort might easily have of heightening rather than lessening international tensions. Briand's exhortation is as pertinent to the question of human rights today, as it was to the minorities question some twenty years ago. The primary and paramount purpose of the United Nations is the maintenance of international peace, and not the realization of domestic justice, mostly impervious to international action short of war.

The danger that the effort to secure the protection of human rights by international law is likely to impair rather than to further international peace is due to the same reason that is bound to deprive the system of its effectiveness. International law has in the last decades made deep inroads upon the province of municipal law. If the covenant on human rights is going to materialize in one form or another, international law will have conquered constitutional law, the citadel, as it were, of municipal law. But the technical structure of international law and international society has remained basically unchanged. The beneficiaries of human rights are to be individual persons. However, technically they are going to be the objects only of a covenant on human rights. States alone will be authorized to bring an infraction of the covenant to the attention of states which are not giving effect to its provisions. Human rights are made the subject matter of international law because the international community as a whole is assumed to have a vital interest in their observance by all states. But the international community, though organized today as a confederation, lacks genuine governmental powers, and must therefore, in trying to secure the performance of the covenant, rely on the cooperation of the very state which is alleged to have violated it. As Bourquin remarks in a penetrating analysis of the problem, one finds in the contents of international treaties regulating relations within nations no truly interstate matters. "Mais si, au lieu de considérer l'objet de l'opération, nous portons nos regards sur son aspect technique, le tableau change radicalement. Les bénéficiares du régime disparaissent. Il n'a plus en scène que les Etats."[22]

There is, of course, nothing immutable about the traditional structure of international law. The classical view that only states can be subjects of rights and duties under international law has gone by the board together with many other nineteenth-century notions, not any longer tenable in the face of recent developments in positive law. If the parties to the covenant on human rights want to grant to individuals not only the right of petition, but the status of a party before an international tribunal of human rights as well they can do so. Nor does international law as such block the conferment of enforcement powers on agencies of the international community. The fact is that the individual as subject of international law would in terms of physical power still have less chance than a protector state to effect the performance of the covenant by his own government; and the establishment of a supranational government strong enough to enforce the covenant against a recalcitrant state is politically out of the question.

As it has repeatedly been observed,[23] the covenant on human rights is designed to impose upon the states parties thereto limitations upon their power over their own citizens which under the American constitutional system have by and large been imposed upon the states of the union only after the Civil War had overthrown the political power structure expressed in the Constitution of 1787 and the first ten amendments. As a matter of fact, the nationalization of liberty through the vehicle of the fourteenth amendment has been accomplished not earlier than in our times. The first ten amendments to which the covenant on human rights corresponds in contents were intended to protect American citizens against arbitrary actions of the newly established federal government and not of the historically older state governments. As regards the Constitution itself, the federal limitations upon state powers were to serve the uniform regulation of inter-state relations rather than of relations within the single states. The only provisions of the federal Constitution intended to protect American citizens against encroachments upon their rights and freedoms by their own state governments are those of Article I, Section 10 forbidding the states to "pass any bill of attainder, *ex post facto* law, or law impairing the obligation of contracts. . ."

The parties to the prospective covenant on human rights are thus aiming at an objective American history has proved to be attainable only under a federal government of a highly centralized type. Nor does any other historical experience support the hope that an international system of human rights and freedoms can secure men in their actual enjoyment. Be that as it may, the great significance of the idea cannot be doubted. It is one of the many symptoms of the profound crisis that international society and international law, as they have evolved in modern times, are going through today.

The idea of human rights and freedoms under international law is a challenge to and a denial of practically all basic concepts upon which international law has during the last centuries been resting. It refutes the traditional doctrine on the contents of international law as well as the division of powers between the international community and its members to which that doctrine corresponded. It implies the rejection of the traditional notions on the structure and the subjects of international law. Last, but not least, it is in fundamental opposition to the concept of sovereignty, the very core of modern international law. In short, the idea is the most radical manifestation of the tendency to develop the law of nations into world law.

Nor are the symptoms of this crisis confined to the theory and practice of modern international law. In fact, the latter are rather the expression of moral, political, and economic forces incessantly working and undermining the foundation of the nation state, the basic unit of modern international society. Indeed, many trends in the realm of ideas and of facts recall the period of transition from the ancient city state to wider forms of political organization, based on new principles of human association. The picture Fustel de Coulanges has drawn of this transformation seems to describe our century as well.[24]

The end of the road leading through the present period of crisis and transformation is shrouded in the mists of he future. All history suggests is, unfortunately, that such periods of transition are not ages of peace. Thus it gives little comfort to see the United Nations indulging in grandiose visions of human rights, as long as it does not attempt to restore the humane laws of war that have been the great achievement of modern times, but are abandoned now. International law of today, we are told, recognizes and asserts, contrary to the traditional international law of the past, the worth and dignity of the human being. The claim obliges us to apply humanitarian principles also to the regulation of warfare, once one of the proudest accomplishments of traditional international law.

FOOTNOTES

[1]Hans Kelsen, *Das Problem der Souveränität und die Theorie des Völkerrechts (Tübingen: J.C. B. Mohr, 1920, pp. 124 ff.; General Theory of Law and State* (Cambridge: Harvard University Press, 1949), pp. 363 ff.; *The Law of the United Nations* (New York: Frederick A. Praeger, 1950, pp. 770 ff.

[2]A. Esmein, *Eléments de Droit Constitutionnel Francais et Comparé* (Paris- Librairie du Recuil Sirey, 1921), I,, 554.

[3]International Labor Office, *Report of the Conference Delegation on Constitutional Questions on the Work of Its First Session* (Montreal: 1946), p. 32

[4]International Labor Conference, Thirty-second Session, *Report of the Director-General* (Geneva:1949), pp. 126 ff.

[5]*Ibid.*, p. 128.

[6]See, e.g., International Labor Conference, Twenty-ninth Session, *Reports on the Application of Conventions (Article 22 of the Constitution)* (Montreat: 1946), *passim.* The Committee of Experts on the Application of Conventions suggests that disregard for conventions has not been due to war conditions only. See *ibid.*, Report V (Appendix), p. 5.

[7]See International Labor Office, *Report of the Conference Delegation. . .*(cited in n. 3, above), pp. 37 ff.

[8]F. L. Oppenheim, ed. by H. Lauterpacht, *International Law* (6th ed., London: Longmans, Green, 1947), I, 662.

[9]See International Labor Office, *op. cit.*, p. 50.

[10]P. de Azcárate. *League of Nations and National Minorities* (Washington: Carnegie Foundation for International Peace, 1945), p. 27.

[11]*Ibid.*, pp. 59 ff.

[12]C. A. Macartney, *National States and National Minorities* (London: Oxford University Press, H. Milford, 1934), p. 275.

[13]Jacob Robinson and Others, *Were the Minorities Treaties a Failure?* (New York: Institute of Jewish Affairs of the American Jewish Congress and the World Jewish Congress, 1943), pp. 187 ff.

[14]*Ibid.,* pp. 196, 238 f.

[15]Report presented by M. Tittoni and adopted by the Council of the League of Nations on October 22d, 1920, reprinted in: League of Nations, *Protection of Linguistic, Racial or Religious Minorities by the League of Nations,* Resolutions and Extracts from the Minutes of the Council, Resolutions and Reports adopted by the Assembly, relating to the Procedure to be followed in Questions concerning the Protection of Minorities (Geneva: March 1931), p. 7.

[16]Robinson, *op. cit.,* p. 111.

[17]Azcárate, *op. cit.,* pp. 66 ff.; Robinson, *op. cit.,* pp. 122 ff.

[18]League of Nations: Ninth Assembly, *Record of Plenary Session,* p. 82 (quoted in Macartney, *op. cit.,* p. 279). Three months later, in December, 1928, Briand as president of the Council made another speech more reassuring for the minorities. He emphasized the "sacred" character of their rights and promised that minorities matters will always be considered by the Council "with the deepest respect for the interests in question." *League of Nations Official Journal,* 10th Year (January, 1929), pp. 59 f. (quoted in Robinson, *op. cit.,* p. 242).

[19]"Report of the Sixth Session of the Commission on Human Rights," Economic and Social Council, *Official Records, Fifth Year: Eleventh Session, Supplement,* no. 5 (1950), pp. 15 ff.

[20]On the question of limitations see H. Lauterpacht, *International Law and Human Rights* (New York: Frederick A. Praeger, 1950), pp. 330 ff., 365 ff.; and Zechariah Chafee, Jr., "Legal Problems of Freedom of Information in the United Nations," *Law and Contemporary Problems,* XIV (Durham, N. C.: School of Law, Duke University, Autumn, 1949), pp. 567 ff.

[21]R. S. Baker, *The Public Papers of Woodrow Wilson: The New Democracy* (New York and London: Harper, 1925–1927), I, 206. Quoted in E. H. Carr, *The Twenty Years' Crisis 1919–1939* (London: Macmillan, 1940), p. 43.

[22]Maurice Bourquin, "L'Humanisation du droit des gens," *La Technique et les principles du droit public,* Etudes en l'honneur de Georges Scelle (Paris: Librairie générale du droit et jurisprudence, 1950), I, 27.

[23]Zechariah Chafee, *op. cit.,* pp. 550 ff.; and Arthur N. Holcombe, *Human Rights in the Modern World* (New York: New York University Press, 1948), pp. 120 ff.

[24]Fustel de Coulanges, *La cité antique* (Paris: Hachette, 1912), V.

IV

POLITICAL THEORY

THE PRACTICAL USES OF
POLITICAL THEORY*

Dr. Jonas has given us a breathtaking philosophical account of the relentless onward march of modern science and technology. What has been the effect of its sweep upon theory and practice in politics?

The new necessities and miseries to which the modern pursuit of knowledge has given rise are most notorious in the realm of politics. The magnitude and complexity of the political problems that statesmanship is expected to solve are today, and will be in the future, infinitely greater than they ever were prior to the scientific age. The prospect is the more frightening because the political ordering of human affairs was never a simple matter. Unrest and change have throughout history sapped the foundations of political societies and institutions almost as soon as they were established. How much stronger are the dynamic forces pressing on political life in all parts of the world now that mankind seems to be definitely committed to "the endless thrust into the ever-new and unknown"! How much more

*Reprinted with the permission of *Social Research*, Summer 1959 (Vol. 26, No.2).
This final essay, a commentary on a philosophical essay by Professor Hans Jonas, published in the same issue of *Social Research*, is intended to provide some insights into the author's understanding of the nature and the uses of political theory.

difficult is the governance of modern mass society, which the unceasing series of technical inventions and economic changes has brought into being, than was the governance of the smaller communities of the past! How much more complex is the problem of international peace when its dimensions are global, as they are today, than it was when nature, not yet conquered by man, assured the coexistence of at least those whom its barriers kept physically apart from one another! Finally, how much less terrifying was the specter of war then than it is at present! By delivering things into man's power, by achieving his mastery over nature, science—whatever it has accomplished for the betterment of life—has brought the self-extinction of the human race within the reach of the possible. Indeed, politics today means dealing with emergencies, one following the other ever more rapidly.

The greater magnitude and complexity of the practical problems to be solved is not the only effect that the pursuit of science in modern times has had on politics. Its influence on the theory of politics and on conceptions of its practical uses has been no less profound. In fact, time and again it has been asserted that while the progress of the physical sciences may have aggravated the practical problems of politics, the progress of social and political science, if only it follows the path of the former, will eventually provide mankind with the technical tools for coping with those problems successfully.

Only lately, however, practically only in our own time, has this vision of a political science patterned on the model of the physical sciences led to massive and concrete attempts to transform the vision into reality. For a long time the influence on political science of the procedures used in modern natural science was negative rather than positive. Thus the insistence on applying to the study of political phenomena requirements and methods similar to those to which the natural scientists have subjected themselves set in motion the lengthy process that resulted in the separation from one another of political philosophy, political theory, and political science. In his work, *Political Theory*, Arnold Brecht has given us a masterful account of that momentous process.[1] Moreover, the increasing prestige of the physical sciences could not fail to effect a depreciation of political philosophy and theory in so far as their objects and procedures place them outside of what came to be considered political science proper.

Attempts actually to realize the vision of a political science based on the rigorous application of the principles of the physical sciences have taken shape somewhat slowly. The most radical manifestation and the very culmination of this development are the current efforts of an increasing number of political scientists, mostly American, to engage in strictly empirical investigation of all facts bearing on human behavior in politics.

Their ultimate and most ambitious objective is to build a scientific system or general theory of human political behavior, and to make scientific the conduct of politics, international and domestic. While originally one could speak only of a common "research orientation" as the uniting bond of these scholars,[2] they have rapidly grown into a school, setting itself apart from political scientists working along more traditional lines of research.

Needless to say, empirical research holds a rightful place and is likely to play an increasingly important role in political science. Its recent concentration on human political processes rather than on the machinery of government has helped us to realize the limits set to the effectiveness of political and legal institutions, once greatly overrated by political scientists. The study of human behavior in politics is not only a worthwhile pursuit of theoretical knowledge; it can also be useful from a practical point of view. Nor is there any reason to object to its employment of quantitative methods, or to deny the significance and the validity of its results. Doubts begin to arise, however, when the moral realm of man, a free agent, is equated to the realm of physical things, and when the absolutist claim is made that the quantitative approach to the questions of politics is the only scientific and promising one.

How little such a claim is justified is borne out by the narrow sphere in which the quantitative approach has so far proved fruitful. It is indeed no accident that the search for uniformities of political behavior has been directed chiefly to the investigation and analysis of electoral behavior. Only mass behavior offers a sufficiently large number of comparable instances on which relevant generalizations and predictions can be based. But even in this limited field, quantitative measurement is a problematic and insufficient means for piercing through the political realities, and is bound to remain so, all possible and likely future technical improvements of the methods of measurement notwithstanding. In the first place, the selection of the factors to which the voting behavior is correlated is determined by conclusions founded on preconceived, not necessarily valid ideas on what motivates political attitudes, as is clearly suggested by the overemphasis in voting studies on the economic motive. Moreover, the actual reason why a person votes one way or another is ultimately inscrutable. Unlike the physical scientist, with his canons of experimental testing, the social scientist is hardly ever able to identify all variable factors in the situation he is exploring, or to repeat his experiment under the same conditions.

More recently the study of political processes and political behavior has been extended to decision-making on the governmental level, in relation to both domestic and foreign policy matters. The empirical investigation of decision-making "as an action process," "analyzed in terms of a generalized conceptual scheme," is expected finally to yield the components of a general behavioral theory. Again it is undoubtedly a worthwhile undertaking to find out how legislative, executive, and judicial bodies actually arrive at their decisions. Moreover, theory can undoubtedly contribute to the rationality of decision-making, in so far as it can help to clarify the choices open to the decision-maker. But it is an entirely different matter to assume, as the behaviorists do, that refinements of the methods applied in individual case studies and refinements of the theoretical formulations will sooner or later enable us "to predict, within limits, policy outcomes from a knowledge of processes.[3]

The basic fallacy of this expectation is that it underrates the degree to which decisions are bound to remain based on contingent factors, varying in varying combinations from one case to the other. For this very reason Edmund Burke not only denied that theory can provide the light needed by practice but also insisted that history, from which he thought "much political wisdom may be learned," is valuable for the statesman only "as habit, not as precept."[4] Indeed, though one can very well visualize that the future statesman will be surrounded by brilliant experts in decision-making, one wonders whether he will therefore be any the less a lonely man, acting and having to act on hunches and in compliance with the commands of his conscience. Discretion is an ineradicable element of decision-making, and the limits set to reducing it are narrow.

There is a strange irony about the efforts of the behavioral school. Their advocacy of a strictly empirical theory and science has been largely prompted by a desire to narrow, if not to close, the gap between political theory and practice. Admittedly, some behavioral investigations have actually added to our knowledge of political realities and enriched the knowledge of usable political techniques as well. But one wonders how many more have yielded only irrelevant results, or merely confirmed what we have already known through the application of less rigorous methods. In fact, the most ambitious and ingenious adepts of the school have become bogged down in purely methodological exercises, or, as one critic has put it, in a methodology of methodology.[5] They are paying the price for disregarding Aristotle's warning that "it is the mark of an educated mind to expect that amount of exactness in each kind which the nature of the particular subject admits." The remoteness from practical life, characteristic of these methodological inquisitions, is strikingly illustrated by the esoteric jargon in which they are presented. One need not be Molière's M. Jourdain not to recognize it as prose.

In spite of the increasing distance that actually separates this type of empirical theory from the practical concerns of politics, the fact remains that its proponents envisage and advocate a blending of political science and practice, similar to the merging of physical science and practice that Dr.

Jonas has described to us. The political ordering of human affairs is looked upon as a task of social-political technology or engineering, applying the behavioral laws of politics.

One is entitled to wonder how an allegedly purely descriptive theory of political behavior, which purposely dispenses with moral speculation, could be able to fulfill the normative function of setting the goals of political society. The answer to this puzzling question must be sought in an entirely unscientific assumption—"unscientific" from the point of view of the scientists themselves. The ends, according to this assumption, are some-how or other given. Moreover, they happily coincide with the ends of democratic society. Thus, like the technician, the political scientist has to concern himself only with the means for attaining preestablished ends.[6] This assumption, or belief rather, reveals more clearly than anything else the utopian streak in behavioral science. "Never forget," Erasmus wrote in the sixteenth century, "that 'dominion,' 'imperial authority,' 'kingdom,' 'majesty,' 'power' are all pagan terms, not Christian. The ruling power of a Christian state consists only of administration, kindness, and protection."[7] In the nineteenth century utopian and scientific socialists were foreseeing and foretelling the advent of the day when the government of men over men would be replaced by the administration of things. In our own time comput-ing machines are added to the technique of manipulating reified man.

The persistence of the political realities suggested by the "pagan terms" is what limits the theoretical value and the practical usefulness of a political science that cannot possibly enlighten us on those central political concepts, or on the political problems they signify.[8] At the same time, the persistence of the perennial great issues of politics justifies, nay makes imperative, our perseverence in the traditional approaches to the study of the vital and pressing political problems. True, political scientists who follow the tradi-tional lines of deductive theorizing and descriptive approach cannot claim, and do not even attempt, to prove by exact scientific procedures the validity of their conclusions and observations. But their contributions to the knowl-edge and practice of politics need not therefore be any less substantial and relevant, as the record of the illustrious political writers of the past con-vincingly proves. If political scientists today want to live up to the standards set by those writers, they must, in particular, shirk as little as their pre-decessors did the discussion of the great moral issues of the political world in which they live. They must not even shirk the greatest of those issues, raised anew by the destructive potentialities of modern science and technol-ogy. Dr. Jonas has suggested that the course of knowledge must not be stopped. Surely, such an unqualified dictum, if it is meant to be unqualified, is open to challenge, and deserves probing. The question of the substantive criteria to be applied in controlling the pursuit of knowledge is no doubt as formidable and difficult to answer as is the question of the authority that ought to exercise such control. But it can no longer be shirked.

FOOTNOTES

[1]Arnold Brecht, *Political Theory: The Foundation of Twentieth-Century Political Thought* (Princeton 1959).

[2]See Henry S. Kariel, "Political Science in the United States: Reflections on One of its Trends," in *Political Studies,* vol. 4, no. 2 (June 1956) p. 113; also D. E. Butler, *The Study of Political Behaviour* (London 1958).

[3]Richard C. Snyder and Glen D. Paige, "The United States Decision to Resist Aggression in Korea: The Application of an Analytical Scheme," in *Administrative Science Quarterly,* vol. 3 no. 3 (December 1958) p. 343.

[4]See Leo Strauss, *Natural Right and History* (Chicago 1953) pp. 294 ff.

[5]Arnold A. Rogow, "Comment on Smith and Apter: or, Whatever Happened to the Great Issues?," in *American Political Science Review,* vol. 51, no. 3 (September 1957) p. 765.

[6]See Kariel, *op. cit.,* pp. 120 ff.

[7]Quoted by Fritz Caspari, "Erasmus on the Social Functions of Christian Humanism," in *Journal of the History of Ideas,* vol. 8, no. 1 (January 1947) p. 95, n. 38.

[8]See Hans J. Morgenthau, *Dilemma of Politics* (Chicago 1958) pp. 29 ff.